The Molly Maguires And The Detectives

ENTERED AT THE NEW YORK POST OFFICE AS SECOND CLASS MATTER.

Allan Pinkerton's GREAT Detective Stories.

70

A. LAN PINKERTON

Mollie Maguires
AND THE Detectives,
by ALLAN PINKERTON.

DILLINGHAM CO. PUBLISHERS, 119 & 121 WEST 23° ST. NEW YORK.

THE

MOLLY MAGUIRES

AND

THE DETECTIVES

ALLAN PINKERTON,

AUTHOR OF

"THE EXPRESSMAN AND THE DETECTIVE," "THE MODEL TOWN
AND THE DETECTIVES," THE SPIRITUALISTS AND
THE DETECTIVES," ETC., ETC.

NEW AND ENLARGED EDITION.

NEW YORK:

G. W. Dillingham Co., Publishers.

8 | 1 | 1 | 9

Mollie Maguires

THE MOLLIE MAGUIRES

AND THE

DETECTIVES.

CHAPTER I.

AN EXTRAORDINARY PROPOSITION.

EARLY in the month of October, 1873, I was in Philadelphia, and one day received a note from Mr. F. B. Gowen, President of the Philadelphia and Reading Railway Company and the Philadelphia and Reading Coal and Iron Company- saying that he desired to see me at his place of business. I immediately responded to the invitation, accompanied by Superintendent Franklin, and met the gentleman in his private apartment, in the Company's elegant building on Fourth Street.

"I have sent for you, Mr. Pinkerton," said the President of the two great Pennsylvania corporations, after we had exchanged greetings, "upon business of importance."

I made known my willingness to hear what it was.

"The coal regions are infested by a most desperate class of men, banded together for the worst purposes—called, by some, the Buckshots, by others the Mollie Maguires—and they are making sad havoc with the country. It is a secret organization, has its meetings in hidden and out-of-the-way

places, and its members, I have been convinced ever since
my residence in Pottsville and my connection with the
criminal courts as District Attorney in the county of Schuylkill, are guilty of a majority of all the murders and other
deeds of outrage which, for many years, have been committed
in the neighborhood. I wish you to investigate this mysterious order, find out its interior workings, expose its evil
transactions, and see if the just laws of the State cannot
again be made effective in bringing criminals to justice. At
present, whenever an assassination is consummated, and, as
a consequence, a trial is instituted, a convenient *alibi* steps
forward and secures for the prisoner his freedom. Municipal laws are thus incapable of execution; sheriffs of counties
are powerless, and the usual run of detectives are of as little
value as the open, uniformed police of the different cities.
All of these have been tested, and all have failed. Now, if
you cannot disperse the murderous crew, or give us grounds
upon which to base prosecutions, then I shall believe that it
never will be effected."

I considered the proposition for a moment, turning over
in my mind the magnitude of the labor to be performed.

"Let me think of it a little," I answered; " and, in the
meantime tell me more about the Mollie Maguires."

"As far as we can learn, the society is of foreign birth,
a noxious weed which has been transplanted from its native
soil—that of Ireland—to the United States, some time within
the last twenty years. It lived and prospered in the old
country considerably earlier. Its supporters there were
known as Ribbonmen, the White Boys, and sometimes
as Mollie Maguires, but their modes of procedure were
the same as now pursued in the coal regions. Men
were then, as they are at this time, killed—sometimes
in broad daylight, sometimes at night, and invariably by
strangers—persons at least unknown to chance spectators,
parties violently put out of the way. Suspected

individuals would be apprehended, but in the end nobody could be found able to identify the criminals. It was only after a protracted struggle in Ireland that the proper evidence could be elicited to convict the tools doing the bloody behests of the society. I suppose it will not be easy to do this in Pennsylvania. The same minds, the same combinations, are to be encountered here. The Mollies rule our people with a rod of iron. They do this and make no sign. The voice of the fraternity is unheard, but the work is performed. Even the political sentiments of the commonwealth are moulded by them, and in their particular field they elect or defeat whomsoever they may please. They control, in a measure, the finances of the State. Their chiefs direct affairs this way, and that way, without hinderance. Men without an iota of moral principle, they dictate the principles of otherwise honorable parties. In its ultimate results this complexion of affairs in Pennsylvania touches, to a considerable degree, the interests of the citizens of the whole country. Wherever anthracite is employed is also felt the vise-like grip of this midnight, dark-lantern, murderous-minded fraternity. Wherever in the United States iron is wrought, from Maine to Georgia, from ocean to ocean—wherever hard coal is used for fuel, there the Mollie Maguire leaves his slimy trail and wields with deadly effect his two powerful levers : secrecy—combination. Men having their capital locked up in the coal-beds are as obedient puppets in his hands. They have for some time felt that they were fast losing sway over that which by right should be their own to command. They think, with some show of reason, their money would have profited them as much had it been thrown to the fishes in the sea, or devoted to the devouring flames. Others, wishing to engage in mining operations, and who are possessed of the capital and experience necessary, are driven away. They cannot intrust their hard-earned property to a venture which will be at the beck and call of a fierce and sanguinary rabble and its heedless and reckless directors. They wisely turn aside and seek other and less hazardous uses for their talents and their means. The entire population of this State feel the shock, and it is in due season communicated to the most distant parts in which anthracite is used and ores reduced or smelted."

I had heard of many assassinations by these Mollie Maguires, and also about those performed by the Ku-Klux and similar political combinations in the Southern States. It had always seemed to me that it was a sacred duty which Pennsylvania owed to herself, to her own citizens, and to the country at large, to clear her garments of the taint resting upon them and bring to punishment the persons who, for so many years, habitually outraged decency, spilt human blood without stint, and converted the richest section of one of the most wealthy and refined of all the sisterhood of States into a very golgotha—a locality from which law-abiding men and women might soon be forced to flee, as from the threatened cities of the plain, or from a spot stricken with plague and pestilence.

" I will enter upon the business, but it will require time, sharp work, and plenty of both ! "

" Yes ! We duly appreciate this," responded Mr. Gowen, " What we want, and everybody wants, is to get within this apparently impenetrable ring ; turn to the light the hidden side of this dark and cruel body, to probe to its core this festering sore upon the body politic, which is rapidly gnawing into the vitals and sapping the life of the community. Crime must be punishable in the mountains of Pennsylvania, as it is in the agricultural counties, and in all well-regulated countries. We want to work our mines in peace, to run our passenger and freight trains without fear of the sudden loss of life and property through the malicious acts of the Mollie Maguires ; we want people to sleep unthreatened, unmolested, in their beds, undisturbed by horrid dreams of midnight prowlers and cowardly assassins ; we want the laboring-man, of whatever creeds or nationalities, protected in their right to work to secure sustenance for their wives and little ones, unawed by outside influences. We want the miner to go forth cheerfully to the slope, or the shaft, for labor in the breast or in the gangway, wherever it may seem to him for the best, void of the fear in his heart when he parts from his wife at the cottage-gate in the morning, that it may be their last farewell on earth, and by evening his bullet-riddled corpse may be taken back to his home the only evidence that he has encountered the murderer—the agent of those who would compel him to refuse all employment unless the regulations of the order were complied with. The State cannot attain these things ; she has repeatedly tried, and tried in vain. You can do it. I have seen you tested on other occasions and in other matters, and know your ability to conduct the business ; we are willing to supply everything within our power to make your task a success."

"I believe that it can be acomplished, but I am also aware that it is a stupendous undertaking. I accept the responsibility, however, with its accompanying consequences, which I perceive will prove no small burden to bear. I also see that I shall encounter no little difficulty in detailing from the many able and trustworthy men in my force one perfectly qualified for this very unusual charge. And an error in the outset would bring irreparable disaster before the end could be reached. It is no ordinary man that I need in this matter. He must be an Irishman, and a Catholic, as only this class of persons can find admission to the Mollie Maguires. My detective should become, to all intents and purposes, one of the order, and continue so while he remains in tne case before us He should be hardy, tough, and capable of laboring, in season and out of season, to accomplish, unknown to those about him, a single absorbing object. In the meanwhile, I shall have to exact from you a pledge that, whoever I may dispatch upon this errand, ne shall not through you, become known to any person as a detective. This is highly necessary to be strictly attended to. If possible, you should shut your eyes to the fact that I have an employé of my Agency working in the mining country. If you can do so consistently, it might as well be given out to everybody interested that the idea of investigating the Mollies through the means of detectives, if ever thought of, has been abandoned as a hopeless job, and that the present status of affairs in the mines is totally incapable of being changed. Take the further precaution that my name, and those of my superintendents and employés, do not appear upon any of your books. Keep my reports in your own custody, away from all prying eyes. I would also ask, if my agents are engaged for one week, for one month, or for years, that these requests still be complied with; and further, whatever may be the result of the examination, no person in my employ—unless the circumstances are greatly changed and I demand it—shall ever be required to appear and give testimony upon the witness stand."

"To all of this I give willing consent. I see how necessary it is. As I said before, we will dc anything in our power, and within the bounds of reason, to aid you and protect your detectives."

I then agreed that the operation should begin as soon as I might make the proper arrangements, and, after some further conversation, principally upon the purely financial portion of the engagement, took my leave.

Immediately after leaving Mr. Gowen's office I telegraphed for Mr. Bangs, General Superintendent. He arrived from New York early the ensuing day, and a consultation was held in my private parlor, over the business offices of the Agency, at No. 45 South Third Street, Mr. Bangs, Mr. Franklin and myself forming the parties to the council. The details of the case were discussed at length and a general plan of operations decided upon, after which I started for my return trip westward.

It was the ending of a delightfully cool and pleasant Indian summer day, and as I was being rapidly whirled through the most beautiful portion of New Jersey, my face toward the open window, inhaling the invigorating atmosphere, and enjoying a view of the fast-fading, swift-passing panorama of plain and valley, village and stream, I continually dwelt upon the service in which I had recently enlisted. Forgetting the sunset, the agreeable evening, and every immediate surrounding, my mind was absorbed in contemplating the subject then nearest my heart. Mentally I brought in review the different devoted attachés of the Agency, who, through nativity and early training, were eligible to the place to be filled. All were trustworthy, as far as that went; all were courageous, faithful and efficient in positions and under circumstances ordinarily calling for the exercise of these qualities. But the man now wanted was to meet peculiar dangers. He must be perfectly qualified in every respect, or he would not do. It was no discredit to my corps of detectives, that I quickly dismissed many of them as inadequate for the duty. It was not their fault. Had I one man who would go against his life-long habits, early impressions, education, and his inherited as well as acquired prejudices? Was there one who held sufficiently broad and deeply-grounded notions of the real duty of a true Irishman to his country and his fellow-countrymen to intrust with this great mission? I believed that I had, but which one was it in the number thus, in my mind, competing for the honor? He must be able to distinguish the real from the ideal moral obligation, and pierce the vail separating a supposed from an actual state of affairs. He must have the gift of seeing that the misguided people of the mining districts who had joined this order were unquestionably working evil, and only evil, to Ireland, Irishmen, and the church, in lieu of doing their

native land and their kindred at home and in America a
service

While Bishop Wood, of Philadelphia, had early placed his
seal of condemnation upon the Mollie Maguires in the coal
regions, and the clergy had followed, almost to a man, in
bringing the individual members of the clan before them
and their congregations, and heaped dread maledictions upon
their heads, calling the persons by name in public, and even
cut them from the church until such time as they should
renounce their membership, still I knew many good Catholics, and honest men at heart, were remaining in the organi
zation, and that, in some more peaceable sections of the
State, the priesthood, if not tacitly countenancing the society said little against it.   To their credit be it stated,
however, they were unanimous in their abhorrence of the
violent acts of the Mollie Maguires in Schuylkill, Carbon,
Columbia, and Luzerne counties.   I had to find a man who,
once inside this, as I supposed, oath-bound brotherhood,
would yet remain true to me; who could make almost a
new man of himself, take his life in his hands, and enter upon
a work which was apparently against those bound to him by
close ties of nationality, if not of blood and kindred ; and
for months, perhaps for years, place himself in antagonism
with and rebellion against the dictates of his church—the
church which from his earliest breath he had been taught to
revere.   He would perforce obtain a reputation for evil conduct, from which it was doubtful that he could ever entirely
extricate himself.   Would the common run of men think
such a position at all tenable ?   Would they consent to
ostensibly degrade themselves that others might be saved ?
My man must become, really and truly, a Mollie of the
hardest character, attend their meetings, and possibly be
charged with direct participation in certain of their crimes.
He must face the priest, and endure the bad opinion of his
countrymen even until the end.   For an indefinite period

he was to be as one dead and buried in the grave—dead to his family and friends—sinking his individuality—and be published abroad as the companion and associate of assassins, murderers, incendiaries, thieves, and gamblers. In no other way could I hope to secure admission to the inner circle of this labyrinth of iniquity. By no other plan could the clan be exposed and its volume of crime clasped forever. Another thing: The Mollie Maguires were working in opposition to the Welsh, English, and German miners. Their hatred of the English, especially, they had imbibed with their mothers' milk. I was, if possible, to destroy the Mollie Maguires. Therefore, my operatives must be the instruments of that destruction. Then how difficult for any Irishman to enter upon the warfare? If he had the ability to see far enough, however, it would be understood that the leaders of the obnoxious society were simply apostates—men disloyal to the land of their birth—engaged in an unholy effort, and one which, successful or not, reflected discredit upon all of their countrymen. Beholding and understanding this, the detective would not be working merely to right the wrongs of this man or that man, but to wipe off a dark blot which had fallen upon the escutcheon of Ireland, and which clouded the fair fame of every Irishman in America. Then he would meet the cry, in the mines and elsewhere, of "persecution for opinion's sake," and the danger of "a conflict between capital on the one side and labor on the other." Would he be shrewd enough to detect the untruthfulness of one and the insincerity of the other? Surely here was a task for me, in the very outset, the fellow of which I had not encountered since the war of the rebellion.

CHAPTER II.

THE MAN FOR THE WORK.

By the time I had reached headquarters, in Chicago, I imagined that I might need a man for the Mollie Maguire operation, who, among other acquirements and qualifications, was also a practical miner. My plans had even partially assumed shape for a flying visit to some of the coal districts of Southern Illinois and Ohio, where it was possible I might chance upon a person of the needed character. Then it occurred to me, even though I could secure an experienced worker in the bituminous shafts and drifts, he would naturally be almost as much at fault in the art of delving in the slopes and gangways of the anthracite fields as one entirely unedu- cated in mining. He might have the trained muscle and capacity of bodily endurance, yet possess no available knowl- edge of the anthracite branch of the business. Then a party of this sort must necessarily be a stranger to the intricate duties of my profession, and have about everything to acquire from the lowest round of the ladder upward. There was another objection—and it had more weight than everything before enumerated: I could not rely upon the truthfulness and faith- fulness of a new acquaintance as I might upon that of one who after years of training under my own direction, had made him- self an expert in the detection of criminals. Clearly, then, I must select my operative for this case as for any other, from my regular force—at least employ a detective that had been connected with one or all of the offices in the Chain of Agen cies. Who should it be? This was the all-important question. Several of my best men, who were, in most emergencies, men tally and physically capable of filling the place. I took occa

tion to carefully approach and sound as to their opinions and
acts under certain supposititious and somewhat analogous circumstances but such as were not too nearly similar to those
under consideration, and soon found that they would never
do. One, who was precisely the man called for in other par
ticulars, had an invalid wife and a family of small children,
and I would not ask him to take the position. There was a
chance that he might be disabled, or even lose his life, and
thus leave his mate and their helpless innocents to the cold
charity of an unfeeling world. Another almost as good was
soon to be married to an estimable young lady. A third had
some blemish excluding him from the list, and I had not yet
hit upon the agent to be sent to the land of mountains and
dales and the home of the Mollie Maguires.

One morning, however, as I was riding from home to
Fifth Avenue—standing, as usual, upon the rear platform of a
crowded West Side street car—I recognized in the person of
the conductor an operative previously escaping consideration. He was engaged working his part of a delicate job
connected with the railway interest, and for some months
had not been in a position in which he was called upon to
report to me personally. The thought instantly found lodgment in my mind: "If this man is mentally correct, and
willing, he is just the instrument fitted for my mining operation." I was satisfied that he could be spared from his car
and the case he was assisting in, and another detective put
in his place, and immediately upon reaching the office, sent
a note to the young man's boarding-house, asking him to
meet me at my rooms as soon as his day's work was ended,
as I had something to submit for his consideration.

James McParlan, the detective alluded to, was born in the
province of Ulster, County Armagh, Parish of Mullabrack,
Ireland, in 1844; consequently, at the date mentioned, was
in his twenty-ninth year. His father and mother were living.
He had been a member of my force for about a year. Com

ing to America in 1867, having previously seen some service
in chemical works, at Gateshead, County Durham, England,
and subsequently, in the same capacity, at Wallsend, England, the first place he filled after landing at Castle Garden
was that of second clerk in a small grocery house on Ninth
Avenue, city of New York.   At a later period he became
salesman for a country dealer in drygoods, named Cummings,
at Medina, Orleans County, in the same State.   His salary
was exceedingly small, and besides, not easily collectible;
and, after a short apprenticeship to the profession of coun
ter-jumping and measuring ribbons, laces, and calicoes, he
resigned, and adopted Greeley's advice to young men, with a
course of travel due westward.   Reaching Buffalo, he tarried
there but a few days and then came to Chicago.   After filling
different situations, he applied for and secured employment
in my establishment.

Of medium height, a slim but wiry figure, well knit together; a clear hazel eye; hair of an auburn color, and bor-
dering upon the style denominated as "sandy;" a forehead
high, full, and well rounded forward; florid complexion,
regular features, with beard and mustache a little darker
than his hair, there was no mistaking McParlan's place of
nativity, even had not his slight accent betrayed his Celtic
origin.   He was in fact a fine specimen of the better class
of immigrants to this country from the poet's

"First flower of the earth and first gem of the sea."

He was passably educated, had beheld and brushed
against the people of a considerable portion of the New World
during the short time he had been in it, and earned a reputation for honesty, a peculiar tact and shrewdness, skill and
perseverance in performing his numerous and difficult duties,
and worked himself into the position of a firm favorite with
those of my employés intimately associated with him.   Thus
far I certainly found no particular fault with McParlan.

The same day McParlan, clad in his ordinary but cleanly citizen's attire, entered my private office, and I invited him to take a seat. The conference which immediately followed was long, confidential, and interesting to the two taking part in it; but particulars need not be given here, as results achieved will exhibit the nature of the conversation, which has also been foreshadowed in the preceding pages. More light will be thrown upon the subject during the progress and development of events. Suffice it that in James McParlan I recognized the very person to whom I could safely and confidently intrust my plans for the campaign in Pennsylvania. While he was not left in the dark as to the dangers to be encountered—and, in fact, these were as fully explained as it was possible to perceive them at the time—he made known his desire to assume the part, and said he would experience pleasure in being sent where he could be of use to me and to his country.

"I will do my utmost to bring the job to a speedy and successful termination," he remarked with earnestness.

"Remember, McParlan," I urged, at the close of this portion of our interview, "your refusal to accept the responsibility—while I can but acknowledge it would prove a disappointment—will not injure you in my estimation, or prevent your employment by me in the future."

"Mr. Pinkerton," answered the operative, rising from his chair, "I am not in your Agency to object to such a thing as this seems to be; on the contrary, I am anxious to go, and ready to start at the word of command!"

"That settles it, then," said I. "Report to me to-morrow forenoon, when your instructions and credentials will all be prepared and you can take the night train for Philadelphia."

Seemingly satisfied, the young man went his way.

It was easy to see, by the expression of his countenance, that McParlan's sympathies were earnestly enlisted in the case, only the bare outlines of which had as yet been com mitted to his care, and if he failed it would not be from wan of zeal, or lack of earnest desire to well and truly perform his duty.

"And so Mr. Pinkerton is after sending me to England, as he kindly says, for the betterment of my health, an' to look after the King Bee of all the forgers," remarked Mc-Parlan, in his pleasant way, the next afternoon, to my cashier, as he received the advance of money for his expenses. He repeated about the same manner of adieu when handed his papers by the chief clerk, and it soon spread throughout the apartment, among the clerical force, that the happy man was "to take the tour of Europe at my expense." After bidding all good-by, and the reception of a warm grasp of the hand and an earnest word of caution from me to "have a care of himself," McParlan left the Agency.

The man had been found, and was at last entering upon his extra-hazardous mission—not bound for England, however. It was well enough, under the circumstances, that all of the detective's personal friends and acquaintances—especially those outside the office—should believe that he was about to cross the wide Atlantic.

McParlan's instructions were as complete and comprehensive as they well could be made at short notice; but of course, after generally counseling him concerning the true object of his labors, considerable had to be confided to his own judgment and discretion, at least until fairly launched upon his undertaking, when all would see what was best, and not best, to be done. Leaving the detective to perform his difficult *rôle*, under my directions, I shall now proceed to give, in detail, a description of his acts, as represented in the reports. It should be understood, however, though the fact may not appear in this narration of events, that McParlan was almost daily in communication with me, through Mr. Franklin, the Philadelphia superintendent, and was required

to keep us aware of his every important movement, by letter.
He was particularly enjoined to use discretion in the sending of messages and documents, and a plan, not necessary to
be divulged, arranged by which all interruptions through the
mails would be prevented. I was to know where and how
to connect with him any day of the week, and all changes
of locality were to be noted as early as might be possible.
The detective's adventures in the mountains of Pennsylvania
are sufficiently romantic and attractive, if properly related,
to satisfy the most exacting reader, without the author
having recourse to the smallest amount of extraneous matter, employing any of the powers of the imagination, or the
tricks of the professional novel-writer in enchaining attention. As

> " Loveliness
> Needs not the foreign art of ornament,
> But is, when unadorned, adorned the most,"

so with the simple truth; in this instance it demands no
elaborate decoration, no enchanting *couleur de rose*, to make
it entertaining.

CHAPTER III.

THE DETECTIVE SEEKS THE HAUNTS OF THE MOLLIES.

AFTER several days very profitably spent among the coal,
canal, and dock hands, in the vicinity of Philadelphia,
acquiring some knowledge of their habits and occupations,
and at the same time, in a measure, habituating himself to
the wearing of a rather novel and uncomfortable costume
with which Mr. Franklin had been kind enough to provide

him, the agent, according to orders, returned and reported to the superintendent that he was fully prepared to commence his work in the mining country.

When the young man glanced at his figure, as reflected in a mirror, he found it difficult to believe he was really himself and not some wild vagabond who had usurped his place. The transformation was satisfactorily complete. He beheld in the glass the shadow of a man of about his height and proportions, it was true, his head covered by an old, dilapidated and dirt-colored slouch hat, with plentiful space for his cutty-pipe in its narrow, faded band; a grayish coat of coarse materials, which had, from appearances, seen service in a coal bin, and, while never very fine in make or fashion, was considerably the worse about the cuffs and skirts, both being frayed out to raveled raggedness, from rough usage by its former owner. The vest was originally black, but the years had come and gone in such numbers since, that the dye was washed away, and with it had fled the surface of the cloth and most of the worsted binding in the region of the pockets. The pantaloons, of brown woollen stuff, were whole, but too large for him in the body, and worn strapped tight at the waist with a leather belt, which, from its yellowish and broken condition, might have been a former bell-thong off the neck of some farmer's cow, appropriated after exposure to all kinds of wear and weather for a series of years. The bosom of a heavy gray shirt was seen beneath the waistcoat, and exhibited no visible vestige of a collar ; but a substitute was formed by a red yarn cravat, or knitted comforter, drawn closely around the wearer's neck and tied in a sailor's knot in front. The under garment had that which ordinary shirts are seldom supplied with—a pocket, at the left inner side, for tobacco. His boots were of the stoga, hob-nailed, high-topped style, and in their capacious legs easily rested the bottoms of the pantaloons. With face unshaven for a week or ten days, and hair quite dry and straggling, from want of proper attention, it is probable that McParlan's mother, had she been present, would have refused him recognition. He could only be convinced that he was himself, by reference to his voice, which sounded familiar to the ear. In his satchels, ready packed, were supplies of writing paper, envelopes, stamps, etc. ; also a suit of clothes a little better than that upon his person, for occasional Sunday wear. Razor and strop he had none. Their absence was no loss, however, as he did not propose shaving his face until circumstances might call for the resumption of his natural character.

Monday, the 27th of October, 1873, was an eventful day at the Philadelphia Agency, and formed an epoch in the life history of at least one man, remembrance of which will never fail until his latest breath. Then it was that James McParlan, attired and accoutred as just described, his heart hopeful for the future, but in fact unknowing and unknown, kicked the dust of the city from his heels, at the Callowhill street depot of the Philadelphia and Reading Railway, and after purchasing a ticket for Port Clinton, depositing his two valises—which bore every outward evidence of having seen much tough usage and extended travel in domestic and foreign parts—in the seat beside himself, in the smoking-car of the afternoon train, set out upon his voyage of discovery in the stronghold of the Mollie Maguires. He was James McParlan no longer—but James McKenna, as I must hereafter call him—and he looked backward upon the receding town, and considered whether he would survive ever again to take his old name and place in the world and see the broad, teeming streets, handsome structures, and beautiful girls of the Quaker City. To him it then seemed he was cutting loose from all the nether world. Those who knew him best would pass him by unheeded in his transforming disguise and adopted name, and even his intimate associates—excepting Mr. Franklin and I—in Chicago and elsewhere, fully believed

him to be adrift upon the blue waters, shaping his course
to lands "beyant the seas," only to return after the lapse of
many months. Would he *ever* return? That was a question,
he soon decided, which, for a favorable response, rested with
himself and the manner in which he conducted his researches.
He was sure that I watched anxiously over him, and that
Mr Franklin was prepared to do everything for his good,
but very largely would he be the worker-out of his own des-
tiny. His life and success, or his failure and death, reposed
in his own strength, guarded by his own intellect. While
these and similar thoughts crowded upon his brain, the detective was traveling onward. Smoothly and swiftly the cars
glided over the track, past Belmont Glen, and beyond the
outskirts of the city. Then came Fairmount Park, Laurel
Hill, seen from the far distance, and closer at hand the broad,
still waters of the Schuylkill, of which Ireland's great poet
sang and on wnose shores he once found that repose which
his weary head had elsewhere sought in vain. It was not
within the heart of a man of McKenna's temperament, or in
one born on the soil of the beautiful land that gave him birth
to resist the temptation to search out Tom Moore's cottage
and feast his eyes upon its walls and roof; and he raised
the blind, admitted the sunlight, and his senses drank
in, in everent silence, the variegated and pleasing landscape. After a time came Valley Forge, the scene of
so much suffering by the American soldiers under General
Washington, in the memorable winter of 1777–8. Indeed,
the country throughout this vicinity is replete with points
bringing to recollection interesting dates and facts of history.
Through the kindness of a fellow-traveler, who sat smoking
in a seat near him, my officer was made familiar with some
of these most eventful localities. And still there appeared
to be no end to the succession of hills and vales, wooded
mountain sides and fertile fields. Yet onward swept the
train, bearing its precious living freight.

Passing beyond the populous city of Reading, late in the afternoon, the agricultural lands began, as the stranger thought, a silent struggle with rocks and rills and more rugged mountains. As they still proceeded swiftly on their route, the rough country gained the mastery, and the fleeting shew increased in boldness, culminating in a grand and craggy beauty when the locomotive whistled "down the brakes" at a point some distance short of Port Clinton. By this time portentous clouds had arisen darkly in the west, as the sun sunk to its couch, and there were other premonitions of an impending storm of wind and rain.

Port Clinton is seventy-eight miles from Philadelphia, at a spot where the two great forks of the Schuylkill—the Schuylkill proper and the Little Schuylkill—form a union, both having had their origin, not so far separated, in the distant northern coal-fields.

It was eight o'clock in the evening when McKenna, with baggage swinging from his shoulder, stood for the first time upon the floor of the massive, brown-stone, turret-roofed depot building at Port Clinton and looked about him for a house which might yield him a night's lodging and supper, as he was both sleepy and hungry after his ride and the unusual excitements of the day. Starting out into the increasing darkness, he was unable to see and appreciate the tall mountains towering above him on all sides; but, feeling his way carefully, he crossed the canal bridge and sought a public house. Seeing a bright light not far away, he directed his steps toward it, and in a short time came to a structure which proved to be a village tavern or saloon. Thinking, despite the sounds of revelry heard within, that it might be a proper stopping-place for him, he entered, rested his burden on the floor—weary enough with its carriage, and wishing, thus early, he had been content to leave one-half the baggage at home—and civilly inquired of the presiding genius— a big, burly fellow, with milky-white eyes, a cherry-red nose, and very stiff, black, straight hair, planted widely apart on his bullet-shaped head—who had evidently "too much taken' of the liquids he dispensed to others—when they had funds to pay for them—if he could have supper and lodging at his hotel. He did not half fancy the crowd he had come up with. Mostly of the lower class of Germans, the men were in the midst of a spree that bid fair to last until another day. Liquor had already gained control of their senses, and their personal appearance was even more forbidding than that of the person who so suddenly appeared among them, and for this there was no possible necessity. Those of the number who labored at all found employment in digging a tunnel, which was in course of excavation in the neighborhood. These were a few points which the new arrival gathered from the talk of the occupants of the small, low, smoke-begrimed bar-room. Cocking up one of his eyes very fiercely, the landlord looked scowlingly out of his other, from beneath its black, beetling brow, and insultingly replied :

"No! I geeps no victuals nor shake-downs for peebles like you! Git oud! You wants der beds and der meats, don't ye? Git oud der haus! Go makes your schleeps mit der bigs! Oud of dis blace, or, mein Gott in himmel, I gicks ye right away oud!"

The stranger, not choosing to move as fast as he thought he should, the landlord continued, while he advanced upon McKenna :

"Look dis way, poys! Dish is anoder of dose blundering dramps! Pitch him oud! Teach the skalamag better manners than to pass de country around schteeling peeble's horses, cows, and dings! Put him oud quick!"

Protesting that he was no tramp, but seeing there seemed no hope of securing rest or food under that inhospitable roof, the traveler took up his baggage and hurriedly retreated from the apartment, just as a general rush was made for him by the bystanders, the desire being to seize upon his person with no peaceable intent.

It was not a part of McKenna's business in those regions to have a set-to with half a dozen infuriated and intoxicated men, though he would willingly have risked something to give that inn-keeper a beating; hence, he slackened not his speed until he had reached the middle of the street, where he stopped a moment to consider which direction he should take.

Here was a dilemma! Here was luck for him! To make matters worse, the rain, which for some hours had threatened, began to pour down in torrents. Presently a man made his appearance, coming from the bar-room and approaching the detective. When near him the citizen said:

"Faith, an' ye jist missed being kilt enthirely by the mane scuts there within!"

McKenna gathered hope. This man was an immigrant from the ould sod.

"Where do you come from, and what is it ye'd be afther havin' here?"

"I'm late from New York—later from Colorado—an' what is it I'm here fur? Is that it? What should a dacent Irish lad want whose stomach is full of emptiness and ne'er a morsel of bread or mate in the wallet? What I want is worruk, and somethin' to relave my hunger! A place to slape in wouldn't be inconvanient, aither!"

This seemed to content the man from the tavern.

"An' if ye are sakin' work, you're no thramp. for little's the hand's turn of that they ever do; an' I know you're no thafe, from your accint, which is like me own, barrin' the Dublin twang, so I'll even be better to ye than the Dutchman—who, by the way, is not as bad as he seems. You jist came upon him in an unlucky time, an' the drink at the fore too! Only yesterday it was that a brace of strollers stole away his only cow—begging the pardon of the whiskey barrel, an' its contints is not exactly suitable for swatening the coffee, sure,—and they druv her off to the next neighbor's beyant, where they sold the baste, fur all the worruld as if they owned her—the blackguards! As natural as iver can be, Mr. Staub—that's the tavern-keeper's name, an' mine's Timmins, be the same token—has no love left to squander on tramps; an' takin' you fur one—an' where could have been his two eyes, an' his ears, meanwhiles?—he gives you the back of his hand nately, and the hardest words he can lay his crooked tongue to! He thought you a thramp and he mistrated you as one! Still, Staub's a clever man when the drink's not in him, an' many's the poor fellow I've seen him take in out of the cowld, and give a sup an' a bed, who hadn't the shadow o' sixpence to bless himself wid!"

"Sure, an' I'm no tramp!" answered McKenna, "an' what I wants in the way of atin' an' drinkin', for the present, at laste, I'm able to pay fur! I've two strong arms, an' an honest heart, God be thanked! an' when my cash is all spent, I can dig, or do something honorable for more, without help from such rubbish as big Misther Staub!"

Timmins, the soft-hearted, responded:

"I'll e'en do better by you, me laddy-buck, than the scullions you have left! Come home wid me fur the night, an' stay longer if ye likes; you are as welcome as the birds in spring—an' tho' its comin' late we are, my old woman will give you somewhat for your stomach, an' a bed to rest your tired bones upon, at all events!"

"As an argument in favor of his acceptance of the offer, just at that moment the rain poured down heavier than before, and the wind beat the large drops into the faces of the men with a force which was uncomfortable.

"I'll go wid you, Mr. Timmins—an' many thanks for your kind offer!"

And, taking one valise in his left hand, keeping the right free for whatever might occur, the operative committed the remainder of his portable property to Timmins' care. Permitting that personage to lead the way, they started.

"I wonder if I'm about to be robbed and murdered, thus early in my career in these mountains," was the thought that flitted through the detective's mind as he followed the form of his retreating host, with his right hand resting on his repeater, which he had convenient in his coat pocket. But nothing to further excite his fears occurred. Timmins only appeared anxious to keep the traveling bag from the rain, by tucking it carefully under his arm, and covering it with the folds of the cape of his heavy cloak. They advanced rapidly, and Timmins, in default of a lantern, exerted himself to illuminate their devious way with sharp sallies of genuine humor, elicited in original comments upon the state of the weather and "illigant condition of the highway." The stranger laughed heartily, which was compensation sufficient for the jester, who was merely trying to make himself agreeable.

"An' here we are, betimes, hard by the home of Mr. and Mrs. Timmins—and that's me an' my good wife—but divil a glimmer of a light is there in the windy, which is something uncommon with Mrs. Timmins!"

The conclusion of these remarks brought the pedestrians, soaking wet, and desirous of putting themselves beyond the reach of the rain, by the side of a large wooden structure, which might be tenantless, from all that any outsider could hear, or see, for that matter, in the darkness of the night.

"Phat's up now, I wonder?" said Timmins, who found his effort to enter the place stubbornly resisted from within. There was no bolt or bar, he said, but come open the door would not. A soft, partly yielding but insurmountable obstacle, resisted the pushing of the two men, who unitedly tried to shove in the barrier.

Then movements were heard inside, and presently came a woman's voice:

"Is that you, Tony!"

"Yes! It *is me!* An' phat the wonder is it that fastens the door? It's kaping myself an' a stranger out here in the drinchin' rain, ye are!"

"Wait a minute, Tony. An' glad I am, sure, that ye came as ye did, and I not cold as a stone, fit fur me grave clothes! Let me light the candle an' maybe I can help yez ' It's the body of a man—whether alive or dead, I can't say, that so bolts the door agin yez! An' me an' the wee childer here all alone until this minit! God be praised, ye came in the very nick of time!"

Here was a denouement for the detective's first day's work, and one he was not well pleased with. His companion, Timmins, from the manner in which he spluttered and tore about the front yard, was either very badly frightened or very mad, McKenna could not decide which.

"I'll soon see who the scoundrel is, an' dead or alive, I wouldn't stan' in his boots for any small sum! When I get at him, I'll——"

A light now appeared within, and the man's threat was cut short by hearing the creaking of boards, as if some person carefully crossed the floor. Then Timmins put his face to the entrance, and a whispered consultation between himself and his wife took place, the purport of which the traveler could not comprehend.

———◆———

CHAPTER IV.

STIRRING UP A WASP'S NEST.

THEY were not long in suspense, as Mrs. Timmins, after closing the interview with her husband, gathered resolution to grasp the seemingly inanimate body by the arm, and to drag it away from the entrance. McKenna and his friend then went into the place—used as kitchen, washing, and dining-room, in accordance with the prevailing custom of the locality. Anthony Timmins at once seized upon the pewter candlestick, held the flame of the taper close to the face of the supposed dead man, almost scorching the eyebrows in his eagerness to discover who it might be; then, breaking out into loud laughter, he returned the light to Mrs. Timmins, raised his two hands above his head, slightly bending his knees as if about to sit down on the floor, his hat falling off sidewise meantime, and fairly shouted, between the rapidly following explosions of uncontrollable mirth which had quickly taken the place of his former anger

"By the hill o' Howth! An' its only poor ould man Fox, of the wee patch beyant the mountains, as harmless as a suckin' dove, but, to his own sorrow, a great drunkard! He's now what wan might call down, dead insensible wid the poteen he has taken."

And Timmins could scarcely postpone more laughter long enough to introduce his companion to Mrs. Timmins, after which brief ceremony he said:

"No wonder on earth that we couldn't open the door wid all this lump of fat an iniquity braced forninst it! He weighs two hundred poun' 'f wan ounce; an' besides, the heel of his shoe wor caught in the crack under the door—which by the same token is wider nor will be comfortable next month—holdin' it like a wedge, nate and tight against us!"

"Oh, what a dawshy clodhopper I must have been," said Mrs. Timmins, in an excellent brogue, "to be scared at ould man Fox! He's his own worst inimy, is Paddy Fox, an' he came here unbeknownst to me—as to who he wor, at laste—just as it grow'd dark, an' before I had lighted the candle, an' he stumbled into the kitchen, an' I didn't know him from the deil's own grandfather; an' I jist ran into the bedroom, the childer wid me, an' fastened the door, expectin' every minute he'd rouse up an' begin to rob the house! I supposed he wor a tramp, for all the wurruld, an' I didn't dare make a noise, or strike a light, for fear we'd be murthered outright! An' how glad I wor when I heard your steps on the gravel outside!"

So the fright about a dead man barring the door was not much of a scare after all. At least, there was very small cause for disturbance, as a drunken person was not such an extraordinary thing to see in that house. Fox was allowed to remain where he was, Timmins having thrown an old quilt over him to keep him warm, saying that he would "be all right by the mornin'!"

Mrs. Timmins, good woman that she was, rekindled a fire and prepared an excellent supper for the stranger, consisting of bacon and eggs, and baked potatoes with strong coffee, to which McKenna helped himself with unwonted relish. After satisfying his appetite, he and Timmins played a couple of games of euchre, took a few drinks from a keg kept in one corner, supported on a couple of sticks, and which was under the exclusive control of Mrs. Timmins—she sold the liquor to her customers from a tin cup—then the wet, weary, and sleepy traveler retired to his bed quite in the dark, in a room in the second story of the building, first having thrown his damp clothes down the staircase to Mr. Timmins, with a request that they be allowed to dry before the kitchen fire.

Anthony Timmins and his wife kept what was known as a railroad boarding-house or tavern, for the accommodation of laborers employed on the adjacent tunnel, and a fair living, and something smart beside, did they realize from their trouble and toil, Mrs. Timmins being not at all assisted by the three tow-headed children which followed close to her heels wherever she went, and called her "mother."

The slumbers of the detective were sound and unbroken

until the hour that the sunlight of another day fell full on his face and disturbed, and finally awakened him. Looking about, he discovered there were three beds in the low room —one, by way of compliment, devoted to his own particular use, while each of the others held two men, of whose presence the previous night he had been entirely ignorant. Waiting until his room-mates had gone out, McKenna went to the door and shouted to Timmins for his garments, which were soon brought up by that personage, wishing him at the same time "the top o' the mornin', an' many happy returns of the same!" The clothing was warm and dry, and the officer felt greatly refreshed by his season of repose. At the breakfast-table he learned, not greatly to his surprise, that the company he had to keep was none of the most select ; still it was as good as he had reason to anticipate under the circumstances. In fact, he thought if he should secure, for the future, equally decent associates, he might consider himself fortunate. The men about him asked no questions, but devoured their meal almost in silence, and then set out for their work on the tunnel.

The long table of unplaned boards—covered with a coarse oil-cloth, which had once been of a variegated mahogany color, but had faded with much rubbing and use to a dark dirt hue—was flanked on either side by equally rough wooden benches of the same length, on which the boarders sat when they partook of their food. There were no chairs in that house; those too proud to occupy the benches while at dinner could stand up and welcome. Furnishing the table were broad tin plates, common horn-handled iron knives and forks, which the landlady had not for months found time to give the polishing rub of "brick-dust and a split potato ;" pewter table and tea spoons; a can for vinegar; salt-cellar and pepper-box of japanned tinware ; pint cups, also of tin, for the coffee ; a quart measure for the milk ; another for molasses—sugar was not permitted on that table. There

was fresh bread in plenty, and meat and vegetables, especially white, mealy potatoes, cooked to a turn, with their
jackets on, in absolute profusion. Butter appeared in boun-
tiful supply, but it was too vigorous, some of the boarders
said, for any other use than to harness to a carriage to draw
grist to mill. In other words, its flavor was rank and taste
abominable. McKenna felt that such food was not good for
him the moment he entered for his breakfast, and, using
everything beside that was nourishing, he quietly gave the
butter a deservedly wide berth.

After the morning meal, and having given some attention
to his boots, which were drawn on with difficulty—first
having to soak them well with melted tallow—McKenna
took a short stroll to the railway work, where he had a talk
with the boss, and with some of the hands who were fellow-
boarders. He gleaned from the former that employment for
him, just then and there, must be counted as out of the question. Labor was to be done, but the price was low, while
workingmen were more plentiful than whortleberries on the
mountain. There were too many German miners and laborers in the vicinity for the prosperity of the Mollie Maguires,
he could easily see, without asking. After making a few
other calls, the traveler returned to Timmins', where, in his
triple-bedded apartment, he managed to indite a hurried
report to Mr. Franklin, informing him of his whereabouts
and movements. This he succeeded in depositing in the
post-office. The address upon the envelope was such as to
disarm and thwart suspicion. It had been prepared for his
use before leaving Philadelphia.

In the afternoon rain fell heavily, and therefore no work
could be done outside the tunnel excavation; even inside it
was wet and uncomfortable, and many of the men remained
at home, some drinking, others dancing and singing, and
still others whiling away the time playing various games at
cards. Among these laborers were several members of the

Miners' and Laborers' Union, but they were all re'cent, after concurring in the generally expressed opinion that mining and railroading were dull and money very scarce everywhere in those regions.

The ensuing day the agent settled his bill at Timmins' tavern, and, as the weather had cleared up finely during the night, bid adieu to the landlord, his wife and family, and started for Schuylkillhaven. Arrived there, he found many men at work, but no possible chance for him to earn a dollar. The operations carried on were mostly for the railroad. He encountered a few miners just from the collieries above, and they gave the visitor nothing in the way of hopefulness as to the condition of affairs where they had been. Laborers could hardly find engagements anywhere. And as for his especial subject of pursuit and object of inquiry, the element predominating was still German ; hence, there was very little to detain him in the neighborhood.

The next point attended to was Auburn, about five miles from Port Clinton, a small country place, boasting a couple of planing-mills and a number of business houses. Here nothing transpired of importance, and McKenna toiled back on foot over the mountain, toward the hour of sunset, to Schuylkillhaven, where he had deposited his baggage.

A day later the stranger went to Tremont, and thence to Sweet Arrow. Returning to the first-mentioned place about the middle of the afternoon, he formed the acquaintance of a number of his countrymen ; but they had no hints to volunteer—and he was very far from asking any foolish questions in this connection—showing that they were even aware of the existence of such an organization as the Mollie Maguires

A day later McKenna encountered Nicholas Brennan, a coal-miner from the vicinity of Mt. Pleasant, near Minersville. Brennan gave out that he was also a traveler, engaged in going from one place to another for the purpose of securing work at his calling for the winter. Their pursuits being ostensibly similar, McKenna and Brennan soon struck up an intimacy. After the latter had more than once tasted liquor at McKenna's expense, he thawed out considerably became pliable and talkative, and soon had much to remark about "the power that made English landlords quake." But he gave it as his opinion that such a force could accomplish very little, if anything, in the anthracite country of Pennsylvania, and pretended to believe the Miners' and Laborers' Union, which had recently been formed, would prove of no benefit to working-men. Brennan prided himself upon his discerning shrewdness, and said, early in his conversation with the operative, he knew, at once, upon first fixing his eye on him, that he, McKenna, was a boatman, or canal hand, the correctness of which allegation, for his own purposes, that gentleman felt constrained to acknowledge. Brennan recommended his new-found associate to go to Tamaqua, or Mahanoy City, where he thought mining was moving more briskly than in any other portion of the State—especially was it more lively than in the neighborhood of Pottsville. He concluded his lengthy harangue by remark·ing, in a significant way—referring to the localities named:

"There's the ground where the boys are true!"

"Then they are the very places I want to get work in," responded McKenna, and, watching the countenance of Brennan, he was sure he discovered in it an expression of disappointment, as though the reply made to "the ground where the boys were true" was not exactly the one he had anticipated receiving. Pretending, however, not to notice it, the detective proposed a game at cards, "jist for the fun of the thing," and, after that ended, Brennan was so much under the influence of spirits, his companion was forced to cut loose from him. Nothing more could be elicited, but McKenna was well satisfied that, if not a simon-pure Mollie Maguire, his late opponent in euchre knew more about the society than he cared to impart to a stranger. He made

mental note of the words: "There's the ground where the
boys are true!" and could not help thinking they were in
some way connected with the mysterious order. Brennan
was kind enough to give him the names of some of his friends
in the mines; these he also treasured in his memory, to be
made use of as occasion presented.

The next day Brennan was perfectly sober, and, it being
the first of November and a Catholic holiday, he accompanied McKenna to church, and, after service, introduced him
to everybody he knew as "a young man from Colorado, in
quest of work," the stranger soon becoming quite popular
with a certain class. In the afternoon all adjourned to a
convenient saloon, where McKenna kept up a continuous
round of amusements for several hours, relating wonderful
stories of his adventures in the United States Navy during
the late war, all drawn from his own fertile fancy, but certainly very interesting to his listeners, and by singing, in
good style, some genuine Irish melodies. | Brennan and his
companions started, the same afternoon, for Pottsville, only
three miles distant, and urged McKenna to accompany
them. He excused himself, on the score of being compelled
to await money, due him for work, which had been promised
by post at that place, and the young fellows reluctantly departed without him.

Sunday, the second of November, passed without the occurrence of any incident worthy of note. On the succeeding
Monday our detective rode by rail twenty-four miles, stopping
at Pine Grove, where he found the shafts still some seven
miles distant, over a rough and hilly path, and did not vis't
them. Small was the loss by this, however, as no work was
being prosecuted, and the employés were scattering to various localities until such time as operations should be again
commenced. After an examination of the tanneries there,
with a few small machine-shops, without learning anything
of value, he returned to Tremont, at which place he met a

man named John Delaney, a miner, who was seemingly on a regular lark, disbursing his money lavishly, and imbibing drinks industriously. Delaney was of Brennan's opinion, thinking work would be difficult to obtain in the mines, so few were being operated, and railed loudly against the Philadelphia and Reading Coal and Iron Company, charging all the existing troubles to that corporation. He boasted that they—the miners—once kept the Company and their mines idle for eight long months, and could do so again if goaded to it. He was equally severe in his denunciations of German, Welsh and English miners, and their "butties," alleging that they—especially the Germans—had everything their own way about the vicinity of Tremont, but it was different in Shenandoah, Tamaqua, and other towns. Delaney was anxious to introduce McKenna to all of his personal friends, and, in that regard, was allowed to have his way, the detective properly considering it well that he should know as many men of the right character as possible. They might be useful as references at other localities. He therefore expressed his hearty thanks to Delaney for his exertions in this direction. The following day, having eschewed liquor for a season, Delaney went with his new-discovered friend to Donaldson, where he made him acquainted with the outside boss of the mines, going even as far as to ask for work for the "young man," who, he said, "was jist stharvin' for somewhat to lay his honest, hard-workin' hands to!" The boss could do nothing, however; and, after examining the slopes and walking through some of the gangways, talking with a miner here and there, they revisited the upper air. Again it was discovered the Germans held the ascendency in numbers and power, and managed to keep it; hence, there was no opportunity for securing employment. He must seek elsewhere for a body of the Mollie Maguires—the Donaldson mines were not their abiding-place.

The next point on the list for examination was Middle

Creek, two miles distant, over the mountain, from Tremont where the men were equally unlucky, finding no work. A walk back, through rough roads, over brambles and stones, and dodging laurel and alder bushes, gave the pedestrians appetites for their suppers when they reached Tremont. Delaney here separated from McKenna, after a few farewell glasses, and started for Pottsville, at which place he said he was due, and had friends and relatives.

During the succeeding Wednesday the detective remained in Tremont, and, after dinner, enjoyed a walk on the railway track, the weather being fine, continuing an intimacy previously begun between himself and the switch-tender, an aged Emerald Islander, who was found sitting nigh the entrance to his little box, or cabin—short, stumpy, gray-haired, brown-faced, roughly clad, but honest and sturdy-looking withal—smoking his pipe contentedly, and receiving pleasurably the cool breeze sweeping up the valley. Mike Fitzgibbons, the switchman, was a genuine specimen of the hard-working, steady, reliable Irish peasantry, and he was never known to neglect a duty.

"An' how is business wid ye the day?" asked McKenna, as he came up to the old man's station, preparing his tobacco meantime, and signaling by a significant motion, easily understood by smokers, for a light for his cutty-pipe, which was old and black, as well as fashionably short in the stem. The switchman tendered his doodeen, which, having been employed, the stranger returned to its owner, with thanks.

"Arrah! an' about all days are the same to the likes o me! I am to the fore all the time when I'm not slapin' an atin' wid Betty and the childer. I jist mind the trains, to prevint misadventure. Sure, the Company gives me fair wages, promptly paid, for that same!"

"Thrue for ye," answered McKenna; "an' hev ye any objection to me takin' a seat by ye, on the settle fornins the wall, while I have a puff at me pipe?'

"Not the laste in the worruld!" responded Fitzgibbons, making space for the stranger on the bench. After resting and drawing away industriously at his pipe for a few moments, McKenna remembered a Philadelphia *Inquirer* which he had obtained that forenoon and not yet examined, and, taking it from his pocket, commenced reading. He knew this would excite his companion's curiosity. Soon Fitzgibbons remarked:

"Would ye be plazed to rade to me a bit? Me eyes are none of the best, an' the little I has I save fur the good of the Company. What do the paper say about the State elections?"

"I'll rade to ye wid pleasure," said the agent, and he proceeded to give all that he found of interest. After commenting at some length upon the contents of the sheet, and having his pipe freshly filled with McKenna's fragrant tobacco, the switchman was more chatty. In a little while he entered his box, and returned bearing in his hand a copy of the well-known Boston *Pilot*, which he proffered to his comrade. After skimming hastily over the Irish news and some telegraphic intelligence, he came to an article headed, "The Mobocrats of Pennsylvania." This he read carefully aloud to the old man. It was a scathing blow at the Mollie Maguires, giving them deserved condemnation, and appeared in the shape of correspondence. After finishing it, McKenna asked:

"What is this all about?"

Evidently much excited, Fitzgibbons answered:

"But isn't it a sarching piece, though? It slathers them butcherin' vagabones widout mercy! O, I would like to know who has writ it!"

McKenna kept down his anxiety to learn more, and said nothing, when the switchman continued:

"Ye have heard of the society? Av coorse ye have! An' now they've got across the big say, till America, an' into the mines ! But doesn't that article cut them deep, tho' ? It has created quite a ruction here—and no wonder ! It was a great thing, the getting up of that piece ! It do lay on the lash to the backs of the Mollie Maguires in splendid style !"

The old man was evidently an opponent of the order, or he was endeavoring to draw out the opinion of his friend. McKenna determined to let him know what he was supposed to think, but which was the very opposite of his real convictions.

"It must be that such writin's will damage the interests of the Irish people in the coal regions. Don't you agree wid me in this ? "

Fitzgibbons was touched at a tender spot and flared up in an instant, moving involuntarily further from the operative, his dark but expressive face ablaze with honest indignation, saying vehemently :

"No ! I disagrees wid ye in that altogether ! It is the Mollie Maguires that's doin' the wrong ! Such articles in the *Pilot* will have a good effect, an' do somethin'—of which there's pressin' want—toward breakin' up the clan ! God knows it nades dispersin' an' punishin' too ! Such bodies is a burnin' shame an' disgrace to the men in them, an' they befoul all Irishmen and all good Catholics ! Ye naden't be surprised if ye mate them yoursel' ! They've had 'em here, even, where there live so few from our country ! But Father McLaughlin druv 'em out wid the hardest words ye iver heard from the lips of a clergyman ! God prosper him for that same ! An' since they left, we've had pace an' quiet in town, wid no killin's and batin's."

It would not do for the listener to permit such an opportunity to say a word in favor of his particular friends, the Mollie Maguires, to pass unimproved. While the sentiments expressed were his own, to the letter, he must dissemble and oppose them. Therefore he replied :

" Now, fur the life of me, I can't see why Irish Catholics cannot have a dacent, paceable society of their own—if there be the laste toucn of sacracy about it—widout the papers an' the clergy interloguing and opposing! Wur any warm done by the Masons and Odd Fellows, shure there wouldn't be a word in the public press about it. An' what's the raison that this society should be abused ? "

" You are all wrong ! My experience goes agin' the order ! I knows some men who hev bin members, but they come out of it. They saw enough ! By my sowl, I'd as soon go colloguing wid the devil, hoof, horns, tail and all, as wid the murtherin' rascals ! Harken to this, now ! If any wan of the crew wur discharged from work an' wanted fur to sake revinge—which the same is swate the worruld over—he jist went to the headquarters of the society, or to the president, or whativer they call him, which is the head official, an' made out that it wur from religious differences he lost his place, or because he wur an Irishman ; and then lots ud be cast, sure, an' two or more of the brothers—bad cess to such a brotherhood !—must go, whether they would or no, an' jist shoot down the boss that had cut him off ! O, ye may spake all yer soft words, an' shake yer head, an' not belave me, fur I consider it awfully incredible myself, that Irishmen will do such things ; an' ye may call me distraught, an' all that ; but I knows what I says, an' my advice is not to be afther defendin' the murtherin', thavin' set, if ye want to be respected in this region of country ! Don't ye bother wid the Mollie Maguires ! "

Before McKenna had time for a reply, the afternoon passenger train came shrieking around an abrupt curve, the switchman seized his keys and flag, and ran off to attend to his duties ; and the detective, pocketing the Boston newspaper, intending to return it, retired to his boarding-place. The *Pilot*, he thought, would prove a valuable document to him, from the article he had been discussing

CHAPTER V.

COLD COMFORT IN THE MOUNTAINS.

THE succeeding day McKenna returned to the switch-tender's hut, and, after obtaining permission to retain the Boston *Pilot*, their suddenly suspended conversation was resumed. It is unnecessary to detail its various points, but the detective learned while Fitzgibbons was a decided and out-spoken enemy of the Mollie Maguires, yet he was thor-oughly informed as to their movements throughout the coal regions. This knowledge was secured by a careful study of the local newspapers, and talking with his neighbors and friends formerly holding membership in the organization. It was Fitzgibbons's idea, judging after several years' close con-sideration of the matter, that the home-nests, the chief dens, of the Mollies, might be located at Mahanoy City, Shenan-doah, Shamokin, Pittston, and Wilkesbarre, and that nearly all of the smaller places had lodges of more or less magni-tude. In one of these principal strongholds McKenna must make his headquarters, but in which he could only decide after personal investigation.

By the time the operative had remained a fortnight or more in the mountains, much exposure to the weather and consid-erable out-of-door exercise had wrought perceptible changes in his personal appearance. His apparel fitted more to his satisfaction, and a certain awkwardness in bearing was nota-bly diminished. The cuticle covering his forehead, cheeks, and hands was toughened. His complexion was darkened, while his hair was lighter and longer. The unshaven chin had sprouted and grown a tolerably heavy beard, and no attempt was made, by trimming, to shape it handsomely or

3

becomingly. His understanding of localities was improved —and would continue to improve through travel and examination—and his list of particular associates was rapidly growing larger and more useful.

At Tower City, McKenna found Donahue's saloon a popular resort for his countrymen, and he at once honored it with his presence. Donahue, the proprietor, was one day entertaining a number of his friends living at Mahanoy City when the stranger, "from Denver," entered the room, and, assuming a reckless air, with the signs of having indulged in a few glasses of something more potent than water, soon made himself popular with those present. This impression was increased by the rich stories he related and the rare songs he sung. The next day he discovered, in the same house, a second copy of the Boston newspaper, before alluded to, containing an answer to the slashing attack upon the Mollie Maguires. The later communication dated from Locust Gap, about four miles from Tremont, and the charges of the earlier publication were all completely negatived. Donahue's attention was ingeniously called to the subject, and he unsuspectingly answered that he had read the article, having borrowed the journal from a neighbor for the purpose. In a short time thereafter, the two men being alone, the saloon-keeper said:

"You must know that I was a mimber of the order, for two years and upwards, but gave it up some time since, belaving it is not a good crowd fur any wan, havin' proper respect fur his good name, to be connected wid. Still, a number of excellent friends of mine are holdin' on, and will not listen to raison, or be persuaded to cut adrift from the body. I am sure that, one day, they will learn I'm quite right an' they far in the wrong. It wur very well wid us until the fighting begun at Mahanoy City, betwixt the Buke and Duggan boys, the last showing themselves the more powerful; but, faith, the effects of the battle can't aisily be wiped out, an' these sharp newspaper writin's are part of the results on the contentions. I think the order is losing strength, in being split up, inter smithereens like, by dissensions an' broils, widout an' within."

Donahue was showing himself a man of more than ordinary intelligence. After a judicious invitation to drink, at McKenna's cost, he continued :

" Considerin' the ladership hev fallen into wake an bad hands, an' the mimbers at loggerheads, one anent the other, all the time—to say nothing about the opposition of the Bishop an' the clargy—it would be just as well if the counthry wur clane rid of the entire subject ! "

" Mayhap you're more'n half right, Mr. Donahue, but did ye niver think, fur wan moment, the very order you condemn may be the manes—wid other naded help—of bringin' into union all the Irishmen in the coal ragions, givin' them protection an' securin' them their aqual rights ? ".

The detective was paving the way for future work, and would say nothing against the Mollies.

" I'm more'n doubtful of that same," returned the tavern-keeper, "such mane men are at the helm ! They'll run the machine for their individual profit, an' use the power of the society for evil, an' only evil, purposes ! "

" Fur that matther, this identical charge would hould good agin almost any kind of combination, sacret or not sacret ! Do ye think, now, spakin' out honest an' thrue, we should lay aside a good implement, jist fur the simple an' only raison we are in fear of its employment, by accident or otherwise, fur unlawful ends ? "

" Well, I see you are friendly wid the boys," at last said Donahue, " an' I'll urge no further objection to them ! Sure, I don't belave it will be fur the safety of my life an' me house an' property I should, but I can't help thinkin' I have had plenty an' to spare of 'em ! Don't let on what I've been afther talkin' to ye ! It might do me harum ! If vou wants to hear more about the fellows, I'll refer ye to me paple at Mahanoy City—I hev father, mother, an' brothers there—an' in fact, if ye came to want it, I can send a letther by ye to the ould gintleman, who'll recave ye kindly, widout doubt. I hev an idea ye'll do much better beyant than here, an' perhaps get work right off. Things is mighty dull an' quare hereabouts ; there, they may not be quite so bad ! "

At this time the clergyman of the town entered the saloon —he was a quaint, little, jolly fat man, with long, fair hair, small, blue eyes, and wore his gold-bowed spectacles as naturally as though nature had handily framed his turn-up nose to properly support them. Of course the remarks on the particular topic, so interesting to McKenna, were at once suspended. The priest was engaged in disposing of admission checks to a church fair, to transpire the following Saturday, and hoping the sooner to get rid of him, and despite the utter impossibility that he would be present at the diversion, McKenna purchased a ticket. Donahue did the same, and the reverend gentleman was quite happy when he made his exit. Then Donahue, unfortunately, had work to perform, but promised to prepare the letter to his father in season for McKenna's return from Tower City, where he knew he had arranged to go that afternoon, and the detective set out upon the expedition.

At Tower City the operative had his first experience in a coal-shaft of any great depth. Having previously descended some steep slopes, and examined the machinery for withdrawing the anthracite at other collieries, the interior of an extensive mine he had not yet inspected. While at the Upper Mine of Messrs. Rappalie & Co., in the vicinity, an outside boss, about looking after some business below, invited McKenna to descend in his company.

It was midday, with the sun shining brightly, when the two men stepped upon the movable platform of the elevator inside the shaft-house. In a few moments they were settling swiftly, but at a uniform rate of speed, down, down, as it seemed to the novice in such matters, even to the foundations of the globe. For a brief period they were in total darkness, and a sensation, as of seasickness, came over him. Still he clung to his support and the uncomfortable feeling soon left him. As the lower regions were reached, the traveler thought he would be far more content if again breathing the clear ether above. The system experienced absolute relief when the motion ceased, and the solid bottom of the shaft was touched. But here it was like entering a new sphere. There was dark above, below, and all around, only here and there relieved by dim little stars, which were continually dodging downward, sidewise, and upward, as though held by an unsteady hand. As his eyes acquired familiarity with the situation, he saw that to each one of these erratic satellites was attached the body of a living man —in fact, they were only diminutive lamps which the miners and their helpers wore above the visors of their hats to light them in their labors. The general effect produced in the sombre recesses of the excavation, and the strange and grotesque, as well as picturesque, shadows reflected back from the men's figures upon the walls and buttresses and floors, all defy description, and must be seen to be understood. As far as the eye was able to penetrate, in every direction, almost, the nodding demon with the single, blazing orb, like a star, in the forehead, and bearing glistening pick and bar, and drill and spade, was industriously working away at the breast, tearing out the black diamonds, making more pillars, and piercing further into the lode. Wandering from point to point in pursuit of his errand, the boss kept on, and McKenna followed. In one place he was startled and nearly deafened by the, to him, unexpected explosion of a blast, close to his ear, as he thought, but really at quite a safe distance. He involuntarily jumped aside, expecting that he had been hit, but in a moment recovered his equanimity, seeing he was not injured. They were met cn every side by a succession of heavy supports and gaping caverns, the former serving as props for the rocky roof, preventing the falling in of the ground resting above, and the latter leading to still other channels and gangways from which coal was being brought. The air seemed heavy-laden, damp, and unhealthy, and the path pursued, in many places, passed through lakelets of black water reaching sometimes above the ankles. All was bustle and activity with that army of underground toilers, drilling, blasting, loading, tunneling, tamping down blasts, laying trains, breaking away coal and running it down chutes to the floors, heaping it upon small trucks, which in turn transported it to the base of the entering shaft, whence it was elevated by steam power to the breaker, high above ground. Over all were heard the sounds of the pumps, clangor of chains, and rattling of picks, making harsh and jagged music, to the strains of which the work advanced. It was no pleasant place to remain in, especially as a looker-on, and McKenna was not illy pleased when the boss, taking advantage of the ascent of a loaded elevator, asked him to return to the region of daylight. The sensation experienced upon again encountering the sunshine was painfully peculiar, the bright blaze almost blinding him during the first few moments of the change. But presently the retina was brought in conformity with the surroundings, and eyesight was fully restored.

The breaker in which the coal is crushed, sorted, and prepared for use, in its different sizes, is a long, dark, high and sloping-roofed structure, generally of wood, to the uttermost peak of which, almost, the anthracite, in lumps weighing ten, one hundred, and three hundred pounds, is raised by the steam elevator—that is in shaft-mining—and there emptied, or dumped into a huge hopper, or funnel, leading direct to the crushing machinery. This consists of two immensely large and heavy iron cylinders, provided with massive teeth which, when the rollers revolve, munch the coal into larger and smaller fragments, producing a crunching, grating sound, and finally casting it into a channel beneath that conveys it to a succession of screens, through which it is run, separating the coarser from the finer sizes. Under these immense sieves come other sluices, still on an incline, and, after having the slate abstracted by the hands of a gang of boys, engaged for the purpose, the chestnut, range, stove, little egg, large egg, and steamboat coal glides to the storehouse by the railway track, or, if need be, direct to the cars in which it is transported to market.

The culm—or refuse coal, slate, and waste—is carried off and piled in high embankments, by man and mule power. It is dumped at the outer end of the temporary track, much after the style of a car-load of dirt in building a grade for a railway. These residue heaps dot the coal regions, as dark notes of admiration, showing to the traveler the great amount of riches from which they have been eliminated and how vast the aggregate of wealth yet remaining in the bosom of prolific mother earth.

Returning to his boarding-place, the traveler secured Donahue's letter to his father, and about the middle of the ensuing day took stage, with three other gentlemen, for Minersville, some thirteen miles distant, over the mountain and near Pottsville. Ordinarily but a couple of hours would be consumed in making the trip, but the occupants of the stage were no ordinary people and were not fated to make an ordinary journey. They had not been long out when the sun was obscured by huge, lead-colored clouds, and across the heavens drifted vapory masses of a more fleecy character. Then a heavy snow-storm set in, adding to the prevailing discomfort and making the progress of the mule team more painfully slow. The passengers, none of whom knew McKenna, and none of whom were personally known to him, made light of their troubles and gave jokes plentifully and cheerfully upon the snow, the driver and his rig, and one cerning one another. It was true the conveyance and its propellers and captain sadly needed repairs, the Jehu being in the sere and yellow leaf of his age, having but one leg to stand upon—and that troubled with rheumatism—while the mules were spavined and lame, the vehicle shattered in cover and framework, and uneasy and creaking in its running gear, not to speak of the harness, which seemed made of odds and ends, selected from the refuse of some army collection, idle since the close of the war. Still, up hill and down grade, the animals managed to move at a little better than a snail's pace.

Gradually the hillsides wrapped a winding-sheet of snow around them, as though taking eternal farewell of earth, and the stunted pine and hemlock and mountain ash took on a similarly white and beautiful mantle. The highway, never too clearly marked, was to the eye of a stranger entirely lost sight of, and nothing but an educated sense or instinct on the part of driver and beasts could prevent the stage and its freight from foundering by the wayside, or dashing suddenly and unexpectedly off the brink of one of the numerous rocky precipices, among and around which, in many a serpentine coil, wound the road they were trying to follow. Once, when at its very verge, the driver saw a yawning gulf just before him. He was barely in time to quickly draw in the reins, thus saving himself and his passengers from certain destruction. But the worst was not yet over. The mules would not back, do all their manager could, and the travelers were forced to alight, put their shoulders to the wheels, and extricate the vehicle without the aid of the team. This consumed time, and it was nearly dusk before the wagon was once more in the road and all mounted and ready to proceed.

"Pat. McCarthy, an old friend of mine down on Long Island, would say," remarked McKenna, while pushing at a wheel with all his strength, "that this was almost equal to workin' your passage on the canal—drivin' the horse and walkin' on the tow-path!"

This conceit restored good humor, and the unsteady coach resumed its journey. Before darkness fully closed in the scene the most dangerous portion of the route was traversed, and thenceforward, the course sloping downward, the mules jogged on at a more lively pace, the travelers reaching Millersville by nine o'clock at night, weary, sleepy, and as one of the number truly said, " as sharp-set for supper as a gang of ravenous wolves." When they alighted, the snow still descended, and the prospect seemed good for fine sleighing on the morrow over all the level country.

Entering the principal hotel, McKenna judged that his dress and presence were again a bar to his introduction to respectable society. The gracious and affable landlord—gracious and affable to all excepting the roughly clad gentle-man from Ireland—was with difficulty persuaded to allow him to remain in the house. But finally he did consent, and under its proper heading for the seventeenth of November, 1873, on the hotel register, the detective inscribed the following :

"*Jas. McKenna, Denver, Colorado Ter.*"

The hotel-keeper was on the lookout for disreputable char-acters, as he should be, but his humanity, added to the pro-tests of the detective's late traveling companions, would not consent to his turning a person out in the snow, possibly to freeze to death, even though his clothing were poor and his face, hair, beard, and general appearance the opposite of prepossessing. A five dollar note, which the stranger had changed at the bar, while paying for a hot toddy for himself and the stage passengers—not forgetting the driver—after the bill had been closely scrutinized and pronounced not counterfeit, exerted its influence in determining the matter, and prompted the innkeeper to be generous, even though

3*

there was a remote chance that his business might suffer thereby. The young man, it was decided, should have food for his stomach and a place to sleep in. The supper was spread on a barrel-head, in the cold, dreary slab kitchen, at the rear of the cook-room proper, through the wide chinks in the walls of which the keen blast whistled mournfully, and the snow-flakes stole in with a whisk and a whirl, painting delicate and curiously enameled pictures on the greasy floor. His chair was like that upon which the late James Gordon Bennett, senior, sat, when writing his leading editorials for the embryo New York *Herald*—an inverted and empty nail keg—but the food was warm and palatable, and he ate it in silence, as he well knew that grumbling would result in no good. He was, for the occasion, a wandering refugee, and must necessarily put up with such treatment as those in his condition usually receive from the world's people. He could plainly hear the tantalizing clatter of crockery, inhale the savory odor arising from epicurean dishes, and listen to the conversation of other and more favored guests, coming from the comfortable, well-lighted dining-hall, when the door chanced to be open, and that was all. Later at night he climbed a rough ladder, nearly at the top of the house, he believed, found his loft, with its straw bed and blankets, and an old saddle for a pillow. Extinguishing his candle, he rolled himself, full dressed as he was, in his coverings, and soon fell asleep. Not all the insects in the place, nor the rats that ran over him, nor the cats that made night hideous with their wailings and spittings could, for more than a few moments at a stretch, banish sleep from McKenna's eyelids.

CHAPTER VI.

POTTSVILLE AND THE SHERIDAN HOUSE.

THE detective, after making a casual inspection of the place, during the following day, was in many-respects well suited with it. Usually carrying on considerable trade, he found all the people of the town complaining of dull times, even the collieries employing but few hands. The blast-furnaces were in the same category. Wading through the snow, during his walks about the streets, he chanced upon some men whose faces were not new to his sight, having previously encountered them at Schuylkillhaven, and he naturally resumed the intercourse there begun. Nothing of particular importance resulted, however, excepting wet feet and dread of impending rheumatisms and neuralgias.

He at once changed his quarters from the hotel to a private boarding-house, where the style of living was less pretentious, the price charged patrons not nearly so exhaustive of his finances—and yet the accommodations, as far as this particular boarder was concerned, were considerably more comfortable. Beside, he was quite at home, and in a better position for work. And here were many acquaintances to form.

While insinuating himself into a new town, or community, McKenna properly adopted widely differing devices, but an extended experience instructed him that the best course to pursue, in any given case of the sort, was the one appearing the most natural. It was a cardinal principle, impressed upon his mind, never to make open and direct inquiries regarding people and things of which he was really in search —a place for permanent employment was, as the reader has all along understood, merely a cover for his actual purpose in visiting the coal country. In fact, unless it brought him in close contact with the right men, and revealed to him hidden things, in no other way attainable, a chance for himself to dig in the mines might, for the present, be deferred. It would be well, he believed, after a while, to divert attention from his real occupation. But to look up a job was a good excuse for much traveling, over a large field, with the topography of which he was required to become accurately familiar. Private objects he left to be worked out in a private way, occasionally giving them a slight and unremarked start, or direction, as he went from place to place.

Night was his favorite time for accomplishing progress Then his friends were generally relieved from labor and gathered where they could be reached. He sauntered unconcernedly about, after darkness had set in, and if he heard a row, or "bit of a shindy" going on in a drinking place would enter and make himself in some manner companionable with the persons within—excepting they chanced to be of the character of Mr. Staub, the portly landlord at Port Clinton, who proved so inhospitable, mistaking the agent for a thief—and in that event he usually caused himself to become invisible as rapidly as possible. With an assumption of unlimited assurance, and pretending to be more than half way under the influence of liquor, other conditions being favorable, he broke out with such a roaring, rollicking ditty as he supposed might please those about him, or, if he felt in the mood, began a spirited Irish jig, performed with much agility and many comical contortions of countenance and body, to the measure of no music at all, excepting he chose to whistle a tune meanwhile. In the course of a little time, the out-door training, and the exercise in singing and dancing, made him quite an expert, and his fame preceded him from Schuylkillhaven to Summit, and, as he learned from his companions, had journeyed even as far as Pottsville. As any rate, he never failed, with those in whose company he cared, for the purposes of his undertaking, to be received, in immediately placing himself upon a secure and friendly footing. The climax of miner's friendship was usually reached by asking the persons present to come to the bar and indulge in something to drink, if it was to be had, at his expense; otherwise, the invitation emanated from some one of the company and included the stranger. Either result was equally satisfactory.

If he happened, as he sometimes would, to fall in with rogues—indeed his search was for and among this class—he had prepared a device and history calculated quickly to attract their sympathies and give him a warm place in their circle.

When in the presence of sober, civil, and sedate people—which was occasionally the case—the operative tried another and different scheme, perhaps relating a cheerful ghost-story, or giving one or more of the many pathetic, patriotic, or sentimental ballads, of which he had quite a collection stored away in his brain to be expended upon such associates. In almost any company of his own countrymen he was certain of finding hearty welcome, and, as it was among Irishmen he expected to labor, he scarcely ever essayed entrance to the homes of persons of other nationalities. The time might come, he supposed, should he succeed in his labors, when the doors of most respectable families from his native land, even, would be closed against him—but, at the end, he believed he would be perfectly justified in the course he was pursuing.

The storm, in the opening of which he entered Minersville, continued, snow falling almost incessantly during three or four days, and the operative could not meanwhile accomplish much in the streets. As soon as the sun came out again, and the paths and roads were broken over the mountains, he visited Miner's Hill, two miles away, returned to Minersville, and then took the horse car for Pottsville. His first work in that city was to secure a cheap and decently comfortable boarding-place, which he found at the residence of Mrs. O'Regan, in East Norwegian Street. The widow kept house neatly, beside a bottle of poteen, from which, without paying license, she sold an occasional drop.

A visitor's impressions of Pottsville, when first beholding its spires of churches and evidences of industry and thrift, from the heights above, cannot well be other than pleasing. The scenery encompassing the town is bold and rugged, and the descent by car to the Schuylkill, and Norwegian Creek, on whose high banks it is lodged, rapid and inspiring; and once having arrived in its handsomely-built streets, to one unaccustomed to see cities perched upon steep mountain-sides, the sight is well calculated to evolve surprise. Having some twelve thousand inhabitants, there is in it much enlightenment and great wealth. Abundantly provided with handsome and elegant churches and school-houses, imposing business structures and beautiful residences, Potts-ville enjoys an enviable reputation as a healthful and pleas-ant place for summer residence. One especial point of interest is the costly and artistic monument to Henry Clay. It is of pure white marble, in the shape of a fluted column, rising from a massive square pedestal, and surmounted by a full-length statue of the great Defender. The hotels—among which stand pre-eminent Pennsylvania Hall and the Exchange—are unsurpassed in the State. There is a large and commodious court-house, and a county jail rivaling in size and com-pleteness of officers and appointments some of the larger State penitentaries. It also has an Academy of Music, in which operatic and theatrical entertainments are given by traveling troupes.

Pottsville is the concentrating point for an extended radius of rich mining country, and the depot of supplies for an equally wide circle.

The surroundings in this part of Schuylkill County are, some of them, deserving of national celebrity. Among these is Mount Carbon, towering in height, broad, black, gloomy and stupendous; and, at its base, stand the Mansion House —a very agreeable place of resort—and a number of fashionable residences. Further away is a bit of natural landscape, pronounced one of the most striking in the country. It is "Tumbling Run Dam," which has been painted by several master hands, and, in picturesqueness and sublimity, is worthy the drawing many times more. Here the waters of the stream, cut across by a heavy obstruction of sturdy rock, are turned abruptly aside, and rush, in a foaming, misty torrent, down, down, a steep side descent, torn and divided into innumerable smaller cascades, again uniting with the still, broad expanse below. Tall pines, stunted cedars, and noble oaks border the river on either shore, and, under the shadow of the overhanging barrier, are piled, in artistic confusion, great heaps of sharp and jagged rocks, seemingly rent from adjacent peaks by giant hands.

To change the subject from the sublime to the real and practical:

Among the occupants of Mrs. O'Regan's house was a young man named Jennings, apparently possessing more than ordinary intelligence, and, the afternoon of McKenna's arrival, knowing he was a stranger, this sociable person proposed to show his new-found friend the sights to be seen in the city. McKenna accepted the offer, and the two started out, not intending to be long absent. During the visits made to different places, of course the saloons were not omitted, and both of the men drank somewhat, but no more than to them seemed respectable and companionable. The operative was introduced by Jennings to a number of his intimate associates and friends, but met none of those with whom he was anxious to open communication.

As they were on Center Street, passing quietly along, the stranger read a sign over the door of a liquor store, or tavern, "Pat. Dormer," and said

" Let's go in here ! "

" Its no place for us," answered Jennings. " You are not of ' the stuff,' I guess ! At least, I know *I* am not ! "

" ' The stuff ! ' Phat is it ye mane by ' the stuff ' ? "

" Come away, across the street, and I'll tell you ! Its not the safe or proper thing to be conversing of such things so near this particular house ! "

So saying, Jennings led the way to another corner, where the young men stopped, well out of the sweep of the wind, in the lee of a large building, and the conversation was at once resumed by Jennings :

" Dormer is a *captain !* "

" Captain of a militia company, is it ye mane ? "

" No ! That's not it ! I believe that you are a good sort of a fellow, and I think I may venture to warn you—yet I want you to promise me never to repeat what I say. It might lead to trouble ! "

" Av coorse, I'll be as silent as the catacombs of Agypt ! Niver you fear Jim McKenna fur that, sure ! "

" You must understand, then, that Pat Dormer is a captain of the Sleepers ! "

" One of the notorious sivin, we rade about, is he ? In dade, an' I supposed they were all kilt entirely, more'n thirteen hundred years ago ! "

" No ! Not one of that number, but of the great secret order, here called the Sleepers ! '

" An' phat are the Slapers ? Plaze to explain it—or is it another conundrum you are after axin' me ? "

" The Sleepers are the Mollie Maguires ! There's a heap of them in this district, and Dormer is, or was, an officer high in authority in the organization. You've certainly heard of the society ? "

" Sure, an' I hev heard much about them in the ould counthry ! But nothing till America ! Are you sure they've ever crossed the say ?

They have, and there are thousands of them in this and some adjoining counties. If you stop here awhile you'll read about some of their work! They do not rest long without doing something in the way of murder or outrage!"

The young man then proceeded, with some particularity, to relate to his apparently astonished listener many of the stories he had gathered regarding the Mollie Maguires, with an outline of their known aims and objects. His words do not call for repetition here, as they allude to things already within the reader's knowledge. Jennings, in conclusion, remarked:

"Of course *I* do not belong to the order—would not if I could, and could not if I would—as I am American born and both of my parents not from Ireland. But there are any number of them in the neighborhood. Dormer is a sort of King Bee among the brethren, and his house their rendezvous when in the city. Dormer filled the office of County Commissioner for some six years in all, but was defeated at the last election, through the interference of the society, which, for some reason, during a short time was opposed to him, but I hear it talked that he is in its good graces again, ready once more to run for office, should occasion offer. He was once quite a respectable man, but place and a long lease of power, and bad liquor taken by wholesale, have brought him to moral and almost physical ruin. One great fault that the order found with him was that he had affiliated with some other secret associations popular among Protestants. He was, and is now, comparatively, a very powerful man standing six feet four inches in his stockings, and pulling the beam at two hundred and thirty pounds, he is considered a dangerous individual to tamper with!"

"As my countrywomen are often heard to remark, 'what a handsome corpse he would make, to be sure!' What do Dormer look like, in other regards?"

"His hair is gray, eyes light hazel, and he has a countesance, which, from its mildness of expression, can be taken as no index to his inward character, for he is cruel and bloodthirsty, especially when in his cups. He calls his hotel the Sheridan House—you see that it is popular. There are many people constantly going in and coming out! But such as you and I do not belong there!"

The young man again cautioned McKenna 'o say nothing of his revelations, and, after promising compliance, they entered a saloon, had some refreshments, and then went home in time for supper.

The detective could not retire to his bed that night without at least attempting to see the man he had heard so much about. He might prove the very person he desired to meet. Therefore, excusing himself by saying he needed to make some purchases up town, he procured a lamp, went to his bedroom, carefully examined his revolver, placed it convenient in his hip pocket, and sallied forth. Making sure, after walking some distance, that Jennings was not in the vicinity, he soon reached Dormer's saloon.

CHAPTER VII.

BLOODY RECORD OF THE MOLLIE MAGUIRES.

For the purpose of properly carrying out the *rôle* of a truthful historian of actual occurrences, we will change the scene, for a short season, and, leaving McKenna to seek adventure with Pat Dormer and his associates, in Pottsville, take a view of acts performed in the same portion of the country, several years anterior to the time heretofore alluded to.

The Mollie Maguires were more than usually active and bloodthirsty in 1865. On the 25th of August of that year, David Muhr, superintendent of a colliery, was killed in Foster township. He was shot on the public highway, in the broad light of day, within two hundred yards of the house he was employed in, and where a large number of men were congregated, all of whom heard the report of firearms, and many being involuntary witnesses of the transaction. While this was the fact, no reliable testimony could be elicited by the Commonwealth, when the matter was under investigation, fixing the commission of the butchery upon any suspected party. Nobody knew the men, where they had come from, or where they had flown to. It was reported that signals had been seen burning that night on the hills, soon after the occurrence, and it was surmised they were built by confederates, to aid the principals in the murder to make their way to safety.

Again, on the tenth of January, 1866, Mr. Henry H. Dunne, a well-known citizen of Pottsville, and superintendent of one of the largest coal-mining corporations in all that circuit of country, was murdered on the turnpike, within two miles of the city, while riding home in his carriage, from a visit to a colliery over which he had control. Even up to the present date, no arrests have been made, nor has any information presented itself which promises to lead to the apprehension of the assassins. That they killed Mr. Dunne through complicity in some labor troubles was always the prevailing belief.

To continue the barbarous record, on Saturday, the seventeenth of October, 1868, Alexander Rae, another mining superintendent, was killed on the wagon road, near Centralia, in the township of Conyngham, Columbia County. Several persons were distrusted, and a number arrested, charged with the crime, and a strong chain of circumstantial evidence made out by the Commonwealth against them. The high

way on which the event occurred was that passing from
Centralia to Mt. Carmel, in Northumberland County, and
the exact location of the tragedy at a point distant about a
mile and a half from the latter place, in the neighborhood
of a spring where, for the convenience of travelers, there
had been erected a rude watering-trough, so that men, as
well as animals, might quench their thirst. Mr. Rae was
riding in his buggy, at half-past nine o'clock in the morning,
coming from his home, and going in the direction of the Coal
Ridge Improvement Company's colliery. He was a peaceable, inoffensive, but naturally fearless man, entirely unarmed, and only intent, at the time, on performing his duty
to his employers in the pursuit of his regular calling. The
fatal shots once discharged by the assassins, from their ambush near the road, the actors in the drama, without waiting
to learn the result of their bloody work, fled precipitately to
their refuge in the mountains, and for a long time entirely
avoided capture, or even the shadow of suspicion. The life-
less remains of Mr. Rae were discovered, Sunday morning,
pierced by six bullets, and resting near the spot where the
attack had been made. As a natural consequence of such
an outrage, the utmost indignation pervaded the community
in which the victim had for years been a widely-known and
much-respected resident. The particulars, as far as they
were learned, were repeated from person to person, and the
news spread like wildfire to the most distant parts of the coal
country. Mr. Rae left an estimable widow and six children
to mourn his death. John Duffy, of Mahanoy City, Schuylkill County, Michael Prior, of Branchdale, Thomas Donahue,
of Ashland, both in the same county, and Pat Hester, of
Mt. Carmel township, Northumberland County, *as was then
believed*, were the assassins. Some change in this regard
was made by subsequent events. Pat Hester was a married
man, forty-five years of age, and had several young children.
Prior was also married said to be forty years of age. Don-

hue had a wife and one child, and was apparently forty-three. Duffy was a bachelor, of about twenty-five years. Thomas Dooley, of Palo Alto, Schuylkill County, standing, by his own confession, in the position of an accomplice in the wicked assassination, about a month after the commission of the deed gave out facts which caused the apprehension of the others just named. The cause came up, was heard on an application for a writ of *habeas corpus*, before Judge Kline, one of the Associates of Schuylkill County; and all the defendants were held for and sent to Columbia County jail to await trial, which begun at Bloomsburg, Tuesday afternoon, the second of February, 1869. Donahue, Prior, Hester, and Duffy were brought into court, arraigned by the Prothonotary, and a plea of "not guilty" entered on the part of each. Upon application of Mr. Freeze, for the defense, separate trials were granted, and the Commonwealth elected to proceed against Donahue. Wednesday morning the prisoner entered court, accompanied by the sheriff, and took a seat by his counsel, Messrs. John W. Ryon, John G. Freeze, Meyer Strouse, S. P. Wolverton, and Wm. A. Marr, an array of talent which was well met by that included in the list of counsel for the Commonwealth, Messrs. Linn Bartholomew, Robert F. Clark, Edward H. Badly, M. M. L'Velle, and E. R. Ikler, the last-named the District Attorney. After a patient hearing the defendant was acquitted by the jury, and the prosecution, thereafter, thought it advisable to abandon the rest of the indictments. If Donahue could not be convicted—and that had been demonstrated by the defeat in his case—it was considered by the District Attorney and his corps of assistants it would be impossible, at that time, to fasten the murder upon any of the remaining defendants.

So commanding and pervading in the community was the subtle power of the Mollie Maguires, it was with the utmost difficulty that a jury could be secured to try the cause, and so abject had become the condition of terror under which the people submissively bowed their necks, seeing no possible avenue of escape, that witnesses accredited with knowledge of important points bearing against the prisoners, dare not, in fear of their lives, mount the witness stand.

So united were the Mollie Maguires, or whatever at that time they were called, they swore to *alibis* without number and barred all further immediate proceedings.

The next important outrage of this character, charged to the sanguinary clique under consideration, was that upon the person of Wm. H. Littlehales, Superintendent of the Glen Carbon Coal Company, which occurred March 15, 1869. Mr. Littlehales was also killed on the road, in Cass township, Schuylkill County, while *en route* for his home in Pottsville. The act was witnessed by several persons, but the perpetrators escaped, and, up to the hour that I sent James McParlan, otherwise James McKenna, into the coal region, no information had been obtained concerning the identity of the guilty persons.

Frequent violent outcroppings of the organization also occurred in Carbon County, which adjoins Schuylkill, extending over a period of fifteen years, and including the killing of F. W. S. Langdon, Geo. K. Smith, and Graham Powell, all of whom were either superintendents of collieries, or in some manner connected with mining operations. Mr. Smith was assailed by a body of murderers in his own dwelling and quickly dispatched, almost in the presence of his panic-stricken family. Although several persons were under the ban of suspicion, and supposed to have participated in that affair, it was impossible, until after the lapse of many years, to obtain any information as to the absolute guilt of the mistrusted parties. Some of these were then arrested, put in jail at Mauch Chunk, and in a short time thereafter forcibly rescued, at night, by their associates in the order.

It appeared that superintendents and bosses might continue to be shot down, and there remained no power to the law for reparation. The assassins were sure to es. cape.

The object of many of these dark deeds was doubtless revenge. But the track of the avenger—or supposed avenger —was covered, as with the obliterating leaves of autumn, and not to be followed. The assassinations were all skilfully planned, relentlessly carried out, and the bleeding bodies and evidences on the ground of a deadly struggle were all remaining to tell the tale of cruelty. The country was disgraced, but seemingly there was no help for it.

In 1870 occurred the murder of a man named Burns, near Pottsville, and nothing was learned regarding his assassins.

But the crowning act of the Mollie Maguires, up to the time of my engagement in the matter of their investigation, and the one reaching the culmination of many previous and similar events, which exasperated the good people of the anthracite region to the pitch where endurance ceases to be a virtue, was the unprovoked killing, during the early evening of December 2, 1871, of Morgan Powell, Assistant Superintendent of the Lehigh and Wilkesbarre Coal and Iron Company, at Summit Hill, Carbon County. The murder was done at about seven o'clock, on the street, not more than twenty feet from the store of Henry Williamson, which place Powell had but a few moments earlier left to go to the office of Mr. Zehner, the General Superintendent of the Company. It seems that one of three men, who had been seen by different parties waiting near the store, approached Mr. Powell from the rear, close beside a gate leading into the stables, and fired a pistol shot into the left breast of the victim, leaning toward and reaching over the shoulder of Powell to accomplish his deadly purpose. The bullet passed nearly through Powell's body, lodging in the back near the spinal column, producing immediate paralysis of the lower limbs, and resulting in death two days afterward. The wounded man was carried back to the store by some of his friends and his son, Charles Powell, the latter then but fourteen years of age, and there remained all night. The next day he was removed to the residence of Morgan Price, where his death occurred as stated.

Hardly had the smoke from the murderous pistol melted into and mingled with the air of that star-lit winter evening, when the assassins were discovered rapidly making their way from the scene of their savage deed toward the top of Plane No. 1. They were met by Rev. Allan John Morton and Lewis Richards, who were hurrying to the spot to learn what had caused the firing. Mr. Morton asked, as they stopped on the rigging-stand, what was the trouble, when one of the three strangers answered: "I guess a man has been shot!" One of this trio was described as a short person, wearing a soldier's overcoat, and the second also as being low in stature, but the third seemed taller, and had on a long, black coat. Mr. Morton and his friend passed on, and the murderers started forward, taking the direction in which Mr. Powell had pointed when asked by Morrison which way the attacking party had gone. They paused but a moment, when confronted by Morton and Richards, and appeared to be surprised to see any one in the vicinity. Mr. Morton thought that he might identify the smaller individual, should he see him again, as he was only four or five yards from him when he spoke in response to his inquiry.

"I'm shot to death! My lower limbs have no feeling in them!" was the exclamation of Mr. Powell when Williamson raised his head. Yet who it was that had killed him no one could tell. They were strangers, it was evident, but where they had come from was a dark, impenetrable mystery. Patrick Kildea, however, who was thought to resemble one of the shooter men, was arrested and tried, but finally acquitted, from lack of evidence to convict. This, for the time, was the end of that matter.

CHAPTER VIII.

THE DETECTIVE SINGS, FIGHTS, AND DANCES HIMSELF INTO
POPULARITY.

THE Sheridan House, Patrick Dormer, proprietor, situated
in Centre Street, Pottsville, was somewhat celebrated in
annals of the town, and its reputation among the inhabitants
by no means doubtful or uncertain. While in some regards
the tavern boasted entire respectability, in certain others it
bore a name far from enviable. Its isolated honors were
due to Mrs. Dormer; its many dishonors to her physically
gigantic but morally erratic lord and master, and the calling
he followed. Many were the drunken brawls and midnight
orgies transpiring beneath its steep roof and within its tawny
brick walls ; but against the lady of the house nothing could
be truthfully charged—except she was Dormer's wife. The
edifice was neither private residence nor hotel, but a compound of the two. Three stories in height, having a long,
low extension in its rear, lighted by a skylight, and in which
was located the well-patronized ten-pin alley ; the basement
of the main structure was employed as dining-room, kitchen,
and laundry, and the first, or business floor, front, for saloon
purposes. Just back of the latter was a card-playing and
bagatelle division. Entering from the street, the first place
to the southward, or right hand of the visitor, was the bar,
the counter of which extended as far as the partition divid
ing the tap-room proper from the small parlor In the last
named apartment were stands and chairs for card-players,
and the bagatelle table. From this sitting room admission
was found to a gallery, or small balcony, overlooking the
ball-alley and from which spectators might watch the progress

4

of the game going on below. Leaving the same corridor, or hallway, a staircase led to the sleeping and other apartments of the second story. There were two approaches to the house from the street, one at the south and right hand, penetrating to the rooms above-stairs, without troubling people in the public places, and the other at the centre, reaching directly to the bar room. The latter was a capacious, comfortable affair, and the supply of drinkables in cut-glass decanters, and beer, ale, and porter on draught, always quite large, if not select as to quality and brand. The patronage extended to the saloon was miscellaneous, but apparently very profitable to the keeper.

When McKenna paused before the house, from the interior came sounds of rude music, evidently emanating from some discordant and faultily-fingered violin. He succeeded, however, in recognizing an air to which he had tripped many a jig in the old country. Considering for a moment the course he should take, the detective gave his tangled locks an extra twist, stuck his hat on one side of his head, rolled unsteadily up to the door, fumbled awkwardly with the knob, finally turned it, and stood in the bar room. The picture then presented to his eye was considered not uncommon to behold in the mining district, yet rather striking to and never to be forgotten by an uninitiated spectator. The place exposed to view was about half filled with men, the majority of whom were clad in rough attire—somewhat different from the miner's shifting clothes, however—and, with their companions, stood and sat around a sprinkling of citizens, mechanics, street laborers, and others Pat Dormer, towering high above all, and whose form the detective was not slow to single out and know, through Jennings' description, seemed to be making himself actively useful outside, conversing glibly with his customers, while his spouse, fresh-faced, short in figure, and matronly looking, stood behind the counter, dispensing with steady hand, ready smile, and pleasant word the various stimulants in demand by her patrons.

In one corner, uneasily perched at the top of an empty whisky barrel—stolid of eye and face, frowzy-haired, low-browed, stunted in body, long of arm, and crooked spined—was the spasmodic little fiddler, drawing away industriously at his bow, his sallow cheek resting caressingly on the old violin, and producing semi-musical tones not so easily under stood as entering into the composition of that frolicsome piece, called "The Devil's Dream." With one big, boot-clad foot he kept time irregularly against the staves forming part of his throne.

All in the saloon were perfect strangers to McKenna, but that made no difference. He staggered about near the threshold for an instant, while he mentally measured the people in whose company he was, and made a hurried inven-tory of the immediate surroundings; then, appearing to gather inspiration from the lively squeak of the fiddle, he ad-vanced to the middle of the floor, where remained a few square yards of vacant space, struck an attitude, and, without further prelude, begun his best Irish break-down. The steps were nimble, well chosen, emphasized with heel and toe, and, despite his assumed state of semi-intoxication, the time was fairly kept with the measure of the tune. Dormer looked upon the strange intruder, at first, as though unde-cided whether he should toss him outside his door, as he would a mangy cur, or applaud his terpsichorean perform-ance. Then he gradually absorbed the magnetism of the dance, and the music made by feet and bow and string, and, seating himself on a convenient chair, held his face between his two brawny hands, the elbows resting on his knees, and interestedly scanned McKenna's movements, keeping the rhythm, meanwhile, by swaying his broad shoulders from side to side. The agile shuffling evidently gave him pleasure, and, turning to the sleepy musician he loudly ordered him to "play fasther!" The request was instantly obeyed, and quicker and quicker came the inspiriting notes, faster and faster were the manœuvres of the dance executed, and the more fantastically the dancer turned and whirled, and threw out leg and arm, in gesticulations more grotesque than graceful

> " Nae cotillion brent new frae France,
>   But hornpipes, jigs, strathspeys, and reels,
>   Put life and mettle in his heels."

It was not long before every occupant of the place, Mrs. Dormer inclusive, took up the measure and, while none but the central personage actually indulged in a reel, beat time to the chords the violinist touched.

Dormer, as usual, was somewhat overcome by liquor, but arose at the conclusion of the jig, advanced to McKenna, who stood, for a few seconds, almost exhausted by his exertions, took the detective by the hand and warmly welcomed him to the place, saying :

"Very good! Very good! Be the sowl of me great-grandfather! I've niver seen such a jigger since the days of jolly Dan Carey! Walk up, stranger, an' have a sup of the best in the house; an' be the same token, let everybody else take somethin' at my cost! I am greatly plazed, that I am, to recave such iligant company!"

"Av coorse I hev no objection in the worruld," answered McKenna, returning Dormer's strong grasp with interest, "wid the understandin', if it be quite convanient, that I'm to give all of yez a bit of a song afther the wettin' of me whistle!"

"Sure, an' a stave or so of a song is jist what we're afther the wantin'," responded a man the operative had heard called Kelly.

The drinks were prepared by Mrs. Dormer with even more than her usual dexterity. Then the uncanny fiddler vacated his barrel-head, McKenna assumed his place, hat on head, arms akimbo, and, without any accompaniment, gave the following ballad :

"Pat. Dolan, it's my Christian name,
   Yes, an' my surname too, sir;
An' oft you've listened to me sthrane,
   I'll tell you somethin' new, sir !
In Cavan-town, where we sat down,
   Our Irish hearts to inspire,
There's bould recruits an' undaunted yout's,
   An' they'r led by Mollie Maguire !

CHORUS.

"With my riggadum du, an' to h—l wid the crew
   Wouldn't help to free our nation;
When I look back, I count 'em slack,
   Wouldn't join our combination !

"Said Mollie to her darlin' sons,
   'What tyrant shall we tumble?
That filthy tribe we can't abide,
   They rob both meek and humble;
There is one Bell, a child of h—l,
   An' a Magistrate in station,
Let lots be drew an' see which av you
   Will tumble him to damnation !'   —CHORUS

"The lot's now cast, the sentence passed,
   I scorn to tell a lie, sir !
I got my chance, it wur no blank;
   I wur glad to win the prize, sir !
To swate Bill Cooney's I did repair,
   To meet the parson, Bell, sir !
At his brain I took me aim,
   Sayin' 'Come down, ye fin' o' h—l, sir !'   —CHORUS

"Those Orangemen, they gathered then,
   An' swore they'd kill us all, sir !
For their frien' Bell, who lately fell,
   An' got a terrible fall, sir !
But Mollie's sons, wid swords an' guns,
   Wid pikes—pitchforks—glancin',
Those bould recruits an' undaunted yout's,
   Stepped into the field just prancin'.   —CHORUS

" Those Orangemen, they all stood then,
    To fight they thought it a folly ;
They'd rather run an' save their lives,
    An' leave the field to Mollie !
Altho' I'm in a foreign land,
    From the cause I'll ne'er retire,
May heaven smile on every chil'
    That belongs to Mollie Maguire !   —CHORUS.

" One night as I lay upon me bed,
    I heard a terrible rattle ;
Who wor it but Bell, come back from h—l,
    To fight another battle !
Then at his brain I took me aim—
    He vanished off in fire—
An' as he went the air he rent
    Sayin', ' I'm conquered by Mollie Maguire !'—CHORUS.

" Now I'm in America,
    An' that's a free nation !
I generally sit an' take my sip
    Far from a police station !
Four dollars a day—its not bad pay—
    An' the boss he likes me well, sir !
But little he knows that I'm the man
    That shot that fin' o' h—l, sir !

CHORUS.

" Wid me riggadum du—an' to h—l wid the crew
    Wouldn't fight to free our nation,
When I look back I count 'em slack
    Wouldn't join our combination !"

During the progress of the ditty—the air of which no description can do justice to—the audience, the members of which had gradually drawn nigh the singer, joined in the refrain with a strength of lung and depth of voice causing the casements to rattle and the air to resound. The enthusiasm evolved was so intense and found such loud vent, that some moments necessarily elapsed before quiet was so far restored as to permit McKenna to make himself understood, after descending once more to the floor, as wanting the friends present to " stand furninst the bar an' have a noggin of poteen wid him !" The request, when fairly heard, was readily complied with.

It was very soon revealed to the acute senses of the operative that he had made an impression which could not well fail in being useful to him in the future. The effect, in the landlord's case, was not to be misunderstood, and he, Jennings had said, was a "captain among the Sleepers," or Mollies. The overgrown fellow was zealous in his openly-expressed, newly-awakened regard for the stranger, and after hearing some sentimental and comical songs, seated himself by McKenna's side and entered upon a course of minute inquiry as to the detective's nativity, residence, last occupation, business in the mines, etc. Mrs. Dormer, in the meantime, attended to the drinks, and was not long in perceiving that their visitor—the lion of the evening, in fact—had some money with him, and was, sailor-like, dispensing it freely for the gratification of her guests. Dormer, on his part, was soon in possession of the fact that McKenna was from Colorado—but latest from New York—looking for work, after which he proposed a trial at cards in the back sitting-room, honoring the stranger by choosing him as his partner. Kelly and a scowling, heavy-set, large-boned man, named Frazer, were to be pitted against them. It was euchre that they entered upon, the stakes being refreshments for the four. The game progressed peacefully, Dormer and his friend at first gaining some advantages, but the landlord soon losing his little remaining wit, with accession of more whisky, they began to fall off in the winnings. McKenna was quick to see plentiful cause for this ill-success. Frazer, when dealing, passed himself six cards instead of the proper number, and played other tricks generally classed as among cheats and frauds. The operative seized Frazer s hand and exposed the deceit to the gaze of his companions.

denouncing the swindler in no measured terms. The
game was broken up; Dormer was raving furiously, and
all hands returned to the bar, where many of its former occupants still remained. Once there, Frazer threw off
his coat, and challenged his accuser to fight him, saying:

" I'll mau. the sod wid any cowardly bog-trotter in sivin
counties that says I chate at cards ! "

McKenna, in spite of the liquor he had been compelled to
imbibe, still retained his mental faculties and physical strength
in perfection—although, following the scheme he had started,
he pretended to be more deeply intoxicated than when he first
made his appearance at Dormer's—and he scornfully looked
upon his opponent's portly form as he defiantly responded:

" Do ye think, fur wan moment, that I'm afraid of the
likes of you ? Ye may live to larn better. I'll bate ye fairly,
an' wid the coat on me back, at that ! "

The detective tossed only his hat aside and squared himself
pluckily, while Dormer volunteered to act as his second, giving
the word to his friends, who cheered lustily for the stranger.

Mrs. Dormer had disappeared at the first signs of a rup
ture, and the bar took care of itself.

Kelly seconded Frazer. The ring was formed and the
two men entered it, Frazer confident in his great strength
and the detective relying upon some experience in the manly
art of self-defense. The contest commenced. At the outset McKenna acted purely on the defensive, only seeking to
throw off or evade Frazer's many unskillful but heavy strokes.
He desired to study his antagonist's tactics and test his muscle before using offensive measures. The result was, at the
end of a protracted round, the smaller sparrer was dropped
to the floor by a sledge-hammer blow, fair on the ear. First
blood and first knock-down were claimed for the heavy-weight.
But these were all he secured to boast of during the continuance of the fight—excepting severe punishment—as Mc-
Kenna carried off the honors in five consecutive rounds, at

the close of all of which he deftly sent his opponent to the earth, each time with a new wound of some sort to remember him by. Between the bouts Dormer would take him to their corner, place spirits to his principal's lips, sponge off his face and arms in regular prize-ring fashion, and return him in due season for more work. The opposing man was equally well served by Kelly, but, after so many fast-following and disastrous defeats, his right eye being fully closed and useless, and the other badly damaged, Frazer could not be coaxed or driven to come forward to the mark again. Then his backers gave him up, and Kelly took him away, a badly whipped and quite crest-fallen bully. Victory was proclaimed by Dormer for McKenna, and the Pottsville Giant was in great glee, stroking the shoulder of his new-discovered pet and making grimaces that he intended to be pleasing, but which were more like demoniacal grins than smiles. Dormer shouted as Frazer went out:

"Good! Good! for me laddy-buck from the West! He's the true grit from head to toe! An', hereafter, if anybody in Schuylkill County jist wants to bother wid him, they must deal wid Pat Dormer fust! An' he's no dawshy infant!"

"I'll have the laste taste of gin in mine!" said McKenna, 'an' I belave all here present will join us in drinkin' confusion to all mane scuts and chates!"

The sentiment was applaudingly echoed and the drinks very quickly absorbed.

Among others, one whom McKenna had heard called Tom Hurley, came up and congratulated the victor, hoping he had received no serious hurts.

"Oh! nothing but a wee flea-bite on me smeller," answered McKenna, "which by the mornin' will be all correct again! A scrimmage like this every avenin' in the wake, would only jist give me jints nadeful exercise!"

Thus ended the detective's first experience in the amateur prize-ring.

4*

CHAPTER IX.

DORMER UNDER INVESTIGATION.

KELLY soon returned to the saloon, reporting his principal in the late encounter as well as, under the circumstances, he could expect to be, and hinting that, as far as he was concerned, he was eager to resume friendly relations with McKenna, who, he very frankly acknowledged, "wur quite in the right, an' Frazer far in the wrong!" This proved enough to warm the heart of the operative toward the second of his recent adversary, and the two men, left to themselves, at once inaugurated a close intimacy.

After another jig, to the lively tune of the " White Cockade " —suggested by McKenna for a purpose, and which the fiddler, already fast asleep and unmusically snoring, prone upon a bench, was awakened to execute—the detective called all hands once more to the bar, and, through the use of a little legerdemain, filling his tumbler half full of water—but his friends meanwhile thinking it undiluted gin—he proposed :

"Here's to ' the power that makes English landlords tremble !'   Here's confusion to all the inimies of ould Ireland !'

Tom Hurley, who had been one of Kelly's partisans, enthusiastically thumped him on the shoulder and answered :

"Hurrah !   Them's the sentiments !   Let all here drink to 'em !"

Hurley, Dormer, and Kelly, with the detective, and the remainder of the assemblage, drained their goblets in silence. McKenna, who was on the alert, thought he noticed a communicative wink passing between Kelly and Dormer, but not a syllable was uttered to inform him whether he had hit upon anything of importance in employing his well-remem-

bered toast—first heard at Tremont. No language having the
sound of a legitimate response to it was he enabled to distinguish. In a short time, however, Kelly came over .o him
with a whispered request to repair to the little sitting-room.
He obeyed, and, as he followed to that place, he found
himself discussing in his own mind what might now be in
store for him—what would prove the result of the impending
interview. He was not fearful—but anticipated taking whatever came with as good a grace as possible. After occupying their seats, his companion remarked :

"Didn't I see you at Minersville, not long ago, in company with Hugh Mahan ? "

"Sure, an' may be you did I You might as well as not, at
.aste, fur I war wid him, at that place, only the last month
sometime I"

Kelly scanned the face of the detective sharply for a
second, and then resumed :

"Do you chance to belong to the Emeralds ? The benev
olent society of that name is what I mane I"

"No, I do not I"

"Well, I know Mahan to be a mimber, an' he's been mak
in' himself very free wid *lashins* of people, hereabouts, within
the past few wakes, invitin' tnem t: ioin, an' I didn't know
but you were wan of his sort I"

"Not at all I I niver belonged to any of the nature in
this counthry I In Ireland, once, sure an' I had a little of
what ye might call exparience in that line I"

Before the conversation could go any farther—as Mc-
Kenna thought, quite providentially—Kelly was called out
of the apartment, some person wishing to see him, and
Dormer entered and assumed his place at the table. They
both tasted the contents of a black bottle that the landlord
had brought with him, and then Dormer asked :

"How long is it since ye war made a mimber ? "

"What do ye mane—mimber of phat ? "

"Oh ye nade not be backward, young man! I hev taken a likin to ye, and all in this house are my *friends—an'* yours!"

The word friend was peculiarly emphasized.

"Well," said McKenna, " I never joined wid any body of the sort in America; I didn't know it would be any use to me when I left home, so I jist quit it entirely. Had I stopped long in New York, instead of goin' to Colorado, to dig in the silver mines, I might have acted in a different way, kaping up me ould mimbership!"

"Yes! I see what you intend! Bedad, but New York *is* full of the rale stuff! Indade, I may say it is rotten wid that same! I have been on the inside since I was old enough. But recently I have had a slight misundersthanding, that I nade not mention now, but it's bein' settled, an' the sooner the better it'll suit me! When it is once fixed, I mane to be the best among 'em again! Most of those outside are mimbers. So you see you're safe enough!"

"Yes! but you see, Misther Dormer," said McKenna, sipping the liquor remaining in his glass, "it's been such a long time since I heard anything, or thought anything, of the order, that, as ye might say, I'm almost as ignorant as if I niver had seen the inside of the affair, an' I belave, until I am once more initiated, the best thing I can do is to say as little about it as convanient! Perhaps, after a while, when you all knows me betther, I may be found worthy of active mimbership. I'm not the laste bit afraid but I'll make as good a society man as iver walked on two fate in all Pennsylvania! I'm not at all frightened—don't ye think that of me!"

"Who would belave that ye war, afther the divil's own basting ye gave Fightin' Frazer, an' he all the while big enough to put ye in his breeches pocket an' walk off wid ye, as a boy might wid a pet squirrel? Oh, nobody hereabouts will long pretind to me that McKenna is at all timid!"

Here Dormer—led off by expert hints, made by the operative, quite forgot the object of his interview—which undoubtedly was to fully test the stranger/as to his former knowledge
of the Sleepers—and the conversation became general. Soon
it was wholly interrupted by calls from the bar-room, which
the landlord was forced to give attention. McKenna had
fabricated all that he made pretence of having gone through
with in connection with the order in the old country—being
as much in the dark, as to the interior work of the association there as in the United States—for the purpose of drawing something from Dormer, but he dare not enter far into
particulars, dreading an exposure of his shortcomings. He
thought it extremely fortunate that, thus far, none of his
associates had been able to fathom his assumptions or con-
tradict his assertions. Both of these had been purposely
kept rather indefinite, that he might safely retreat, assuming to have spoken of some other society, should an exposure be imminent.

Presently the saloon was vacated and the doors closed.
The morning of another day was nigh at hand, and Dormer,
donning his coat, went with McKenna part of his way homeward, and would not separate from the new-comer in Pottsville until he secured a promise that he would frequently
visit the Sheridan House and make himself quite at home
there. They parted warm friends, the detective to go to bed,
and the innkeeper to return to his hotel.

The next morning, when, after a few hours of unrefreshing sleep, the detective arose, he felt very much the worse for
his fistic and other muscular exercises of the preceding
twenty-four hours. About every bone in his body ached
fearfully, and his eyes and lips were dry and inflamed. However an application of cold water afforded him some relief,
and, having partaken of a late but hearty breakfast, he again
evaded Jennings and went to the Sheridan House, according to agreement. The landlord greeted him very cordially

and joined in something liquid and inspiring; .hen informed his visitor that, as he was an "old trump" he was just the man to go with him to attend to some business of a private character in another part of the city. They attended church, after which their steps took another direction, landing them inside Capt. Dougherty's saloon, where several of the men McKenna had previously encountered at Dormer's were already convened.

Dougherty kept a real estate office, was a sort of a lawyer, and his son took general charge of the drinking place. The elder Dougherty was present on this occasion, and did not seem pleased that Dormer had brought a stranger along, though he contented himself with scowling upon him and saying nothing particularly hateful. Following a companionable dram or two—one proffered all hands by the new arrival—the men repaired to a back room, McKenna having been previously warned by Dormer to remain behind, unless sent for. In a moment he was alone in the bar-room, while, as he supposed, a body of the bloody Mollie Maguires was in session under the same roof. More than an hour elapsed, and there was not an order sent in for a drop to drink, which, considering the character of the party, was, he thought, rather strange. Still the men remained in council. He was only able occasionally to hear a confused murmur of voices in the adjoining apartment, and could make out nothing that was said. What were they deliberating about? He could not guess, but he seemed to have a certain dread of the result, as though it might affect his own safety. "Perhaps," he surmised, "these fellows are even now considering whether I am an imposter or not, and should they prove successful in showing me up in my true character my life will pay the forfeit of my rashness in venturing among them."

Still he pretended to doze unconcernedly in his chair before the cheerful fire.

But all similarly uncomfortable thoughts were dispersed

and his attention turned in another and more comfortable
direction by the sudden return of Capt. Dougherty to the
bar. And he came not for liquor. He evidently wished to
speak with the stranger, as he advanced toward him, extending his hand pleasantly, saying :

"Excuse me, friend McKenna, for keeping you so long
alone! I must ask your forgiveness for another thing!
When I first saw you here, I made up a rash opinion that
you were against us, and I so charged, as I now see, acting
under a mistaken notion, as I am fully convinced you are all
right, an' 'old head'—an' I desire to see an' know more of
you! Dormer vouches for you—and his word is not to be
questioned!"

"What is it all about, now? What do ye mane?"

"I mean you are all correct! You are an 'old-timer!
That's what I mean!"

"Af coorse I knew it! Why not? I hev no objections to
all that! I'm also agreeable to your better acquaintance!"

And the detective's thoughts were lightened considerably.
A load seemed lifted from him. And, the remainder of the
company soon coming in, he was cordially congratulated by
many, and quickly responded by another urgent request to
"assist in making the disappearance of some more noggins
of poteen." That's the way he fashioned it. All accepted
with alacrity.

In a short time Dormer and McKenna took their leave,
after promising to look in at the saloon again. As soon as
outside Dormer began to inform his friend that a committee
had been engaged in investigating his own case, the charge
being that he, Dormer, was a member of an Odd Fellow's
lodge, but so far they had been unable to fix it upon him,
and he did not believe they ever would. Dormer also
explained that Dougherty had cast doubts upon McKenna's
genuineness, otherwise he would have been invited to take
a seat with the Board. Of course he was not very friendly

with Dougherty for his "impertinence," as he worded it, and said he'd whip him, one of these days, if he was shoved out of the order. As long as he remained in it, he would not dare strike him a blow. McKenna said he forgave the Captain and wanted nothing further done about it.

While making for the Sheridan House, Dormer invited the operative to enter a saloon, and there introduced him to one Deenan, alias Bushy Deenan—called so from his plentiful crop of bristling, bushy hair and beard—where they met a number of old acquaintances and made some new ones. Deenan's was another rendezvous for the Mollies in Pottsville. Not remaining there long, the two once more started for Dormer's house. Arriving there, the landlord and McKenna had the bar to themselves; and sitting in a comfortable chair, and stretching out his huge limbs before the glowing stove, Dormer commented upon one they had just parted from.

"That man, Deenan, is a miserable hypocrite ! I hev my own opinion of the likes of him ! They hev little good in them—barrin' the big talk—an' that puts no whisky in the can. He's all smooth and straight while forninst ye, but when out of sight he's worse nor a rattlesnake. More nor that, he has no backbone in him ! When the trying time comes you don't find him there ! He'll wag his jaw till all's blue, but divil a bit of fight is there in him ! For instance : Last fall, early, when there was considerable excitement among the miners, a fellow was to be beaten, for some reason known to the byes who axed it to be done, in a township not far from this, beyant the mountain, an' the job fell on my nephew, Jim O'Reilly, an' Bushy Deenan. Well, I furnished all the money needful, and O'Reilly, tho' but a broth of a boy, was all ready, cocked and primed, to start for the place, when what should Deenan do but crawl squarely out, like a cur, an' say he'd have nothing to do with it ! Fr'th, he flew the track enthirely ! Phat sort of a fellow would ye be afther callin' that in the ould counthry ?"

"Nothin' more nor less than a craven coward ! An' they'd expel him forever ! I'd soone: be a rat nor such a man !"

"You're perfectly right !" said Dormer, grinning like the ogre in the fairy tale. "I know you wouldn't act that way ! The McKennas, in my part of the country, were always a sould set, an' honest to the heart's core !"

Swallowing this dose of blarney with as good a grace as possible, McKenna asserted :

"Thanks ! I'll try in the future to show that I'm wan of the rale ould sthock !"

At a late hour the landlord was much overcome with drink, and when he bolted the door, after McKenna's departure, he shouted through the key-hole : "Come agin, the morrow, ye thafe of the worruld, or I'll bate ye within an inch of your life !"

Of course McKenna returned answer to this delicately-conveyed compliment that he'd "be sure to do that same !"

Light and elastic was the step, and buoyant and hopeful the heart of the detective, that cloudy morning, when he sought his pillow in widow O'Regan's domicile. He had now been for some two months in the stronghold of the Sleepers, or Mollie Maguires, and labored hard, day as well as night, to reach his present position of intimacy with men prominent in the order. Success, he thought, was about to crown his efforts.

A few days passed, during which McKenna, who had purposely cut the acquaintance of Jennings and been given up by that young man as hopelessly in the snare set for him by Dormer, was continually found at the Sheridan House, gaining fast the reputation of an incorrigibly hard case, but a good singer and dancer, and jolly companion, nevertheless. One day, in the presence of one Arthur L'Velle, who was a Mollie, according to Dormer's report, when the detective was bemoaning his bad luck in getting work, the tavern-keeper said·

"I have regard for ye, McKenna, since ye whipped Fraser so handsomely, fur nuthin' plazes me more'n to see a yout' able an' willin' to put up his hands and take care of number one! Now, L'Velle"—turning to that person—"I'll tell you what sort of an idea has just been runnin' through my brain fur all the world like mice in a potato-bin. I've been thinkin' I'd give McKenna, here, a loud letter to Mike Lawler, of Shenandoah, an' it's my private opinion that, if 'Muff' can't get him a job, he may hunt the mines over all this winter widout findin' one!"

"An' why do ye call him ye spake of 'Muff' Lawler?" asked the stranger.

L'Velle answered:

"Because of a choice breed of chickens that he raises! Dormer, your thought is a happy one! Lawler is a leader, up there, an' I know his friendship will in that way be secured —an' it's valuable to any man!"

"Yes," said Dormer. "Lawler is the big dog in these parts now; beside he kapes a good tavern, and will see no old-timer, or young one either, for that matther, sufferin' from want while he can relieve him!"

Then L'Velle spoke up:

"If it were not that Dormer and I are, for the present time, under a little cloud, I, for one, should insist that you be furnished with a *staff* to guide your steps over the mountains and through the mines! But, by going up there and seeing Lawler, you'll soon be as well provided for! I know Mike'll do all he can for you!"

"I think I understand what ye allude to! I shall be greatly obliged fur the letther! An' as for the other matter, when I gets to Shenandoah, I can look to it. But what is it I see in the Boston *Pilot* about the Bishop bein' opposed to us? Wouldn't it interfere wid me proper duties at the church?"

"Oh, bother!" answered the landlord, "that's very aisy!

Ye lave the body a while—resign, ye see—an' then ye are all
ight wid the praste. If ye wants to go back agin, who's the
wiser? Not the clergy, sure! But you know all about it!
You are too old a head not to understand. An' in Luzerne,
I hear, the prastes are more'n half way favorable to us—be
the same token, more will be afore many months! Oh, I can
tell you, it'll not do ye the laste harrum in the worruld, an' it
may do ye much good! Then, as ye are an 'old one,' we
wants ye in the order, for it nades some such to put sinse in
the fool-heads of the many new and spooney boys—an' there's
plinty of them, an' to spare!"

McKenna promised, after some palaver, to think seriously
on the subject.

As the reader is aware—but as the Mollie Maguires were
not aware—the detective was only too anxious to place
himself within the pale of the order; yet, when the matter
seemed so nigh accomplishment, he believed it best that
he move slowly, and it would not do to exhibit too much
anxiety. Great haste might spoil all and end in disappointment.

In about a week's time from the date of this conversation,
armed with a complimentary letter from the landlord of the
Sheridan House to Lawler, the operative started for Shenandoah. At that place, if anywhere in the mines, he made up
his decision he would necessarily locate his headquarters.
There, if at all, he must solve the mystery surrounding the
Mollie Maguires.

CHAPTER X.

FATHER BRIDGEMAN GIVES JACK KEHOE A BLAST.

THE night before the one on which McKenna had determined to take his departure from Pottsville, while in Dormer's saloon, some words passed and a quarrel arose between the detective and a young person named Philip Nash, and the drunken desperado undertook the task, it seemed, of teaching the stranger some of the tenets of the Molly Maguires by actual demonstration. Whipping out his revolver, he made known his intention of finishing him just then and there, and, had not the operative been on the alert, and immediately covered Nash with his own weapon, it is more than probable that at least one career of usefulness in the mining region would have met with a speedy termination. As it transpired, Nash appreciated it was life for life, which was far from his sort of game, and he waited action until Dormer, with his powerful person, arrived and stood between them, when he quietly lowered and put away his pistol, McKenna following the example set, but taking especial care to have the protector within ready reach of his right hand.

"Phil Nash!" exclaimed Dormer, "what is this you're after doin' now?"

"I'll whip this fellow, or me name's not Nash!' was the angry response.

"Two can play at that trick!" retorted McKenna.

Then the combatants came together again, despite the presence of the big pacificator, Nash aiming a swinging blow with his fist upon the detective, but happily missing him. McKenna was more fortunate. His stroke, full at the side of the face of Nash, hit the mark, stopping with force behind his opponent's left ear, and tumbling him to the floor as if he had been a felled ox. When able to do so, he regained his feet, and, for the second time, essayed to draw his revolver; but Dormer, seizing both the young man's arms, held him in a vise-like grip, as a mere child, saying:

"No you don't, Phil! You've tried that once too often already, and I now recommend ye to drop the matther directly! McKenna, here, is an old-timer, an' was inside the ring when you were a wee gossoon! An' you're breakin' the rules in attackin' him!"

It was strange to see how quickly Dormer's words wrought a change in the irate bruiser. He released himself, promising to obey the saloon-keeper, and, saying he'd make it all right, caught both of the operative's hands in his own, and abjectly begged to be forgiven for his violence.

"Sure, an' I didn't know ye wur wan of us!" he said.

Of course McKenna, who was unhurt, and had not been knocked down, could well afford to be generous, and freely forgave the miner. They exchanged civilities, and drank a noggin with Dormer, to seal peace and reconciliation.

During the short walk to the depot, the ensuing day, McKenna was accompanied by Dormer and Kelly, now his warm and inseparable friends. At the train, the tavern-keeper took the detective aside, and gave him, beside the letter to Lawler—which he had previously put in his possession—several separate slips of paper, bearing the names and addresses of a number of leading Mollies. Among them were John Gallagher, of Coaldale, and John Mahoney, *alias* the Cat, of Gilberton. Each slip contained the information that the bearer was a particular friend of the writer, looking for a job of work.

"Jist plaze to remember," said the Pottsville giant, "that you're not to brathe a blessed word to any wan, that I tould ye a single point! You see I'm out, at the present an' it wouldn't be the right thing to be makin' myself too forward like, wid even an old head in the business! So, kape dark! None of 'em will refuse ye help in gettin' work, depind on that!"

"I'll jist mind well what ye say, an' many thanks for your kindness, beside!" returned McKenna, as the bell struck thrice, warning passengers that the cars were about to move.

"Good luck to you, anyhow! An' be sure ye come to my house for your Christmas!" were Dormer's parting words, as he clasped McKenna's palm closely. Dan Kelly was equally warm in his requests, and profuse in regrets connected with their separation. Promising to be back in Pottsville by the holidays, if he could possibly make it convenient, the traveler stepped aboard the coach, and sped away on his journey.

The detective, thinking it inexpedient to go direct from Pottsville to Shenandoah, decided upon visiting some other localities before stopping there. Perhaps he might secure valuable points which would set him before the Mollies in a favorable light. He had, early in the week, directed Superintendent Franklin to forward any letters of his to St. Clair. Stopping over, therefore, at that town, he received from the postmaster a missive containing instructions, to go to some of the neighboring places, and then repair to Shenandoah. He answered these, and also wrote to Dormer, saying (what was not true) that he had met and agreed with a man to work on a new water basin, in the mountains; hence should slightiy defer his visit to Shenandoah. He also told the innkeeper that he need not write, as it was impossible to say where he might remain, but agreeing to give him the proper address as soon as it could be decided upon.

The next point to honor with his presence was Girardville, where McKenna knew there were many Mollies. Arriving there, he secured a room at a second-class hotel and started out to see the place. At one of the saloons he encountered a man, who was named to him as Tom Durkin, *alias* Lanky, a tall, raw-boned, ugly-looking fellow, who was drinking very heavily. This party the detective easily attached himself to, and soon learned that he was about to go to Shenandoah, to see some relatives and old-time associates.

"Do you chance to know one Muff Lawler?" inquired the detective.

"Know him? Do a child know its mother? Know him? Be the staff of St. Patrick, that I do! Right well! An' are you acquainted wid him?"

"Not personally," answered McKenna, "but I'm on purty good terms wid Bushy Deenan, Capt. Gallagher, Dan Kelly, and more of his friends in Pottsville. An', sure, they're a jolly crowd!"

"Faith, an' I've been in this country, it war four years last Michaelmas, an' never met their equals, nowhere! An' you knows that set do ye?"

Lanky shook hands with the detective, making much show of pleasure, and put his right forefinger to the right side of his face in a peculiar style, at the same time watching the movements of his companion. Then he asked:

"Do you know anything about it?"

"Not just at present," responded McKenna, "but in the old times I was well posted!"

Of course this was enough for Durkin. They were companionable, fraternal, convivial, and thus traveled about the town together, Lanky introducing his new friend to all his associates as "a fine chip of the old block," or employing words of a similar significance. Finally, it was with some difficulty that McKenna shook him off, late in the day, and, pleading business as an excuse, left him to finish his spree solitary and alone.

Here was another point gained by McKenna. One of the best signs of recognition of the Sleepers, or of some simi-

lar society, was in his possession. But he did not dare to
use it, well remembering an unpleasant episode previously
occurring to him at Pottsville. On that occasion, having
encountered Fenton Cooney, a miner from Wadesville,
at Dormer's, he was spoken of as an ancient Mollie—
Cooney being actually what the detective assumed to be,
and a sharp one at that. Cooney at once proceeded to
test the new-comer, who, fortunately, was acting as though
greatly intoxicated. Quickly apprehending that he was
no match for the inquirer, from the direction that his
questions took, he imbibed a stiff glass of grog at the bar,
with his interviewer, and shortly thereafter fell over on a
bench and immediately passed into a state of semi-uncon-
sciousness, from which even Dormer himself, by a powerful
shaking, failed to arouse him. Cooney was very angry, and
told the innkeeper that he had a notion to kick the drunken
man—drunk only in simulation—from the house. Dormer
proved a friend, and insisted that it was all a mistake ; there
was no doubt in his mind of the man's former membership ;
but he was a victim of liquor—which was his only noticeable
failing—and, if taken when duly sober, he had faith that
Cooney would recognize him as all he represented himself
to be. Some things he had forgotten, it was true, but he
remembered enough to satisfy him that he was all right.
Cooney, not so easily deluded, roundly swore that he could
never believe the stranger a true friend until he produced
his clearance card from the body to which he had belonged.
Escaping so narrowly from this impending trap, the detective was more careful thereafter. Evidently he must see
clearer and travel further before successfully imposing upon
well-informed Sleepers. It proved also quite fortunate that
he cut adrift from Lanky, as, before night, that besotted individual found himself under arrest for an aggravated assault
upon a man who had indiscreetly spoken against the Mollies
in his presence.

It was the middle of December, 1873, that the detective made his *début* in the pleasant little town of Girardville. One of the first persons for him to meet was Pat Birmingham, a school-teacher, who addressed him :

"Stranger, didn't I see you, a few days ago, at Dormer's place, in Pottsville ? "

" Faith," responded McKenna, " ye did that ! I remember ye perfectly ! I wor just a little under the influence, on that occasion. An' it's that way I am much oftener than is good for me moral character ! But I'm jist reformin' a bit now—by the same token, will ye have a sup wid me ?—I'm flush, an' don't mind tratin' ! "

" I don't care if I do have a taste," answered the school-master.

During their trip to a saloon where the pedagogue said they kept the best Irish whiskey in town, McKenna gave out that he was just in receipt of his pension from the government, granted him on account of wounds he had suffered from while serving, under Commodore Davis, on the flag-ship Blackhawk, at the capture of Memphis, in 1862. And it was well taken by Birmingham, as was the liquor, when they had found it. McKenna managed to water his portion considerably, so that its effect upon him was not noticeable.

" I suppose from the company I found you in at Pottsville," said the teacher, " that you are an Ancient ! "

" An' phat is that ? "

" A Mollie Maguire ! "

" Sure, an' you're wrong there ! That is a thing I've heard of, but know nothin' about."

" Just the way with all of them ! I believe if I asked Pat Dormer, he'd deny being a member, point blank ! It's all right, though ! Every man to his faith ! But I've known some who are Mollies and, at the same time, quite decent people and honorable citizens. Now there's Jack Kehoe, for example, in the tavern over the way. He's the most

5

staunch man in the business, but, for all that, a very good neighbor, an' I never saw him drunk in my life, or beating anybody, inside or outside his saloon. That you can't say of everybody, Mollie or not Mollie!"

"I have heard of Kehoe," said McKenna, "but I have not the pleasure of his acquaintance. Before I lave the borough, I mane to give him a call. Still, I wants ye to understand that, tho' rough-appearin', an' given to rather hard company, I'm not quite a Mollie Maguire!"

This was thrown out as possibly suggestive to the citizen that he invite him into Kehoe's; also, by denying all knowledge of the society, to cause the hearer to more firmly believe in his membership. Birmingham did not, or would not, take the hint, and neglected to ask the new-found friend across to see Kehoe, but, as had been intended, he did gain strength in the idea that McKenna was connected with the mysterious brotherhood. Some further talk ensued, when the men separated, the pedagogue to attend to his pupils, and the operative to pursue his investigations.

The afternoon of the following day McKenna left his hotel, fully determined to secure an acquaintance with Jack Kehoe. The weather was stormy, business dull, and he would probably find a number of men congregated in the tavern. Kehoe's residence—the Hibernian House—which is expected to play an important part in the pages of this work, was and still is a two-story frame building, situated convenient to business, not a great distance from the Catholic church in Girardville. Having its gable to the street, and a single square window at either end, directly beneath the peak of the roof, the usual supply of casements and doors for a structure of the size, and painted a dull, red color, on the ground floor, front, was the bar-room, and in the rear of that the kitchen. From the latter apartment a staircase gave access to the living rooms of the family in the story above. There was also a door from the bar, leading to the cook's domain. Throughout the interior the arrangements for occupation were of a comfortable but inexpensive character, and everything was cared for in a manner evidencing the capacity of Mrs. Kehoe, in the *rôle* of housekeeper, as better than ordinary. It was also reported in the town that she was the sharper member of the hymeneal firm, and fully in accord with her husband on the Mollie Maguire question. She probably approved his membership, not because of any particular bloodthirstiness in her disposition, but because the affiliation brought money to their family purse and politically elevated Jack Kehoe.

Kehoe, as the operative had already heard, was a native of the city of Wicklow, Ireland, some twenty-seven miles from Dublin, and a man of but common education. His wife had been a Miss O'Donnel, of Mahanoy. Their family consisted at the time of five children.

When the detective entered the saloon, he found several miners within, clad in their holiday suits, showing that they had not been working that day, or were on the night shift. The proprietor of the place, in person, was behind the counter, evidently in good humor, and everything passing to his satisfaction. McKenna stepped modestly to the bar, ordered a drink, swallowed it, paid the reckoning, and then occupied a seat on a bench while he filled and smoked his short pipe. Some pleasant words, dropped to a man near him, regarding the weather, were answered cheerfully, and soon the conversation took a wider range, engineered by the new arrival, and culminated in that person's second call at the bar to inquire of Kehoe as to the prospect for work brightening up, and asking about the chances for a stranger getting employment. Kehoe responded quietly, without a very pronounced brogue :

"Well, times are rather hard here at present, but there's a show of their soon mendin'. I hear that some collieries now lying idle, are to begin operations in a short time. If they do, then more hands will be needed. Perhaps some of the men here may know, better than I, the opportunities for immediate jobs. They are mostly miners. I say, Mike," turning to the man McKenna had previously been speaking to, "is there a show for work, for a stranger, that you know about?"

"Shure, an' I don't mind me of any! But some one else may!"

And Mike, as he was called, with several others, came up to the bar, as if willing to be consulted. McKenna, thereupon, acting as he seemed to be called upon, under the circumstances, very promptly set forward drinks for all, which Kehoe prepared and the company disposed of with evident relish. The general expression, however, was that the operative would hardly be able to secure a job until more collieries commenced active work.

While Kehoe stood concocting the different beverages, the detective embraced the opportunity, without appearing to do so, of observing the man more minutely. He was seemingly two or three years past forty, but time, in his flight, had been lenient, and left few noticeable traces upon his countenance. There were some impressions of crow's feet at the outer corners of his small, sharp, light-blue eyes, occasionally a gray hair among the plentiful brown ones of his head and in the equally dark, full whiskers and mustache. The beard was noticeably lighter in color at the far ends, as though somewhat faded. The eyes were set too close together to give a square, honest look to the face, as a whole, which was slightly cadaverous in appearance. The nose unnaturally sharp, as though pitted by small-pox, assisted in forming for Kehoe a fox-like and cunning look, and the forehead was straight and reasonably high. It was the impression of McKenna that, if Kehoe should ever get others into a difficulty, he would probably manage to keep out of it himself. He was athletic, erect, and could hold his own in a crowd, but did not seem inclined to quarrel, or risk his person too rashly in an encounter from which ingenuity could extricate him. Not above medium height, or weight, his shoulders were square and strong, and his limbs muscular and well proportioned. His hands, which had seen labor, now looked fair and white. Generally agreeable in manners to strangers as well as acquaintances, he claimed a number of friends, yet no really warm and devoted personal followers. Formerly a miner, the tavern proving more profitable and less laborious, he had of late years done very little manual labor. Whisky-selling and politics were giving him plentiful money and power, and he liked both exceedingly well.

McKenna's proffered treat had touched the feelings of Kehoe in a tender place, favorably introduced him to a portion of the Girardville community, and it was not so very long before he was on the best of terms with all in the house. Finally finding that his reputation in that line had preceded him, and having been invited to do so, he was prevailed upon to strike up a song, and gave, without accompaniment, "Larboard Watch," followed soon by "Kathleen Mavourneen." At the request of a native of Scotia present, he then sung, in fair voice and accent, the "Collier Laddie," by Burns, beginning :

> " Where live ye, my bonnie lass ?
>   An' tell me what they ca' ye ;
> ' My name,' she says, ' is Mistress Jean,
>   And I follow the collier laddie.
>   My name,' she says, ' is Mistress Jean
>   And I follow the collier laddie.' "

This particularly pleased the miners, one of whom felt so merry over the strain that he called up the crowd and proposed a toast to "Bobby Burns, Mistress Jean, and the stranger singer." It was drank with highest honors, and then the landlord could do no less than follow suit This business was kept up until nearly night.

When the hangers-on had dropped off, one by one, to their homes, Kehoe stepped from the bar, sat down by the stranger's side, and showed himself unusually communicative. He ended by calling McKenna to the counter and drinking a toast, which, from its sound and sentiment, he was positive must have been a Mollie signal; but the detective knew too well the result to try a response, and contented himself with drinking it in silence. Kehoe went further and gave him the identical sign, with the hand to the face, which he had noticed Lanky using the day before. To this also McKenna remained blind. He was not to be caught.

" I see that you know nothing at present," said Kehoe at last.

" Faith, an' that's exactly true for ye," responded the detective. " It's a very long time since ever I was within."

" That makes no difference, for I am also an old-timer, dating back to '66."

And Kehoe peered suspiciously at the stranger from his half-shut eyes, while he awaited some identifying movement or word from McKenna.

Here was more trouble. Another Ancient had been encountered who was not to be trifled with. It was no longer stolid Pat Dormer who stood before him.

" Now for it," thought the bothered detective. " Deil a thing have I to trate him wid, barrin' some balderdash that I gave in Pottsville, an' which I'm positive 'll not fool Kehoe."

Once again fortune favored him. At this very opportune moment a man from Pittsburg, called by the saloon-keeper Tim Gallagher—a traveling liquor dealer, opened the door, entered, and greeted Kehoe as an old acquaintance. He was introduced to McKenna, who was treated by Kehoe and his friend as a true Ancient Order man, and informed that the last arrival was at the head of the society in Pittsburg. Several other persons now coming in, Kehoe forgot all

about his investigation and the operative was very far from
giving him any hint to return to it. Just before supper-time,
Gallagher, Kehoe, and McKenna—who that day by chance
wore his Sunday suit of clothes, the weather being too cold
for his first costume—all sallied forth, leaving the tavern to
the charge of Mrs. Kehoe, to make a few informal calls upon
city friends and companions. Gallagher, as they walked,
enlightened his co-member upon the condition of the order
in Western Pennsylvania. He said the part of country
named was full of the spirit of the order, and they had everything their own way, the clergy being with them very
cordially, if not inside the ring. During their round they
stopped at the house of the resident Catholic clergyman,
Father Bridgeman, who, despite his many and violent denunciations of the Mollies, was a personal friend of Gallagher. After the usual greetings the Pittsburg man asked the
priest, jokingly :

"Have you ceased scolding the Sleepers yet ? "

"No, I have not ! " said the clergyman, "and never shall
while they remain as they are."

"Why is it that the Church in this part of the State acts
so differently in this regard from the Catholics in Pittsburg ? "

"The cases materially differ," answered the priest, warm
ing up quickly. "With you, in the west, the members have
something like friendship for one another, and the order is
not managed in the interest of politicians, tavern-keepers,
and other bad men. Here it is in the control of a few un-
scrupulous fellows, who care not for God or man, only for
themselves and their own pockets. Yet they call themselves
Irishmen ! They can sneak around and whip and kill some
unfortunate person—some mining boss, or superintendent,
or destroy property, thus scandalizing those in the Church
of the same nativity— but they do not dare to turn out in
regalia on St. Patrick's day with honest Irishmen, for then

they would be known and marked for the murderers and assassins they are. Oh, it's a bad, bad society; A withering curse rest upon it, and upon all in any way connected with it!"

The priest evidently felt every word that he said, and, though one of the most generous of men, could find no good language to waste upon the Mollie Maguires.

Kehoe listened to the denunciation, his head slightly bowed, but said nothing in reply. The color of his face changed a little and his lips quivered perceptibly, yet no words escaped him. Gallagher spoke evasively, and the detective remained silent. After some talk over other and more pleasant matters, the party took leave of the priest. He made no excuse for his harsh language. He believed that it had been deserved, and had, therefore, nothing to take back. In the streets Kehoe maintained a moody silence. His small eyes wandered from object to object, however, resting on nothing long. He was wounded by the imprecations of his clergyman, yet could find no means of escaping their weight. Gallagher and McKenna endeavored to rally his sunken, sullen spirits, but in vain. Up to the time of their separation he seldom spoke. Excusing himself, the operative returned to the hotel for supper, and spent the evening writing in his bedroom. After sealing his report and preparing for an early start for Shenandoah—where he determined to go at once and encounter the lion, Lawler, in his native jungle—he retired to his bed and wooed repose.

CHAPTER XI.

A KILKENNY AFFAIR AT TAMAQUA.

TAKING cars over the Shamokin branch of the Philadelphia and Reading road, the ensuing morning, McKenna started for his destination ; but, overhearing a conversation occurring in the seat before his own, between two rough-looking men who boarded the train at a station not far from Shenandoah, during the course of which he learned that Muff Lawler had gone on a short visit to some friends in Pottsville, he concluded it would be best to shun the locality for the present and proceed at once to Tamaqua, a city that, thus far, he had devoted very little attention to. When the train stopped, therefore, at the point named, he took up his satchel—having left the remainder of his baggage at the hotel in Girardville—alighted at the depot, and, proceeding at once to the Columbia House, which he had understood from Dormer was frequented by the Mollie Maguires when visiting the city, secured a room and made the acquaintance of the innkeeper, named Marks. Although by this time somewhat accustomed to rough society and unruly transactions, he soon acquired the information that, of all the cities, towns, and villages he had seen in Pennsylvania, to Tamaqua, at that date, must be awarded the palm for holding prominence in these particular characteristics. It appeared to be the centre of attraction for a flock of unemployed stragglers, discharged men from adjacent collieries, tramps, and other reprobates. Liquor flowed unrestrainedly, and was largely consumed in the various saloons and taverns. A storm of wind, rain, and sleet prevailed, and the streets wore a deserted appearance, while the grog-shops and gam-

5*

bling-rooms were all crowded and in full blast.   There were
other disturbing elements at work in the community, one
being the strike of the miners, which had just been inaugurated.   A basis for the settlement of differences existing
between the proprietors and the employés of collieries, had
only recently found the miners prepared with a prompt neg
ative, and, without some agreement—and that seemed far
away—not a man among the laborers would dare begin operations.   Hence idleness prevailed—"an idle brain is the
devil's own workshop," in the coal regions as elsewhere—and
bad habits, bad deeds, were among the results accompanying this unsatisfactory state of affairs.   While some of the
miners had gone elsewhere, seeking jobs for the winter—a
portion to Luzerne, and others to Columbia County—there
were many who, having families and homes thereabouts demanding attention, yet remained, waiting for some change to
better their condition.

Tamaqua was filled with excited men and exciting whisky
Not long after reaching the city, who should present him
self to McKenna's notice but the identical Dan Kelly, left,
not so long before, in Pottsville; the man who became his
friend, and who, somewhat earlier, had backed Fighting Frazer
in his contest in Dormer's house.   Of course they expressed
themselves as mutually glad to see each other.   The operative explained to Kelly that the party for whom he was to
have worked in the mountains, on the mythical water basin,
was found to be a first-class deception; and, leaving him in
disgust, he had visited the adjacent country in search of
work.   All of this Kelly received with perfect faith in its
truth, however untruthful; and that personage told the
detective, in turn, that he was more fortunate, having obtained a paying job at Boston Run Colliery, less than two
miles from the borough of Tamaqua.   In fact, the reason of
his visit to town that day was to buy a suit of shifting clothes.

Kelly at once insisted that the operative should accompany

him to a saloon and partake of something warm and stimulative. This constituted an invitation not easily refusable under the circumstances. It was accepted, and the drinkables enjoyed. After this, and following some talk about mining and acquaintances in Pottsville, the detective went with Kelly to the train, and saw him safely off for home. Kelly had remarked that Tamaqua was no place for men like himself and companion, as there were no friends in the town, the nearest being at Old Mines, some five miles distant. Occasionally a few straggling brothers accidentally convened at some tavern in Tamaqua, but no regular organization had ever commenced or been maintained in the city; several times, however, the thing had been started, and as often fallen through.

Upon returning to the Columbia House, and while partaking of supper, McKenna was accosted, in a friendly way, by a man who had been introduced to him as Gillespie:

"Are you posted as to the standing in the community of the man with whom I just saw you at the depot—I mean the one carrying the bundle on his arm?"

"An' why not?" answered the detective, still maintaining more of the brogue than was natural for him. "Why not? Do I know Dan Kelly? Sure an' I lately made meself a companion of his, at Pat Dormer's place, in the borough of Pottsville. An' didn't he back Fighting Frazer agin me fur the first bit of a scrimmage I ever enjoyed in Schuylkill County? That he did! An' he war gentleman enough not to harbor malice agin me! On the conthrary, I flatter meself that he an' I are rather warrum friends at the prisent moment! What should I be inquarin' as to his character for? He's all correct, isn't he?"

"Manus has been very unfortunate."

"Manus who?"

"Manus Kull, sure!"

"Manus Kull? Is that the name ye give the person I saw off on the train, beyant?"

"Certainly! That's his name!"

"Well, Mr. Gillespie, I hev regard for ye, but must say that ye labor under a mistaken idea! It war Dan Kelly, a miner—an' he has work not so far from this town—that I saw to the train the day!"

"Oh, I know what I am talking about!" said Gillespie a little nettled by McKenna's unbelief. "He is Manus Kull! I insist upon that, say what you may! Haven't I known him since he was knee high to a rabbit? and, sorry I am to say it, since he came to the age of maturity it is very little I've learned to his credit."

"Kelly's the name I've always heard him called—Dan Kelly, at that—an' sure I didn't take him for wan of those havin' occasion to dale in double names an' deceptions!"

"He is none other than Manus Kull; tho' since his troubles he may have adopted some other man's name, having doubly dishonored his own. And, what is more to the purpose in my speaking with you, to put you on your guard, lest you make an intimate associate of him, to my certain knowledge he has served a term of three years in Luzerne County jail for biting off a man's ear, in the course of a rough-and-tumble fight, at the town of Wilkesbarre. And upon one court-day there were not less than eight or nine warrants out and in the hands of officers for his arrest, for offenses ranging all the way from assault and battery to burglary and highway robbery. He has broken his poor mother's heart, has Manus Kull!"

The talk continued in this strain for some moments, during which the detective learned—as before he had more than half suspected—that Kull, *alias* Kelly, was only one among many hard cases usually congregating at the Sheridan House. Expressing some surprise, however, that he should be thus misled, he continued his meal in silence.

During the same evening two miners, named Mullhearn and McGinly, arrived at the hotel from the neighborhood of Mauch Chunk, both in a state of semi-intoxication and ready for any sort of adventure that might come within reach. The large bar-room gradually filled with people. Finally the two strangers, concluding a deal of loud talk plentifully interspersed with oaths, managed to get up a wrestling match in the apartment, a ring being cleared for the purpose. Then all was noise and confusion. Some, not particularly interested in manly sports, were engaged in drowning sorrow, from lack of work, in deep potations at the bar. Others sat, nodding stupidly in their chairs. After a protracted struggle, in which several heavy falls were given and received on either side, Mullhearn was fairly thrown, his antagonist coming down upon him with great force, and McGinly declared the victor. The result of this decision was the formation of two parties in the assemblage, a McGinly party and a Mullhearn party; this culminated, as might have been expected, in the usual Kilkenny fight, in which all participated, battering skulls, blacking eyes, breaking noses, and spoiling countenances generally. During the prevalence of this hurly-burly, one Dougherty, who commanded a crowd of roughs like himself, and who was affected more than those about him by the liquor he had drank, pulled out a pistol and commenced discharging it into the walls, ceilings, floors, counters, or whatever eligible objects he chanced to see. Fortunately, the supply of cartridges was quickly exhausted and nobody hurt except the ruffian himself. One of the missiles from his weapon, rebounding from the hard wood of the counter, came back with force, striking Dougherty in the left hip, inflicting a painful but not deadly wound. The shooting had been in sport, and, the practical joker, having received merited reward for his ghastly jest, the disturbance was quieted, and while his injury was examined almost silence reigned. McKenna, saying he had some experience in the surgical line

volunteered to dress Dougherty's hurt. His navy service was again alluded to, and, as there was no doctor nigh, the duty finally devolved upon him of staunching the blood and binding up the injury. A little whisky and water, properly applied, soon performed the first, and, a keen pen-knife quickly laid bare the bullet, which had not penetrated deeply, and it was deftly extracted by the fingers. Then more whisky and water cleansed the hurt, while a plaster was procured from a neighboring drug-store, applied, and, tne patient, feeling quite easy, before the borough police had discovered who had done the shooting, Dougherty resumed his carousal with his associates.

Marks, the proprietor of the hotel, was able to breathe more freely when the Dougherty crowd vacated the premises. McKenna earned many plaudits from Dougherty's friends for the skill he had exhibited in amateur surgery, but Dough- erty himself said that he had cut him more and deeper than necessary, and he would never forgive him for it. Unrea- sonable as this certainly was, his followers earnestly endeav- ored to convince the drunken fellow of his error, but the liquor in him had turned his brain, and it is presumable that he might have sought to punish the detective, who had as- sisted to preserve his worthless life, had not others prevailed upon him to defer it until the morrow, and finally succeeded in coaxing and dragging him off to another tavern. In a short time he was as drunk as ever. Some of the Dougherty crowd said if they ever wanted a doctor they "would send for that fellow just from the Rocky Mountains."

As much to get out of the way of the intoxicated men as from any other reason, McKenna, the hour still being early, left the bar-room and hunted up Pat Nolan, to whom he bore a letter from Dormer, finding the man soberly at his home. Nolan read the epistle and said he was happy to meet any friend of Dormer, but was sorry to say that work, for the present at least, was simply out of the question. They had

some quiet games at cards, and passed a couple of hours
pleasantly, when the detective bade all good-night, and, at
about eleven o'clock, went back to the Columbia House.
Before midnight, leaving the place well filled on the ground
floor, t.. retired to his bed—but not to sleep, as fate or circumstance ordained. Too much noise rang upon his drowsy
ear to make slumber possible. He had been between the
sheets, tossing uneasily from side to side and enjoying such
brief intervals of repose as he could catch betwixt waves of
uproar and riot rising from the depths beneath him, during a
couple of hours, perhaps, when there was a resounding rattle
at his chamber door. Without moving, he asked, in no pleasant tone:

"Who the divil's there?"

The answer was not particularly reassuring:

"We want to get in!" said somebody in a thick, gruff
voice.

McKenna quickly appreciated the fact that Dougherty
and his unruly crew were looking for him.

"Go away, an' don't bother me!" shouted the operative.
But this had no other effect than to increase the force that
some person was exerting upon the bolts of the bedroom
door. Visions of sanguinary Mollie Maguires, and an unpleasant feeling that they might possibly have penetrated
his disguise, discovered his deception, flitted through his
weary brain. But instantly dispersing all such thoughts as
mere dreams—

——" Interludes, which Fancy weaves
When the monarch, Reason, sleeps"—

he leaped from the bed, making considerable stir, lighted a
lamp, and said, in a loud, determined, and unfaltering voice:

"Now, get away out of that, ye spalpeens or I'll ist blow
the head off some of yez!"

The shaking of the lock soon ceased, and the steps of several persons were heard retreating. Once more seeking his pillow, the weary man endeavored to obtain some repose. But in a little while he again distinguished the stealthy fall of human feet nigh the entrance of his apartment. Dougherty, for the second time, was trying to force admission to his presence.

"We *must* get in!" exclaimed the drunken man.

Exasperated at this long-continued annoyance, McKenna turned out, struck a light, donned a portion of his garments, suddenly unlocked and opened the door, and brought the forbidding, dark muzzle of his heavy seven-shooter plump in Dougherty's face, demanding his business with him at such an hour and such a place. Hesitating somewhat, and dodging his head from side to side to escape McKenna's aim, he faltered out:

"I can't find me partner! Didn't know but he might be in this room!"

"I don't know anything about your partner, if you have wan, an' I give ye due notice that I've had plenty and to spare of you an' your eternal racket! So get out of this, quick! An' don't ye come banging about here any more! Sure, an' if ye do, I'll make serious trouble wid ye!"

Perfectly quieted down by the pistol, the detective's undaunted front and resolute language, Dougherty and his companions took themselves off, invoking anything but compliments upon the man who had sent them away so unceremoniously. Again McKenna extinguished his lamp and courted repose. For a short time he slept fitfully and ill at ease, but, about an hour before daylight, he was aroused by sounds of a desperate row in progress below stairs. Pistol-shot after pistol-shot echoed along the corridors and through the rooms, making the hearer think that a small army of bushwhackers were attacking the house, and practising to see how many bullets they could lodge in the weatherboard ing. He finally started up, unable longer to bear the confusion, and, after putting on his clothing, took the light in his left hand, and with the right resting on the butt of his revolver, which he held ready for immediate use, in his outside coat pocket, noiselessly opened the door, made his exit, and moved toward the supposed scene of conflict. Not much accustomed to the sense of fear, the detective thought, as he bent his steps in the direction of the warfare, and as the jar and other evidences of deadly strife smote more clearly upon his ear, he really experienced a feeling akin to that of a soldier when receiving the "baptism of fire" upon his initial battle-ground. At least there was a queer creeping of the flesh, a chilly blast over his back and shoulders, a novel rising up of the scalp, as he entered the dark, deserted bar-room, and still heard, as though in the distance, the rattle of small arms. The fight was evidently losing none of its intensity. "Perhaps it has been transferred to the kitchen or dining-room," he thought. It must be in one or the other, and in which he could not decide. Upon opening the entrance of the latter place, however, the mystery was quickly solved, and a strange spectacle presented itself to his vision.

———◆———

CHAPTER XII.

McKENNA MEETS A MORNING ADVENTURE.

BEFORE him was the long, low, dark dining-room, only a small portion of which, at one extremity, was illuminated by a single tallow candle, trussed to the wall with an old rusty, bone-handled fork, and the flaring lamp held over his own head. On a line with, and at one end of the deal table, which extended nearly from one side of the apartment to the other, and at a place properly described as the head of the board, were grouped in deep shadow, only broken by fitful flashes from McKenna's light, a number of men, all sporting revolvers, rapidly loading and firing, without regard to order or regularity, at the target—a rough, white hat, loosely nailed to the partition not far from the candle. Every member of the reckless gang was more or less intoxi-cated. Among them the spectator saw several of Dougher-ty's friends, but the leader himself had been put in bed—otherwise under the dresser—about an hour earlier, and there he reposed, his uncovered head—rough, long-haired, and pallid as to face—supported on the bent right arm, as helpless as an infant and almost as still as a stone model of the spirit that he evidently worshipped—Bacchus.

"Halloo! here's the docther!" exclaimed a short, ruf-fianly fellow, wearing a huge fur cap, thrown backward from his forehead, showing his front hair, black, short, and stiff, and holding in his hand a revolver full half a yard long, which he had just discharged a dozen times at the mark with-out once coming within the length of his weapon of hitting it. "Halloo! Give the docther a chance!" ·

"Yes! Give us a taste of your marksmanship!" said the frightened publican, who had remained with his gentle and lamb-like patrons to protect his furniture as well as he could and prevent the wild madcaps from firing the building in the course of their innocent gambols. As it was, the thin barrier of plank, separating the dining-room from the kitchen, was thickly perforated with black apertures, ranging from the size of a pea to that of a musket bullet. Luckily, at that hour of the morning, no person was employed, or chanced to be in, the culinary department of the house, and hence injury to life and limb had not resulted from the careless use of fire-arms. The wall only was shattered, and it, while made of wood and neatly covered with light paper, bore the appearance of having been irregularly pierced with innumerable circular openings for purposes of ventilation.

Promptly accepting the invitation, as he was certainly in for it by reason of his appearance on the spot, the detective deliberately raised his pistol, and, in rapid succession, fired two shots, both of which struck the target near its centre.

"Bedad! He's as good at firing bullets as he is cuttin' them out of wounds!" shouted the individual with the fur cap, putting away his pistol. "He's bate the best shot; an now I move that we quit, before the policeman comes an interferes wid our little divarsions!"

The suggestion was taken advantage of by Marks, the guttered candle extinguished, and, headed by the operative, all made their devious way to the bar-room, where, from the reason of his close firing, McKenna was informed he would be expected to stand treat. This he willingly did, and the men—excepting such as were found physically unable—soon began to disperse. The few remaining were disposed of as expeditiously as possible, some in bed-rooms, and others in seats beside the fire, where they would be in no danger of freezing to death. Then the disgusted landlord and the worn-out detective retired to their respective apartments. McKenna gained his bed, prepared for a nap, while the sun was ushering in another day.

As a natural consequence of passing such a horrible night, the agent slept late, and it was near dinner-time when he arose greatly refreshed. The same day he received a line from John Deenan, *alias* "Bushy,' in response to one he had previously sent the tavern-keeper. As Deenan's epistle forms a portion of this eventful history—although its author has long since been gathered to his fathers—it is printed in full, as follows:

POTTSVILLE, JAN. 19, 1874.

DEAR SIR:—I received your welcome letter, which gave me a great deal of pleasure. I was glad to hear from you. I have written to Alex. Campbell to inform you of what is going on there, so you can go to him and he will tell you all about it. He lives at the upper part of Tamaqua. He keeps a tavern. We are all well at present.

Yours truly,

JOHN DEENAN.

This presented an opportunity for forming the acquaintance of Campbell, which the sojourner in the land of the Mollies was not slow to embrace, immediately calling at the locality indicated. He was cordially received by the landlord, who was a tall, bony, angular-shaped personage, dark of hair, moustache and imperial, sharp of eye, the forehead being rather low and straight, the nose long, sharp, high-bridged, and with a curved indenture either side of the arch. His age might have been forty years. His wife and several children formed the entire family. All united to make the honored guest welcome during the remainder of that day. Campbell was found a sharp, shrewd man, and fully aware of his consequence in the order. He said that Bushy Deenan had advised him of McKenna's intended arrival, but, under the circumstances, he could not see how he would be able to accomplish his wishes in securing employment. Should work be resumed, he would gladly do all in his power to find a place for him, or say or do anything where his influence would be for his visitor's advantage. As concerned any other business toward which Deenan might have hinted, he could only refer him to Muff Lawler, who had all such matters in charge. After a pleasant season, and carrying with him rather more liquor than he felt absolute need of, McKenna returned to the Columbia House in time for supper. There he met, for the first time, one

Christopher Donnelly fated subsequently to be associated with some of the chief actors in my narrative, a leading Mollie, and at the time ostensibly engaged in preparing banners and regalia for the Brotherhood, to employ in the approaching celebration of St. Patrick's day, when the Mollies proposed publicly appearing in the procession with the Benevolent and other Catholic societies. Donnelly was a man of ordinary appearance, above thirty in years, having lightish brown hair, with mustache of the same color, light eyes, and, as he stood, the detective estimated, about five feet seven inches in height. His features were thin and small, but not unhandsome, the face having disfiguring marks of coal and powder, showing that he had followed the business of mining. He was married, and the father of a family. After four years' service in the army, he came out, at the end of the war, with a fair record for bravery and good conduct. McKenna was of the opinion that Donnelly was in some way connected with the treasurership of the society's funds. He was soon on intimate terms with the stranger, and the friendly feeling was strengthened when McKenna informed him of his service in the United States Navy. Not too communicative, crafty, calculating, and fairly educated in the common English branches, Donnelly was somewhat above the average, in the way of intelligence, among miners. He departed by the early train for his home at Mt. Laffee.

The detective now thought it time that he turned 'oward Shenandoah. He therefore took his baggage to the depot and procured a ticket for that place. Bidding the few friends he had made at Tamaqua farewell for the present, he mounted the smoking-car and soon afterward found himself in the then hot-bed and grand centre of the Mollies for Schuylkill County. Framing the usual excuse, that he was looking for a job in some colliery, he managed to extract the information, without exactly making inquiries, that Law ler was still absent in Pottsville and not likely to return for several days. He at once determined to go there and make the gentleman's acquaintance, if possible, in Dormer's saloon, where he knew he would be surrounded by true and faithful friends. The weather was freezing cold and he would have a good reason to urge for the short journey, in that his wardrobe sadly needed replenishing. An overcoat and some other articles of comfort were in pressing demand. Consequently he remained in Shenandoah but a few hours, going by the next train to Pottsville. It was not long before he was again at the Sheridan House, in company with his former companion and fellow Mollie, big, smiling, ugly Pat Dormer. The innkeeper was so highly elated to once more behold McKenna, that he quickly entered upon a grand spree, that bid fair to last him a week, during which time he would do little more than guzzle whisky and beer and sound high the praises of the " d——st best Irishman in the whole of Schuylkill County," as he frequently designated his particular friend from Denver. Without appearing too deeply interested, the detective discovered that Lawler was yet in Pottsville and habitually frequenting certain bar-rooms more industriously than seemed exactly incumbent upon a perfectly sober citizen. Hence he waited the time when he should arrive at Dormer's house.

It was Wednesday, the twenty-first of January, that the detective encountered the object of his secret search, Michael Lawler, upon entering the Sheridan House, after breakfast. Lawler was deeply in his cups thus early in the day, yet sufficiently sober to walk erect and know exactly what he was about. It was cloudy, rough, and stormy outside, and the sort of day well calculated to tempt men to seek comfortable corners. A number of prominent and active Mollies were in Dormer's place, with Lawler, when McKenna made his appearance there. He recognized, in the man he had been looking for, a rather prepossessing personage, something past forty in years, above medium height, heavily but not clumsily built—yet more fleshy than the generality of miners—with black hair and heavy side whiskers of the same dark color, the chin being shaven; eyes a deep hazel, and withal, "Muff" was slightly bald at the crown of the head. His cheeks wore a ruddy and healthful look, and the skin was fair and clear. As McKenna subsequently learned, Lawler claimed a wife and six children, the oldest of the offspring a girl of eighteen, and the youngest a boy past three years of age. He was quite pleasant in manner, free-spoken, and used a noticeable shade of Irish accent. He bore the reputation of being a steadfast friend, as well as a relentless but not subtle enemy. His absorbing passion was cock-fighting, and a rare breed of game chickens, which he raised and bet upon, called mufflers, gave him the *sobriquet*, among his intimates, of "Muff" Lawler. A practiced miner, strong, able-bodied and industrious, he usually obtained work at some of the collieries if such a thing was to be had in the vicinity.

Upon the introduction of the detective to Lawler, by Dormer, which ceremony was performed in the grim giant's most fascinating style, the Shenandoah man remarked:

"I'm plazed to meet you, Mr. McKenna! Through your friend, and mine, Pat Dormer, I've heard about you, and begun to wonder where you were taking yoursel' to—had expected to see you at my house in Shenandoah!"

"Bad scran to me, but I'm glad that I've come up wid ye!" replied McKenna, "an' I'm just from your town, where I stopped only a few hours. As work war dull there an' I had no frien's, you bein' away, I jist rode over here to take another glass wid Dormer, an' who should I run right forninst but the very person I have wanted to see! I shall only buy my-self some warmer clothes an' then go straight back to Shen-andoah, where, if I can get work, an' a dacent, comfortable boardin'-place, I propose stopping most of the winter—that is, providin' some swate frien s of mine, who are mighty pressin' in their attentions, but that I don't crave to see jist at this present moment, may not come afther me sooner. Av coorse I shall attind church while I'm here, as it may be me last chance for some length of time !"

" An' I can't do that same !" said Lawler, with some regret in his voice, "for I am too deeply in somethin' of which the clergy disapprove! I'm fixed about as high in that, however as they make them in the county ! I suppose that Dormer has given ye that information already ? "

" Yes ! I have heard as much ! "

" By the same token !" here interrupted Dormer, "I sint a bit o' letther to ye, Mike, by McKenna, an' now that he's met you, sure, the line will be of no use !"

" That's so ! " said Lawler. " It'll be all the same ! Any friend of yours—any old head especially—will be sure to meet a warm welcome at my house !"

Here one of the men forming the company directed Lawler's attention to an article in the daily *Standard*, stating that the Philadelphia and Reading Coal and Iron Company was about to bring five thousand raw men into the county to work their mines. Lawler was very much interested in this, and read the entire extract aloud, commenting upon the same :

" I'm a man of learning, I am, have some small sense, and know a little of what's going on in this region of country, and I can tell you all that, if Mr. Gowen, President of the Philadelphia and Reading Company, undertakes to do any-thing like what this piece in the paper sets forth, in place of having the State Militia here to protect his men in the mines, and keep his breakers, shafts, and depot buildings from the torch, it'll take all that force and all his time and skill to protect his own life !"

" That's so ! That's so ! " was the hearty response.

" I look a person in the eye myself, an' I know in wan single moment whether I spake to a true man or not !"

"I admire your courage an' ability, Mr. Lawler, said McKenna, "an' I'm of the opinion that Mr. Gowen—if that be his name—will think over it a long while afore he'll trust a force of raw men in his mines! At any rate, he'll soon see, if he tries it, that such a thing will not work in this country."

This agreement with the boys gave McKenna standing with them at once.

The subject was discussed at length by all hands, and the universal opinion was, if the Company tried to butt against the society, the society would soon show the management of the railway, and the coal organization, of what kind of metal it was composed.

During the ensuing day Lawler was more sober, and, saying that he had already been too long from home, made preparations for an immediate return to Shenandoah. Before leaving, however, he very cordially invited McKenna to call when he reached his locality, saying :

"I'll make you as safe and secure as you can be anywhere !"

From this significant remark the detective inferred that, as he had all along intended he should, Dormer had given a hint to Lawler that the stranger was a hard case generally, and engaged in concealing himself from certain officials in Western New York, who were in search of him for having killed a man in Buffalo a year or so before. It was more than probable that his reputation as a dealer in counterfeit money had also been discussed by the same worthies.

"I'll accept your offer wid pleasure," answered McKenna, "an' I think it'll not be many days before you'll see me face in Shenandoah ! 1 believe it'll be just the place for me !"

The detective and Dormer attended Lawler to the cars and bid him good luck on his journey.

After Lawler's departure time hung rather heavily upon the agent's hands. He had nothing particular to attend to

6

that was of importance in his calling, excepting to make the acquaintance of as many Mollies as possible, impress on the mind of Dormer the necessity of covering his tracks from the New York detectives, and secure the names of such persons as would be likely to listen to propositions connected with his counterfeit currency schemes. He pretended that he might soon have a supply to be disposed of. Dormer would sit for hours in his chair, when customers were not plentiful, and drink in, with open eyes and gaping mouth, the wonderful tales the detective related of his strange adventures in foreign lands, the different people seen, and the narrow escapes he had made from capture and drowning while in the naval service. The little trouble experienced with another man in Buffalo, in which his antagonist chanced to be killed, was often repeated, with such embellishments as his inventive genius supplied. Once in a while he would exhibit a genuine bank-bill and tax Dormer' acuteness of vision to the utmost in finding out the difference between it and those he knew to be genuine issues of the same bank. He was hardly able to distinguish the peculiar secret mark which, McKenna sagely told him, "spotted the 'flimsy' as of the sort called 'queer.'" That it was spurious, however, was evident, from the fact that the exhibitor said he could "sell any needed quantity of similar bank-notes at the exceedingly low rate of forty cents on the dollar." His word was not to be doubted.

"For the life of me, I can't see why it is not of the genuine issue!" Dormer would remark, with a puzzled look on his naturally sardonical face. "I'm no bocaun, as you're aware, but may I niver die till I see me own funeral, if the wan bil isn't every bit as good, to me, as t'other!"

"Faith, an' wan is jist as good as the other," McKenna would reply, sotto voce, "for two-thirds of all them bills is as false as Sam's masther—the devil—but don't say a word about it ! As long as the paple don't know the truth, where's the difference ? "

Of course the detective never kept a dollar of spurious money in his possession, never intended to, and never permitted himself to be drawn into any sales of that which he had given out as bad. It was sufficient for him if he made his companions believe that he was driving a profitable business selling the stuff, and further, that he was in regular receipt of a pension from the government, to account for getting on in the world without much work, and at the same time appearing to have plenty of funds for his personal wants. This he managed to do, for Dormer told several cronies, and they spread it among the Mollies.

While McKenna was in Pottsville on this occasion—about the 24th of January, 1874—transpired news of the murder, at Miner's Hill Gap, of a man named Bradley. The information reached him through the columns of a newspaper. He at once determined to go to Shenandoah, see Lawler, and find out, if possible, whether the Mollie Maguires were the perpetrators of the deed. He waited until the close of the Mission in the church, and then, on the twenty-ninth of the month, prepared to leave. Dormer, who had recovered from his debauch, with a sober face informed the detective that, hereafter, he would have nothing to do with secret societies, intended faithfully to perform all his church duties, and in fact become a better man than he had ever been before. He advised the trip to Shenandoah, and said, when once there, Lawler would, if he so desired, make him all right in the society. It was Saturday, the 31st of January that McKenna found himself, for the second time, in the handsome city of Shenandoah. If he snould now prove successful, it would not be so long before he would see the inside workings of the Mollie Maguires.

CHAPTER XIII.

MUFF LAWLER AT HOME.

THE day following the one on which he arrived in Shenandoah was the Sabbath, and, believing Lawler would be unemployed. McKenna put in an early appearance at the gentleman's house. The landlord was apparently much gratified to meet him. After a number of calls to the bar—for only a portion of which the detective was allowed to disburse his money, the remainder coming as so many warm expressions of good-will from the proprietor of the place—McKenna threw out some feelers which brought up a discussion of the circumstances attending the Bradley homicide. Lawler spoke of the affair with apparent frankness, but could not, or would not, make even a guess as to who had prompted or committed the crime. Not desiring to push the subject, and saying carelessly that "possibly the man merited all he had received"—to which insinuation the saloon-keeper made no direct or audible response—the subject was dropped, and the conversation turned upon other things. Lawler affected to have known nothing about the case until he saw a statement of it in the Shenandoah *Herald,* and, as that paper was bitterly opposed to the Mollie Maguires, of course he was not exactly prepared to credit everything appearing in its columns.

IN a few hours the stranger was invited to partake of dinner with the family. He accepted, of course, and received an introduction to Mrs. Lawler and the children. Knowing how to make himself agreeable to the mother, he praised her child, said he had her eyes, etc., and concluded, after the meal, by swinging the boy upon his knee, and singing a simple refrain which amused him greatly. Lawler and his wife were pleased with the attention paid—even by this apparently rough, uncouth wanderer—to their youngest, and soon themselves became more communicative. In fact, Lawler, as far as he was concerned, needed no farther argument than his record as a jolly, good fellow, the least bit tempered with rascality, as obtained from Pat Dormer, to induce him to feel kindly toward McKenna. Mrs. Lawler was accustomed to think much as her husband did in most matters, and she, true woman that she was, looked with the eye of friendship upon him. How greatly these first impressions upon both sides influenced acts and events which followed, the careful reader will be able to determine. It is sufficient now to say that the traveler had praised Mrs. Lawler's progeny, gaining a welcome seat in the family circle, and was certainly better pleased with the company than with any he had enjoyed since leaving Philadelphia.

Lawler informed his friend that he would do all he could to secure employment for him in the mines, but, should he succeed, the wages would be low, at the highest not above ten dollars a week, and the labor severe. He must naturally begin at the bottom round of the ladder, and gradually, if at all, rise in the scale to the rating of a miner. It required time and hard work to reach that position. The place of "butty," or helper, even, was not so very easy of acquirement. McKenna here put forward the idea that he was accustomed to manual labor—which was not exactly the truth, though, in the old country, he once worked on a farm, and had his muscles hardened by considerable out-door exercise. Some years had elapsed, however, since his hands were employed in real toil and he had earned his bread by the sweat of his brow. Still, he expressed his willingness to try and said that he would accept anything yielding him a decent compensation, his principal object being—as Lawler had doubtless been informed by Dormer--to remain *perdu*, out of sight and quiet like, until certain people should lose all trac of him. He believed, he told Lawler, in a whisper intended to impress the hearer that there was a mystery surrounding him, that the depths of a slope and a miner's attire, with the grime and dust incident to delving in a colliery, would about as effectually cover him from the pursuit of those so anxious to come up with him, as anything in the way of disguise he could wear, or any calling he could engage in. Muff coincided in this opinion.

Lawler's residence, in which the detective was making himself quite at home, was and is a respectable but unpretentious wooden structure, painted outside of a brown color, and two stories in height above a low basement. In the front part of the first floor was the usual bar-room, the counter extending across the northern side of the apartment. Behind the counter were exhibited the commonest saloon fixtures, glasses, decanters, bottles, etc. At one end of the eastern side was a door, opening into the kitchen, employed also as a dining-room, from which latter apartment extended a staircase reaching to the upper story. On the second floor there were but two partitions, forming three compartments. In the rear of these were two beds, for the elder children. In the middle room was one double bed. In the front room, much more spacious and better furnished than the rest, was the couch occupied by Mr. and Mrs. Lawler. There were also the usual bureaus, tables, chairs, and other furniture of similar habitations, with a stove, sofa, rocking-chair, mirrors, and pictures. It was far from a bare and unsightly place of abode. Rather the contrary, and showing, in the neatness and order prevailing, that Mrs. Lawler was a good and careful housekeeper. It was, in fact, the best room in the house.

In other parts of the dwelling, the arrangements for home comfort were not extensive or expensive, yet all that could well be expected of people in Mr. and Mrs. Lawler's sphere in life.

Passing the time very pleasantly at Shenandoah, which is an agreeable and growing city of some three thousand inhabitants, the detective made occasional trips—as he informed his new-found friend, with an expressive wink, of the eye, "upon particular business"—to the town of Colorado, where he encountered and became intimate with one Hugh Mulligan, then to Rappahannock and other points, in all of which localities he made good friends among the Sleepers. He eventually took up his abode at Lawler's house, occupying the bed in the centre apartment, up stairs, in company with Mrs. Lawler's brother, and paying a reasonable compensation for room and board.

Situated as he now was, in the midst of the hardest characters and most devoted Mollies of the whole country, living in the house, and on most intimate terms of friendship, with the leading spirits of the organization, though not yet a member of the murderous order, it was plainly incumbent upon the detective, if he cared for preserving his own life and promoting the success of the Agency, to exercise more than ordinary prudence and discretion in all of his words and movements, that he might not be thought other than the wandering vagabond, fleeing from justice, that he was generally believed to be. It seemed especially necessary that his correspondence with the Philadelphia office should not be discovered, or even imagined. The precautions and safeguards placed about that portion of the business before McKenna started from the city, would baffle all inquiry, in the end, if once set on foot, but even the breath of suspicion should not be allowed to arise. Men have been murdered from the mere supposition that they might be guilty of acting as detectives, in Ireland, and the same spirit pervaded the ranks of the Mollie Maguires here—hence matters calculated to excite a surmise must be deeply buried. The detective's compulsory letter-writing, if made public, even though its object and destination were ever so well disguised, might place him in a dangerous predicament. Thus he was alert, and continually vigilant. Excepting it might be in inditing a letter to relatives in the old country, and then only at long intervals, he seldom wrote anything—that is, as far as his companions were apprised. His daily reports must, however, be prepared as usual. This was mandatory upon him, and in no case to be omitted if the duty could be safely performed. Occasionally a day or two might be unavoidably missed, and then the consolidated report would go forward in one envelope. Sometimes he was forced to take a short journey to an adjacent town, secure a room at a second-class hotel, and there indite his letters and mail them to the proper address. Thus they would quickly reach Mr. Franklin. Writing-paper and envelopes he could with safety keep in his possession. They might rest in his satchel, which he frequently left unlocked, without danger of causing those to wonder who might curiously open that receptacle. But any large supply of postage stamps would hardly seem consistent with the character he assumed. He must not purchase them at the Shenandoah post-office, but a quantity were forwarded to him from Philadelphia. These came to him in due season. With the envelope containing them in his hand, he sat upon the side of his bed, and the question arose: "What shall I do with these troublesome little things?" He first thought of hiding them in some of the many pockets with which his rough clothing was furnished. But the chances were that some time, when he was enacting the *rôle* of the deeply intoxicated man—as he had done, and undoubtedly would again be called upon to do—he might be searched and the mischievous stamps discovered. Besides, from exposure to inclement weather, he was frequently drenched to the skin, and the stamps would in such a case be reduced to pulp and destroyed. They must be concealed—but where? When did one of his countrymen ever give over as hopeless any scheme or plan, when exertion of ingenuity might supply the bridge that would safely bear him over an obstacle? The instances are rare, and McKenna was not to be the subject of one of them. "Can't I put them under my stocking, next the sole of my boot?" he asked himself. No, that would never do. Moisture, friction, and his weight would combine soon to deface and ruin the stamps. An expedient, in this connection, however, now occurred to him, and, taking out his pocket-knife, he made a small, narrow opening in the sheepskin lining of the leg of one of the heavy top boots, and betwixt that and the heavy leather formed a pouch, the mouth of which was almost invisible, in which, after wrapping them in some strong paper, he deposited the postage-stamps. In this safe place, as long as he remained in the vicinity, he continued to carry them. He was reasonably sure of having them always convenient; and, as he had but one pair of boots at a time, could hardly forget to take those with him, however suddenly he might be called to remove from one point to another.

Another thing which troubled him not a little was to obtain a constant supply of good ink. Several small bottles, which he procured and kept hidden in his room, froze solid, and the fluid was spoiled. The Lawler family was not literary. Its members made small use of pens, ink, and paper, and a fragment of red or white chalk employed upon a portion of the bar shelving, and well out of sight behind bottles and cigar-boxes, formed blotter, journal, cash-book, and ledger for Mike. His was a cash business, calling for no account-books. Ink was a superfluity in his house, the absence of which could well be pardoned. Both of the heads of that family believed firmly in meddling with writing as little as possible. But McKenna must have ink. Fortunately for him, Mrs. Lawler was an excellent laundress, and employed liquid bluing to give proper clearness to her husband's linen. This coloring matter the detective frequently made use of, and there is abundant evidence in his reports, sometimes in

6*

the shape of blots and patches not necessary to the adornment of the sheet, that the landlady's indigo bottle suffered
considerably from the inroads made upon it by his busy steel
pen.   The latter instrument, in a common tin case, he
easily managed to carry, with tobacco, keys, cartridges, bits
of string and nails, in some of his convenient pockets.   Many
a time did he creep down the stairs and across the bar-room
in his stocking feet, bearing his boots in his hand, of a cold
winter night, light a tallow candle, or a miner's lamp, and
sit shivering by the kitchen table, with a miserably dim and
uncertain flame, writing up his report, and consuming his
substitute for ink, at Mrs. Lawler's expense.   On one or two
occasions, in fact, he was reduced to the strait of comming-
ling soot from the fire-place with water for writing purposes,
when he had no pencil, the indigo vial was absent from its
accustomed place, or the supply of fluid had given out.
After completing the composition there came the enveloping
and stamping.   Diving into his corner in the old boot-leg,
he would take out the amount required and carefully replace
the remainder.   Then, not daring to retain the dangerous
missive over night in his possession, he must don his overcoat, and, by the illumination granted by the stars alone,
wend his way to the post-office, where he could deposit his
parcel in the outside box and no person be the wiser.
Sometimes he had to return from these short nocturnal jour-
neys completely saturated with falling rain, or having, in the
darkness, stumbled into a ditch or mud-hole, his clothes
would present a terribly soiled appearance when he could see
them.   To save himself trouble in answering unpleasant
questions, he would, in such an event, kindle a fire in the
cook-stove, dry and cleanse his garments, and then, before
retiring, sit up and watch the embers until they expired, in
order that Mrs. Lawler might find nothing to make inquiries
about.   Very luckily for him, his bedfellow was a sound
sleeper, and never once awakened when he left the room or

returned. Had he done so, however, the detective had ready contrived an excuse which must have silenced suspicion, in any reasonable man, that the absentee was engaged in work not unnecessary for one in his physical condition. All in Lawler's house slept deeply. This greatly favored the detective's wanderings at night. But he was not long in discovering that he must find a place where, however small and inconvenient, he could occupy some sort of an apartment quite by himself. Otherwise his reports would be few and scattering, brief and unsatisfactory. He therefore began the search for another boarding-house, with a valid reason for cutting away from the Lawler residence.

One day, not long after McKenna had reached this conclusion, Lawler came home from the colliery some hours earlier than usual, and meeting the stranger, inquired if he had any clothes suitable for use in the mines.

"Faix, an' I hev these same that ye see me afther standin' in," said McKenna, "wid my Sunday suit beside!"

"Oh, botheration!" exclaimed Lawler, impatiently. "Those will never suit the work in the slope, with the smoke, an' the dirt, an' the wather!"

"Well, then, I suppose wan can buy others that will do! Just tell me what's wantin', an', sure, I'll see about it! Now in the silver mines, in the West, a man can wear most anything—still, I must acknowledge that the chaper the cloth the least money thrown away, even there!"

"True for ye!" said Lawler. "And if you can't raise the funds—of the right sort, you know—I'll go security for you till pay day for such things as you'll need—my credit's good at the store—for the boss has sent me to tell you that in a short time he can put you on a job loadin' coal in the slope. I'll inform you, beforehand, that it'll be hard work, but I guess you can stand it a while!"

McKenna made known his desire to try it, at all events.

The heavy-soled boots, miner's lamp for his hat band, the

tin dinner-pail and canteen, a pair of coarse denim overalls, a loose jacket tied with a strong string at the waist, or buckled in with his trusty strap, and an old, nearly worn-out hat, formerly worn by Lawler, completed McKenna's shifting suit. The prospect of soon entering the mine to labor was pleasant. It would give him a better opportunity to see and know a greater number of Mollies, and at the same time gain more familiar footing with Lawler. But when the appointed day arrived, the boss received orders from his employers to discharge old, instead of hiring new men. Still Lawler did not despair. His time would come, he confidently declared.

At about this date the whole country was covered with snow, which fell heavily during several succeeding days, and travel, with teams, or even on foot, was dangerous. For more than a week communication between places not connected by railway was almost entirely suspended.

When Sunday came, McKenna, as was his custom, put on his best garments, combed out his matted hair a little, washed his face, and attended the church of his faith, where he sat and listened, silently concurring, to a powerful denunciation of the Mollies by the officiating clergyman, Father O'Reilley, who, after reading to the congregation a communication from Bishop Wood, of Philadelphia, on the same subject, launched out feelingly and bitterly against the Ancient Order of Hibernians, White Boys, Buckshots, etc. etc., otherwise the Mollie Maguires, characterizing the men who could belong to such bodies as scarcely less than damnable. Lawler held a talk with the detective, after Mass, and, alluding to the anathemas of the priest, said that the Sunday previous he had himself been in the church and received a scoring of equal severity. He pretended not to care the snap of his finger for it, and bade McKenna not to be down hearted over so trifling a matter. He said :

"For my part. I am a member of and officer in the

society and will remain so until I see good reason for changing!"

Ed. Lawler, a nephew of the landlord, some months previous, had engaged in a quarrel with an Englishman, named Brophy. He finally fired upon and severely wounded his antagonist, and only escaped immediate arrest by suddenly leaving the vicinity. Brophy recovered, and, the Sabbath spoken of, came to Muff Lawler with propositions for settlement of the affair. The arrangement consumed most of the day, and was completed, Lawler paying Brophy twenty dollars to have the prosecution abandoned. That same night word was forwarded to the young exile—who was not yet twenty-one years of age—that he could return to his home and his relatives. In a short time Ed. made his appearance in Shenandoah, was introduced to and conceived a wonderful liking for McKenna, and, had the detective been willing, would have made himself very intimate in his companionship, but that personage had his own ideas concerning his associates, and did not care to have many so reckless and juvenile as the man in question. Ed. was notoriously bad—and there was nothing to attract McKenna to him, nor could anything be gained by seeking his society.

The officer felt, from day to day, that, as long as he remained outside the order of Mollie Maguires, so long would he be in the power of a bad, reckless and changeable set of men, who might, at almost any moment, turn from friends to inveterate enemies. Hence, without seeming to press the subject upon Lawler, he caused him to move a little faster in the proper direction.

CHAPTER XIV.

THE DETECTIVE ACHIEVES A VICTORY.

THE operations of the detective as a laborer in the coal mines were destined to be of brief duration. Commencing nigh the middle of February, 1874, working a few days loading coal-wagons from the chute in the slope, to be run to, and then emptied in the breaker, he soon had all that he cared for in that particular line of industry. A day's apportionment was considered to be about eight of these wagon loads of the mass coal, comprising pieces varying in weight from a few pounds to several hundreds of pounds, all of which he was expected to place in the body of the small truck for removal to the upper regions. He was supposed to be in the shaft from half-past six in the morning until about five or half past five o'clock in the afternoon, which was the day shift, when other workmen took his place. Everything, at first, appeared very strange to him, and the close air made him sick and giddy. Each wagon would transport some two and one-half tons of coal, hence the shoveler's ten hours' stint would be equal to handling twenty tons of anthracite *per diem*, a task that one, accustomed, for mere pastime, to shovel into a cellar, handily with a scoop, his ton or half ton of grate or range coal, can hardly appreciate. He may come near it, but the strength required to lift the larger pieces he cannot properly estimate. And this wearisome occupation must be steadily pursued, from early morning until the hour for luncheon, and from one o'clock P.M. until time to be relieved by the night force. It constituted much heavier work than McKenna had ever been accustomed to, hence it is not to be wondered at that his hands were worn quite raw when he left the shaft-house at the colliery, after his first day's experience in it. Indeed, had there not occurred an accident, in which some of the apparatus by which the loaded trucks were elevated to the hopper of the breaker gave way, it is more than probable that, before quitting time, he would have found himself entirely disabled and compelled to vacate his post. As it was, the condition of his bruised and bleeding fingers, when he returned to Lawler's for supper, after a good cleansing in the kitchen, was quite deplorable, and he employed his knife and fork awkwardly and painfully enough during the meal. He made no wry faces, however, as this would have been an admission that he had never before had anything to do with mining of any sort, but bore the pain in gritty silence, retiring early to his apartment, not to write or sleep, however, as the tortures he experienced interfered with the use of the pen, and kept his eyes open, in spite of his exhaustion and desire to become oblivious to sublunary affairs. It was almost time to rise and prepare for another laborious day, before his eyelids closed in broken and fitful slumber.

The second day, the detective was approached by a miner, seemingly at the head of the society, who demanded a view of his card from the Miners' and Laborers' Union. As he had none, the request could not be complied with, and the man, named Mullaly, was so informed. The man told McKenna that, unless he joined the organization, he could not labor in that calling. Of course the operative was willing to do this as soon as able, and so expressed himself, when, after some further words, Mullaly took his departure.

The severe pain in his hands and limbs left the detective after five or six days, and he felt well enough to roam abroad in the city soon after supper. But it was very little he cared about sitting up late following a day's digging in the shaft, and nine or ten o clock at night generally found him in bed. But an accident that befell him on the seventeenth of the month put him upon the shelf for some time. Having his hand severely injured, by being crushed between two car-wheels, he was unable to pursue any laborious occupation until it healed. On the succeeding day, Mrs. Lawler was suddenly attacked with serious illness, and all the boarders at the tavern, McKenna included, were forced to leave and secure other accommodations. Mrs. Lawler was not ex-pected to sufficiently recover to return to her duties very soon, and no proper substitute for her could be found in Shenandoah. Excepting the bad health of Mrs. Lawler—for which he really felt sorry—the occurrence furnished that which the detective had lately been seeking for—an excuse to change boarding-places—and he soon obtained a room passibly to his liking at the residence of Fenton Cooney, who had moved to Shenandoah. The little bedroom that he tenanted was rather cold and cheerless, but there was one thing about it which fully compensated—he was to be its only occupant, unless, when the house might be crowded, he chose to share the bed with some of his friends. There was one slight objection to the apartment, which, however, he soon obviated. It came in the shape of a large hole in the wall separating him from another room, just in the cor-ner, at the head of his bed, caused by uneven settling of the foundations of the building, through which a man might thrust his arm. Not that he particularly cared for the draught of air, but when he came to composing his reports and using a lamp, which was generally late at night, it would not do to have any chance observer in the hall, or prying servants, see a gleam of light emanating from his bedroom. This was prevented by stopping up the large aperture with such old clothes as he could spare from his satchel—taking the precaution of packing them away again in the morning before vacating the premises—and hanging his old shifting hat on the knob of the lock, over the keyhole. After these preparations, he was enabled to work in safety. A small bottle of ink, however, which he procured and secreted in the room, froze as solid as a rock the very first night, and he was reduced, for several days, to the expedient of trying a lead pencil. Subsequently, he used a newly-patented copying pencil, but had poor luck with it, as the nearly undecipherable reports he sent in abundantly testify. By employing a portable inkstand and filling it frequently out of Mrs. Cooney's bluing bottle, which, happily for him, was left near the fire, in the kitchen, he managed to do better until an event occurred that rendered such a proceeding unnecessary. Cooney, who was no scholar, chanced to have a number of letters to send to Pottsville, and, learning that his new boarder, McKenna, could "use the pen iligantly"—as Lawler expressed it—he was pressed into the service, first having been sent to the nearest store for some ink. He took care to buy a middling-sized bottleful, and, after completing his task for Cooney, put it beside the bluing in the same place, and all he had to do when he needed to perform some work in his room, was to take away a quantity in his pocket stand and throw out what was left when he concluded his labors. Mrs. Cooney was particularly cautioned to keep the ink-bottle where it was, and, without asking any questions, complied. Thus was this trouble, for a time, wiped away. These details may seem trifling, but the emergency demanded great caution.

It was at this time that McKenna formed the acquaintance of one Frank McAndrew. A friendship immediately sprung up between these two men that, notwithstanding the trials and troubles through which both have passed—in fact, danger and adventure seemed to strengthen the feeling—remains, to this day, unimpaired and unshaken. McAndrew held true to McKenna in his darkest hour, through good and bad repute ; and as he must play a conspicuous part in the course of this relation, some reference to his *personnel* may prove of advantage to the reader.

Of Celtic descent, McAndrew was twenty-eight or twenty-nine years of age, fair to look upon, of medium height, having round and well-proportioned limbs. His hair was of a lightish auburn, somewhat wavy, fine in texture and worn rather gracefully. He had a mustache of sandy hue, good teeth, blue eyes, regular features, and a complexion sometimes described as florid. His nose was rather long and sharp. Usually clad in good and decently-fashioned clothing, when out of his shifting suit, Frank was, if anything, generally more presentable than the usual run of men brought up to the calling of a miner. He was married and the father of two children.

It was from McAndrew that McKenna, about the middle of February, heard that a man named Lanaham had been shot the preceding day at Centralia. The crime was by some charged upon the sheriff, or his assistants, and by others upon the chain-gang, but, as McAndrew remarked, 'the Mollies would have to bear the blame, whether guilty or innocent." The probability was that they had something to do with it.

About the close of the same month, McKenna, only suffering the loss of some of his finger-nails, as the result of the mining accident, was sufficiently recovered to return to coal-shoveling in the shaft of the West Shenandoah colliery. McAndrew was employed in the same mine, not far from him, and they had Mike Lawler as a companion almost within speaking distance. During their dinner hour Mike Lawler suggested that he wanted McKenna well inside the ring before St. Patrick's day, so that he could appear in the procession. It was then the intention to make as good a show as possible on that occasion. McAndrew readily acceded to the proposition, and the operative assenting, it was agreed that his name should be taken in at the ensuing regular meeting. But McKenna did not march in the procession on the seventeenth. A few members from a country division came out. The majority of the Mollies, preferring to remain incog., did not attempt to walk with those belonging to other societies.

About the beginning of March the times were so hard that a number of men had to be discharged from the colliery, including McKenna and his companions. They were promised work when business was more lively. In the meantime, the detective's efforts—which could not be very active without attracting undesirable attention—to gain admission to the Ancient Order, as it was sometimes called, were unavailing. Lawler sometimes referred to his promise, but seemed unwilling or afraid to proceed. McKenna was aware of the fact that he had not been black-balled, and all now wanting was a fairly attended meeting to call for his admission. McAndrew and Lawler had lately fallen out. They did not openly quarrel, but Lawler wanted to be re-elected Bodymaster of the division, and McAndrew thought it was due to him. Lawler urged that, as McAndrew could not read or write, he was ineligible, and there were a few members who sided with him. Others contended that lack of education made no difference. McAndrew being McKenna's warm friend, that fact might have had something to co with the delay by Lawler in having the applicant initiated.

Matters remained in this condition, McKenna and his friends working part of the time and then for weeks being unemployed, until about the thirteenth of the following April. Thinking to accelerate action a little, the detective, one day, proposed to Lawler, that, in a little while, he would have to bid him good-by, alleging that work was so dull he had concluded to go to Luzerne County, and there pass the spring and summer. He knew he could get work in Wilkesbarre, or find an old friend who had proposed to set him up in business—that is, give him a supply of bogus bank bills to be disposed of on commission. "Anything," he remarked, "is better than idleness." This had the desired effect.

McKenna had been instructed to take some such course, but not to push the matter.

Lawler stirred himself, said he did not want McKenna to leave, informed him that a meeting would soon be held, and his case should certainly be acted upon. He had his own reasons for desiring McKenna to remain at Shenandoah, and for getting him into the division; but he wanted first to be sure that he would support him (Lawler) for Bodymaster. In default of this, he wished to be elected County Delegate, a lucrative and high position then held by one Barney Dolan, of Big Mine Run. A hint of this was all McKenna needed. While he could not promise to go against McAndrew, he could, and did, say that he would do his utmost to put Lawler in Dolan's position. Thereupon Lawler exclaimed, with a chuckle of satisfaction: "At the very next meeting we'll see you made all right!"

As the division held its sessions at Lawler's house during these days, the would-be Mollie made it his business to be present nearly every evening. But it was not until the night of Tuesday, the fourteenth of April, that his watchfulness earned its merited reward. He was at Lawler's, after supper, as usual, and Mike had been drinking more than needful, assisted somewhat by McKenna, who wished his friend to be in good trim for doing something generous, as he had heard it was the date for the regular monthly gathering of the society. Presently, as nine o'clock arrived, there dropped in at the tavern several well known Mollies, among them Ed. Ferguson—called Fergus—Pete Monaghan, Thomas Hurley, Frank McAndrew and Tom McNulty. In a little while, seeming to take their cue from Lawler, who left his wife to attend the bar, the rest of the family having retired, they one by one dropped into the kitchen and quietly ascended the stairway leading to the second floor. McAndrew and McKenna were thus alone in the beer room with the landlady. The former appeared to be acting as a sort of outside guardian of the division. Very few words were exchanged by the two men.

The thoughts which passed through the brain of the detective at the moment, as he sat listening to the retreating footsteps of the Mollies, may possibly be imagined by those who have been in similar positions, but others can have small conception of their meaning and effect, and to describe them is quite impracticable. His heart stood almost still during the following few minutes of suspense, and only beat regularly and calmly when he heard a quick-descending tread, and then the same sound approaching him from the kitchen. He breathed more freely when he saw that the arrival was Pete Monaghan, who made a signal that he should accompany him upstairs, still leaving only McAndrew below. The decisive period, for which he had labored, watched, and waited during five long, weary months, had at last arrived. It was a trying and critical crisis in the detective's experience, and he felt within him keener evidence of mental excitement than he remembered having been the subject of since entering the State. As he ascended the steep steps he endeavored to take in, comprehend, and forecast the probable result of the act he was about to take part in, and mentally asked himself, more than once, if it would end in failure or success. This cast of thought was turned from its course by arriving at the door of Mike Lawler's sleeping apartment, which, it will be remembered, was reasonably large and decently furnished. Space left within, on account of the wide bed, the tables and chairs, was a little circumscribed, yet enough remained to tolerably accommodate the sparse assemblage of brothers. A large lamp burned brightly on the bureau, before the oval mirror, at one extremity of the room, between the two heavily draped windows, and another, giving a lesser light, rested upon a stand, or table, at the opposite end of the apartment

Behind the small table Mike Lawler, the Bodymaster of the Division, stood, holding in his hand a slip of paper, which at the moment he was intently and earnestly studying. The other men were ranged, standing erect with arms folded around the room, leaving a clear spot of carpet in the centre of the floor. Each Mollie devoutly made the sign of the cross as Monaghan and McKenna entered. The latter was instructed to similarly bless himself, and promptly obeyed. He was then taken to the middle of the room and, still standing by his side, Monaghan proclaimed all in readiness to proceed.

"The neophyte will kneel !" said Lawler.

"Now get down on your prayer-bones," whispered Monaghan; and McKenna knelt upon the carpet.

Here all the members, at a given signal from Lawler, drew nearer the initiate, leaving room for the Bodymaster, who came also, still holding the mysterious paper in his hand.

"I will now proceed," said the presiding officer, in a pompous and affected tone of voice, "to explain to you the objects of the Ancient Order of Hibernians : ' We are joined together to promote friendship, unity and true Christian charity among our members, by raising money for the maintenance of the aged, sick, blind, and infirm. The motto of the order is, Friendship, Unity, and true Christian Charity ; unity, in uniting for mutual support in sickness and distress ; friendship, in assisting each other to the best of our ability ; true Christian charity by doing to each other and all the world as we would wish they should do unto us.' It is the desire to promote friendship among the Irish Catholics, and especially to assist one another in all trials. You are expected to keep all matters occurring within the division room a secret in your own heart. None of the workings of the society are to be recalled to those not known to be members."

Here there was a short pause, and the initiate was asked

He subscribed to all these things, to which he made audible answer in the affirmative.

"I will then proceed to administer the solemn and binding obligation with which all present have already pledged themselves. You will repeat these words after me:"

McKenna, still upon his knees, and guarded by Monaghan, repeated the oath, or obligation, as Lawler read it from the paper, as near as may be, as follows:

"I, James McKenna, having heard the objects of the order fully explained, do solemnly swear that I will, with the help of God, keep inviolably secret all the acts and things done by this order, and obey the constitution and by-laws in every respect. Should I hear a member illy spoken of, I will espouse his cause, and convey the information to him as soon as possible for me so to do. I will obey my superior officers in every thing lawful, and not otherwise. All this I do solemnly swear!"

Then McKenna was told to cross himself once more, the surrounding brothers doing the same, and the test-paper, as it was called, was handed to him by Lawler, and, still in a kneeling posture, he reverently kissed it, and was prompted by Monaghan to rise.

This concluded the brief initiatory ceremony. Afterward, the new-made member walked to the treasurer's table, which was the bureau, and there paid three dollars, the sum assessed as the initiatory fee.

He should have subsequently signed his name in a book containing the constitution of the body, but this was omitted, as were many other things which in regular lodges of the order of Ancient Hibernians are always insisted upon. All present now came forward and warmly shook hands with McKenna, welcoming him as brother.

The next thing was the instruction of the new member in the passwords and signs—or secret work—commonly called "the goods" of the society, by Lawler, as follows.

"The sign of recognition, which is changed every three months, for the present is made by putting the tip of the little finger of the right hand to the outer corner of the right eye, thus: and the Bodymaster made the sign, which McKenna was requested to imitate. He did so, and the officer resumed:

"The answer to this is, to catch the right lapel of the vest or coat, with the little finger and thumb of the right hand, in this manner;" and Lawler performed the answering signal which the novitiate imitated as well as he could.

Lawler continued:

"There are a number of toasts, or hailing signs and responses, by which members of the order recognize each other. When the signal just furnished cannot be seen, what is called the drinking toast for the quarter is employed. It is this:

" 'The Emperor of France and Don Carlos of Spain.'

"And is answered:

" 'May unite together and the people's rights maintain.'

"The password, now used in entering a division, is this:

" 'Question: Will tenant right in Ireland flourish?'

" 'Answer: If the people unite and the landlords subdue.'

"The quarreling word, to be employed when a brother is in doubt if one with whom he is about to dispute or come to blows is a member of the order, or not, is as follows:

" 'Question: Your temper is high!'

" 'Answer: I have good reason!'

"The night word, to be used when two men meet in darkness, is:

" 'Question The nights are very dark!'

" 'Answer: I hope they soon will mend!'"

This concluded the ceremonies, and the meeting, without transacting any further business of importance, adjourned, all going straight to the bar, where, as was expected, the newly initiated Mollie spent some money in treating his comrades. When, at about midnight, McKenna and McAndrew left for their respective homes, Lawler was on his way to bed, more decidedly mellow than he had been seen since the detective's arrival in the place.

In the cold, silent room at Fenton Cooney's, very late that night, before retiring, McKenna indited the most important report he had ever written, minutely detailing, as here given, every particular of the ceremony attending his initiation into Shenandoah Division of the Mollie Maguires, with the signs, toasts, passwords, and other matters of interest. His concluding sentence was:

"So you see victory is won at last!"

It was not until that report had been sealed, stamped, and deposited in the post-office box, that the detective sought repose, thinking he would not immediately leave Shenandoah.

CHAPTER XV.

MORE WORK OF THE MOLLIES.

THE detective was now competent to encounter modern as well as old-time Mollie Maguires. He apprehended no more trouble from the questions of Dormer, Lawler, or even Jack Kehoe himself, and felt that however imperfect his introductory work with the order in the coal country might have been, he was then prepared to meet all members of the order, and enabled, from his late instructions, to suit his companions. The danger coming from sudden inquiries, made by strangers, he no longer dreaded. Just as well posted in the mysteries of the society as anybody well could be—he had already learned that there were no degrees beyond the initiatory in the Ancient Order—he believed he could work his

7

way into a division, or into the good graces of the people as well as any man with whom he had conversed. In fact, his memory, which was retentive to a degree, treasured every sign and password and toast much better, he discovered, than did the minds of many of his associates, some of whom had joined the body many years before, and who would therefore be presumably far more familiar with its interior workings than a mere tyro in the business. As a general rule his comrades were wholly uneducated, and their laborious occupations debarred mental exercise. In this regard McKenna held an advantage, and was really better qualified for office in the division than any member he had ever met. He had not been long in the order when this was apparent to his friends, and they commenced talking of him in connection with one of the chairs to be vacated at the next annual election.

Surely, he must not for the present leave Shenandoah.

This was a strangely inconsistent society. Having for the public eye a motto to all appearances as elevated in tone as that of any secret order in the land, and professing the noblest moral principles, its members were, with some exceptions, assassins, murderers, incendiaries, thieves, midnight marauders, gamblers, and men who did not scruple to perform almost any act of violence or cowardice that a depraved nature or abnormal animal instinct might conceive. Having "unity and true Christian charity" as its ostensible guiding-star, its constituent parts were at war each with the other—excepting in the perpetration of dark deeds, in which they stood firmly together—and one member jealous of the power obtained by another. Professing benignity and the utmost benevolence, it was a combination of enmity and malice for purposes of blood and outrage, brutally manufacturing widows and orphans—not caring for and cherishing them. Its adherents were certainly not particular as to the moral endowments of their initiates. McKenna was quickly accepted, yet he had not been at all cautious in concealing from Lawler and his friends that he was—at least, professedly, an escaped manslayer, and one who would not hesitate to deal in counterfeit currency, or pursue any other calling by which money could be made or old grudges repaid.

Then there was Dormer, who had formerly stood well with the organization; yet he was by no means angelic in disposition or reputation. Nor were Lawler, Monaghan, Kehoe, Dolan, and a dozen others, with whom McKenna had come in contact, at all of the character called saintly.

It was easy to see how fair the aims and objects of the original fathers of the society might have been when beginning the movement. It could even be believed that, in some parts of the country, the primal endeavor might yet be in force, but, in the mining districts of Pennsylvania, surely they had long since disappeared from view. Evil had taken up the reins and obtained undisputed sway. Acts of beneficence and charity had been succeeded by scenes of violence and carnage. Wicked-minded and reckless persons were at the helm, and made choice of their kind to fill the ranks. Good men had no chance. A murderer, an assassin, a violent party was sought after and coveted by the divisions, while one of known rectitude of purpose and strict integrity was not wanted, and sure of being rejected were his name by accident proposed. Hence it was well that McKenna took the course he did when first arriving in the coal regions. His jolly, devil-may-care manner, his habit—not really a habit, but an assumption of one—of being nearly always intoxicated, ready and willing to sing, shoot, dance, fight, gamble, face a man in a knock-down or a jig, stay out all night, sleep all day, tell a story, rob a hen-roost or a traveler—just suited those with whom he daily came in contact.

Returning to a date preceding McKenna's induction to Shenandoah Division, let me bring in some of the acts committed by the Mollies and their opponents, forming a kind of introduction to others of wider celebrity, if not of greater magnitude, which it will soon be the chronicler's duty to narrate.

It was the middle of March, 1874, that McKenna was invited to witness one of the milder amusements of the rougher portion of the people of the mining country—a dog-fight. The canine contest was appointed to occur at Number Three Breaker, and McAndrew, Ferguson, and Monaghan were the detective's companions. The locality was only a mile from town, and the attendance was large, some two hundred men and overgrown youths having gathered to see the expected ferocious proceeding. But all were fated to disappointment. From a failure to come to time on the part of one of the owners and backers, the ring was just one dog short. The animal on hand had to be taken home, his pugnacity unsatisfied, and the spectators, unable to get up a battle between two human beasts, were compelled to disperse, considerably disgusted with this peaceful result of what earlier bid fair to be a savage and enjoyable sensation. On the route homeward, McAndrew said he would stop at a house were he was acquainted, and see if a dog could not be procured. The attempt did not succeed, but as the men were standing near the place, Dr. Shultz, who was known to nearly all the party, came that way. He paused to chat with McAndrew, and among other matters stated that a man, named Peter McNellis, had been shot the previous night at Jenkins' Patch. The deed transpired at McNellis' own house, and was the work of one Canfield, whose father was shot, but not mortally, the preceding Saturday. McNellis had been attacked while in his dwelling, but the doctor could not say if he were dead, or would die, but the hurt was pronounced very serious by the attending surgeon. McNellis' brother had been three times notified by the Mollies to quickly leave the neighborhood, or accept the consequences. The missives conveying this delicate bit of information all bore the signature of " Mollie." The

McNellis family, it appears, chose to accept the consequences."

When the doctor had ridden away, Ferguson exclaimed,
referring to McNellis:

" May he never rise again, the scoundrel ! "

In which wish all his comrades heartily concurred, and
McKenna, seeing that he was expected to express himself
regarding a Sheet Iron lad, complied, saying :

" An may the divil fly away wid his sowl ! "

On the morning of the twentieth of the same month, one
Dougherty was shot while passing from home to his work.
It was reported that the victim in this case was a Mollie,
and the outrage had been brought about by some of the
dreaded Iron Clads.

This made the third or fourth person that had been killed
during the time of the operative's residence in the vicinity
of Shenandoah—and all before he had become a member of
the organization of Mollie Maguires. I make mention of
this, in the present connection, from the reason that enemies
have undertaken to instruct the public that until my detective was sent to and appeared in the coal region, and was duly
constituted a member of the order of Mollies, the murderous
society lay comparatively dormant. This endeavour to have
it seem that McKenna fomented discord and caused crimes to
be perpetrated which led to the arrest and punishment of his
companions and intimates, is so absurd, that only those who
desire to do so, put any faith in it, and for such persons and
their wretched opinions I have supreme contempt. McKenna
was constantly instructed to avoid prompting outrages. He
obeyed his orders faithfully. The truth is, he entered the
stronghold of a gang of assassins, and, despite his presence,
they succeeded in doing a few murders He could not stop
them. Before closing, I shall show some of the troubles
that he did succeed in preventing. Dating from 1868, and
from that year down to 1873, murder and other violence ran

riot in the coal districts. Since the authorites have been able, through our exertions, to punish assassins and conspirators, there has been a noticeable decrease in acts to be punished. When the Mollies' ever-convenient *alibi* was shattered and scattered to the wind, they had nothing left to fall back upon, and there was no chance for them. They were forced to flee the country, or remain and behave like good and orderly citizens.

When McAndrew heard of the last act of blood—the shooting of Dougherty—(this was not the man of the same name—who was no Mollie—causing so much trouble at Tamaqua, as related in another and preceding chapter)—he was very indignant, and passionately exclaimed that "if such things continued, there would soon be regular war in Skuylkill county !"

These words must have reached the ears of some of the Chain Gang—or those who were not Mollies—as, only a few days subsequently, a message was received by Muff Lawler that a portion of the Modocs (Germans) and Sheet Irons had made common cause against McAndrew, Monaghan, Garritty, Ferguson, Lawler, and several others, all of whom would meet the fate of Dougherty if they did not cease their cruel work, or depart from that portion of the State. When Monaghan heard about this, he said :

" Some fire will fly and some blood be spilled before *I* get out of this neighborhood !"

He evidently did not intend to be frightened away with merely hard words.

An incident, which may be given in this connection, was related by Lawler to McKenna, one night, after his return from a meeting of the Miners' and Laborers' Association, to which Muff also belonged. It was about a Welsh boss in one of the mines, not far from Shenandoah, and had only recently occurred. According to Lawler, this superintendent, whose name was not given, had been discharging all the

Irishmen operating under him and putting his country men in their places. The natural result was, the Mollies notified the boss that he must leave. He disregarded the injunction, saying that it would "make no difference, if he obeyed, as the proprietors would run the colliery if he were in h—l!"

A few days after using this language, a man visited the exasperated Welshman and gave him a warning letter.

"Where are you from?" asked the boss.

"From h—l!" answered the messenger, and quickly disappeared.

This boss did not listen to the warning, and as a consequence, the Mollies, in a body, demons as they were, went to his house, at the dead hour of night, broke up his furniture, ill-treated his family, and taking the stubborn fellow into the yard, in his night garments, beat him with clubs until he was nearly dead. He was satisfied from this treatment, which might be called striking evidence, that the colliery was not exactly a healthy place of residence or refuge for him, and, as soon as able to do so, removed to Pottsville. In this case, as in many others, no arrests were made, and no efforts put forth to hunt up the guilty parties. It could hardly be expected that there would be, when it is considered that the Mollies controlled the magistrates and other officials of the city, and partly those of the county.

McKenna, judging from Lawler's manner while relating the story, more than from the words he used, suspected that the beating of the Welshman had been performed by him, or at least by men acting under his orders. Still, as he was not yet a member of the Mollies, he could not be expected to have reliable information on the subject. Mike concluded his story by saying that he never allowed his men to know about his movements, and ordinarily, when anything was to be done, he preferred attending to it himself rather than let others into the secret.

"So there's a ring within a ring!" mentally ejaculated the detective, as Lawler left him to attend upon a customer at the bar.

The strike of that winter, which has before been alluded to, ended nigh the first of April, 1874. About this time McKenna heard, from one Foley, living near Indian Ridge colliery, that at the water station a man named Keating had been shot and instantly killed. The event occurred about five o'clock in the afternoon, and, as usual, the murderer made his escape. It was again charged that the Sheet Iron lads were the guilty parties. Lawler and the detective were at the colliery looking for work to do, when they learned about Keating's death.

Another of the more innocent diversions of the Sleepers was the indulgence in cock-fighting. In this, from his known intimacy with Lawler, the operative was naturally expected to take part, and he did not disappoint his friends. Knowing that whatever he did he must, under the circumstances, gain fast hold upon the good will of Lawler and the remainder of the gang, thus exhibiting his qualifications for a good Mollie, he strained every faculty with that view, and even consented to take charge of the interests of the tavern keeper in the impending chicken-fight, acting as trainer, manager, and all hands, in getting ready the birds for the great occasion. As fortune would have it, in his boyhood he had received a few lessons in the art, hence was not wholly unprepared for the position and its duties. Having ten of the game chickens to commence with, he devoted considerable time and attention to their breaking-in for the pit.

The opposing birds were bred in the vicinity of Girardville, coming from the flock of, and to be handled by, one Dennis Murphy.

Here is something of the style in which McKenna trained Lawler's pets. In the first place the chickens were clipped and gaffed in scientific style ; that is, their spurs were skilfully amputated and steel gaffs, or artificial spurs, fitted in their places. The fowl were then physicked with a soft compound consisting of oil, bread, and milk, and some sugar which reduced them somewhat in weight, the process continuing until the proper shrinkage had been accomplished. Empty barrels were taken, and a piece of one stave carefully removed, forming a coop, which was properly ventilated, and each chicken thus given a separate shelter. After their usual strength had returned, daily exercise of a peculiar kind, calculated to give them muscle and endurance, was entered upon. McKenna would get upon his knees, on an old mattress spread on the ground in the back yard of the tavern, for the purpose, and taking a bird between his two hands, toss it high in the air, then catch it again and repeat the process, until he was weary or the rooster was nearly exhausted, when it would be returned to its coop. Every bird had to take this lesson once each day, and under it all rapidly gained in fighting qualities. No soft food was now permitted, but they received plenty of water and corn, wheat and oats. If one refused to feed he was immediately presented with a supply of raw apples. Out of the ten thus treated only seven came out capable of contesting in the pit. Some of them, less than one year of age, were called stags. Those more than a twelvemonth old assumed the dignity and cognomen of game-cocks.

On the occasion selected for the match, Lawler's house and grounds presented the characteristics of a grand gala-day. Murphy was early on the spot—scarce two hundred yards from the tavern—where were congregated men, women, and children to the number of two hundred or more, all interested in seeing and enjoying the exciting sport.

There was at first a great difference in opinion as to who should be the winner, the bets ranging from five to ten dollars each battle, and being plentiful for both sides. Of course Mike Lawler was reaping at the same time a plenti

7*

fu. harvest through the sale of drinkables at the bar. I employed his own services and those of his wife to keep pace with the impatient orders of the thirsty ones. Mean time, McKenna, dressed for the occasion in his Sunday clothes, with his hair straightened out and his beard trimmed, wearing a new, soft hat, which was the envy of all the men and the wonder of all the women, was attending to his part of the business.

At first the odds ran heavy in favor of Murphy's brood, —and they certainly were very handsome chickens; but when McKenna put aside the brand-new hat, and, with a red bandanna handkerchief wound in the shape of a turban round his red head, a strap encircling his waist, coat and vest off, sleeves rolled up, and game chicken in hand, entered the ring; the betting changed, and the difference was two to one in favor of the mufflers. They were certainly ferocious-look-ing bipeds.

It is needless to attempt a description of the chicken-match. Appropriate language fails. But it is sufficient to say that Lawler's mufflers carried off the honors. As a consequence, McKenna acquired a wide-spread reputation throughout the mines as a manager of such affairs.

Murphy accepted defeat all in good part, as everything had been fair and above-board, and challenged Muff Lawler for a return match, to take place early the next month, at his house, near Girardville. This was promptly accepted by the Shenandoah party, and time named, when the crowd dispersed, leaving the innkeeper to count over his day's gains, which were not inconsiderable.

Of course McKenna's services were once more in requisition to train the birds, and afterward to fight them. When the morning arrived he had to c— e chickens on his back, in a bag, a distance of over three miles to Connor's Patch, where Murphy lived. The road was rough, his bur-den not light; and when he returned, again the winner of the fight, to Shenandoah, late at night, from Girardville, he was weary enough, and heartily sick of cock-fighting as a profession, or even for amusement.

There was a great crowd assembled at the Patch—if any thing, larger than the one Lawler had secured—and Murphy, though twice defeated, said he was "enthirely contint wid the results!" So were most of those in attendance.

Lawler gave a treat to all the "boys" that night, as he was confidently expected to do after winning two fights in succession, and everything passed of smoothly, with a single exception. One Dick Flynn, charged to the muzzle with bad liquor, and being naturally of a fiery disposition, was very mad because he had lost five dollars which he ventured on Murphy's chickens, and wanted to fight Lawler, to secure his revenge. The innkeeper having other duties to attend to, besides being in a sportive humor from the success of the day, only laughed at his big antagonist, telling him to "call at another time, when he could have all the fighting he might feel in want of."

Flynn lived in the town of Colorado, was a known ruffian, capable of shooting a man from behind a bush, or performing almost any infamous act, and it is more than probable that Lawler had rather make no attack upon him. Be this as it may, Flynn left late at night, swearing many oaths and loudly threatening that he would beat Lawler or kill McKenna, his ' butty,' if he had to wait a dozen years for the opportunity. It would appear, from an incident transpiring a few weeks later, that Flynn had a good memory, and did his best to carry this promise into execution. The event, however, will have to await relation in another chapter.

CHAPTER XVI.

A ROUGH JOURNEY AND A THRILLING ADVENTURE.

A FEW days after McKenna's initiation into the Mollie Maguires, he was surprised, upon entering Lawler's bar-room, to find his friend with one limb bandaged, sitting by the fire, in an easy chair, while Mrs. Lawler busied herself behind the counter attending to the spirituous wants of several acquaintances and patrons, and Mike commenting upon some serious difficulty which had befallen him.   In response to an inquiry by one of the new arrivals, the landlord, between groans and grimaces, informed those present that he had received a shot in the leg, the night before, while attempting to quell a difficulty in front of Cleary's drinking place.   He was quite seriously wounded; his countenance wore a pale and anxious appearance, and Mrs. Lawler, only recently recovered from a protracted and dangerous illness, was nervous and low spirited.   McKenna promptly gave assistance, made himself generally useful about the premises, and also attended to some outside business for the tavern-keeper.   When the people had all dispersed, Lawler proceeded to show him his hurt, which the quick eye of the detective was not long in discovering must have occurred as a result of Mike's careless handling of his own revolver, and not through any assault by a second person.   The bullet penetrated the anterior portion of the right thigh, ranged downward, deflecting a little toward the left, and finally found lodgment near the skin immediately above the knee-joint, whence the scalpel of the surgeon had already removed it.   There was a long, painful and dangerous channel ploughed through the muscles, but happily for Lawler and his family no important vein or artery had been severed. If properly cared for, tnere was reason to believe the healing process might be accomplished by nature without the sloughing away of the coats of the femoral artery. Should these finally give way, the end would certainly ensue, as nothing could save the victim from bleeding to death.

"Tell me, thrue and honest now," said McKenna, "how this thing happened. It is plain enough that it wor your own hand that did it."

"Why the d—l do you say that?"

"Sure, an' you needn't take me for a *gomersal, cruddy* from the bogs! I kin see, wid half an eye, that nobody could iver shoot ye like this, exceptin' Mike Lawler himself!"

"Thrue fur ye!" unwillingly answered Lawler, making a comical grimace and groaning aloud with the pain, as he reached for his staff. "That's the raal fact of the matther! But how the d—l you came to know 't, is more'n I can tell!"

"O, its aisy enough! Men don't lie down, as a general thing, to get shot; then there's no hole in your clothing, so the pistol must have been in your pocket when it exploded!"

"Well, never mind that now," whispered Lawler, turning an uneasy glance toward his wife, who was jingling the glasses as she cleansed them, and hence heard nothing of the communication. "Will ye kindly act as me crutch 'till I goes to the docthor? He made me promise to have it dressed the day; an' by me sowl, I'd about as soon hev the leg cut off at wonst!"

"Certainly," said the agent, "I'll help ye wid pleasure!"

And he aided the injured man to rise; but he could no stand, and was eased back into his chair.

"*Mo-vrone!* But ye can't walk! Ye must not try it! I'll go fetch the docthor right here! So kape quiet, an' I'll soon be back. An' while I'm gone, I'll jist s'ep in at the carpenter's and tell him to make ye a crutch; fur sure, as if ye iver intend for to save yer leg y'll want a substitute for a while !"

Muff Lawler was so nigh a dead faint that he could not thank McKenna, who scampered away to bring the surgeon. The wound once dressed, and Lawler comfortably reclining on his bed, upstairs, McKenna volunteered to act as nurse, while the good woman of the house gave attention to the bar and all below. Then it was that the operative learned how the injury had been inflicted. As he shrewdly guessed, Muff had hurt himself while awkwardly returning a revolver to his pantaloons pocket, where he carelessly carried it, with the lock set preparatory for sudden use. Lawler closed the revelation with this unexplained but furtive statement :

" An' hadn't it been for the accident, Fergus would have made bloody work somewhere before the mornin' ! "

Of course McKenna did not press an inquiry as to the job he and Fergus were attending to, knowing that Lawler would tell it of his own accord, if left alone. All that day, and until late at night, the operative was employed as a nurse to the wounded Bodymaster.

A few days later the last meeting in April occurred, at Lawler's, and a young man named Dean was duly initiated, McKenna prominently assisting in the ceremony. Dean subsequently admitted to the agent that he had been better than a year endeavoring to reach the interior of that division, but somehow his moral character was either too good or too bad all the while; but a little serious trouble that he had recently fallen into made him a desirable applicant, or removed an objection, and he was at once notified of his acceptance. It seemed to McKenna, under such a state of affairs, that he was extremely fortunate in gaining for himself such prompt admission to the order.

McAndrew, it appeared, had not been inside a division room in more than three months, having, as will be remembered, only acted in an outside capacity at the detective's initiation—as he had temporarily resigned—which was an accepted custom in the society, since the troubles with the Church—to attend for a season to his neglected religious duties. Now, having been good during one-quarter of a year he could come back and enact the part of a Mollie Maguire for the remaining three-quarters. This ingenious and handy manner of compromise also brought home a number of the brothers, lately absenting themselves for the same purpose, and Lawler's living room was soon uncomfortably small for their accommodation.

At the same meeting Lawler gave a rather remarkable address, in the course of which he said the time had nearly arrived for the annual meeting of their State Convention at Pittsburg, and he was requested, through a letter from Barney Dolan, County Delegate, to advise his division members of the necessity for raising—the amount and the request to apply to all the bodies in Schuylkill County—the sum of nine dollars toward paying the Delegate's expenses to the west, and also to New York. In the last-named place he would see the National Secretary, on important business. Without this action it would be impossible for the Division to secure the "goods"—signs and passwords—for the current quarter; and Mike eloquently urged that it was always desirable to keep the body in fair standing with the State and National officials. The pompous Bodymaster, still suffering considerably from his wound, kept his chair while he enlarged upon the prospect before the brotherhood. He believed, if the fraternity would stand by him, he could swell their ranks to at least one hundred good men and true, before the commencement of another year. Of course the speech, or talk, was purely conversational, rough and uncouth, and not particularly coherent, but it touched its hearers and was received with applause—which, however, was necessarily suppressed, because of the family being so near. It was not long, after the close of the harangue, before the needed funds were in the Bodymaster's possession. The meeting closed soon afterward, and the hours following to midnight were passed in carousal, singing, and card-playing, when the house was deserted, the doors fastened, and the Lawler family presently dreaming the dreams of the just.

At about this date, appreciating the fact that he would not soon find remunerative labor, and still desiring to remain in the mountains, McKenna saw the necessity for a fresh source from which ostensibly to obtain the amount of money that he must, in due course of events, disburse in the community. The cash must be spent, and a valid reason for its expenditure, a natural origin for the fund, must be furnished, otherwise his associates might begin to suspect there was something about him they did not fully comprehend. It was then he took Mike Lawler further into his confidence and told him a new secret, to the effect that he, McKenna, owned a certain house and lot in the city of Buffalo, New York, which was leased from year to year, and, through the medium of an attorney, named Clinton, who was in his interest, and who knew the address of some of his relatives in Philadelphia, he received twenty-five dollars a month as rental for the property. This story served two purposes. It covered up occasional letters that the postmaster of Shenandoah must know he received, and increased his income enough, with the alleged pension from the government and the money made in his pretended disposal of bogus currency, to account for all he spent in the mining country. His wearing of poor clothes and wishing to stay in the vicinity was consistent with his mission, which was, outwardly, to escape the eyes of the officers of the law. It seemed hardly possible that, under these safeguards, his real purpose would be revealed.

The fourth day of May, Lawler, having so far regained the use of his leg as to hobble about on a crutch, aided by a blackthorn stick, determined to visit Barney Dolan, at Big Mine Run, in person, obtain the "goods" for the quarter, and turn over the collection made for the use of the County Delegate. McKenna was invited to accompany him. His arm was needed in helping Mike into and out of the buggy—besides, he liked to have some one about who could listen as well as talk. It was impossible for the agent to refuse, had he so desired, which he did not. He might learn something of importance, at small cost, and make the acquaintance of Dolan, who was then looked up to as the highest Mollie in all the county. So McKenna started out with his Body-master for Big Mine Run.

Riding over the country, although the air seemed chilly, was not really unpleasant, and the trip among the collieries, enlivened by cheerful conversation and spicy anecdote, in which both of the men participated, came to an end before either person expected. The big, good-natured County Delegate, who kept a small roadside shebeen-shop, patron-ized by all travelers and miners, was very much pleased to see his company, and he came out to the buggy, before they alighted, to greet the men, personally helping Lawler to per-form that, to him, slow and painful act.

Barney Dolan was a large, muscular man, of some forty years, much after the style of Dormer, of Pottsville, in face and feature, but by no means so tall or heavy.

After putting Mike in a chair, of course Dolan had to be informed of the particulars of Lawler's accident, brief men-tion of which he had seen in the Shenandoah *Herald.* The old story, of being fired upon by an unseen person, who he more than half suspected to be Dick Flynn, of Colorado Colliery, with whom he once had a difficulty, was related to Barney, with many adornments. As another matter of course, Dolan was profuse in sympathetic condolements with the in-jured man. When the County Delegate's back was turned, Muff Lawler sent an audacious wink of intelligence to McKenna not to spoil his story by letting slip the truth. The detective, who was contentedly smoking his short pipe and sipping some strong poteen, sagely shook his head, as much as to say : " Don't fear ! I'll keep your secret !"

Barney—whose name, from his habit of smooth, sweet talk, evidently should have been Blarney, for he must have kissed the famous stone on that famous Irish castle more times than once—proceeded to dilate upon the able manner in which he would represent the county in the State branch of the order, the great things he was about to do, and how, to sum up all, he believed it was the bounden duty of the Mollies to re-elect him Delegate at the ensuing county convention. To all of which egotistical bombast Mike and his fellow-traveler listened with an appearance of wrapped attention reflecting credit upon their capacity for acting that which they could not feel. Both really enjoyed his self-sufficiency—especially Lawler, who was afflicted with the same difficulty, as he was well aware, when he got about half-seas-over. After dinner, which was spread in the rear apartment, and the enjoyment of parting glass number one, at the invitation of the detective, the visitors proposed to leave.

Dolan made a little speech over the toast : " The Ancient Order—may it prosper and be peaceful !" offered by McKenna, and among other things remarked :

" Be them five crasses, but I'm glad indade to have *coshered* wid ye, *mabouchal !* An' when ye come here again, let it not be for a mere *kailyee*, but bring your clothes wid ye, and stop as long as ye plaze ! An', Mike Lawler—bould fellow—you'll show yourself a *gorsoon-bo*, if ye let that lad slip away from your town at all ! Kape him there ! Ye greatly nade such stuff as he's made of to bring the body up to the correct standard ! Not to say that ye are a wake Body-master, by any manes, far ye are not, as I give ye credit for doing hapes of good things ! But ye can have many more powerful members, now that ye have made the proper commencement ! What you do is done oately, an' if I do say it, you have some few fellows over there capable of doin' ' a

clane job,' an' what ye want is more of 'em ! Be the same
token, I may tell ye, Mike, that Shenandoah Division is the
very first to send in the allowance an' take away the 'goods' !
Oh, bad 'cess to me, but I'm gone *a shaughran*, an' come
near forgettin' to remember that ye have paid yer money,
but not got yer property ! Well, never mind ! It's all owin
to the poteen ! Jest step in the other room—McKenna will
excuse us—an' I'll instruct ye in the shortest time possible !"

"Business is business !" said McKenna. "Certainly I'll
excuse ye !

The succeeding conference between the County Delegate
and the Bodymaster was of short duration, and, after parting
glass number two, or three—the last one through the
thoroughly aroused generosity of Barney—the visitors really
bid the host farewell and made their departure.

The "goods," Lawler had learned from Dolan, were given
out in Ireland, the transatlantic headquarters of the society,
and thence transmitted to this country by a man named
Murphy, employed as a steward on one of the Inman line
of steamships plying between Liverpool and New York.
From the latter city the National officers distributed them
to the different divisions in this country.

No incident worthy of mention occurred to the two
Mollies until they reached the vicinity of Colorado Colliery,
where they paused to see Hugh Mulligan, a friend of Lawler's,
who was, and for some time had been, very ill. Knowing they
had reached a dangerous locality, as this was the stamping-
ground of Dick Flynn, an inveterate enemy, yet they had
no apprehension that they would come across him, and indeed were not of the class of men much reckoning upon
serious consequences should they prove thus unfortunate.

Hugh Mulligan lived in a large frame house, at the top of
the hill. When they stopped, finding that Mulligan was in
bed, in the second story of the building, to his disappoint

ment, Lawler, from his lameness, was quite unable to see his
friend, but unwillingly compelled to remain in the parlor on
the first floor. He had suffered pain enough, he thought,
through alighting from the buggy, without climbing and descending a pair of stairs immediately thereafter. He sent
along his compliments by McKenna, and made himself
easy by the stove, awaiting that person's return. Mrs.
Mulligan and another lady who had just stepped in to see
the family went up with the detective. They found the sick
man seemingly very low, in the last stages of pulmonary
consumption, slowly coughing his life away. He was wan and
attenuated, with features pinched, sharp, and anxiously drawn
up, eyes unnaturally large, dark of color and suspiciously
bright, and the glossy black hair contrasting strangely with
waxlike forehead and cheek. The hands, with which he nervously picked and clutched at the counterpane, were thin,
the fingers talon-like, and nails long, white, and rounding outward in the middle. With barely sufficient strength to raise
his arms, he lay, a pitiable object, that once had been a large
and powerful man. Just able to recognize McKenna, Hugh
was seen to smile faintly, quite gratified that two of his comrades had shown their regard by calling to see him. In a
feeble voice he asked his wife to bring some beer to the
chamber, and give Mike Lawler the best the house afforded.
Mrs. Mulligan obeyed, quickly returning with two bottles of
Cronk beer, one of which McKenna opened, presenting a
glass of its contents to the lady visiter.

The sick-room was small, with reasonably high walls,
lighted by two windows, fronting the public road and at the
side of the invalid's bed. Its furniture was poor and scant.
There was an old-fashioned chest of drawers, not as high as
a bureau, but taller than a trunk, made of pine, painted a
dark red, on the lid of which stood some medicine bottles
and an empty tumbler and spoon. Near by was a bit of
cracker, which the sick man had nibbled with his teeth when

besought to take some nourishment. The bedstead had high posts, and the bed and coverings were barely comfortable. Near the foot of the bed stood a high-backed, splint-bottom rocking-chair, with neat tidy over the top. Two or three other chairs and a small table completed the furniture of the apartment. No carpet concealed the floor, the boards of which were scrubbed white and clean. Plain bleached cotton formed the looped-up window curtains, and along the wall were nails, on which hung a soldier's overcoat, a hat, a heavy teamster's whip, and then several articles of female costume. At the head of the couch was a cheap print of St. Patrick, without a frame, and on the opposite wall a cross, entwined with real shamrock, the emblems worked with a needle in red worsted upon some gilt pasteboard. A door led into the hall, at the head of the stairs. At one side of the center of the room was a sheet-iron heater, fed through a pipe from the apartments below, which came up through the floor by a tin thimble, or protector, and kept the atmosphere warm and equable. A small hat-stand supported the bottles of beer and a couple of common flaring beer tumblers.

Mrs. Mulligan, a motherly, kind-hearted woman, with blue eyes and plentiful iron-gray hair, a cap, and becomingly clad in black, stood at the side and partly toward the foot of the bed, knitting work in hand, a pitying glance resting upon her suffering husband. The lady caller, her bonnet and cloak unremoved, sat not far away, while McKenna was at that moment in the act of helping himself to a tumbler of beer, which he had not yet poured from the bottle. This was the condition of affairs, when the detective heard a heavy and hasty step upon the staircase, the door of the chamber was rudely thrust open, and big Dick Flynn, with pistol presented in one hand and a long knife brandished recklessly in the other, strode in and paused before the entrance. His aim was directed upon the sick man in the bed. Mulligan uttered a despairing wail, and, nervously throwing up the coverings, drew his head beneath them. Mrs. Mulligan, almost paralyzed with fright, dropped her knitting, raised her hands and screamed "murder!" at the top of her voice, while the lady visitor, without pausing to say "good-by," flew past the intruder and down the stairs like a frightened deer. McKenna, who had paused in the work of decanting the contents of the bottle, heard Lawler hobbling, with crutch and stick, over the floor below, and, looking from the corner of his eye, soon saw the brave Bodymaster making rather rapid time, for a lame man, toward the gate, where his horse and buggy were standing. Then the agent had no doubt he was left to cope, single-handed, with the savage brute before him. He took in this idea in much less time than it has consumed to record the fact, and arrived at the conclusion that only calmness and the exertion of ingenuity could save his life. Dick did not shoot the sick man, who he was quite sure was Mike Lawler, but stood ready to fire. McKenna finished pouring out his beer, took up the second glass and the bottle, and with supreme impudence advanced a step toward Flynn, saying, not even forgetting his assumption of the brogue that he had used while in the country:

"Sure, an' is it yourself, Misther Flynn? An' its tired indade ye are, afther your long walk! Tak' a drap of the beer at Hugh's expense!"

And he proffered the bottle and glass.

Flynn was, in turn, thunderstruck by the coolness of his enemy, muttered something between his shut teeth, was undecided what to do, wavered, and at last, depositing knife and pistol on the little table, took the tumbler in one hand, the beer bottle in the other, and proceeded to drink.

No sooner had McKenna released bottle and glass than his right hand quickly, yet cautiously, sought the side-pocket of his coat, where rested his trusted seven-shooter. With a sud der twist of the wrist, holding a firm grasp upon the pistol stock, his thumb brought the hammer of the lock to full cock. Still he did not display the repeater.

"By heaven! I've got Muff Lawler this time!" said Flynn. "Ye can't chate me! Pretendin' to be sick, or lame, won't save ye! I'm here to kill ye!"

His wild, insane look rested uneasily on the half-concealed figure in the bed, as he said this, not perceiving the fact that McKenna had quietly changed position, and now stood somewhat nearer to him than before.

"Oh, I'm not Muff Lawler!" painfully gasped Mulligan, exposing his white, almost spectral features. The voice was stronger than usual. He had summoned all his vital powers to repel that which he might well believe a hateful vision. "I'm only poor, sick, disabled Hugh Mulligan!"

Turning his eye to the window, Flynn beheld Lawler, driving away in the buggy, the horse's head turned toward town. Then he fiercely faced McKenna, and exclaimed:

"You've saved Muff Lawler, but you are his 'butty,' and I'm here to kill one of the two—so it seems you are the one!"

"I guess not, me swate raparee! Not by these lights!"

And the detective drew his weapon, bringing it close to the man's face, until the dark muzzle rested, deadly, sullenly cold, in close contact with the ruffian's bare cheek. Flynn, drunk and infuriated as he was, could not resist that forbidding and blood-chilling argument. It was plain that the lock was set, the man's finger resting on the trigger. He began to tremble like a poplar leaf in the wind, his color shifted from red to white, the features relaxed, the corners of the mouth fell down, and his whole appearance was fearfully changed.

CHAPTER XVII.

A PECULIAR WEDDING CEREMONY.

FLYNN obeyed. He could do nothing less, finding himself completely in the power of the enemy and that menacing revolver. It was far from his intention to lose his life, when, by merely complying with McKenna's simple command, he could insure its immediate or temporary preservation.

At this late moment Mrs. Mulligan recovered her voice, and throwing herself between Flynn and her husband, cried out :

"Oh, don't hurt my Hugh ! He's never done anybody any harrum, *sheeling avourneen !* Sure its dyin' the poor boy is, the moment ! An' its right down cruel of yez to come disputin' about, disturbin' us an' makin' him the worse ! Oh, kill me, if you want to, but don't hurt a hair o' him ! "

"Faix an' I don't see that Flynn is about to shoot any body jist at the present moment ! " said McKenna, still keeping the weapon nigh his adversary's head. " I am in the firm belaif that the boot's on t'other foot, this time ! "

Meanwhile the detective slowly retreated, still facing his opponent, to the table on which the drunken man's weapons rested, and, without changing aim or lowering the revolver, proceeded to deposit the knife in his pocket. The second loaded pistol he retained in the left hand, ready for use should his own miss fire or the cartridges be exhausted.

At this stage of proceedings, Flynn, whose reason seemed partly to have resumed sway, through fright, thought death was sure to follow and his legs would no longer support him

Falling prone upon his knees, the tall hat came off, and he held up both hands, begging abjectly, like the arrant coward he was, that life might be spared, saying :

" Don't kill me, McKenna ! For my poor childer's sake, don't shoot ! "

" I don't intend to shoot, right here, in the presence of Hugh an' the good lady—but you had no such hesitation. Do you see that opening the carpenter left in yonder wall ? What I now want is, that you get up from the floor an' betake yourself down thim stairs as fast as ye can go ! "

" I'll do anything ye say ! " answered Flynn.

And the big, lubberly fellow, completely cowed and almost sobered, moved slowly toward the door, McKenna following close upon him, his weapon steadily directed full upon Flynn's bushy head. Down the staircase in this order of procession they slowly continued their march.

" Get ye in here ! " said the detective, and he opened the door of a sort of vault, where Mrs. Mulligan stored her bottled ale and other liquors. " Step quickly," was added, as the result of an evident hesitation on the part of the prisoner. The dark muzzle of the pistol emphasized the language, and made it impossible for him to disobey ; so in he went.

" It is well you got in," said McKenna, " fur I had brought ye to the place where I intinded fur to kill ye ! "

" I'll niver hesitate agin ! " said Flynn, and he looked about the dark recess. McKenna shut the door with a bang, shot to its place the bolt of the ponderous lock, withdrew the key, and placed it in his pocket. Then with a heavy piece of timber, which had been employed as a support for whisky barrels, he propped the massive oaken panels in their position, resting the upper end of the brace against the boards and the lower portion behind a solid brick-and-mortar projection, forming part of the chimney. Thus was Dick Flynn safely caged. To make sure that he remained where he had confined him, the detective closed and fastened all

8

the shutters to the windows, locked and barred every outer
entrance to the lower part of the house, took possession of
the keys, and then, only pausing a few moments to inform
Mrs. Mulligan that she was perfectly safe, and that he would
send an officer to her relief, with the frantic cries and oaths
of the imprisoned man ringing in his ears, experiencing a
feeling of gratitude that he had escaped, he started for
Shenandoah, following the track left by the carriage which
had borne away his wounded companion.

McKenna had not gone far when he met Lawler returning to Mulligan's accompanied by a deputy sheriff.

" Hurrah! " shouted Lawler, when he saw the young man,
apparently unharmed.   " Then ye are not kilt enthirely ? "

"An' phat did ye run off afther ? " queried McKenna,
appearing greatly offended.   " I think ye might 'ev stopped
at laste to carry away me dead body, afther the matin' wid
Dick Flynn, the murtherous thafe of the worruld ! "

" Didn't I ride away, wid all me power, to get me revolver,
which, like a looney that I am, I had left snug at home?
An' wasn't I so disabled, from me wound, that I couldn't tak'
any part in the pother?   Didn't I think there'd be nade of
an officer, sure—an' isn't wan here ?   Faith, ye kin now take
the boy to jail in a twinklin' !   But where is Dick Flynn, the
insanity that he is ! "

" Well, a poor excuse suits ye as well as any ! " answered
the operative.   " But I forgive ye, seein' as how I wur successful in handlin' the man !   You'll find him, all swate an'
cooled down like, in Mrs. Mulligan's beer closet, an' all ye
hev to do is to put a revolver close to his head, an' he'll walk
quieter nor a lamb, wherever ye may wish.   I have his
knife and pistol—here they are—an' the kays to the doors—
take thim along, too—you kin do wid the fellow as ye
wish !   Right here, I wash me hands of the business enthirely ! "

McKenna handed the weapons and keys to the officer

and, stubbornly turning on his heel, rapidly journeyed homeward.

Flynn was removed to jail, at Shenandoah, where he remained a few days and was eventually released, the witness for the State having been coaxed by Mrs. Mulligan not to appear against him. The poor woman was afraid that, if punished, Dick would make her home too hot for her. Thenceforward, however, Flynn bore himself quite decently toward both of his former enemies, and gave McKenna a wide berth if he chanced to find himself where he might possibly encounter him.

This may be set down as one of the many adventures of a critical and dangerous nature which the detective experienced during the course of his first year's residence in the anthracite region. He had still others, but they will receive attention in an appropriate place. With these tragical rencounters there arose also occasional experiences which were of a more pleasant sort. Among the latter was his participation in a Polish marriage ceremony, transpiring in the vicinity of Shenandoah only a short time subsequent to the sudden meeting with drunken Dick Flynn, just alluded to.

Pete Monaghan, Ed. Fergus, and Tom McNulty accompanied my representative on the trip. In view of this fact, and their future relations with our work, it may be best more particularly to introduce them to the reader's attention.

Monaghan seemed about four years past his majority, was of fair complexion, hair of the color denominated sandy, full, florid face, light blue eyes, and wore no beard or mustache. In fact, he was a middle-sized, boyish-looking man, a little above medium height and weight. He was at that period a miner, but subsequently attended college about a year and finally settled down in Shenandoah as a staid and sober green-groceryman, in which place and position he yet remained at last advices. He is not to be confounded with Ned Monaghan.

Ferguson, *alias* Fergus, was also a miner, but a personage whose figure and face were a contrast to those just described. Of dark complexion, wearing a black, full beard and mustache, of which he was so proud that he constantly stroked and petted them with his rough hand; a foxy little face, red nose, that turned ever upward; large, broad, and capacious mouth, which was seemingly filled with long, wide, shovel-shaped teeth; staring, hazel eyes, ready to wink comically at the faintest possible chance; his shoulders tending to form part and portion of a human interrogation point, he was neither large nor small, heavy nor light, but about a medium in both; a person to be remarked upon the street, and as full of genuine wit as he well could be. While Fergus was wild and frolicsome, Monaghan was quiet and good-natured.

McNulty was a compact fellow, of swarthy complexion, black hair, dark gray eyes, round face, pug nose, and would steal like a born thief. Work and he had evidently early fallen out and never become reconciled. A fearful consumer of drink, he was never trusted by the Mollies, and there were few who knew him that would leave sixpence in his reach if they cared ever to see it again.

These were some of the every-day companions of the operative.

The natives of Poland, quite numerous in the vicinity of Shenandoah, were most, members of the Catholic Church, affiliating readily with the miners from England, Ireland, Scotland, and Wales, and, when of the same religious belief, even with those of Germany and Scandinavia. Still they were located in particular sections, and tenaciously held to many of the fatherland social peculiarities. Their habits and customs were mostly novel to the average American reader, and their nuptial ceremony notable as among the most curious of those belonging to a queer community. In the first place, although it was generally known when and where a wedding was to

transpire, yet no persons were especially invited to participate, and none were asked to stay away. All, as it was
generally understood, would find welcome on the occasion.
Preparations were entered into for great sport, and plenty
of it, as an accompaniment to the ac. of uniting " two hearts
that beat as one." There was, on these occasions, almost
total absence of restraint, but perfect decorum being the
prevailing rule, and disorder the exception. The Polish
women were as well-behaved, in every respect, as those of
other nationalities, and, in a locality where two-thirds of the
inhabitants were Poles, cause for divorce, and illegitimacy
were seldom brought to the light.

But the wedding.

Monaghan, Fergus, McNulty, and McKenna attended
the nuptials of Julius Krozepski with a fair maiden, to
whom he had been some years betrothed. It was rather
outside the borough limits and in the edge of the wood that
the girl's parents resided, and this was the scene of the wedding. There were many people already gathered when they
reached the place, although the time was only an hour past
sunset. The view presented to the eye of the detective
reminded him of pictures he had seen of gypsy encampments
at night.

Two forked sticks had been embedded in the earth, the " y "
parts above ground. Across, and resting in the crotches
of these, was placed a heavy hickory sapling, some five
inches in diameter at the butt. Suspended by iron chains
and a hook from the center of this beam was a huge caldron
kettle, made of iron, and under the vessel a hot fire had
been kindled, which, beside serving its culinary purpose
threw out fitful flashes of red light upon the motley assem
blage, giving a garish contrast on one side of each object
to the darkness of night shadowing the other.

As a more voluminous sheet of fire would dart out from
among the pine knots and glowing embers, it illuminated a

space for yards around, and sent the pleasant light far into the building branches of the highest trees.

From the great iron kettle a savory incense arose. After some inquiry, the stranger learned that it came from an admixture of high-wines and common molasses, in about the proportion of one gallon of the latter to four of the spirit, which, when once well incorporated by stirring with a wooden ladle, and brought to the boiling point, was to constitute the wedding refreshment, in lieu of the breakfast, supper, or dinner. The number of guests was large and the liquor boiled made, in the aggregate, several gallons.

There were present miners of all nationalities nearly, with their wives and sweethearts—all outside the house in which the bride sat, as the building was much too small to accommodate one-tenth part of the concourse assembled. Had this been different, the kettle would have swung from the crane in the wide, open fireplace, after the olden fashion.

McKenna and his friends were well received by the people. This was especially the case with the detective, who had dressed himself with more than ordinary care for the occasion, exhibiting, for about the first time since the chicken match, an immaculate linen shirt-front, collar, black necktie and waistcoat, and having entirely eschewed the old leather belt, with its common iron buckle. He was, therefore, in his freshly-trimmed hair and whiskers, a rather gentlemanly appearing young fellow, reputed a fair dancer, and as having an uncommonly fine voice for an Irish love ditty. He was met by several acquaintances, who were at some pains to introduce him to the young ladies and gentlemen. With the former his native modesty was not in the way of his cultivating, to the full extent, their good graces. In fact, some of the men thought he devoted more time than necessary to the handsome women. Be that as it may, despite the rough reputation he had won, he certainly was a prime favorite with the Polish maidens. The Irish girls, also, thought he was about right; one especially—a queenly figure, with dark, waving chestnut curls, and laughing, hazel eyes, whose name, he heard, was Mary, and resided in, or very nigh to, Tamaqua—was the particular object of his regard, and Fergus suggested, more than once, that the western chap had in her met his fate. It is true that McKenna was deeply struck with the lady's beauty, vivacity and amiability—seen at a distance. He was now intent on business, and believed, after that night, would never see her again.

But the wedding.

The seething blackstrap was pronounced ready for use, and a lady, a long-handled tin dipper in hand, stood at the kettle dishing out its smoking contents to the company. It rapidly disappeared, and, as it diminished and was imbibed, the fun and hilarity proportionately increased. The fluid was greatly relished by the Poles and their families.

The young couple having been united by the priest, after the ritual of the Roman Catholic Church, the clergyman partook of the spirits and departed for his home. Then the bride was seated at her place in the best room—which was the kitchen—having a small table near, on which stood a steaming pitcher of the blackstrap and a tin pot. In the open fire-place blazed pine knots and light-wood, giving a genial brightness to the place, which was devoid of lamps or candles A dresser, with its array of polished tinware, reflected back the flame and made each corner like open day. By the chimney jamb, on a bit of log, fashioned into a rude stool, sat the aged grandmother of the bride, gray, wrinkled, and trembling in limb, but rigged out in a white ruffled cap, and smoking a brand-new clay pipe. Chairs there were none, excepting that devoted to the queen of the occasion —fair, comely Mrs. Krozenski, with her hair done up in a knot behind her head, combed flat at the sides of the face, and the whole surmounted by a high tortoise-shell comb—

who bore her honors gracefully, and was supplied with a
dress pocket, capacious enough to contain a small fortune
in silver.

This was the style of her reception : Her male friends,
one after another, came in, saluted her kindly, wishing her
the usual good luck, calling her by her new name, and each
one helped himself to some of the liquor, handing the bride a
present—always in the shape of money, and ranging from
one dollar to ten dollars, according to the ability or generosity of the donor—then kissed the lady three times. She
nowise disconcerted, placed the cash in her purse, and was
ready for the next person.   The room was well filled with
ladies and gentlemen, the groom, meanwhile, busying himself
with out-door affairs. McKenna watched this part of the proceedings for a while with interest, rather liked it, and then
walked up, paid his money, enjoyed his small share of the
lady's lips, and stepped back a little to give others a chance.
Following him happened to be the young woman from Tamaqua.   She tripped gaily to the bride, took her dainty sip
of the liquor, tendered a bank-bill, and then, her roguish Irish
eye resting upon the detective, she suddenly swooped down
upon him, rested one little hand for a second lightly as a
snow-flake on his shoulder, and, before the defenseless man
could prevent, kissed him once, twice, thrice, on the cheek,
then as swift as the wind almost, turned, ran away, and disappeared.

The laugh which was raised at the detective's discomfiture
was both long and loud, and he was forced, after he had
recovered from the astonishment, to take part in it.

It seems that the young lady had done nothing at all
indecorous or uncommon. The rule, as McKenna subsequently saw exemplified, permitted any of the ladies who
saluted and feed the bride to kiss the woman just married,
or if she so chose, any of the gentlemen present. Hence
the agent had unwittingly placed himself in a position to

become the subject of Miss Mary's little trick. He was not
at all sorry for it, and the sensation of pleasure, caused by the
kiss, visited his cheek for weeks thereafter.

The money thus donated to the bride—and this part of the
ceremony might be continued for some days—was employed
in furnishing the house of the wedded pair. It closed at
midnight, after which the lady and her husband could join
their friends and indulge in a polka or waltz.

The dancing of the Poles consisted of redowas, waltzes,
polkas, mazourkas, and schottisches, some of which McKenna
was taught; but, after all these, he liked best the lively jig
and the rattling reel. Following some of this amusement, he
was called upon to sing a song and dance a favorite fling,
both of which he did with success. The song he gave
eliciting most commendation was as follows, and called:

THE WEDDING OF BALLYPOREEN.

On a fine summer morning at twelve in the day,
The birds they did sing and the asses did bray,
When Patrick, the bridegroom, with Onagh, the bride,
With their bibs and their tuckers, set out side by side.
    The pipers played first in the rear, sir;
    Maids blushed, and the bridegroom did stare, sir--
    O Lord, how the spalpeens did swear, sir,
        At the wedding of Ballyporeen.

They were soon tacked togither, and home did return,
To make merry the day at the sign of the Churn.
When they sat down togither, a frolicsome troop,
The old Shannon's bank never held such a group.
    There were turf-cutters, thatchers, and tailors,
    Fiddlers, and pipers, and nailers,
        At the wedding of Ballyporeen.

There was Bryan McDermott, O'Shaughnessy's brat,
There was Terence O'Driscoll and platter-faced Pat;
There was Norah McCormick, likewise Bryan O'Linn,
An' the fat, red-haired cookmaid that lived in the inn;

8 *

There was Shelah, an' Larry the genius,
Pat's uncle, old Darby McGinniss,
Black Thady an' crooked McDennis,
    At the wedding of Ballyporeen.

The groom he got up an' made an oration ;
He pleased them all with his kind botheration ;
" Since you all have met here "—then he swore and he cursed :
" You can eat till you swell, boys, an' drink till ye burst ;
    The first christening I hev, if I thrive, sirs,
    I hope ye all hither will drive, sirs.
    You'll be all welcome, dead or alive, sirs,
        To the christening of Ballyporeen."

The bride she got up and she made a low bow,
She twittered—she felt so—she couldn't tell how—
She blushed, and she stammered, and a few words let fall ;
But she spoke it so low that she bothered them all.
    Then the mother cried out : " Are you dead, child ?
    For shame ! Now hold up your head, child ;
    Tho' sixty, I wish I were wed, child,
        I would rattle all Ballyporeen."

Well, they sat down to ate—Father Murphy said grace ;
Smokin' hot were the dishes, an' eager each face ;
Knives and forks they did rattle, spoons and platters did play
They elbowed an' jostled an' walloped away.
    Rumps, shins and fat sirloins did quake, sir ;
    Whole mountains of beef down were mown, sir ;
    We demolished all, to the bare bone, sir,
        At the wedding of Ballyporeen.

The whisky went around an' the songsters did roar ;
Tim sang, " Paddy O'Kelly "—Nell sung, " Moll Asthore ;"
When a motion went around that their songs they forsake
And each man took his sweetheart, their trotters to shake.
    With the pipers in couples advancin'—
    Pumps, brogans, an' bare feet fell a prancin,
    Such pipin', an' figurin', an' dancin',
        Was ne'er seen at Ballyporeen.

Here's to Patrick, the bridegroom, and Onagh, the bride ;
That the Harp of Old Erin be hung by their side ;
An' to all the people, whether old, gray, or green,
Drunk or sober, that jigged it at Ballyporeen.
  Until Dan Cupid does lend you his wherry
  To trip o'er the conjugal ferry,
  I hope you all may be as merry
    As we were at Ballyporeen.

Just as McKenna had concluded this effort, a great screaming and rushing of the ladies was heard in another part of the house, accompanied by heavier voices of men, mingling curiously with the music of the fiddle and the barking of the dogs. The three friends, with almost every person in the vicinity, quickly started for the field of disorder, which seemed not far from the residence.

CHAPTER XVIII.

A ROW, A REMOVAL, AND A RAFFLE.

THE true cause of the disturbance was not at once disclosed, but its progress and bearings were easily determined by the eye and ear of the spectator. Such a reign of confusion and roar of voices ; such a Babel of tongues, it had never been the fortune of the operative to see or hear. In the center of a considerable group of persons stood the young husband, Julius Krozenski, brandishing a long stiletto and loudly swearing that he would take somebody's life. Meanwhile a friend, less under excitement than the bridegroom, firmly held the angry man back by the collar. Facing the Pole, somewhat in the shadow of a large tree, stood an athletic Irish miner and his equally muscular wife, both much wrought up, but neither exhibiting or employing any more deadly weapon of offense or defense than their unusually acrimonious tongues, which they exercised with all their strength. Soon Mrs. Krozenski made her appearance, and, walking straight to the side of her newly-made liege lord—but by no means, as the sequel will show, her master—she scientifically seized him by the left ear, told him to "put away his knife," and then, with an affectionate and effective twist of the imprisoned auricular appendage, hauled the irate man away. The burst of laughter which followed this evidence of power on the part of a wife was highly exasperating to Julius, and he slipped his tether, again drew his knife, and rushed back toward his opponent. Once more Mrs. Krozenski caught him by the ear, once more he had to replace the weapon in his belt, and once more the victorious lady led him in the direction of the house. This escaping and catching process was repeated several times, and on each occasion, the peacemaker succeeded in capturing and carrying away her husband. At last he was safely returned to the kitchen and seated on a log of wood at the wife's side, where, for some moments, he remained as mild and quiet as possible.

Now the reception ceremonies were continued, and nothing more occurred to disturb the usual routine of proceedings until O'Neill and his wife ventured to enter the apartment. This was too much, and Krozenski burst out afresh, worked himself into a new frenzy, and quickly rising, again reached for and produced his long-bladed knife, which, unfortunately, his spouse had permitted to remain in his possession.

The detective soon learned the cause of the difficulty.

It seems that O'Neill, who was a miner, and an intimate associate of the bridegroom, had formerly entertained the hope that Julius would marry a maiden sister of his own—was, in fact, somewhat angered that he did not—and, in Krosenski's presence, made the remark, while dancing, that Mrs. Krozenski was not as graceful in the polka as that gifted young lady. This was a very mild criticism for O'Neill to make, but it was heard by Krozenski, who had imbibed too much of the blackstrap to have any great amount of sense remaining in his head, and he resented it by calling the Irishman a liar and following the hard word with a stinging blow in the face. As was perfectly natural, O'Neill came in to take a hand, backed by some of his immediate neighbors. In the mêlée the bridegroom had drawn his knife and been joined by some of his countrymen. This part of the fracas was ended by the masterly manner of Mrs. Krozenski, whose principal idea appeared to be to have her reception continued and prevent her husband from thus early leaving her a widow.

It was all very well until O'Neill, having armed himself with a revolver, entered the kitchen, which was crowded with men and women. This was more than the husband of Mrs. Krozenski could possibly endure, and as before stated, he rushed once more to the deadly fray. He could not bear to have O'Neill there to gloat over his abject submission to Mrs. Krozenski. O'Neill, nothing loth for a further continuance of the battle, promptly fired upon the bridegroom, narrowly missing a lady standing near, and not hitting the target by a foot. This was enough to cause all the Polish, German, Welsh, and English miners in the room to side with Krozenski, while those from Ireland were not backward in joining the O'Neill and his plucky little helpmate. McKenna's friends, promptly deserting him, or expecting that he would follow, entered the field. The detective, being duly sober, saw at a glance that the Irish element was in the minority, and, despite abundant courage and considerable experience in such matters, would inevitably meet defeat, and he assumed the *rôle*, for the first time that evening, of conservator of the peace. There was imminent danger, in view of the proclivity of the Poles for using sharp knives in such troubles, that some of his companions might be dangerously injured, if not killed.

Beside, the Mollie Maguires, as a body, were not interested in the affair.

Krozenski had gone in with the full intention of killing O'Neill; and O'Neill was equally intent upon performing the same kindly office for the Polander. Each man was backed by his corps of partisans. The tumult that developed defies powers of pen and pencil to depict, and, in point of vocal and physical performances, exceeded all that the agent had ever heard or read of in the same line at famous Kilkenny, or equally famous Billingsgate. Bricks and stones were the principal missiles employed; pistols and knives played their part; heads were broken, and faces and noses contused; crabsticks crossed; eyes draped in beautiful black and blue, teeth lost, shins bruised, chops swollen, and shillalahs fell with telling effect. The shouts and cries that rent the night air were guttural Teutonic, Gallic, Celtic, Anglo-Saxon, Welsh, Polish, and sometimes a mixture of all, perfectly unintelligible to any of the nationalities participating. Dust arose in clouds, and was almost suffocating in density. The whole affair much resembled the common idea of a miniature bedlam, and was in truth a small pandemonium let loose—chaos come again.

When the turbulence was at its highest pitch, while it was difficult to think of, and utterly impossible to hear anything, excepting the medley of noises immediately surrounding him, McKenna's attention was drawn to the part taken in the fight by the aged grandam of Mrs. Krozenski, who seemed greatly to enjoy the rumpus going on around her. Jumping hither and thither, like a veritable witch without her broomstick, the little, frisky old lady, her broad lace ruffles and straggling gray hair flying about her withered face, with shrill tone and violent gesture urged on her countrymen to the contest, and added at least her share to the general disorder. At last, when the police had arrived, and been driven away with clubs, when the combat had been resumed, and shouts and shots and rattling of many sticks again filled the air, the grandmother of the bride climbed upon the back of a common chair, which had been brought in by her granddaughter, and standing as erect as possible, she loudly clapped her bony hands and screamed in her cracked treble voice :

" Oh, jolly noise ! *jolly noise ! !* JOLLY NOISE ! ! ! "

This genuine burst of enthusiasm roused the energies of the detective, thus far held firmly in reserve, and he drew his revolver and fired three shots, in rapid succession, into the floor, directly under the crone's perch, shouting in a double-bass voice, as loudly as he could, after each explosion :

" Peace ! " " *Peace ! !* " " PEACE ! ! ! "

The aged dame beheld the flame and smoke issuing from the revolver, and heard the reports ; then, thinking that she was certainly hit, if not killed, she toppled over backward to the floor and straightened out in a dead faint. McKenna at once dragged her insensible form out of harm's way, and then joined those who were trying their utmost to quell the disturbance.

The pistol shots, and the loud voices of McKenna and Mrs. Krozenski—the latter having quit the fray to attend to her relative—soon caused the belligerents to hesitate. In a few moments their fury evaporated, and comparative quiet was restored. Shortly thereafter those who were able limped away to their homes.

" Faith, an' I've had enough an' to spare of all *such* weddin's ! " said Fergus, examining with care an extra curve that he wore in his turned-up nose, and wiping the gore from his face with the sleeve of his coat. " When you catch *me* goin' to a Polish war again, I give ye good lave to put me in me coffin first ! "

Monaghan had two eyes in preparation for mourning, which he was sure they would assume by another day.

McNulty was the only lucky one, having escaped personal injury—and found a silver watch, as he explained, "rolling along on the floor, widout any kaper or owner bein' around!" He intended merely to retain the timepiece until the loser should call for it. But McKenna never heard that anybody ever saw the value of that watch, through having retrieved it from the thief.

The Polish husband and wife, with O'Neill and his spouse, and a number of the originators of the riot, were taken to jail by the officers, who returned with increased numbers for the purpose.

These scenes read like romance, but they are simply the truth.

Nothing here related is intended to reflect upon the Poles as a portion of the inhabitants of the coal regions of Pennsylvania. They are, as miners, industrious and frugal, and, though slow workers, very reliable and trustworthy. The men are large, robust, muscular, and capable of great endurance. The women are also far from sylph-like, but many of them beautiful in form, face, and figure; with dusky olive complexions, dark eyes and hair. They are excellent wives and mothers.

Let us now return to the Mollie Maguires.

The next meeting of the midnight clan was held on Sunday, the tenth of May, and his own room being too small, the Bodymaster notified the members to convene on the mountain-side near the house. All were present excepting Fergus, who was not fairly recovered from the blows received at the Polish wedding. Several of his teeth had disappeared, his nose was badly bruised, and his beauty—of which he had little to part with—entirely destroyed. He thought it advisable to remain within for a few days, having, as he remarked, a great respect for the children of his acquaintance.

and not wishing to be the means of frightening any of them to death by his untimely appearance in their midst.

Bushy Deenan, from Pottsville, being in Shenandoah on a visit, was present at this meeting in the bush. About all done was the giving out of the "goods," received from Barney Dolan by Lawler. McKenna was careful to commit all to memory. They were as follows :

The password :

" That the troubles of the country may soon be at an end ! "

The answer :

" And likewise the men who will not her defend."

The quarreling toast was :

" You should not dispute with a friend."

The answer was :

" Not if I am not provoked ! "

The night password was :

Question : " Long nights are unpleasant ! "

Answer : " I hope they will be at an end ! "

The sign of recognition was the front or first finger and thumb of the right hand touching the necktie, or top button of the shirt.

The answer was given by rubbing the right hand across the forehead, just touching the hair.

About this time the detective had his first portion of the process of inuring himself to the mountain region. It came in the form of fever and ague, and, during a number of days subsequent to the meeting of his division, he suffered intensely, at times, from chills, with the succeeding torrid sensations, which confined him to his room and his bed at Mrs. Cooney's. Those who have enjoyed the rigors of this unpleasant complaint need no description of the detective's symptoms—that, in this instance, " ignorance is bliss," let those who have not shaker be content to believe.

As a matter of necessity, the officer soon settled the slight difficulty in which he and Muff Lawler were involved. It was foolish, as well as unnecessary, to keep up a quarrel with a man so bound to him and in whose movements he was so much interested. Should he separate from Lawler, at this juncture, the division would look upon him with coldness, if not suspicion, and it was his idea to remain on the most intimate terms with his friends, the Mollies. Lawler made a feint of going over to Colorado Colliery, to fight out the trouble with Dick Flynn, and borrowed McKenna's revolver for dueling purposes, having little confidence in his own weapon, after injuring himself with it, but the cowardly Flynn would not come to time, ending the interview with Lawler—as related by that veracious individual in person— by falling upon his knees and asking the Bodymaster's pardon. Thus ended the affair, without having further recourse to weapons, or the law.

It was now the duty of the detective to collect statistics connected with the order of which he had been made a member. That he might accomplish this object, he must travel from place to place. Therefore, saying his health demanded rest from work in the mines—even should labor present, and of this there were serious doubts—he prevailed upon Lawler to grant him a traveling card, directed to the officers of all divisions in the United States, through which— with the "goods"—admission could be secured in any city, town, or village. This card had to be countersigned by Barney Dolan, County Delegate, before it was valid. The name was easily gained, through a short trip to Big Mine Run.

Night and day during the spring, fall, and winter, McKenna had been exposed to all sorts of weather and late hours, and it told upon his constitution, which must have been of iron to have held out so long, and he grew thin. cadaverous, and his strength perceptibly and rapidly failed. The symptoms were aggravated by a dry cough, which drove off refreshing sleep.

Although it was not his intention to stay long away from Shenandoah—which place, from the material in and surrounding it, he believed to be the grand center of the field of operations of the Mollie Maguires—and so informed all his friends—the. parting between McKenna and McAndrew was a scene of mutual regrets. All disliked to have him leave. This was especially the case with Cooney, Lawler, Monaghan, Fergus, and little McNulty. But, after many good wishes from the men and women, and promises on his part that he would return as soon as fully recovered, the detective occupied a car on the Lehigh Valley Road, the evening of the fifteenth of May, 1874, and reaching Wilkesbarre, Luzerne County, the same day, took up quarters at the Railroad Hotel, of which Daniel Shovlin was then proprietor.

Some bitter experiences were in store for McKenna. There must be the bitter with the sweet.

Bearing letters from Lawler and others to William Kirk, County Delegate of Luzerne, he encountered no difficulty in forming the acquaintance of the chief Mollies of the vicinity. He found that there were at that time only a little less than thirty divisions, or bodies, in the county, all of which were in a prosperous condition, as many as thirty or forty persons being added to the lodge in Wilkesbarre alone during a single night.

County Delegate Kirk was a gentlemanly person, kept a store, and was kind enough to say that Schuylkill County, from which his visitor came, "was, from its course, a disgrace to the Ancient Order of Hibernians, and should be cut off, root and branch, until there could be a complete remedy for the difficulty in reorganization."

He received McKenna cordially, however, and said he was not to blame for the condition of the order outside of Shenandoah, and complimented him for the manner in which the business and finances of that division, as far as he had heard, were being managed. He also took especial trouble to introduce the operative to the chief men of the society in Luzerne. It was learned that there were about four thousand Mollies in the county.

After remaining in Wilkesbarre a few days, McKenna visited the division at Pittston, and saw and talked with the Bodymaster, whose name was Melvin. He then visited Kingston, Plymouth, and the adjacent towns, familiarizing himself with the faces and names of the officers and members, quietly adding to his list, acquiring a better knowledge of the manners and customs of the people, and the modes of procedure within and outside the division room. Among others, he encountered Mike Hester, own cousin of Pat Hester, of Shamokin, who had not the violent reputation of his kinsman, but appeared to be a decent young man. The detective had not been long absent when he was the recipient of a letter from Muff Lawler, inquiring after his health, and particularly cautioning him not to use the new "goods" in Luzerne, as the members of the society in that county had not yet been instructed in them. This the operative had already discovered, but, as his memory was good and he had remembered those of the previous quarter, he encountered no difficulty in that respect. He also met Ned Lawler, the degenerate nephew of his uncle, and found that he had gained no wisdom by the taking on of years, but was the same rollicking, reckless fellow he had been while in Shenandoah. Kirk, when McKenna next visited his place, showed him a letter from Mike Lawler, pompously worded, but inquiring kindly after the health of his *protégé*, in whom he said he was more than usually interested.

The matter then most canvassed by the Mollies was a conference, held on the twenty-seventh of the month at Scranton, between Bishop O'Hara and five clergymen on one side, and a delegation of twenty-five Bodymasters from all

parts of the country, on the other, to discuss certain changes
in the constitution and by-laws, as well as in the secret work
of the order. Mr. County Delegate Kirk, and Peter Duffy,
of Hazelton, represented Luzerne County. The proceedings
of the convention were harmonious, but no conclusion was
arrived at, excepting in hearing the Bishop's *ultimatum.*
The clergy insisted that there must be a thorough revision
of the rules regulating divisions; that they should cease
holding meetings in bar-rooms, and consent to have a priest
for spiritual adviser, before the Church could recognize or
affiliate with them. The sentence, "If I hear a brother illy
spoken of I will inform him of it," was also to be expunged
from the obligation. They did not seem to interfere with
the secrecy, and the signs and pass-words, and little was
said about the murderous acts which had been done by
the Mollies. It was, after much argument, left in about the
same condition as before. No mere county convention
could abrogate work done by the National Board, or the
Board of Erin. Indeed it was doubtful if the Mollies would
ever consent to any changes, Church or no Church, and
whether Bishop O'Hara would not, after all, have to follow
the example of Bishop Wood, and proceed to deal in anathemas and excommunications.

Remaining in Luzerne until the fifth of June of the same
year, McKenna then received orders from Superintendent
Franklin—under whose immediate supervision, guided by
Mr. Bangs and myself, he had all the time been acting—to
report at once in Philadelphia, and he immediately obeyed.

It should have been mentioned, in its proper connection,
that, while waiting at the Shenandoah depot for the arrival
of the train to Wilkesbarre, on the fourteenth of May, Tom
Hurley had cautiously dropped something heavy into Mc-
Kenna's outside coat pocket, whispering at the same time:

"Jim, don't you say I never made you a gift of anything!
You'll have a hard set to deal wid, over in Luzerne, they're

tellin' me, an' my billy 'll come mighty convenient to have
at hand for your defense ! "

Of course the operative expressed his thanks. When he
arrived in Philadelphia, having no use for such a thing, he in
turn presented the life-preserver to Mr. Franklin, who will ever
treasure it as a relic of the Mollie Maguires. This weapon
is composed of a piece of untanned cowhide, now as hard as
horn itself, some six inches in length, twisted or braided into
a sort of handle, and covered from end to end with woolen
cloth. One extremity is loaded with three-quarters of a
pound of lead ; to the other is firmly attached a loop, large
enough to admit a man's hand, formed of strong linen cord,
and intended to allow the billy to hang loose from the wrist
and at the same time prevent it being lost or wrenched from
the grasp of its owner. At close quarters, it proves a very
savage and formidable arm of defense, resembling, but being
much more dangerous than the ordinary slung-shot in daily
use by policemen and others. Twelve ounces of solid lead
and raw-hide, dashed against the thickest skull by a strong-
armed ruffian, would as effectually silence a man as an
ounce of the same metal discharged from the bore of a
Springfield rifle.

While at the Agency in Philadelphia McKenna prepared
a complete list of all the Mollies whose acquaintance he had
formed, as well as a regular enumeration of the officers and
members, so far as he knew, belonging to the different
divisions in Schuylkill and Luzerne Counties, after which
he was instructed to re-enter the field of operations, in Carbon County, and to particularly investigate the circumstances connected with the assassination of Morgan Powell,
occurring December 2, 1871, and alluded to in chapter
vii. of this volume. It was suspected that the deed had
been perpetrated by men residing in the vicinity, the system
of exchanges between Bodymasters not having on this occasion been observed. Taking the proper line of railway, the

detective was soon in Mauch Chunk, one of the most
romantic and ancient-looking towns in the entire State.
Here, however, for the present, he need spend but little
time. His business was at Summit Hill, and, taking the
cars over the Switch-back, he was soon in that locality.
Going at once to the house of Thos. Fisher, who kept a
tavern and acted as County Delegate, he was well received,
after making himself known by throwing the proper sign,
which was promptly responded to by the Mollie. There
were several members present at the moment, and McKenna
was introduced to them. Among these were Daniel Boyle,
the Bodymaster, John Gallagher, and Pat McKenna—of
those of the last name given the detective heard there were
a large number in the neighborhood—naturally they must
be relatives. Here he also saw Maguire, the State Secretary of the order, from Pittsburg, who was canvassing in
the interest of his newspaper, the *Hibernian*, which was the
acknowledged organ of the A. O. H. in this country. It
was here he heard that big, blarneying, blundering Barney
Dolan was in disgrace at headquarters and there was a
chance that he would be removed from his office as County
Delegate of Schuylkill, and never receive any more "goods"
for the divisions, simply because he had, in a fit of anger,
loudly cursed the Bishop and the holy Church of Rome.
All agreed that Barney should have been more respectful,
and in using such language had richly merited the punishment of expulsion for life.

McKenna, the detective's namesake, was a young man,
above the average in intelligence, but loved his dram as
well as any of his countrymen in that vicinity.

Fisher had been tax-collector of the county, with other fat
positions, and was considered the big man of the Mollies in
Carbon County.

The detective's kinsman was even at that early day
suspected of having been engaged as a principal in the

murder of Morgan Powell, and Pat very naturally became an object of interest and a person whose company Mc-Kenna wanted to keep. That young man was at first rather shy, but a few songs and dances, some drinks, and a distant cousinship once having been discovered, the heart of the real McKenna gradually warmed toward the party bearing, for the time being, the same name. The companionship was kept up for some days, and finally the detective was invited to McKenna's residence and introduced to all of his relatives, girls and women, boys and men. There he made himself comfortable for a short time. He was also quite welcome, because of the stories he told the women, and the drinks he gave the men, while with the younger crop of McKennas he was a great favorite from his lessons in dancing and singing.

During the latter portion of June, bidding farewell to Summit Hill and its inhabitants, and promising to call again some day—an engagement that he was determined to fulfill —the detective thought to return to Luzerne, but stopping over at Hazelton, during his stay he was invited to attend a dance and raffle at Buck Mountain, and accepted. The chances were only a dollar, and the article to be won by somebody was a brass clock, the property of a widow woman named Breslin. The lady in question kept a shebeen-shop on the mountain, and her husband had, some months before, been killed in the mine by the sudden falling of a pillar near which he was at work. Tickets were for sale in every saloon in Hazelton, and having procured one, McKenna started, in company with some thirty or forty Mollies, to walk to Buck Mountain. At least more than half the distance, from the steepness of the ascent, had to be made on foot as no vehicle could be drawn up by horse or mule.

The party was held upon the grounds surrounding Mrs. Breslin's mansion—if mansion it could be called, consisting as it did, of one small room—and the company was as miscellaneous as it was numerous, there being several hundred men, women, and girls in attendance. But all could be accommodated, as there were plenty of torches, any amount of level earth, and seven or eight fiddlers to furnish the music.

Mrs. Breslin—a fine figure of a woman, but one somewhat along in years—was celebrated the country over for her good liquor, which, on this occasion, had been prepared in a large kettle, and was dealt out steaming hot—in fact, it was the Polish blackstrap over again, with some scraps of lemon added, by way of variety, and honored with the name of punch—hot whisky-punch.

The operative received an introduction to many of the men and all of the women, among the latter to a handsome lass, of rather uncertain age, named Kate McIntyre. Con O'Donnel gave him the acquaintance of this handsome and sprightly lady. She evidently became smitten with the young man, and despite the image of the Tamaqua queen, Miss Higgins, who still held a place in his memory, he paid her considerable attention, engaging her hand in several successive and successful reels and round dances. He treated Miss McIntyre to some of the prevalent beverage, found that she liked it, and took sufficient himself to make him feel jolly. In fact, a little after ten o'clock at night, the whole assemblage was funny, and after the clock had been raffled for and won—the winner gracefully making the widow a present of the timepiece—the mirth merged into hilarity and gradually into boisterousness. Then the time passed until midnight, when there was a short recess, during which Mrs. Breslin added to her profits by disposing of a cold collation, consisting of chicken, sandwiches, and hard-boiled eggs, of which the parties partook with appetite.

Miss McIntyre and her gallant, after having refreshments, walked around the grounds, arm in arm. While near the shanty of Mrs. Breslin, they nearly stumbled over the pros-

O

trate form of a man, who had evidently absorbed too much of the liquor. The drunken fellow slowly opened his eyes, saw Miss McIntyre, and, rising up on one elbow, with a gesture called her to him. But she gazed on him in blank astonishment, merely turning on her heel, with a look of disdain, and they walked away.

" An' who is your friend ? " asked McKenna.

" I don't know the man at all," said Miss McIntyre, " and I'm sure he does not know me ! It was the act of an idiot, who could think of nothing else ! "

" Well, but for his helpless state, I'd just go back and bate the brute for his impertinence ! " said McKenna.

Kate looked admiringly upon her companion, out of her large, dark eyes, and they passed on and once more joined n the dance.

<hr/>

CHAPTER XIX.

SNARED BY KATE—HONORED BY " MOLLIE

CON O'DONNEL, who stood nor far off, noted the drunken man's remark and was seen to smile significantly as McKenna and the lady moved from the spot.

The festivities were continued until nearly break of day, when the detective, learning that his partner had no male attendant, politely volunteered to accompany her home, which she said was no great distance away. Miss Kate accepted the proffer, as McKenna afterwards thought, with slight evidence of embarrassment, and looking furtively about her, as though in search of some one she had rather expected to see. But if there was any person present, her roguish eye failed to discern the fact, and, placing one hand upon the arm of her escort they were soon lost in the darkness.

Con O'Donnel was still looking after the couple, around the protecting and shaded corner of the widow's shanty, from which, with a sly chuckle, when the coast was clear, he quickly emerged and walked to the vicinity of the drunken man. That he was bent upon mischief those who saw the merry twinkle in his eye were well convinced.

It is unnecessary to enter into a minute description of the pleasant walk that McKenna enjoyed with Miss McIntyre. Knowing well that his companions from Hazelton would await his reappearance among them—as the majority were in no condition, from the poteen they had imbibed, to under-take the home journey—he and his fair lady did not hurry toward the protecting paternal roof. On the contrary, as has been the usage since the days of Adam, they made haste slowly, enlivening the trip with cheerful conversation, refer-ence to the festive occasion and lucky chance that brought them together, with such other talk as would naturally suggest itself to a pair in their exact mental and physical con-dition. It was a long story—and a wrong story, too, it ap-pears—that vivacious Miss McIntyre related to her im-promptu beau, about her parents' home, the family, and the trouble they had to get along during the suspension. Mc-Kenna was already hinting that, if he were a little better acquainted, perhaps he might be bold enough to ask the father to part with his child, press her to change her condi-tion in life and become Mrs. McKenna, and Miss Kate had started and blushed—but that could hardly be seen in the dusky gray of the misty morning—when both distinctly heard sounds of footsteps coming swiftly toward them from the direction of widow Breslin's place. Miss McIntyre suddenly withdrew her arm from that of her chevalier, paused in her tracks and listened breathlessly for a moment, then, in a faint and trembling voice ejaculated :

"My God! It is my husband! Our lives are in danger! He will kill us both! What shall I do?"

"Your husband, is it?" inquired McKenna, realizing the joke that had been put upon him and fully alive to the awkward predicament in which he was placed. "Your husband? Sure, didn't Con O'Donnel introduce ye as a single lady? Faix, but we are really in a purty kettle of fish! Tell me, is yer husband of the jealous sort? An' do ye think that's him, whose feet I hear makin' such a racket over the path?

"Don't stand here askin' questions," answered Mrs. McIntyre! Oh, why did I fall in with Con O'Donnel's wicked deceit? I might have known he would bring it about to punish me! He's just gone and roused Danny, and I don't doubt, if he catches me in your company, there'll be murder done upon the very spot! My husband 'll shoot us both! Oh, that I should ever have been so foolish!"

McKenna had more than once heard of Danny McIntyre, but without for a moment suspecting that he was any kin to the young woman with whom he had been walking, dancing, and making himself generally agreeable.

"I'm jist of the mind to step out into the road and shoot that husband of yours before he has a chance to say a word or do wan single thing!"

"For mercy's sake, don't talk that way!" whispered the lady, trembling all over like an aspen leaf.

"We must not be seen! Here—get you behind this tree! The underbrush will hide me! Keep quiet until he goes beyond!"

And, without a moment to spare, they disappeared from view. When the man passed their place of concealment they were as still as death. McIntyre carried a pistol in his hand, and was walking as rapidly as his mellow condition permitted, surging from one side of the path to the other as he moved, but finally, without discovering the fugitives, he was lost to their sight.

When his heavy tread could no longer be heard, the couple stood again in the road. At least one of the two breathed more freely—and that was McKenna—when the husband's form could no longer be seen. He had caught sufficient, while he was going by, to convince him that he was the identical personage who had spoken to his lady companion near Mrs. Breslin's, and to whom Kate had, in his presence, refused recognition.

The feelings of both had undergone a sudden revulsion. McKenna was very angry with Con O'Donnel, as well as with the woman who had assisted that person in playing such a practical joke upon him, and Mrs. McIntyre was naturally much mortified to be caught in such an embarrassing situation, being also fearful of the treatment to be expected from her husband should he reach home before her. With a cold and crusty "good morning, sir!" for the gentleman to whom she had so recently been saying all manner of sweet things, she added that she " could take a short-cut, with which she was acquainted, and, going across lots, make their mutual place of destination before Danny." Then Kate took her departure.

It was still too dark, though almost daybreak, for a person with the sharpest eyes to see very far in any direction, and the probabilities were that the woman would get to her residence first and succeed in fooling the half-intoxicated McIntyre with the belief that she had deserted the dancing place before midnight.

McKenna gave utterance to a long, low whistle, somewhat expressive of surprise and partly seeming like a sigh of relief, as he returned by the road over which he had so recently passed.

He walked alone and hurriedly this time.

Arrived at the house of Mrs. Breslin, he went directly in pursuit of Con O Donnel, but that individual was not to be found. He had made his exit. Throwing himself, therefore, upon a bundle of straw, under the branches of a tree, the detective soon forgot his wrath and his troubles in sleep. He had not been long in the land of Nod when he was aroused by the sound of a heavy voice calling loudly from different parts of the premises for Con O'Donnel. Near-ing the operative's improvised bed, McIntyre—for it was he —exclaimed:

" Jist tell me where I'll find that spalpeen, Con O'Donnel, an' I'll tache him to be afther playin' practical jokes on me I I'll larn him to tell me that Kate's gone off wid that Jim McKenna ! Jist let me lay these two han's on the mane scut, an' I'll mash the life out o' him ! Sure, an' me wife war slapin' in her bed, as a dacent woman should be ! Oh, tell me where to find Con O'Donnel ! "

But nobody seemed to know where the object of McIn-tyre's anger had taken himself to, and the husband was compelled to satisfy himself with some more whisky-punch, and then subsided, by the wall of the sweet-smelling pig-pen, into a drunken stupor, from which, had he appeared, even Con O'Donnel would have failed to arouse him.

So Mrs. McIntyre had succeeded in duping her husband ! This was sufficient to send the weary operative off again into slumber, and it was an hour after sunrise when he awoke. As he had expected, only three or four of the Hazelton Mollies were fit to return. The remainder could not be made sensible, and were scattered in various grotesque atti-tudes, like bodies on a sanguinary battle-field, about the dancing-grounds, oblivious to all surrounding them, where they were left to take care of themselves, while the detec-tive and his more sober comrades pursued their path down Buck Mountain to the village.

Con O'Donnel was not foolish enough to put himself in the way of the Shenandoah Mollie during his short stay in Car-bon County, but the story being far too good to keep bottled up was related to his boon companions, with many extra sdinary embellishments, not well calculated to please Mr. and Mrs. McIntyre, or suit the ideas of McKenna, and in this way soon reached general circulation in a gossiping community. While the detective was able to laugh it off, and soon get away from the locality, Danny McIntyre, when he heard what was being said, went on another extended but still fruitless search after the defamer of his household. The man who had imposed his wife upon a stranger as a single lady, having business and employment offered him in another part of the State, accepted the opportunity and soon removed from the neighborhood. Still threatening vengeance that he was unable to wreak, McIntyre was forced to quiet down and endure the result as best he might. Thenceforward the agent was more than ordinarily on his guard, and extremely careful how he volunteered to see unprotected maidens to their homes, without first making diligent inquiry if there chanced to be one Con O'Donnel thereabouts.

Carbon County having been well gone over, during the early part of July McKenna returned to Shenandoah.

The few events following, to the first of August, may thus be summarized:

The detective soon found all his Shenandoah friends about him. Lawler, Cooney, Hurley, Monaghan, McAndrew, and the rest were very glad to see their fellow-Mollie.

After the Fourth had passed, during which the members engaged in a general good time, celebrating the day of national independence, they commenced talking about securing a new Bodymaster for Shenandoah division, Lawler not having given satisfaction in several particulars. He seemed simply doing nothing. The boast that he would rapidly increase the membership had fallen short. Numbers were leaving, not liking the style of the presiding officer, instead of flocking in and joining the order. It was hinted to McKenna by several, that if he would accept, he might have the place of Bodymaster. He very wisely refused the tempting bait, but returned answer that, if they must honor him in this style—and for such an elevation he was by no means anxious—it should be in the bestowal of some subordinate position.

It was at this date that there arose considerable talk among the Mollies about one Gomer James, who had not long before shot and killed a member of the order named Cosgrove, living near Shenandoah. James was arrested, but secured bail and would soon be at large. Ned Monaghan and several others were desirous that Lawler should get some men from an adjoining body and have Gomer James quietly put out of harm's way, but, somehow, Muff could not, or would not, comply with their wishes. Therefore, ex-constable Monaghan—not Ed. Monaghan—expressed himself in favor of having an officer who would and could perform the job. Barney Dolan was sent for, and Lawler forced to send in his resignation, so that the Country Delegate might appoint a successor.

To make matters more unsettled, and the Mollies more lively, a general suspension of active operations occurred on the sixth of July, all the collieries belonging to the Philadelphia and Reading Coal and Iron Company, as well as those the property of, or leased by, individual operators, closing business and refusing longer to keep on at a loss, with expected permanent detriment to the mining interest. Labor of nearly all kinds was at a standstill. Thousands of men were without employment. The vicious and unprincipled of these being left to idleness, and naturally ready for anything, it was anticipated that outrages would quickly follow. Such always had been the case, and probably always would be, under the prevailing system of managing the coal regions. But one or two collieries kept at work in all Schuylkill County. Many of the miners and their helpers sought for getfulness in liquor. Among this number were several of McKenna's associates, Hurley being notably one of the first to begin and the last to terminate a spree. He loudly and openly cursed the Modocs, and ended by saying that Gomer lames, and those like him, who were responsible for hard times, must look out, as some of them would sup sorrow during that summer. How they could be chargeable with a stoppage of the works he did not pretend to explain, but put it upon them, without explanation, merely because he did not know where else to place it.

On one occasion Hurley exhibited a handsome set of brass knuckles, that he had borrowed of Martin Deane, and which were intended to be used upon somebody. Shortly thereafter, Deane left for Loss Creek, and he had been gone only a few days when a man named Reilly was shot and mortally wounded, by one Anthony Shaw, known to be Deane's butty. Suspicion fastened upon the latter as an accomplice in the shooting, but there was no evidence pointing him out as the accessory.

In the meantime, Frank McAndrew was the prominent candidate for Bodymaster, and, on the fifteenth of July, the big County Delegate, Barney Dolan, appeared in Shenandoah, saying something should be done, and done at once, otherwise their organization in the town should be disbanded. Dolan sought an early interview with McKenna and came out plainly with the wish that the detective should accept the Bodymastership; but he firmly refused, saying his conscience would not let him take it when there were so many more worthy men in the division; and he clinched the statement by hinting that he did not know at what moment the officers from Buffalo might pounce upon him. In such an event the division would be disgraced. No! he could not fill that office! Whatever he did must be in a subordinate position, or as a common member. The same day, Hurley, Monaghan, McAndrew, and the detective met in Lawler's house, at once shut Mrs. Lawler in the little, back kitchen, off the bar locked and bolted the door against her, and pro

9*

ceeded to hold a special meeting, one man having been stationed without to give warning, should any straggling stranger chance to stroll to the vicinity. After some desultory conversation, Frank McAndrew was duly appointed Bodymaster for the remainder of the term, and instructed in the duties of the position. He was informed that he must make all the members pay up their dues, or be cut off. Dolan said that, hereafter, it must be a beneficial society. The charge had gained circulation that charity was not among the virtues practiced by the A. O. H., and it should be disproved. After some more talk of this sort, the County Delegate, quite muddled with drink, and well satisfied with himself and his official acts, left for home.

That very night, at a late hour, as McKenna and Monaghan were passing the house of Gomer James, the obnoxious young Welshman, on the route homeward, the ex-constable pulled out his revolver and wanted to fire into the building, saying, if he "only knew where Gomer James' head rested he'd send a bullet there." He was only prevented from putting his project into execution by McKenna, who seized the pistol and compelled its owner to put it away. There was nothing in the programme of the detective authorizing him to become an accomplice in outrage when it could be avoided.

At the ensuing regular meeting of the division, held in McHugh's house, on the eighteenth of July, an election took place. McAndrew was confirmed as Bodymaster for the current term, James McHugh elected Treasurer, James McKenna, Secretary, and all were regularly installed. It was really a business meeting. James O'Brien, Charles Hayes, and John Travers were accepted, subsequently initiated, and other persons proposed as members.

Lawler was not present, having gone into a fit of the sulks, because of his removal by Barney Dolan, in the first place, and from the failure of the members to re-elect him Body master, in the second place. He temporarily resigned membership, but promised, after he had been a quarter of a year in the Church, that he would resume active participation in their proceedings. This was perfectly satisfactory to those concerned.

All things considered, Shenandoah Division succeeded better than before. Although McAndrew was troubled to read writing, and even perused print indifferently, he soon made, with McKenna's assistance, a very fair presiding officer. The detective had to go to his assistance in the ceremony of initiation, was called upon to deliver the obligation, or test, as it was sometimes described, and instruct the novitiates in the signs, pass-words, and toasts, but otherwise McAndrew managed affairs exceedingly well. This election to the Secretaryship gave the agent standing with the members, furnished him a safe place in which to write his reports, and also an excuse for carrying on considerable correspondence. Should suspicion thereafter ask a single question, he could plainly answer: "Am I not the Secretary? And nave I not the writing of the division to attend to?" While instructing the members in the "goods" his memory would be stored with their salient features and he be enabled the more correctly to report them to the Agency. The Mollies being generally uneducated, such a position gave its occupant high standing in the order.

It was not long after McAndrew's succession to the Body-master's chair, that he commenced, spurred on by Monaghan and Hurley, arguing seriously with the detective, whenever he found an opportunity, about the case of Gomer James, the murderer of Cosgrove, and to perfect plans for the Welsh-man's sudden taking off. He often referred to the timber of which Shenandoah Division was composed, and regretted that it had no suitable men to do a clean job. But he said there was encouragement now, as new members were fast coming in, and it could not be long before the right sort would be plentiful. When he found the persons for the deed he would not be slow in selecting and sending them upon the track of the enemy. One John Gibbons, who, about this date, came to the town with a letter from Barney Dolan, he had hopes of. He was looked upon as about the manner of man needed for any outrageous business, and certainly appeared bad enough to the eye, and consumed sufficient whisky to constitute a first-class ruffian.

McAndrew was excessively proud of the eminence to which he had been conducted, and acted as though not far from parting with his senses when a delegation of neighboring Bodymasters, comprising " Bucky " Donnelly, of Raven Run, James Munley, of Rappahannock, and several other promi-nent Mollies, called in a crowd at his house, with their con-gratulations upon his good luck, and wishing him every suc-cess in office. As a natural consequence of such a shower of compliments, McAndrew treated several times to the best that could be found in the city, and, after making a day of it, went to bed late at night as drunk as a lord, when he had bid his visitors farewell at the train by which they departed.

It was a considerable task for McKenna to teach McAndrew the prayers with which every meeting of the Mollie Maguires was opened and closed—for these men of blood did not hesitate to introduce and canvass their mur-derous acts and begin and end their councils, at which the taking of human life was deliberately discussed, with a peti-tion for the blessing of the Father to rest upon them—there fore, after receiving one or two lessons at the house, and in the bush, the Bodymaster said if the operative would reduce the forms to writing he would have his wife repeat them to him until they were fixed in his memory. When this was done, and McAndrew had secured some instruction in par-liamentary usage, the new-fledged President considered his education complete.

At each and every conference of the two men, McAndrew now would say to the detective that Monaghan, or some other party, had once more been urging the necessity of doing something with Gomer James. McKenna endeavored to make the Bodymaster believe it useless to pay any attention to these demands, holding that they would soon cease and their cause be forgotten. But that official, while he did not wish to assume any such responsibility, was not able to see the road by which it could be avoided. And McKenna, on his part, did not dare oppose too strenuously. Such a course would cause McAndrew to drop his communications on the subject, and then possibly the work might go on without his Secretary's knowledge. One day the head of the division arrived at the decided stand that, as soon as the number of members should justify, he would levy an assessment, and collect a fund to pay for the services of men from some adjoining division to come over to Shenandoah and " put Gomer James off his legs."

McKenna saw that McAndrew's mind was firmly made up in this direction, hence gave no further check to the business. A contrary plan, he was well aware, would prove of no avail, and, resolving merely to watch closely the course of events, he remained silent. Should the Mollies undertake to murder the young Welshman, as he feared they might, his duty was plain. He must, while appearing to favor the deed, do all he could to prevent its consummation, and at the same time keep Mr. Franklin well informed in every stage of the game, to the end that the Superintendent might, if he deemed it advisable, capture the criminals before the act, or notify James of his danger. It did not trouble the brain of the agent much, as he was fixed in his belief that nobody could attempt the crime without his knowledge. And he felt sure that, being fully advised as to what was going on, he would be in good time to preserve the intended victim's life.

He quickly found out that there was a general complaint, which neither Bodymaster nor Secretary could afford to overlook. It was in the shape of an inquiry, set on foot by Monaghan and Hurley, asking : "Why is not something done for the removal of Gomer James?" There was but one response to be made to this question, and that must be : "It shall have attention."

Having done all he could to counteract this demand on the part of the Mollies, McKenna visited Pottsville, where he found his particular friend, Pat Dormer, of the far-famed Sheridan House, in a terribly shattered condition of mind and body. After a long debauch, during the course of which Pat had driven his wife almost insane, and finally out of doors, he was suffering the consequences of his errors and keeping house by himself, which was lonely enough to make the giant quite distracted. In fact, he was about as miserable a piece of six-foot humanity as ever the detective looked upon. He brightened up a little, however, when he grasped McKenna's hand and heard his cheerful voice, and tried to become more like his former jovial self, but it was a failure, and ended with subsidence into a deeper fit of despondency than had before possessed him.

McKenna exerted himself to bring Dormer around to his senses again, partly because he hated to see him so wretched, partly to learn what he knew of the Mollies, and finally so far succeeded that Dormer invited him to enjoy a carriage ride over the mountain. During their journey Pat begged his companion to visit Mrs. Dormer and try to induce her once more to return to his and her home, engaging faithfully to go before the priest and take an oath never to drink another drop of liquor if she would forgive him. This the detective had to promise. He did, later in the day, try his hand as family peacemaker with the lady in question, but without success, as she utterly refused ever to have anything to do with her husband. She said he thought nothing of an oath, and might break it within thirty days. Her life would be in constant danger, and McKenna could hardly blame her for preferring a comfortable and quiet home, where she was, to the trouble and disorder in which Dormer was always embroiled.

After wandering over the mines, calling upon the principal Mollies, and thoroughly sounding the miners on the subject of the suspension, the Secretary returned, about the first of August, to Shenandoah. There he was gladly received by the officers and members of his division, and soon learned that, on the fourth of the month, there was to be a meeting of County Delegates at Tremont. It now became his special object to lay his wires in such shape that he would be reasonably sure of discovering, at an early day, the general purport, if not full particulars, of the business transacted by the convention.

Could it be that this arrangement foreshadowed evil to Gomer James ?

CHAPTER XX.

A FRIGHT, A FIGHT, AND A FUNERAL.

TIME passed, however, and the murder of Gomer James was not accomplished. In truth, it was little spoken of. Political excitements and the occurrence of other absorbing events appeared to cause the Mollies to bury, if not forget, their enmity to the young Welshman. But, as facts distinctly indicated, their vengeance was only sleeping, to be awakened, in the future, with added strength and fury.

Barney Dolan, as my agent at about this time learned, encountered fresh trials. There was a movement on foot to get entirely rid of him. It culminated in the meeting of the County Convention, consisting of Bodymasters of all the principal divisions, at Mahanoy City, upon the peremptory call of the State Delegate, Captain Gallagher. As a part of the proceedings, which were promptly reported to the Secretary by Frank McAndrews, Dolan was cut off for life from all participation in, or benefit from, the order—in other words, expelled—and fined in the sum of five hundred dollars on account of his failure to report and pay over to the State officials certain collections that he had made for the current year. While this summary action fell particularly hard upon Barney, constituting an act for which he appeared wholly unprepared, it was not unexpected by McKenna, who, it will be remembered, heard the topic hinted at by the State Secretary, Maguire, while visiting, some weeks before, at Summit Hill.

The Convention then proceeded to nominate and elect— as it seemed to have the right to do—Dolan's successor in office, and John Kehoe, of Girardville, was declared the unanimous choice. That cunning wire-puller and artful dodger, it seemed, had his tricks ready prepared, long before the day set for the Convention, and it was the easiest thing possible for him to slide his thin feet into Dolan's big shoes.

The decision of the meeting was also expressed, by vote of a majority of those present, that something more should be done to make the world look upon the Ancient Order of Hibernians as purely and simply a benevolent institution, in the coal regions, as it was supposed to be in other portions of the United States. It must no longer be accused of murders and assassinations, and lesser outrages, but, on the contrary, gain credit, at home and abroad, as the tried support of the widow and orphan, and the source of relief for the laborer, when unable to work, or when otherwise thrown out of employment. The real Mollies laughed in their sleeve, meanwhile, and none more heartily than John Kehoe the newly-elected County Delegate. Capt. Gallagher might say and do what he would, the County Conventions, the State Conventions, and their officers, might pass resolutions, and issue orders and commands, and, after all, the small yet potential ring within their circle, encompassing the counties of Schuylkill, Carbon, and Columbia, would manage affairs and shape results, through the use of the order, to suit themselves. If murders and outrages were to be wrought, the Mollies had the organization, and the society held the men in its midst to perform them quickly and well. The State Delegate could return to his home in Pittsburg, if he so pleased, and set forth to the other officials that he had permanently fixed affairs in the anthracite regions, might even flatter himself that he really had accomplished something in the proper direction; still the Mollies knew better, being fully aware that, at the moment of holding this Convention, the lives of men were being threatened by themselves and their associates. These menaces were soon to be consummated. The machinery sometimes, moved tardily, but, like the monster engine that propels the largest vessel, it performed its work remorselessly, almost noiselessly, and effectually.

The Convention passed its resolves and adjourned.

Several violent outrages, of more or less importance and cruelty, were perpetrated at this date. About one of them McKenna learned from Frank McAndrew, the night after the Convention, when he had retired to his room at Cooney's and prepared to sleep. The Bodymaster came at a late hour, roused the landlord, and demanded admittance to the Secretary, which Cooney could not well refuse, went up to the room, and, sitting on the side of the bed, informed that weary personage that he, McAndrew, having just left "Bucky" Donnelly, of Raven Run, from that person had received the particulars of a fight between the Mollies and the Sheet Irons, at Connor's Patch, a night or two previously.

Phil. Nash, John Brennan, *alias* ' Spur " Brennan, and Donnelly were engaged in it, opposed by a large force of German and Welsh miners. From the narrative of Mc Andrew it seemed to have been another edition of Donny-brook Fair. Two of the Sheet Iron lads received wounds from pistol shots—one being considered as mortally hurt. After McAndrew had taken leave, McKenna sought slumber, but was once more awakened by Tom Hurley, who desired to give his version of the affair. He fully corroborated the story McAndrew told, and added :

" Sure, then, Jack Kehoe went the bail of ivery mother's son of 'em yesterday, at the coort ! "

" That accounts for the big vote from that part of the county cast for Jack Kehoe for County Delegate ! "

" An' you're right, there ! " said Hurley.

After thus filling the listener's brain with subjects for fright-ful dreams, Hurley also left the room, and McKenna was not sorry to be alone.

The operative did not quickly recover from his illness, and, during several weeks, was constantly under the doctor's care, yet managing to be about the city, part of the time. After paying a visit to his physician, one morning, the report reached his ears, through a friend, that, as a supposed leader of the Mollie Maguires in the county, his life was in imminent danger. Father Bridgeman—so ran the story—was joining hands with the avowed enemies of the order—in fact, standing at the head of the Iron Clads, everywhere de-nouncing the Mollies and giving all perfect freedom to hunt out and shoot them down wherever found. It was hardly probable, the operative believed, the priest would ever carry his resentment thus far. But should the tale prove true, bloodshed was sure to follow. For his own part, he would now have double duty to perform. One, for the Agency, in following up the work of the society, and if possible, bring ing the perpetrators of crime to punishment, and another the care of his own life, which was liable to be lost as a consequence of his complete assumption of the guise of a Mollie Maguire. The task had been difficult before. Now it was assuming gigantic proportions. To complicate and retard matters, he was ill, and necessarily confined much of the time to one place, if not to his sleeping-room.

After recovering somewhat, McKenna accompanied Mc-Andrew on a visit to Jack Kehoe, at Girardville, to find out if certain rumors about the County Delegate threatening to refuse recognition to Shenandoah Division were true or not. When the question was put to Kehoe, he laughed hypocritically and replied :

" Far from it ! on the conthrary, I am prepared to say to y'z, that, upon the payment of its back dues, Shenandoah Iivision can not only go on swimmingly, but, by applying to the County Secretary, Gavin, this very day, if you wish, you kin recaive the 'goods' for the quarther. An' let me say, by way of explanation, that whoever started the story I ver intended differently is a liar, an' I'll say it to his face !"

This was satisfactory to his visitors, the matter was soon settled, and they left to call on Gavin.

They also went to see Barney Dolan, the great deposed, finding him very despondent. He said his trial before the Convention was a one-sided farce, and as for fining him five hundred dollars, it was simply infamous. Thinking that there might be a chance for his case before the National Board, he had already written to Campbell, the National Secretary, at New York, but that worthy answered him briefly and to the point, that he, Dolan, was cut off, root and branch, and could only be reinstated by vote of the State Convention, upon settlement of all arrearages and suffering three months' probation.

" All of which," said Barney, " shews that I am in the minority now, and for the present Jack Kehoe is boss ! But, by the rod of Aaron, and Moses too, I'll be back again.

one of these fine days, spite of King Kehoe an' all who are
forninst me ! Wait a while and see what'll happen !"

And Barney winked his dexter eye in a winning way, as he
placed the bottle of whisky on the counter for McAndrew
and his Secretary.

Some articles appeared in a Western paper, at this date,
charging that the Mollies determined who should act as assassins by lot, or with dice. This we knew very well to be
untrue, but no attention was given the report. The truth
was, the Bodymaster of a division, having himself conceived
the necessity for an occurrence of the kind—or, upon secret
or open petition of any influential member of the order to
have some man put out of the way—at once called upon
the proper men to perform the deed. Their plain duty was
to obey, without questioning as to the why or wherefore.
So blindly did the Mollies follow their officers in this, as in
other matters, that they seldom failed, in the end, to accomplish all that was required—then the order gave the assassins
protection, through an *alibi*, or aided with money to be em
ployed in flying from the country. There was no need of a
game of chance to decide. It wanted only the decree or
request of the Bodymaster, which was to be complied with
implicitly, and from which there was no appeal. McKenna
apprehended that, in due course of events, he might be called
upon by McAndrew—from his late acquired reputation as
a violent character—to perform some work of this sort.
However, by feigning intoxication, and in reality making
way with a great quantity of liquor—when he could not, by
exchanging glasses, or by some hocus-pocus or legerdemain,
make those present believe he imbibed when he did not—he
endeavored to create the impression among the Mollies—and
he had already caused the general public to believe it—that
he was quite unreliable, as he was too often under the control
of drink. That he succeeded in this he soon became satis
fied from conversations transpiring in his presence, while

seemingly soaked to the point of stupidity in whisky, sodden and insensible, on the bar-room floor, or limply resting upon a bench in the corner.

On one occasion he heard Hurley say:

"Jim's a splendid fellow, a good scholar, as far as book larnin' goes, an' a fighter not to meddle with—when he's McKenna. But he's too often somebody else! Whisky's too powerful for his head, an' a good job might be spoiled by givin' it in his charge!"

"That's so,' said McAndrew, who was standing near.

They little thought their associate's love for and indulgence in liquor was all assumed, and that, at the very moment, he was, in reality, as sober as a judge and taking mental note of every word and act of the surrounding squad of Mollies. The emergencies of his great work, had he been otherwise inclined, which he was not, would have kept my emissary from over-indulgence during a residence in that particular vicinity.

Thus was McKenna made safe for the present. While he could listen, and learn, without danger of having to participate in troubles, for a season, yet he knew that such a game would not long serve his purpose, as he must be dragged in at last, or lose the confidence of those now placing their trust in him. It was well he adopted the ruse, however, as he knew not when his time might come.

On the tenth of August, 1874, at the regular meeting of Shenandoah division, the new "goods" were given out as follows:

The password was:

"What do you think of the Mayo election?"

"I think the fair West made a bad selection"

The answer was:

"Whom do you think will duly betray?"

The quarreling toast was:

Question—"Don't get your temper high!"
Answer—"Not with a friend!"

The sign was made by placing the thumb of the right hand into the pocket of the pantaloons.

The answer, by putting the thumb of the left hand on the lower lip.

McKenna faithfully reported these things to Mr. Franklin the same night, despite his illness, and mailed the letter before retiring to his apartment.

The morning of Tuesday, the eleventh of August, the detective was awakened by his boarding-master, Cooney, with the information that two men, whose personal appearance he minutely described, and did not like, had called for and wanted very much to see him. Cooney put them off, saying McKenna was not at home, but would be by nine o'clock. He thought it prudent to do so, and also to warn his lodger to have a care for himself. They were gone, but would soon return. This person could not remember ever having seen parties of their exact shape and size, and it struck him that possibly they came from the Sheet Irons to assassinate him, because of the recent permission granted by the priest. This impression it was impossible to shake off while he was dressing. Before going down to breakfast, therefore, he examined the cartridges in his revolver, tested the condition of the lock, and left the weapon—carelessly, it must be admitted—at full cock, deposited in his right-hand outside coat pocket, convenient for use, in case of an emergency. He ate the morning meal in no pleasant frame of mind. But all was made clear, and his preparations for active hostilities shown to be unnecessary, by the coming in of his callers, who were only Peter Duffy and Manus O'Donnell, of Hazelton, with whom he had fraternized during the eventful dance and raffle at Buck Mountain. He suspected they were absent on some murderous errand.

but had no fear that he was their supposed victim. The Secretary received his friends cordially, and after an invitation to Cleary's saloon, and laughing over a few jokes upon his escapade with the fascinating Mrs. McIntyre, McKenna endeavored to find out the business the men had in Schuylkill County, but they continued stubbornly reticent, saying they were only going to see some relatives, at Locust Gap, which possibly was the cause of their trip, work being dull at their homes. The new-comers were introduced to the principal men of Shenandoah Division, and, after a pleasant time in the city, in the afternoon took cars for their point of destination.

The operative slept soundly through another night. But his dreams were not blissful.

About this date, or perhaps a little earlier, a schoolmaster, named O'Hare, living near Tuscarora, was severely beaten by four men, who might have killed him had not some stout German girls, his pupils, driven them off and held the door against their return, thus allowing the victim to make his escape to the high-road—O'Hare's crime consisting in being inimical to the Mollies and refusing to obey their notice to leave the region. He had in some way offended one John J. Slattery, a Bodymaster. A few nights after the day assault at the school-house, a band of the same order, headed, as was reported, by " Yellow Jack " Donahue, Bodymaster, went to O'Hare's residence, while he slept, set fire to the building and barn, burning both to the ground, O'Hare barely escaping with his life. He was left penniless, excepting the small sum due him as salary from the school-board. This was another straw, showing the direction of the wind. Evidently disorder was on the increase in the neighborhood.

A little later, one O'Brien, a Mollie, beat his butty, an Englishman named Clements, in so cruel a style that his life was put in jeopardy.

To strengthen the organization, and make it, if possible, more malignant, Muff Lawler had his nephew, Ed. Lawler, come home from Luzerne County, the old trouble with Brophy having been amicably arranged.

At the same time, to gain outward color of reformation, another meeting of the Bodymasters of the county was convened at Girardville. Muff Lawler, Tom Hurley, and John Gibbons were brought to trial, and, after discussion, cut off from the order during life ; Lawler, for allowing a man to be robbed in his house, Hurley, for committing the crime, and Gibbons upon general principles, his particular offense not having been recorded. Dennis, *alias* " Bucky " Donnelly, was also expelled for exhibiting cowardice at the Connor's Patch affray, the second of the month, with the Sheet Irons, and for another offense—showing outside the division a letter which should only have been seen within the confines of the order. No other business of importance was transacted, the convocation dissolved, and the day terminated in a free fight, lasting twenty minutes, during which pistols and knives were resorted to, but without deadly effect. The reformatory measures of the Mollie Maguires, as it appeared, met strenuous opposition from certain quarters.

Later still, the month saw a row at Raven Run, when a Mollie by the name of Barnett received two bullets in his body, and Phil. Nash one through the left wrist, as he informed the detective, laying bare the wound. He said he took the pistol from a man in the opposing crowd of Sheet Irons, broke the weapon, and played havoc generally. After being shot, he employed his own pocket-knife to cut out the ball, which job he successfully accomplished. Barnett was dangerously injured, and it was doubtful if he would survive.

On the seventh of September 1874, the resumption of the collieries had, for a time, a pacifying effect upon the irrepressibles of the coal country, and quiet seemed about restored. But Shenandoah Division grew in strength and numbers meanwhile. At a meeting held on the fifth of the month, Andrew Murphy, of Loss Creek, John Dean, John Carey, and John Walsh were accepted and duly initiated. A brother of the Bodymaster was rejected, at the suggestion of McAndrew in person, as he urged that the man proposed was continually in trouble and would surely bring disgrace upon the honorable brotherhood.

During the latter part of September occurred the decease of old Mr. Raines, a crippled miner, who for several years, through rheumatism and hurts received under a falling pillar, had been unable to perform any labor. From the same causes his body and limbs were bent forward into the shape of an irregular crescent. There was to be a loud wake, and McKenna having nearly recovered his health and good spirits—but being not yet cured of his adopted habit of drinking—received an invitation to be present. He was ready for a spree, or anything else, and went. The Raines place was near the Rappahannock works, on the road from Loss Creek to Girardville, where were situated a number of "patches" belonging to different collieries. The family was large, its range of acquaintance extended, and over a hundred men and women gathered to do honor, in their usual way, to the departed. The corpse was laid out in the largest and best room of the house, with candles at its head and feet. There was a dilapidated table in the center of the apartment, which for many seasons had seen service in parlor, dining-room, and kitchen, and now supported pipes, tobacco, and two bottles of liquor, with a generous supply of lucifer matches. At one end of the room was a cook-stove, but as the weather was yet genial, no fire shone through its door. Benches and blocks of wood served as seats for the men and women, who were ranged about the walls and table, the majority of the men wearing their hats, and the ladies, with lace caps or without them, as accorded with their respective ages and circumstances in life. As

10

old-fashioned pendulum clock, with weights, and a face as smoky as the surrounding walls, hung against the plastering at the other side of the place ; there were a few pictures ; and the last almanac issued by Dr. Jayne swung from a nail under an ancient square-framed looking-glass, which was inclining forward just above. But the principal thing to attract the eye of the detective, when he and his companions—Hurley and Monaghan—entered, was the corpse, to honor which all the people had assembled. The coffin could not yet be used—and for a good reason—the body would not fit into it, but the plain, walnut case rested in another room. Stretched out on a sheet spread over a rough board, which was supported at either end by a common chair, reposed all that was mortal of old Mr. Raines, clad in shroud and grave-clothes, and the head resting on a pillow. In order to overcome the difficulty accruing from the bent and contorted condition of the body and limbs of the deceased, which would not assume a straigh* position, even in death, a light panel door, taken from an unoccupied room, had been put on top of the defunct and loaded down with rocks and a heavy piece of iron, the latter being, apparently, part of a cylinder to a disåbled coal-breaker. This, it was hoped, would relax the contracted muscles, and the curved spine and limbs, so that, on the morrow, there would be no trouble in placing the corpse in its casket.

The remainder of the scene was peculiarly striking only to those who had never beheld its counterpart.

The men from Shenandoah, though just as welcome as others, were left, as is the custom, to look out for themselves. They did not uncover their heads, but, squatting on their heels, or any other convenient seat by the wall, proceeded to smoke a pipe with the rest. It was not, and is not to this day, the etiquette of the miners of this nationality to get up from their chairs and offer them to strangers, nor for visitors to remove their caps, or hats, upon entering a neigh-

sor's house, no more than it is to knock at the door—except-
ng it be at night—before opening it.

McKenra looked on in silence, while the mourners proceeded with their wailing, crooning hymns to the dead, and
the men helping themselves to *lashins* of poteen, while the
bonneens stuck their faces in at the door and joined in the
keene, or *caoina-song*. The eldest lady of the party raised
her hands and cried out :

" Forcer ! Forcer ! Mo-vrone ! Mo-vrone ! Ochone ! Ochone !"

Then the *keene* would be raised to a higher pitch, and the
wail for the dead resumed, louder and more piercingly
mournful than before.

This was kept up until midnight, when an incident
occurred which bid fair to terminate this portion of the
funeral ceremonies with a fight. One young lad, named
Flaherty, a slouchy, shock-headed fellow, as full of mirth
and rascality as he well could be, growing weary of the
ordinary solemnities, fired by having taken more of the
liquor than was needful—and many more were by that
time in a similar predicament, from the same cause—determined to vary the monotony somewhat and have some
sport, and made his arrangements accordingly, as it turned
out, only perceived by the agent, who placed no obstacle in
his way. All at once, when the attention of those present
was centered upon the drink and the table for tobacco, etc.,
there was heard an unearthly yell, as of horror, the weights
rolled, with the thin, little door, off the corpse, and the
vital flame seemed to have returned to the dead, as old Mr.
Raines started up, whirled quickly and mechanically about,
and fell headlong to the floor.

Such a mixture of swearing, groaning, shrieking, praying,
screaming, and screeching was never before heard in that
neighborhood, and in the space of a minute the room was

nearly vacated, McKenna, the corpse, the candles, and furniture being left sole possessors of the field. Some of the demoralized friends of the deceased did not pause before reaching their own homes, and many not until well outside the house, while a few of the more courageous rallied in the kitchen. Flaherty, whose actions the operative had watched attentively, was among the first to stick his freckled face in at the door and inquire if "anybody were kilt." He found McKenna trying to lift up the corpse, rearrange its disturbed funereal costume, and replace it on the board.

"Come here, ye *gorsoon-bo*, an' lend a hand to hoist the old man back to his restin'-place!"

The lad at first refusing, the detective had but to hint that the piece of cord, with which Flaherty had cunningly pulled away the door, still remained attached to a hinge, and if he did not carry it off, his trick would be exposed, to bring the young man in to his assistance.

"Lay holt wid me, and I'll say nothing about the string! Refuse, and you'll suffer! D'ye think I didn't hear ye scrame like a young locomotive?"

"Sure, an' I only meant to have a bit of fun!" explained Flaherty; but he entered and helped to replace things. When all was as before—and it took but a few minutes—Flaherty called out to the crowd:

"Come back! Come back! Daddy Raines is all right!"

Then the men and women who had not gone home returned, their eyes sticking out, and each person treading on tip-toe, perhaps expecting to see a *banshee*, the gentleman in black—or his counterpart in hoof, tail, and horns, with nostrils breathing fire and smoke—and were much amazed to behold everything exactly as arranged before the sudden rising of the dead; the candles burning, the table undisturbed, and old Mr. Raines just as quiet and decent a corpse as any of them had ever helped to wake; while McKenna and silent on his billet, at the side, smoking his pipe as calmly as if nothing out of the ordinary course had transpired.

Young Flaherty kept the secret, through fear of the consequences should he reveal his share in the ghastly joke, and the agent did not care to undeceive the people. Hence the strange occurrence was spoken of for some weeks thereafter, in the vicinity, as about the eighth wonder of the world. McKenna was highly complimented for his nerve by men and women, and Monaghan himself said he " believed that nothing would ever scare that fellow—excepting it might be Auld Nick in person ! "

CHAPTER XXI.

CONTEST WITH A CONSTABLE.

NOT long after the wake, it was made evident to some of the members of Shenandoah Division that Frank McAndrew was not fitted by nature or education for the important office of Bodymaster, being far too generous, too much inclined to leniency—in fact, not half bloodthirsty enough. Among those who saw this more plainly than others were McHugh, at whose house, in those days, the Mollies held their meetings, Tom Hurley, John Gibbons, and Fergus, *alias* Ferguson. McKenna said little on the subject, but while lying, apparently tippled to a state of insensibility, in Cleary's, late one night, he heard sufficient to convince him of the existence of a plot, at the bottom of which stood Jack Kehoe, to replace McAndrew with a person that they were pleased to denominate as of " better material." The officer in question, when spoken to upon the subject, the ensuing day, said he knew full well why so much dissatisfaction was growing up around him. It had its roots deep planted in his own unwillingness to engage in the schemes of murder and outrage that his opponents evidently desired should be immediately executed. McHugh was especially loud in denouncing him for failing to have Gomer James killed, as he also had been of similar inaction under the leadership of Mike Lawler, when that party was equally opposed to the same job under like circumstances. So far had McHugh committed himself in this direction, that he made no secret of demanding McAndrew's expulsion from the organization. McAndrew's argument, beyond its claim to compatibility with the impulses of humanity, was perfectly sensible, as well as unanswerable, and when brought out in the course of conversation, caused most of the decent and orderly persons in the division to coincide with him. His logic was that, when Cosgrove had been murdered by Gomer James, Mike Lawler, then Bodymaster, acted promptly—but without choosing to trumpet it over the county, keeping the thing to himself—and, among others, appointed an own cousin of Cosgrove as one of the avengers. That nigh relative of the man for whose death retaliation was to be sought refused to act, and Lawler at once, and very properly, excused all the rest. McAndrew thought it rather late in the day for utter strangers to dig up the hatchet, unless there was a money reward offered by some one for the knocking of Gomer James into eternity. Of that he was not so sure. If something of the sort was not in the wind, why were such men as Hurley, Gibbons, and McHugh so exceedingly anxious?

To this query my agent in the coal regions could return no response. Nevertheless, nothing was done, though much was said, regarding the taking off of the young Welshman. How quickly action might be taken he possessed no means of judging. But that Hurley and his backers would, sooner or later, seek to kill Gomer James, if he continued to live in the vicinity, he harbored no reasonable doubt. Upon the reception of this suggestive conclusion Mr. Franklin searched for and obtained means of warning Gomer James, advising him to get speedily out of the country. This, at first James firmly refused to do, but, subsequently, securing paying work in another county, he did temporarily remove. He remained away only a little while, being quite convinced that, if the Mollie Maguires were after and wanted his life, they would come up with him, wherever he might be. At the date of the latest talk by McHugh, James was engaged as a night watchman in one of the collieries, and, as far as could be learned, performed his duty honorably and faithfully.

McAndrew maintained his ground, saying that he knew he would be sustained by the State and National Boards, whatever the new County Delegate might say or do in the premises. This pleased McKenna, who wisely refrained from joining either party engaged in the controversy, merely putting in a word, to one or the other, when compelled to do so, to the effect that everybody knew him as a bad man, and it was best that he keep his mouth closed on subjects which might, in time, come to him, whether guilty or not. For his part, he said: "I am willing to do my duty by the division, for the protection it affords me from those that I fear in an adjoining State, but it is not for such as I to do much talking."

So the business of the division was still intrusted to McAndrew, and the detective managed to be sober long enough, each month—somewhat to the surprise of his intimates—to write up the books and carry on such correspondence as his office demanded. At about all other times he was engaged in some game, attending a fair or chicken-fight, or training some dog, which was to "whip out all creation" when ready for the ring. He followed other occupations. If a man was needed to doctor a sick horse, mule, or cow, in the borough—or out of it—who should be sent for but handy Jim McKenna? Should a man have his hand hurt in the mines, who bound up his wound and nursed him tenderly until recovered? Why, the self-same vagabond, red-headed Jim McKenna. If a hen-roost was to be robbed by Mollies, ducks or geese stolen, and thereafter surreptitiously roasted, Jim McKenna was invited to take a hand. And sometimes he was found sober enough to give the latter freaks attention, but not often.

If a young lady wanted to send a *billet-doux* to her sweetheart in a far-off country, she knew that, by the simple calling, she might have the help of "the handiest man at the pen in all Schuylkill County," and that, in the general opinion, was Jim McKenna. As a matter of natural consequence " Jim " was, with maids and mothers, boys and girls, fathers and sons—of the rougher sort—a great favorite. There was nothing under the sun to be done, scientific or culinary, agricultural, surgical, artistic, or mechanical, that " Jim," in the opinion of his countrymen, could not do— certainly very little he would not attempt, merely to oblige those who needed him. To a certain class his name was synonymous with fun, frolic, dance, and song, and his face indicative of good nature and genuine Irish humor. To others, he was terror personified. Some of his best friends said that he might comb out his hair somewhat oftener, and drink less whisky, but very generally these slight and prevalent defects were overlooked in the benefits McKenna conferred upon those with whom he associated.

As before stated, there were also those who seriously believed that the agent was really an assassin, had murdered a man in Buffalo, and was in constant communication with counterfeiters and black-legs. Those who knew these things—or supposed they knew them—did not often speak of them outside the Mollie ring. One fact could not be gainsaid: if there was a ball, a charity, a dance, a picnic, or a man or woman in real want, Jim McKenna always had a dollar to give. If there was a treat where he chanced to be, none put up glasses more liberally than that same McKenna. These contradictory opinions rather surprised the good people of Shenandoah who canvassed the subject. How he could be such a favorite with the miners was more than they could fathom.

During the latter portion of September, 1874, there was a grand fair at Ringtown, and, as it was stated that the Sheet Irons were to be present in great force, with the express intention of whipping out their enemies, the Mollies, several of the latter determined to go, armed and equipped for the purpose of defending themselves and seeing how much their adversaries would really accomplish.

This fair was similar to those called county agricultural shows in the Western and Southern States, and sometimes from one thousand to fifteen hundred persons, men, women, and children, would congregate daily, for five or six days, on these occasions.

At Ringtown there were found people from Shenandoah, and other parts of Schuylkill, and from many towns in Columbia County. There were the usual attractions, sideshows, ugly dwarfs, scrawny giants, slimy anacondas, and a fine display of fat bullocks, sleek cows and sheep, thorough bred horses and mules, improved pigs, geese, ducks, and chickens, and the ordinary collection of ingenious and useful machines for manufacturing and home uses. There were foot-races; races in sacks; games of catching the greased pig; climbing the greased pole; lady equestrianisms, and all the gayeties that attend exhibitions of the sort. All were taken in by the Mollies from Shenandoah, as well as by those from Catawissa, Centralia, and the entire Mahanoy Valley. There was music and dancing and drink *galore* at night, and a full brass band, hailing from an adjacent city, discoursed "concord of sweet sounds" at the grand stand

during each day's regular performances. And the song
seemed to be :

> "The butcher, the baker,
> The candle-stick maker,
> All, all are gone to the fair."

McKenna's friends flattered him by saying that he was
the wickedest and toughest, as well as the roughest-looking
vagabond seen at the county fair.   But the crowd in his
company was not by any means conspicuous for good behavior or lamb-like undertakings.

After one day's experience at Ringtown, finding that no
Sheet Irons made their appearance, the greater portion of
the Shenandoah collection of Mollies were disgusted and
went home.   The detective thought he saw business, and
remained.   He had to sleep in the fair enclosure, however,
as, at the hotels, he was invariably, from his bad name and
appearance, refused admission.   One tavern-keeper named
Fencermacher, showed him out, saying :

"I keeps no dramps and such-like caddle in mine blace !
Geh zu hause ! "

He may here learn, for the first time, who it was that he
turned away.   But the German was perfectly excusable.
The applicant for lodgings seemed rough enough to prompt
any respectable landlord to pursue the same course.   It
was sufficient to know that "Jim McKenna" was the inquirer
for accommodations to cause any well-regulated hotel door
to close with a bang against his face, almost of its own
accord.

During his recent sickness the operative lost his hair—a
ttle circumstance that has not been alluded to—and had
been supplied with a wig of about the color of his former
natural growth, which, as he was not a barber, seldom received proper dressing, and gave its wearer a very uncouth
and shabby appearance.   But it seemed not quite as bad as

going around completely bareheaded, especially in chilly weather. His beard and mustache were also very long and bushy, and scarcely ever cut away ; his face was red and sunburnt, but somewhat thinner than when first reaching Pennsylvania. He wore the clothes he had bought the year before—saying to the Mollies that ill success was making him a little careful of his expenses—and a white shirt was rarely seen upon his back. A coat of many colors, badly patched and darned, soft hat—new ·when he first fought Muff Lawler's chickens for him—and a pair of heavy miner's boots, completed an inventory of his visible personal effects —excepting the two loaded revolvers which he constantly wore at his back. He could hardly be deemed a likely customer to take into a decent tavern ; but he was not as bad as he looked. His deeds were not criminal, however unseemly he appeared, and his duty was ever uppermost in his thoughts.

McKenna was constrained to sleep the little he did sleep, when first in attendance at the fair, upon the bare ground. During part of one day, however, he superintended the bar for a respectable Irish lady, Mrs. Corcoran by name, and that night she left him to occupy the booth, while she went home, showing that this woman, at least, reposed confidence in him, despite his generally accepted bad character.

He participated in only two fights while at Ringtown. The first of these occurred on the third day of the fair, when a Dutch constable, from Dark Corner, had trouble with a man named McBain, and the operative entered the row in the interest of peace. The official gazed at McKenna with astonishment and said :

"Look here ! you seem like what you are—a d——d thief ! "

This was too much to be taken quietly, and the detective quickly knocked the representative of public justice down with a blow from the fist, and then administered to his body a good kicking with his rough boots, which settled the prevailing question in his favor. The constable cried "enough," and was allowed to escape without further punishment.

The second affray came very near resulting seriously, and was a consequence of the first. At about nine A.M. of the last day of the show. the defeated constable returned to the fair grounds, in company with six or seven other men, of about the same ugly appearance. McKenna was at that time attending a booth for one Whalen, who was absent. They came up exhibiting knives and other weapons, and swearing they would kill the man who had beaten their friend. The detective had been deserted by the Mollies, knew not which way to turn for support, and so determined to help himself. Rushing out of the stand, he seized a small wooden bench, which was kept for the convenience of customers, and swinging it wildly about his head, hit the first Dutchman, who fell; he struck the rest in rapid succession, and soon four were knocked over before they could use their weapons The others fled, leaving him, for the moment, master of the situation. Then, knowing that they would still make good their threats, if he waited for their courage to muster, he ran, jumped into a passing wagon loaded with country people and was driven rapidly away.

After that, whenever McKenna wanted anything in Ring town, there were plenty who would run to his assistance.

In this way he added to his reputation—or kept it up—as the wildest Irishman of the mountains, and the most unprincipled Mollie in the whole country.

When he got back to Shenandoah and visited the post-office for letters, McKenna found, to his extreme satisfaction and relief, that he had a missive from the Philadelphia Agency. As he handed it to him, the clerk remarked, exhibiting a second missive enclosed in the same kind of an envelope, apparently superscribed by the same hand, be addressed to "James McParlan, Shenandoah."

"Here is a letter I nardly know what to do with; but it is not for you! It has been here several days, and is still uncalled foi. Perhaps you know something about it, as I see it seems, from the hand-writing and post-mark, to have come from the party that has been writing you!"

The clerk looked at the uncouth young man very critically, and, as he imagined, very suspiciously.

The operative "thought of ten thousand things at once," as he described his sensations to me afterward, but Irish wit and readiness for reply did not desert him in the emergency.

"Yes," said McKenna, with all the assurance imaginable, and without a second's hesitation. "I *do* remember, now you spake of it, but the thing had before gone clane out of me head! Jim McParlan? Why, sure, an' he's a crony of mine, over at Wilkesbarre, beyant, an' faith, when I wor there last month, he said that I should inquire here for a letther for him, as he expected at wan time to come over an' work wid Frank McAndrew as his butty, but got a better chance in Luzerne! Bad 'cess to me memory! I think there's somethin' in the whisky they hev in Shenandoah that sinds me wits all a wool-gatherin'! But never mind! Wid your permission, I'll jist forward the letther to Jim, and write an' tell him how it have been so delayed!"

The suspicions of the clerk were dissipated in a moment, and he readily gave the document into McKenna's hand. Had the recipient exhibited the least confusion or embarrassment, the probabilities were that his letter—unhappily misdirected by a new clerk in Philadelphia—must have gone to the Dead Letter Office, in Washington, where it would have been opened and returned to Philadelphia. In the meantime both Mr. Franklin and McKenna would have felt much disturbed by its loss. The operative realized the mistake in its full extent, and sat down and wrote a line asking that, so long as he remained in the coal country, such accidents might be carefully guarded against; and his wishes were obeyed.

The strike of the miners against the rates paid for labor, for 1874, began in October, with the usual result, the first to kick being the men in Luzerne County. This was not a Mollie movement, and its ringleaders were promptly arrested by Sheriff Whittaker. But the end was not yet.

At about the same date Kehoe received a scorching letter from Capt. Gallagher, the State Secretary, saying the chances were that, at the next meeting of the State organization, the Mollies of Schuylkill County might be severed from the body, as a punishment for their past misdemeanors, and Bishop Wood, of Philadelphia, would also officially excommunicate them by name from the Church. He suggested that a meeting of Bodymasters might be held at Pottsville, at an early day, and the bad men of the order, who were probably known, all summarily expelled, when possibly the remainder could be saved. If the body was purified the good members might not lose caste. Here was a muddle for the emissary. He was sure to be among the first men cut off, and, should the movement succeed, his career of usefulness in the neighborhood would be very short thereafter. It should not be! Whatever was done, he must retain his position. Happily for him, Jack Kehoe simply laughed at the recommendation, and remarked that Mr. Gallagher might attend to his own business, as he would call no such meeting. So no convention was held, and the Mollies were still triumphant. It was not for Kehoe's interest that they should be as mild as lambs. In reality, the worse they were the better King Jack would be suited.

CHAPTER XXII.

HORRORS UPON HORRORS.

THE strike was yet in progress, in November, 1874, and the consequent want of work produced the very result anticipated—the Mollies were as active as a community of hornets whose nest a schoolboy has invaded with a club. There followed a number of sanguinary encounters, some of which terminated fatally. One of these, the shooting and subsequent death of Mr. George Major, Chief Burgess of Mahanoy City, transpired on Saturday, the 31st of October, in the year mentioned. McKenna was in Shenandoah at the time, but received early intelligence of the event. McAndrew, feeling very anxious to learn the full particulars, it was an easy matter to induce him to detail the operative and Chas. Hayes to go to the scene of the encounter and gather them. This they were willing to undertake, starting out from Shenandoah on the second of November.

The request of the Bodymaster formed a good excuse for McKenna, who had early been directed by Mr. Franklin to investigate the murder, to go to Mahanoy City. Without McAndrew's order, suspicion as to his calling might have been created among the Mollies of his division. It was all very proper, when the Secretary was known to have plenty of money, and little else to do, for him to chance around at localities where murders and other crimes had been perpetrated, but at this particular time he was putting on a sorry face, declaring that his income from rents had run several months behind, the county officers suspecting him of leaguing with counterfeiters—hence he could not safely get rid of his bogus currency—and, in fact, dressing very badly

so that he would not be expected to have funds to expend
in too many treats for his guzzling and expensive companions.
Furnished with a safe cover from which to carry on his ob-
servations, he at once commenced hunting up the facts con
nected with the shooting of Major.

The Chief Burgess, as that official—usually the Mayor of
a town—is called in the State of Pennsylvania, was not yet
dead, but could hardly be expected to live more than a day
or two with a bullet resting in a vital part. Major had been
shot through the left breast, two inches above the heart.

McKenna went to Clark's house, the known rendezvous
of the Mollies, of which I shall have more to say hereafter,
and, finding the proprietor alone, started a conversation with
him.   Clark was an old man, and not a member of the order,
but his two sons were Mollies.

"An' how is it about the bit o' scrimmage ye had over
here last Saturday?" commenced the operative.

"Oh! it's a bad affair altogether!" answered the landlord
of the Emerald House.

"Who fired the shot that brought the Chief Burgess
down?"

"That I can't, fur the life of me, tell!   There's two
stories about it; wan of them puts it on Dan Dougherty—
but I belave him jist as innocent as the babe unborn—an'
the other charges it on Major's own brother, William, hittin
him be mischance, when firing afther the Hibernian company's boys—for ye must know that the whole trouble came
about thro' a quarrel betwasen the Hibernian an' the Citizen
fire companies.   Wan is wholly made up of our countrymen,
an' the other of Modocs—English, German, Welsh an' what-
not!   I suppose ye know that?"

"Yes!   But who started the row?"

"I am sure, from what I can learn, that Dougherty didn't!
He never has a pistol about him!   There was a bit o' fire, on
the night, as ye must know, an' both companies was out an

we had considerable excitement, an' not a little whisky
Afther the fire, in comin' home, over the strate, the firemen
got in a jangle, an' blows were being passed, when the Chief
Burgess, Geo. Major, came out, flourished his revolver, and,
during the confusion, shot a dog that was barkin' near by.
This led to more shootin', an' some one in the crowd took off
the Chief Burgess, an' Major's brother shot Dougherty, who
has a bullet in the neck, below the left ear! Oh! it's a
bad business! A bad business! Do you know, I am thinkin' no good can iver come of it?"

"Yes, a shookin' bad thing!" assented McKenna.

Finding that Clark really knew very little about the
minutiæ, the operative, who had purposely separated from
Hayes, went to see other friends, hoping to find some one
who might be able to give him information.

Meeting Clark's brother, who was a Mollie, he accompanied him to Dougherty's house, which was only guarded
by an old constable, named Litchenberger, who was too
tipsy to do either good or harm. Several men were standing
around, but the excitement seemed quietly subsiding, and
there was little trouble in gaining permission to see the
wounded man. They ascended to his room. The injured
Mollie was slightly touched in the brain, and barely recognized his friends, but, turning over in bed, exhibited his hurt,
which appeared to have been produced by a heavy, large-
sized bullet. His left cheek and eye were greatly discolored
and puffed up, the side of the neck being quite black. The
ball still rested in the muscle, the surgeons thinking it unsafe,
at that time, to probe for or attempt its removal. The visitors remained with Dougherty but a few moments, and they
repaired to McCann's boarding-house, the landlady of which,
at first, said the man inquired for had gone out, she did not
know where; but, when the operative and Clark made
themselves known by name, she changed her tune and
cordially invited them upstairs. The person visited they

found in bed, but not at all averse to conversation. This was satisfactory to the detective. McCann said there had been no disturbance whatever in the street when Chief Burgess, Major, fired the shot at him, and, before he, McCann, could catch the revolver and take it from him, he discharged three shots.

Hayes, who had joined the others, was anxious that James McCann should swear out a warrant for the arrest of Major before he would die, charging him with an assault with a deadly weapon. That, he contended, would place McCann on the witness-stand and prevent him from being brought to the bar as a defendant. Others who were present desired McCann to make his escape. McKenna did not venture any suggestion. The general belief was that Major would die, and this was all in the case that gave the Mollies any satisfaction. They were united in protesting that Dougherty must remain where he was, saying that a removal to Potts ville, in his precarious condition, would be sure death for him.

The Chief Burgess succumbed to his wounds Tuesday, November 3, and received burial, with suitable honors, the ensuing day. Dougherty was still unable to be removed, when the operative, having obtained all the information possible, returned with Hayes to Shenandoah, and reported to the division the issue of his trip. He had previously sent Mr. Franklin daily bulletins of his inquiries and their results.

Dougherty was subsequently moved to Pottsville, where he recovered, had his trial, and was acquitted.

Mike Lawler now managed to attach himself once more to the order, having been received by Wm. Callaghan, Bodymaster, into his division at Mahanoy Plane. Lawler still maintained friendly relations with McKenna, despite his aversion to the Shenandoah Mollies, as a body, and one day visited the Secretary in company with Callaghan, who chanced to be in the city on personal business. While the three were together, walking leisurely over the mountain, Muff related, with much particularity, a circumstance occur ring some eighteen months before. Two Mollies named Doyle, brothers, residing at Jackson's Patch, had recently been attacked and beaten by Sheet Irons. The Mollies had a meeting among themselves and deliberately prepared a scheme to wreak terrible vengeance upon the whole community at the Patch in question. The idea was to burn down every building, after midnight, when all the inhabitants were sleeping, having the torch applied almost simultaneously over the entire place. Afterward the Mollies, well armed with guns and revolvers, were to stand closely guarding the blazing houses, and whenever any—man, woman, or child—attempted to escape, deliberately shoot him or her down. Not one was to be spared to tell the tale. The division went so far, even, as to appoint the night on which this dastardly outrage was to be perpetrated. They convened in Shenandoah for the business, but Lawler—so he claimed—assisted by Callaghan, managed to get up a discussion on another subject, thus diverting the attention of the ringleaders, and they forgot what they had gathered for, adjourning at too late an hour for their purpose, thus postponing operations until a future time. Finally the job was abandoned. Lawler and Callaghan accorded great credit to themselves in having, at the risk of their own lives, saved the unsuspecting inhabitants of Jackson Patch, thus averting one of the most sickening wholesale assassinations that the heart of savage ever conceived. Through inquiries in the proper quarters, which the operative made, he was satisfied that the story he had listened to was not drawn from imagination. Previously aware of the fact that there were men in his division who, to secure revenge, or when under the excitement of enmity or drink, would perform deeds that might make angels weep, and throw the acts of the Indians in the shade, still he was shocked by this recital. He must perforce maintain friendly relations with these persons, drink of their liquor, share their orgies and listen to their blood thirsty plans. It was no pleasant duty to perform.

The strike continued. It was not alone Luzerne County that was interested, but disaffection and desertion of works spread over the anthracite region. It was the intention of the Mollies and the Miners' and Laborers' Association that work should entirely cease. To this end those men who desired to labor for the support of their families were notified. If they failed to stop, they were beaten, or assassinated, and the hand that consummated the deed was hidden in the secret recesses of the hearts of the Mollie Maguires.

On the eighteenth of November McKenna obtained information that a number of outrages had occurred the preceding Saturday—denominated by the *Miners' Journal,* of Pottsville, as "a horrible day."

In the first instance, a man named Pat Padden was discovered in the streets of Carbondale, dead, with two bullet holes in his skull.

Secondly, Michael McNally was mysteriously murdered in the same locality, and found with his throat cut from ear to ear, and body otherwise mutilated.

In another part of the county, a man, whose name was not learned, had been come upon by some farmers, nearly dead, in a most novel but painful predicament. It seems he had refused to give heed to the notices the Mollies gave him; was one night taken from his home, carried to the mountains, and thence to a deep morass, where there was nothing surrounding them but water, high trees with branches closely interlocked, and fallen timber. There the inhuman monsters prepared to leave him to die a slow death by starvation. Iron spikes were driven through his coat sleeves, tight to the wrist, the man lying upon his back lengthwise of a solid pine log, the arms bent backward so as to form the shape of a cross; then his feet were similarly pinned to the log with the strongest nails. Making sure, as they supposed, that there was no possibility he would escape, the Mollies deserted the place, first having put a gag in his mouth, which they thought he would be unable to remove. For nearly three days, and two horrid, long nights, their victim remained thus secured, praying, at last, for death to relieve him from tortures of hunger and thirst and the dreaded attacks of stinging insects and fierce wild animals. Happily he at last succeeded in releasing the fastenings of the gag, the block of wood fell out, and he made the air resound, about noon of the third day, with his loud and repeated shouts for aid, which were heard by two German woodmen, who at once sought out the cause of the noise. They soon found the man, at once relieved him, and gave him, sparingly at first, food from their well-stored lunch pails. Water was also procured, and in a few hours the victim of the Mollies found himself strong enough to be removed. For some weeks he was a raving maniac and could not tell who he was, where he came from, or the cause of his punishment. When his senses returned he possessed no knowledge of the parties who had perpetrated the outrage. He emigrated from the coal mines, as soon as well enough, and said he "would rather starve in a civilized community than fare sumptuously in a place inhabited by brutes in human form."

Still another. A mining boss, name not heard, but connected with the Erie Breaker, was set upon, beaten, and left for dead, with one of his arms broken.

And another. One Michael Kenny, not a Mollie Maguire, was murdered at Scranton, Luzerne County, and his mangled remains thrown down a steep embankment, where it was supposed they would forever remain undiscovered, but accident revealed their hiding-place. They were encoffined and given burial. The assassins were not known.

The men at Carbon were nearly all Irish and Welsh, the former mostly Mollies, and there were no members of the Sheet Irons supposed to be in the neighborhood.

The miners still refused any reduction from the basis on which they were laboring when the strike was inaugurated. Some were working, but all expected to suspend by the beginning of the New Year.

An event which made the detective's very blood boil, and still one in which he could not interfere, furnishes the cap-sheaf of this array of horrors. It transpired at Fowler's Patch, east of Shenandoah, a little later in the month, and the actors in it were Chas. Hayes, Dan Kelly—called also Manus Kull and "the Bum"—and Ed. Lawler, members of McKenna's own division. They were out on a spree until four in the morning, when they went to the house of a poor old woman, named Downey, who kept a she-been-shop, roused her from her sleep, and, after drinking, robbed her of her money—which was but a small sum—and then forced her to join them in finishing their orgies. They were finally all very drunk, and Kelly took a pail and proceeded to fill it from the landlady's whisky barrel, which sat in a corner, across two large rocks, and the woman interfered. Kelly, at this, had his fiercest passions aroused, and, fired by the liquor, was ready for anything. The woman still resisting, he raised her in his arms, being a muscular and powerful man, carried her bodily to the almost red-hot stove and threw her upon it, face downward, and was holding her there, despite her frantic struggles and loud cries, to be roasted and burned to death, when Hayes came to the rescue, struck Kelly under the ear, knocked him down, and liberated the badly injured old lady. Her hands and face were shriveled, broiled in deep, large patches, and there is no doubt that, had she not been taken off the stove by Hayes, she would have been killed. As it was, she had to remain in bed, and for weeks was not able to sit up. Still no arrests were made.

Kelly challenged Hayes to fight him, for intermeddling with an affair that, he said, belonged entirely to him, and they walked out in the highway, just at daybreak, all by themselves, the old woman still writhing and screaming with pain, and fought ten rounds, Hayes, though a much lighter man than his antagonist, giving Kelly a severe pummeling and coming out ahead in almost every contest, until Kelly gave it up.

Before they left, however, Kelly visited his intended victim, and, striking his fist in her very face, said, with an oath:

"It's about your time! I'll burn your accursed body up yet! So look out!"

He would have set fire to the building and executed the threat, at the moment, only Hayes insisted that he should leave her, which he did. Hayes sent a physician to the woman's house immediately. He found its sole occupant incapable of answering a single question. The little mind the woman had was for the time quite distracted, and the floor on fire, from the upsetting of the stove. Had she been left alone half an hour longer she and her house would have been reduced to ashes.

------◆------

CHAPTER XXIII

GOOD OLD MICKY CUFF.

SHENANDOAH is a handsome little inland town, the center of a productive coal country and the place of residence of many excellent people. This volume, however, will not have much to do with that particular portion of the inhabitants, the Mollies and their associates fully monopolizing and employing the writer's attention. Among those who were not members of the organization, but still wicked enough to be classed with them, was one Micky Cuff, the proprietor of a small whisky shop in the city. The building, the basement of which Cuff and his family occupied, was a two-story tenement, standing nearly flush with the street, and it its cellar part rather low between floors. One night, about eleven o'clock, after coming from a wake, McKenna found himself with Fergus and Ned Monaghan, for the first time inside Micky Cuff's groggery. Having such a brace of worthies to introduce him, he made sure of a cordial welcome, and Cuff shook his hand heartily as he said, in his gruff voice—something between the noise produced by filing a mill-saw and that made in the smaller theatres and called sheet-iron thunder :

"I'm plazed to mate ye, lad ! Make yerself at home here, an' when ye're thirsty come in an' taste our liquor ! If you misbehave—which I suppose ye niver do—you'll be well baten for yer pains !"

The detective had received his cue from Fergus never to dispute Cuff, or find fault with anything in his house, unless he wanted a stroke over the head with whatever instrument was most convenient, and therefore accepted the allusion to a fight without sending back his habitual rejoinder : "Two can play at that game ! " And it was well for him that he did. Without noticing Cuff's captiousness, McKenna proposed : "Drinks for four, or five, if Mrs. Cuff would take somewhat ! '

"Af coorse she wull !" said Cuff; and that dumpy woman with the small face, scanty gray hair, bent shoulders, and meek but deprecatory smile—she felt compelled to express pleasure when her husband told her, as plainly by a look as words could speak, that she must do so—came forward and drank her thimbleful of poteen from the one lonesome, dirty glass, sole remnant of the half dozen she had commenced housekeeping with some thirty years before, and said :

" Thanks ! This is Jim McKenna, is it ? We have heard of you ! I am glad to meet any friend of my husband—and Mr. Ferguson ! "

Ferguson acknowledged the compliment intended, and she retired to the rear of the room, where there was work for her, " doing up " Cuff's linen.

" Sure, an' ye are that same bould Jim McKenna, what docthered Pat Hennessy's colt ! I knew you be sight long ago, but this is the first time you've honored our house with your prisence ! Niver mind ! Here's to your betther health, Mr. McKenna ! "

And good old Cuff drained his half tumbler of raw spirits as unconcernedly as if it had not been one of a dozen odd, similarly large and strong, he had tasted since dinner. Then the four men sat down to a greasy table, located in the middle of the apartment, and, by the light of the single, smoking miners' lamp, essayed the interesting game of poker, the ante being the small sum of one dime.

That room and its contents would rejoice the graphic pencil of a Hogarth, or the facile pen of a Dickens, were these great artists alive to enter its stifling and tobacco smoked precincts. Let me attempt merely to outline the curious picture.

Descending a steep flight of well-worn stone steps, from the sidewalk, a reasonably tall man would have to stoop considerably to save his head from coming in violent collision with the arched lintel. Pushing open the paintless, but by no means colorless, door, the interior premises were at once disclosed to view. No, not at once, as it consumed some moments for the best eyes to penetrate to the most distant walls, by reason of the density and murkiness of the atmosphere, and the prevalence of smoke from some cookery and several tobacco pipes. But there could be no delay in the process of smelling the presence of perspiring humanity in its most filthy forms. It required stomach and lungs inured

II

by extended habit to confinement in similarly reeking, social stews, to enable a person to exist for any length of time in the air of Micky Cuff's castle.   Two low windows at the front gave a dim light during the day, while at night a flaring flame from a small lamp was all the illumination the apartment afforded.   The room was possibly thirty feet in length, and eighteen wide.   The ceiling, which was once whitewashed, and then left for years to accumulate smoke, dust, and moisture, was scant six feet above the dirty floor, and the encompassing walls were of the same piece—adorned here and there with a rusty nail, on which hung either a coat, a skirt, a skillet, or a frying-pan—and in the economy of this particular family it mattered little as to their rotation.   It might be a pan, a dress, and a hat, or perchance a hat, a pan, and a dress.   Across one corner of the further end a string was drawn, and to it a sheet hung suspended.   Behind this temporary screen slept all the Cuff family—man, wife, and five small children.   When the detective entered, a chicken and two pullets were serenely roosting on the top of this convenient bed-room partition, and the curtain evidenced, from its plentiful want of cleanliness, that they were unaccustomed to make their nightly vigils elsewhere—for sleep they could not while Cuff was awake, and that was generally the greater portion of the night.   In that triangular recess the Cuff family reposed.   In that dingy apartment the same persons cooked, washed, ate, drank, and sold whisky to customers—beside keeping two boarders, who occupied a second and calico curtained corner opposite that of the Cuffs. There were no means of ventilation, save through the front door, the windows, and the stove-pipe.   The liquor rested in a five-gallon demijohn, which Cuff denominated his "retail department."

Good old Micky Cuff, as he heard himself ironically called by his neighbors, was not generally looked upon as either good or handsome.   Heavy and tall of figure, he had

plentiful, long, stiff, iron-gray hair, and bristling eyebrows.
His face was broad and retreating at the base, and narrow
and projecting at the top, preceded, when he walked, by a
pug nose, which seemed always heartily ashamed that it was
not large in proportion to the vast expanse of cheek flanking
it on either side, and hence appeared more insignificant than
it really was. But the lack of size in the nasal appendage
was more than compensated by the yawning chasm beneath,
dividing the countenance into two moieties, and commonly
called a mouth. Cuff's mouth was the crater of a miniature
volcano, continually bursting forth with loud oaths, running
streams of tobacco juice and bursts of fetid breath, causing
the face to tremble with the vehemence of the smouldering
fires of the elements within. To make the thing still more
hideous, there were four tusks in the front of the upper and
lower jaw, jutting out slantingly, causing either lip to pro-
trude and assume a grin, which would have made the fortune
of any actor who affected the line of character professionally
dubbed the "heavy villain." When Cuff laughed, which
was constantly—and never more diabolically than when
incensed to the pitch of working violence upon something—
his little, round, black eyes retreated into their sockets, the
nose wriggled felicitously, like the stump of a dog's tail when
begging for meat, and his four broad tusks clattered together, causing his repeated guffaws to assume the tone of an
illy played pair of castanets combined with the before-men
tioned stage thunder. In fact, the big fellow's face was
open, like that of an alligator. Dressed in coarse miners'
blouse and pantaloons, with boots of the usual weight—Cuff
seldom wore his hat, excepting when in the street or the
mine, for he was an expert miner, and labored when he
could by day, selling whisky at night—he was a perfect wonder to behold.

Cuff was not, and never had been, a Mollie, but was
greatly in favor of the organization, and on intimate terms

of friendship with its principal members. He bore the reputation of being a very rough customer, and undoubtedly was, but he may be complimented by the addenda : even he " was not as bad as he looked." His temper was as peculiar as his *personnel*. Once disputed in a favorite theory or belief, his anger was quick to rise, knew no bounds, and the handiest weapon, no matter what it chanced to be—a rock, an axe, or hammer, a bar of iron, a stick of wood—was employed upon the person of his opponent, whether it chanced to be man, woman, or child, and it was a cause of wonder in the neighborhood that Micky had never yet been guilty of murder. In truth, he had not even been arrested for an assault, though frequently guilty of those of an aggra-vated character. His inner consciousness was as utterly in-explicable as his outward general appearance. Nondescript is about the only word in the English language clearly con-veying to the mind of the reader a photograph of the being bearing the name of Micky Cuff, of Shenandoah. And the same syllables equally well apply to his mental and moral attributes—for he possessed both of these in a marked and powerful degree.

Cuff would never refuse a man a quart of whisky, even though he whacked the applicant roundly before he could get off the premises with it. During times of suspension, when few miners commanded ready funds, Cuff is said to have disposed of, without money and without price, barrel after barrel of liquor, showing that penuriousness was not one of his many faults. Those who failed in coming up and settling, among the few to whom he extended credit, when better times arrived and the cash was attainable, the good old man took occasion to remind just once of their indebted-ness. A continued omission to walk up, soon afterward, and pay the score, resulted in the closing of the account—wiping away the chalk-marks from the wall with his huge paw—and the balancing of his ledger by giving the negligent

creditor a broken head the very first time they came to
gether.

"When I give, I gives," said Cuff, "an' when I trusts, I
mane to have me pay, if I have to take it out of somebody's
hide !"

So Cuff's customers were ordinarily model paymasters.
He sold by the gallon, quart, and drink, mostly for money
down. It was most agreeable this way, all around.

Miners, or their companions, who took sick at or near
Micky Cuff's house, were considered fortunate. If Cuff
could have his way, he was the softest-handed, gentlest·
hearted nurse in the world. When he might not do as he
pleased, the invalid was quickly compelled to seek other
quarters. His usual parting salute in such an event would
be :

"Go off now ! Git out of me house ! I'm not *nagerly*,
but ye can't stand here an' dispute the docther—an' by the
same token, that's Micky Cuff ! *Dher manhim !* Ye can't
be sick and docther beside ! Go away—an' the devil go
wid ye an' sixpence ! Here's six eggs to ye an' half a dozen
of 'em rotten !"

With more of the same sort, which would make a stranger
tremble ; but those who knew Cuff were aware that, to those
in misfortune or suffering from illness, his heart was that of a
baby.

When the sick man wisely kept a silent tongue in his
head, and swallowed the remedies provided without word or
grimace, no one could be more compassionate than Cuff.
His principal reliance, in all cases—his *medicamentum* and
cure-all—was a preparation which he called "skelkeen,"
and it was generally to be gulped down very hot, so that his
patients denominated it —but not in his presence—"scald
keen ;" for they said it scalded them sharply in the taking.
Cuff made his skelkeen about in this manner : Taking three
fresh-laid eggs, plenty of sugar or molasses, he broke the

eggs, beat them, with the other ingredients, in a bowl, then added a generous quantity of whisky; putting all together in a pot, or tin kettle, he stirred it while it boiled until reduced to the consistency of cream, when some cayenne pepper was added, and the fiery medicine was ready for use.

"Here! Take this!" he would say, holding a cupful of the steaming stuff in his hand. "If ye wor gone, clane dead, the skelkeen would bring ye to life again!"

Should the patient dare refuse the draught, Cuff would call him vulgar names, not mentionable here, whip him, and end by kicking him out of doors and up the stairs, in the goodness of his heart. It was not often that his friends in this manner incurred his displeasure. Only strangers dare refuse the skelkeen.

Then Cuff had his "mulled beer," suitable for ladies, which he declared cured all the evils flesh is heir to. And many went to his house to partake of this remedy. The ladies' cure consisted of malt beer, or ale, boiled down thick and strong, in some vessel, on the family stove, with molasses enough added to make it palatable, and drunk as hot as the sick one could bear.

"Swallow this! It'll cure you, or I'm a *gaberlunzie*, which by the same token, I never wor!" was the rough language accompanying the presentation of the vile concoction. Woe be unto the woman who dared to turn her head away from the fumes of Cuff's mulled beer! She would be sure to hear such language from the impromptu doctor as would make her repent the act during the remainder of her life. As with the men, very few had the courage to put the cup from their lips. They generally recovered their health, however, after taking one dose of the stimulating compound.

There was an entire absence of spittoons in the place, and as all who visited there chewed tobacco, or smoked, the sanitary condition of the floor may be imagined but not por

trayed. The scrubbing-brush or mop never interfered with
the supreme sway of abominations. An old broom occa.
sionally touched the surface of the boards, or the coating
above them, but soap and water were "too dampening for
the children"—who, by its use, might take sudden colds—to
be placed upon anything in the house, where their use could
possibly be dispensed with. An old tin kettle contained the
smoking tobacco, and as it generally stood on the floor, excepting when being passed from smoker to smoker, sundry
discharged and useless quids got mixed with the article to be
used in pipes, and McKenna was about to refuse to fill his
doodeen when he looked at Cuff, who was regarding him
carefully over his cards, and remembering a caution he had
received, he choked down his rising gorge, employed some
of the tobacco, and handed the kettle to Fergus.

Mrs. Cuff was in most respects a fitting helpmate for
Micky. She was fully as fine-looking as her husband, but
small in figure and undemonstrative in demeanor, implicitly
relying upon the ungainly partner of her bosom as a wonderfully superior being—in truth, as one of the greatest and
best of men. She performed what he might order, in any
emergency, promptly and uncomplainingly, and so lived that
she made not an enemy in the town. True, her progeny
wanted clothing sometimes, and wallowed in the dust, as
dirty as the *bonneens* in the sty, growing up as tough as
maple knots and as uneducated as Hottentots, but it was not
her fault. She had never been taught any better, and as
long as Micky thought it right, the whole world would be
wrong entirely, if found to differ with his expressed opinion.
She worked hard to keep her large family fed and clothed,
but the urchins would climb rocks, and fences, and slide
down cellar doors, and hence their garments would show
holes and rents. They exhibited little evidence in their persons that clean water ran in streams, or stood in wells, and
that soap was cheap at corner groceries. Rather the con.

trary. But they and she had always been accustomed to such a life, and cannot be blamed for believing it them natural state of existence.

After several games at cards, in which Cuff and his partner came out ahead, he proposed that McKenna should give them a song.

"I hear you are a wild boy wid the music an' dance," said the good old man, trying to appear companionable; "an' I have, these many days, been wantin' to see yez, an' hear some of your best!"

"Yes," chimed in Monaghan. "A song! A song!"

"Do, plaze favor us!" echoed Mrs. Cuff, who was now sitting by the stove, mending a bifurcated garment intended to cover the body of one of the younger Cuffs.

McKenna had a very sore throat at the time, but endeavored to comply. The others withdrawing somewhat from the table, he seated himself upon it and began with "The Miner and the Exciseman," the tune being indescribable the words about as follows:

"I know that young folks like to hear a song;
Its something funny—its not very long;
Its of an exciseman, the story I'll tell,
Who thought t'other night he was going to h—ll.

CHORUS.

"With my fal-al-addy, dol, tol-ol-oddy-dol," etc.

"This exciseman went out upon the other day,
He met plenty of smugglers, as I hear them say,
All gauging their liquor, just ready to sell,
This exciseman got drunk, boys, the truth for to tell.—Chorus.

"Well, 'twas nigh to a coal mine this exciseman did lie,
When four or five miners there chanced to pass by;
They took him on their shoulders and bore him away,
Like a peddler's pack, without any delay.   --Chorus.

"It's into the bucket they lowered him right down;
When this jolly exciseman he got underground,
An' when he awoke in great horror and fear,
Up starts a big miner, saying, 'What brought you here?'
—Chorus

'Indade, Mr. Devil, I don't very well know,
But I see that I have come to the regions below;
An' if ye spare me now, as you've oft done before,
I'll never kape robbin' the poor any more!' —Chorus

"'It's what trade did you follow when you were above?'
'I was an exciseman, an' few did me love.'
'If you're an exciseman, why, here you'll remain,
An' you'll never get out of this dark cell again.' —Chorus

"'Or you must give us money —now that we demand
Before you get to one sight of the land!'
'Here is a hundred guineas,' the exciseman did say,
'For I long to get seeing the light of day!'" —Chorus

"Served the skunk right!" said Cuff, rising from his chair, and giving the table a thump with his closed hand which made the room ring, and caused McKenna to get down rather hastily from the perch and look around to see if anybody were injured. Cuff gave him a reassuring wink and continued: "I don't belave there is any one thing, exceptin' a rattlesnake, that I hate more than a gauger—or a detective!"

"Them's my sentiments, precisely!" shouted McKenna. "Come, let's have another smile, all around, and then we'll go home!"

This ended the operative's first call on good old Micky Cuff, but it was by no means his last. He visited there when he could not avoid it, during that winter, but later an incident occurred that may be related here, which terminated his companionship with that party. He does not go to see Micky Cuff any more—and did not, after the event
11*

alluded to, for many months preceding his departure from Shenandoah.

Cuff's four horrid snags of teeth have been mentioned. They were a source of continual annoyance to their owner, and the special aversion of Mrs. Cuff—his one defect, if the word may be permitted. Both thought—and their friends believed—that if the tusks were once removed and their place filled with a new and regular artificial set, he would be an elegant-appearing man. Cuff confessed to his boon companions that he knew the fangs did slightly detract from his beauty of countenance; and said if he had money to spare to fee the dentist he certainly might have them taken out, and a "dacint set put in the mouth!" When Fergus, on a certain occasion, thought of this, he cast a sly wink at McKenna, and said: "Now, Cuff, McKenna and I are your friends. We have noticed your anxiety about those teeth, and, with the assistance of Tom Hurley, Jack Gibbons, an' some more, have got up a raffle, to come off two weeks hence, to raise twenty dollars for you, for the very purpose of getting a new supply!"

"Yes," said McKenna, taking the hint; "an' it'll not be long before the money's all collected. Tom Hurley and I can raise most of it, I do believe!"

Cuff was very thankful, believed all they said, and promised to have the four offending incisors extracted. In a short time Fergus informed the operative that Cuff, taking them at their word, had accordingly had the fangs taken out.

"What I'm thinking of now," said Fergus, "is where you an' I will be after hidin' until Cuff ge's over his anger! When he hears he has been sold, he'll be as mad as Sam's master!"

"Then there was no raffle, after all?" asked McKenna, innocently.

"Sure, an' you knew that all the time! What's the use of your playin' off r did't, a' this late hour?"

Oh, faith! I supposed you had got up a paper for Cuff, an I was ready to pay me share," answered McKenna; but seeing that Fergus did not care to shoulder all the blame, he finally assented to an arrangement by which they were, for a few weeks, at least, to travel always in company, and never in the vicinities frequented by good old Micky Cuff.

The raffle never came off—but the roof of Cuff's house was nigh coming off with the solid imprecations that good but impulsive man indulged in when a neighbor informed him that McKenna and Ferguson had been playing a practical joke on him. No one in the place dared even look suspiciously at the horrid hole left in his jaws, without incurring his lasting displeasure. He went about his affairs with a more hideous countenance than he had sported before the doctor took away his tusks. Two men in Shenandoah never go to drink, play cards, sing and dance with Micky Cuff. When invited, they invariably decline.

CHAPTER XXIV.

HOSTILITIES CONTINUED.

IT was maintained by some that the Mollies of the coal regions were not supported or recognized by the Ancient Order of Hibernians throughout the United States, but there is abundant evidence of this being utterly false, the Sleepers, or Mollie Maguires, being substantially part and portion of the society. That this entire organization, from root to branch, was rotten and corrupt, has been unmistakably shown to the people of the country. As early as January, 1875, the State and National branches of the Hibernians were beginning to feel uneasy regarding their brethren in the mountain country of Pennsylvania. This is exhibited in the fact that John Kehoe, County Delegate of Schuylkill, issued an order to the divisions to send their Bodymasters and officers to Girard-ville, on the fourth of the month mentioned, to confer with the National Delegate, the great head of the organization, known as the Ancient Order of Hibernians, in the United States. This man was named Campbell, and he met the leaders of the Mollies as stated, Shenandoah Division having for its representatives McKenna, Frank McAndrew, and others. Campbell is described as a medium-sized man, with gray hair and chin whiskers; form rather lightly built, aged about fifty-five years and countenance wearing a look of intelligence. The National Secretary, Reilley, was also present, with a band of Bodymasters, as follows:

> PAT COLLINS, Palo Alto.
> FRANK KEENAN, Forrestville.
> NED KEAN, New Philadelphia.
> LARRY CREAN, Girardville.
> JAMES MURPHY, Loss Creek.

It was found that the object of the meeting at Lafferty's Hall was merely to investigate some offending brothers. Barney Dolan was put on trial for embezzling five hundred dollars of the funds, and, after hearing the testimony, Reilley and Campbell retired, but in a few minutes brought in a verdict of "not guilty," and the big County Delegate looked well pleased, yet, when the National Delegate and Secretary announced that Jack Kehoe should retain the position of County Delegate, Barney's face elongated, and its owner was not half as well satisfied as he had appeared just a moment before. The decision was final, however, and Barney could remain a member of the order, but no longer act as County Delegate, excepting he should be duly elected at a State Convention. Of this there was little hope.

When the regular routine of business had been completed

Campbell made a long speech to those assembled, in which he counseled all to behave well, and so generally conduct themselves as to win the recognition of good people, and admission to the Church. He hinted that all the Bishops desired was that the Schuylkill Hibernians should remove the stigma resting upon them, and thus a return to the fold was attainable. But for the acts performed there, the obstacle would long since have been removed. Campbell was given respectful attention, but his words fell on deaf and unheeding ears.

Then the meeting adjourned and the members returned to their homes.

And this was not all. The era of Conventions seemed to have come. On the eleventh of January, in the same year, a meeting was held in Pottsville, again upon Kehoe's requisition, to prepare for a general celebration of St Patrick's Day. McKenna was in attendance, as Secretary of Shenandoah Division. The following Bodymasters also put in an appearance :

PAT DOLAN, Big Mine Run.
CHRIS DONNELLY, Mt. Laffee.
FRANK KEENAN, Forrestville.
JAMES KENNEDY, Mt. Carbon.
JOHN REGAN, St. Clair.
PAT COLLINS, Palo Alto.
WM. CALLAGHAN, Mahanoy Plane.
DANIEL KELLY, Connor's and Patches adjoining.
LAWRENCE CREAN, Girardville.
MIKE O'BRIEN, Mahanoy City.
PETER SHERRY, St. Nicholas.
PETER BURNS, Silver Brook.
JOHN DONAHUE, Tuscarora.
JAMES J. GALLAGHER, Coaldale.
—— BRADLEY, Representing Pat Butler, of Loss Creek.
FRANK MCANDREW, Shenandoah.
JAMES KERRIGAN, Coaldale.
JAMES ROARTY, Tamaqua.

Excepting only Florence Mahanoy Division, of Turkey Run, which was not represented, almost every lodge had present, on this important occasion, a full corps of five offi cers, viz. : President, or Bodymaster, Vice-President, Secre tary and Assistant Secretary, and Treasurer.

After the opening by prayer, Kehoe explained the object of the gathering, and all the members able to purchase were supplied with suitable regalia ; flags were bought and music engaged, when once more the meeting of Bodymasters was dissolved.

Jack Kehoe was fast becoming a man of power in Schuyl- kill County and gaining supreme control of the dreaded Mollie Maguires. It was policy on his part to invite these conferences. While the President and officers of the bodies were together, he could cultivate their acquaintance and push certain plans, political and otherwise, which, in due season, he would carry to completion. He desired to see all the leading men *en masse*, and succeeded. The presence of the national representatives, and the deference shown to Jack by them, in virtue of his office, at the first Convention, gave him eminence in the eyes of those possessing an inferior order of intellect and standing lower in the official scale than nimself. The County Delegate was a scheming, crafty fellow, and looked far into the future, thinking that he could see for himself and his family political distinctions and riches in the deft and continued handling of the Mollies. He did not, however, as the sequel will show, penetrate quite deep enough into the obscurity of coming events. Had he pierced the mystic veil a little further, the ghastly spectre that would have glided before his startled vision might have turned him from his evil pathway, with terror-stricken face and palsied limbs, to seek the bloodless and better course.

Kehoe was now the self-crowned king of the Mollies in Schuylkill. They moved promptly, like so many puppets, at his will, and when he commanded a halt the mysterious clan paused in its deadly work. Would he order a cessation of hostilities? Or must the word be "Forward—march?" Nobody could tell! That the General intended tough work was apparent from the activity he had inaugurated among the Bodymasters, and they were the men who acted as the Lieutenants and leaders of corps for the Commander-in-chief.

At this time one Pat Hester, who had for two months past been in custody, on a criminal charge, was released and went directly to his home, not far from Summit Hill. He was a bad and violent man, and formerly of high standing in the order. More will be heard of him hereafter.

Immediately following the ball at Pottsville, January 20th, in which nearly three hundred Mollies and their ladies participated, and a very brief visit to New Philadelphia and Silver Creek, the operative returned to Shenandoah.

On the twenty-fifth, the country was visited by a snow-storm of unusual severity. The same day McKenna learned from a friend that Pat Dormer had met his wife at a neighbor's, and they engaged in an animated conversation that ended in Pat giving the lady a cruel beating, for which little act of indiscretion he was still suffering in Pottsville jail, where he would have to remain for three months.

At the end of January the detective had another attack of his old complaint, chills and fever, and for some days was ordered by the physicians to remain indoors.

It will be borne in mind that the great strike was still in progress; work was nearly at an end; some of the stores in the mines were closing up business and others refusing credit to miners, causing considerable suffering among those who, during flush times, had improvidently spent their money, keeping none for this sort of emergency. It was no source of surprise, then, that the mere announcement, founded upon rumor, that Col. Cake had been seen at Loss Creek, where he was to sign papers, agreeing, on the part of the Philadel phia and Reading Coal and Iron Company, to the basis in vogue preceding the strike, should create wild excitement over the country. In Shenandoah, nearly all the Mollies entered upon a prolonged debauch on the strength of the story. Frank McAndrew, the President, was entirely overcome by liquor, and meeting the young Welshman, Gomer James, engaged in a fight with him and his companions, during which knives and pistols were freely used, but no persons seriously wounded. McHugh and Travers were of McAndrew's party, and Gomer James and his confederates finally withdrew from the field. McKenna, from his keeping the house, through the doctor's commands, was not a participant in, or present during the time of this little disturbance. He heard of it the next day, when McHugh went to see him. That person was terribly in earnest, swearing big oaths without number that the time must soon come when Gomer James should be made to suffer for his acts. He thought it bad policy to insist upon immediate revenge, but stated, when work was fairly commenced and everything would not be charged upon the society, he and the rest could never be satisfied until two men were obtained to make way with the murderer of Cosgrove. McHugh ended by remarking that "it was a shame and a disgrace to all members of the order that Gomer's taking off had been so long delayed!"

The starting, a few days subsequently, of several large collieries, made the emissary think that, if others were as anxious as McHugh, Gomer James would have to look out for himself. As James had been previously warned, through the instrumentality of Mr. Franklin, he did not deem it necessary to do more in this instance than make due report of McHugh's words. This he did at once, and Mr. Franklin again had the information conveyed to James that he stood in imminent danger of losing his life.

Father McFadden was now visited by a committee of Mollies, asking permission to take part in the general cele

bration of St. Patrick's Day, for which extended preparations
were being made, but he refused, cursing the Mollies and
their committee with the heaviest maledictions. He charged
them with being murderers and assassins, and commanded
them to leave the order. They would do nothing of the
kind.

McKenna was one of the committee, by the request of
Jack Kehoe, but had no hope, at the time, of being successful in the mission. Kehoe and others determined to take
part in the celebration if they had to walk over the priest's
dead body. The detective was apparently as anxious as the
rest, and managed to raise nine dollars—"from where," he
said his friends "could guess"—with which to purchase
himself regalia for the seventeenth of March. They naturally supposed he had disposed of more counterfeit money.

The early part of March a riot occurred at Jeddo and
Buck Mountain, during which three men were shot. The
Mollies, being largely in force there, were accused of bring-
ing on hostilities.

At about this date three hundred men gathered in the
same vicinity to prevent the collieries from working, and extinguished the fires under the pumping boilers, the intention
being to drown out the mines and bar their owners from
operating them for a long time. The country was over-
spread with snow to the depth of a foot, on the level, and
travel upon the mountains was again greatly impeded, making the work of the Mollies easy of accomplishment and their
escape almost certain.

About the fourth of March a so-called Anti-Monopoly Convention was appointed to take place at Harrisburg, having
for its principal purpose a movement against the Philadelphia
and Reading Coal and Iron Company, by individual and
other large operators. The laboring man, excepting he
might be far removed from, and a great consumer of the
product of the coal fields, could have but small interest in

the result of the meeting, yet many of this class attended as delegates and took part in the proceedings. Among them was Muff Lawler, who reported, on his return, that there were nearly three hundred representatives present, and it was decided to ask the Legislature, by resolution, to cause an investigation to be made, by committee, of the officers of the company, and say why their charter should not be abrogated. Lawler further said that the committee would be appointed and the investigation set on foot. All of which did not prove that there was anything wrong in the organization to be investigated.

Had the Mollies been aware of the full extent of Mr. F. B. Gowen's proceedings in the coal fields—as President of the Philadelphia and Reading Railway and of the Philadelphia and Reading Coal and Iron Company—and the work he had instituted years before, to punish the guilty, and clear their confederates from the land, wresting from them by the strong hand of the law the great power they held over the inhabitants, it is believed that his life would have been taken —at least, attempts would have been made upon it. But the President calmly waited his time, which he knew must come, and relaxed no effort, withdrew no force—on the contrary, kept himself more closely down to his work—through all these mutterings and threatenings. His head was clear, his nerves unshaken.

Charles Hayes, who was just from Summit, where he had gone to secure work and see some relatives, reported that the Laborers' Union and the Mollies had made common cause in the fight on Summit Hill, headed by Tom Fisher, County Delegate, Pat McKenna, Bodymaster, and a prominent Mollie named Boyle. They were determined that, unless the collieries submitted to the general demand, they should not have men to do their work.

Sunday, the fourteenth of March, the Mollies of Shenandoah were startled by the reported finding of the dead body of Edward Coyle, one of their number, in the slip of Plank Ridge Colliery, belonging to the Coal and Iron Company. Several weeks before—in fact, some time in January—Coyle had been on a spree and was heard to say that in a few days he would leave the locality and go to Pittsburg, where he was promised employment. He was never seen again alive. When the water had been drawn off, his remains were discovered, the rats having mutilated his flesh horribly. Parts of his fingers were entirely eaten away. His hands were clasped over his head, and there were other evidences that, while going to his boarding-house at night, he had fallen into the shaft and been killed. There was a coroner's inquest, but nothing more than here related elicited. The Mollies held a meeting and resolved to take no action in Coyle's case, not even to reveal that he was a Mollie, as, should they let the secret out, Father O'Reilly would never allow his remains burial in a Catholic cemetery. This was the course pursued. It was also reported, in this connection, that the priest said he was glad the society was to parade as a body, on the seventeenth, as he would be the better able to judge who were and who were not Mollies. He already knew them in the dark, as cut-throats, robbers, and incendiaries, and concluded his denunciation by observing that the curse of God was sure to fall upon them. Father Bridgeman, of Girardville, expressed similarly forcible opinions of the society and all who had anything to do with it. Still the Mollies would parade, and did parade.

Before the middle of the month arrived a man named Dixon was shot by another, called Bradley, at Mine Hill Gap The two had for some time been on bad terms, and, taking advantage of a spree which he was on at the time, Dixon went to and fired upon Bradley's house in the night, but, fortunately, hurting none of the inmates. Bradley, who was an engineer and a man of nerve and resolution, arose, seized his revolver, went out and shot Dixon through the heart, kill

ing him almost instantly. The engineer at once reported
Dixon's death to the authorities, gave himself up, had a trial
and was discharged as having acted purely in self-defense,
a verdict which was generally commended, excepting by
Dixon's intimate relatives and companions. Even the
Mollies in Shenandoah said Bradley was justified by the
circumstances.

The great day—the seventeenth of March—came at last,
and ended without any great disturbance. The members of
Shenandoah Division combined with those from Loss Creek,
and mustered nearly one hundred men for the procession.
There were four hundred Mollies in line at Mahanoy City
After organizing at a hall in that place, Jack Kehoe made an
extempore oration, in the course of which he said that the
parade was looked upon by some of the inhabitants of the town
as a direct and open threat to overpower them, or a signal for
the resumption of a reign of carnage ; and, if any of the Mollies got drunk while in the neighborhood, he would, in person
strip off their regalia, then, if necessary, get an officer, have
them arrested and sent to prison.

" Let us show the clergy," he concluded, "that, although
we bear a bad name, we are very far from deserving it !
There is no truth in what they say, exceptin' when we meet
a party opposed to us—then we do as well as we can. Let
us all act as men—not as boys !"

Kehoe's remarks were loudly applauded. He was followed
by a man named Love, who spoke in a similar vein. but
without the County Delegate's vehemence.

As before stated, the day passed off quietly, and the Mollies returned to their homes in their usual condition.

The same remark does not apply to Number Three Hill,
where, at 10 P.M., there was a savage battle fought between
John Thompson and Martin Deane, on the part of the Mollies, and a crowd of Sheet Irons, headed by a man named
Welch. The Iron Clads, in trying to kill Thompson, shot

a young girl named McHale, sending a bullet through her arm, narrowly missing a vital part. Some of the Shenandoah men, when they heard this news, promptly started to find Welch, who wisely kept out of their way. Had the crowd encountered him, doubtless his blood would have been shed. McKenna was so ill as to be confined to the house after the procession, hence did not join in the search.

Sunday, the twenty-first of March, Father O'Reilly read out in church, almost complete, a list of the Mollie Maguires who had attended the parade, McKenna among the rest, asking the prayers of the congregation for the salvation of their souls. The Mollies merely laughed at the proceeding, when outside the church, where some still persisted in going, and said such exhibitions of spleen would do them no harm.

At the close of the month, a number of strange men arrived at Frackville, to work in the mines, from Philadelphia, with a few engineers for the railway company, the railroaders having long before submitted to a reduction of ten per cent., refusing longer to hold out with the miners and other laborers, but the imported workmen had to be sent home, and dare not go to their employment, so hostile were the demonstrations made against them by the Mollies and members of the Laborers' Union.

Then came the news that the telegraph office at Summit Station had been fired and burnt to the ground. It was supposed to have resulted from the act of an incendiary. Not long after, a railway train, loaded with coal, was thrown from the track and the cars badly smashed up. Many Mollies lived in the neighborhood, and these deeds were probably performed by members brought from a distance

In view of the frequency of these occurrences in the mining country, McKenna now suggested that Mr. Franklin send policemen to different places, with orders to openly make investigations, and also act as a preventive of further difficulties. It was impossible for the operative to do more than he was doing. The magistrates were powerless, and other county officials in the same predicamen

———◆———

CHAPTER XXV.

PLOT TO DESTROY THE CATAWISSA BRIDGES.

BEFORE the opening of spring, McKenna fully recovered his health—at least was well enough to join his friends in many of their midnight and other carousals and sprees. It was afterward remembered by his associates, that as soon as any dark deeds were done, he generally managed, sick or intoxicated, to make his appearance in the vicinity of the occurrences. But these slight eccentricities in the behavior of the wild Irishman of the mountains passed at the time unnoticed by the Mollies. That he came and went they knew, but questioned not the why or wherefore. So little were they on the alert for anything Jim McKenna might do, that, in reality, they seemed to think the very act he performed the most natural for a man of his supposed character under the attending circumstances. While looking after the threatened destruction of the high and costly bridges of the Catawissa Railway—of these more hereafter—the detective had a queer adventure, in the neighborhood of Ringtown Mountain, that his reports make no mention of, but a description of which the writer has verbally received within the past few months. Chancing to be in Girardville, on a visit to Jack Kehoe, the operative encountered Frank McAndrew and a miner named Maguire—the latter being a Mollie by name as well as by nature—both of whom were perceptibly the worse for much spirits they had imbibed during the day, and they found it very difficult to guide their own mov ments, unaided, over the homeward road, which was still deeply covered with snow. Kehoe saved the almost help-less men from freezing to death, by taking them into his house and seating them by the stove; but, through later absorption of a few more drinks at the bar, they were left, in the course of a few hours, in as poor condition for locomotion as before entering the tavern.

"See here, McKenna," said the County Delegate, "I don't see whatever I'm to do wid these fellows! Sure an' they insist on goin' home this very night to Shenandoah, beyant, at all hazards, an' I know, as well as I know I'm now spakin', they'll be stone dead, if they ever live to get off the mountain, wid the cold an' the whisky! You'll hev to go in their company, an' see they don't fraze up en-thirely!"

"Faix an' I am the lad that kin do that same!" answered the Secretary! "But how am I to act wid the obstinate bastes if they jist lie down in the snow an' refuse to move? That might bother me! The divil can't match a drunken man fur obstinacy!"

"Oh, fur that matther," said King Jack, with a cruel blaze in his eye, "if they do that, ye'll hev to build a fire under 'em as we do below a balky mule, an' here's plenty of matches for your use!"

Kehoe handed the operative a box of lucifers and held the light until the three men were well off the platform in front of his house, when he wished them plenty of "good luck" and shut the door, leaving them in darkness.

Kehoe having found out that the men carried a little money with them, and fearing they might be robbed, even if lucky enough to escape death by freezing, should they linger by the roadside, was glad to have McKenna travel in their company.

The path was dimly marked and the obscurity almost im-penetrable, as the young man, with a drunken miner clinging to either arm, attempted to seek the way over the hills to Shenandoah. First, McAndrew stumbled and fell, and McKenna was forced to relax his hold of Maguire and help his superior officer to his feet. While this was being accomplished, Maguire, left unpropped, and unable or unwilling to stand alone, suddenly slipped and went down headlong through the darkness into a deep bank of snow, in which he floundered and sputtered like a struggling novice at a swimming-school. McKenna, at first, tried hard to restrain his temper, and finally succeeded in starting both of his protégés once more *en route* for home. But his patience gave way after three or four repetitions of the same act, varied only by McAndrew rolling down a steep declivity, and coming very near going off a ledge of rock to the bottom, a distance of thirty feet.

"I'll be shivered!" exclaimed McAndrew, when once more in the road, "if I walk another step! What'ser use gettin' all tired out, when its so warrum and nice slapin here? I'm jist goin' to bed!"

So saying, the Bodymaster threw himself flat in the snow-bank, stretched out his limbs, and prepared to stay where he was during the remainder of the night.

"Tha'so!" repeated Maguire. "Move 'long, Frank, an' don't take up all the bed!"

And he quickly followed McAndrew's example. Both continued recumbent, despite the detective's exertions to keep them in the observance of a perpendicular; and before many minutes elapsed, were snoring away in concert, as though safely under blankets in their respective homes.

"What the divil am I to do now?" soliloquized McKenna. "It'll never do to follow Kehoe's advice, beside the matches are as wet as a dog after a bath, wid the snow in me pocket! Here's a raal quandary!" He did not forget his brogue even when talking to himself.

Presently the agent observed a faint light in the distance,

and resolved to make one more effort. He shouted in McAndrew's ear:

"Get up now! Faith an' I see the light in Mike Carey's shebeen! Sure they're awake yet, an' ye know the sort o' liquor they sells? Get up, an' we'll rouse that drunken Maguire—not that you're touched at all yourself—an' go on a few steps, an' I'll stan' trate when Mike Casey puts out the stamin' whisky-punch!"

"What-yer say about 'whis-sy-punch?'" drowsily inquired McAndrew, turning over on his side and filling his mouth with snow, "Was-is—it bout 'whissy-punch?'"

"I say old Mike Casey's place is jist beyant, an' that I'll trate!"

"Enough said! Give me a lif'," begged McAndrew, and he strove to rise. "I—I—belave I really am gettin' uncommon thirsty! 'Swonderful how atin' snow'll make one take to the drink!"

The drunken fellow blew the snow away from his eyes, nostrils, and mouth, and truly stood alone, while the sober man turned his attention to Maguire. That besotted individual at first flatly refused to get up, but finally made out to rise to his feet, and McKenna, once more taking an arm of each, marched away in the direction of the light.

The shebeen-shop of Mike Casey and his wife—an elderly couple, living on the mountain by themselves—was reached after much difficulty, and the detective, puffing like a porpoise, from over-exertion, released his protégés and knocked at the unpainted door. When left to themselves McAndrew and Maguire fell in a limp and confused heap, like so many damp rags, upon the ground.

Soon there were heard footsteps within and Casey opened the door, saying:

"Who the divil comes here at this time o' night?"

'Oh, it's McKenna an' two belated travelers," answered the operative.

12

"Well, whatever have brought *you* here? But niver mind! Step in, an' in a jiffy the old woman will be out te help you!"

"Its very well to say 'come in!' an' *I* can do it, but these two spalpeens here, are too drunk to do anything! Just get on some clothes, plaze, an come help me to house the rascals!"

In a few moments, by dint of hard pulling and much tugging at hands and feet, McAndrew and Maguire were at last hauled inside the cabin, where they reposed on the floor, a couple of as wet and uncomfortable bodies as can well be imagined.

Casey's shanty consisted of a single room, and a half loft overhead, to which latter place access was had by a wooden ladder. In the lower apartment slept the man and wife, on a bed in one corner. In the same room they also ate, drank, did their washing, cooking, and sold whisky and tobacco. Only one window, the door, and a big chimney gave light and ventilation to the shop. It was a rough retreat, but far better and warmer than out-of-doors, and quite acceptable under the circumstances. Old Mrs. Casey—blind of one eye, not exactly handsome-looking, and only partly dressed— was by this time ready to wait on her unexpected but not unwelcome customers. By again shouting "whisky-punch" in McAndrew's ear, the detective managed to put his friend upright, and, after imbibing more drink, assisted him to ascend the steep ladder, to the only spare bedroom in the building Maguire had to be shaken for half an hour, some matches set off under his nose, and one slightly touched to his cheek, before he could be sufficiently awakened to drag himself to the same portion of the cabin. Covering the men with the hay forming their couch, and all the clothes he could find, McKenna left the drowsy worthies. The loft would only contain two.

"Now phat are we to do wid you?" inquired old man Casey.

"Oh, I kin sit up !   Its not long 'til mornin' ! "

" An' ye shall do no such thing ! " said Mrs. Casey.   " I knows a trick worth two o' that ! "

She then went hunting about the room until she found an old shawl and some bags, the latter suitable for holding corn.   These she spread on the floor before the hearth stone, beyond which was a rosy, red bed of anthracite resting upon a novel grate, made of railroad iron and smaller bars, and which was sending a genial warmth throughout the apartment.

" Auld man !   Get ye to bed ! " said Mrs. Casey.   He obeyed the command, and his wife piled upon the recumbent McKenna—who had placed himself, dressed as he was, on the improvised mattress, in accordance with an imperious gesture of Mrs. Casey—her husband's lately vacated coat, and other garments.   Then she said :

" Now, lad, shut your eyes ! "

McKenna did so, and presently heard a rustling, as of changing garments, and felt his coverings greatly augmented in weight.   Mrs. Casey retired to the scant and only bed the place afforded.

" I hope ye'll slape comfortably ! " said Mike, laughing.

The operative knew that the kind-hearted old lady had heaped her own woolen garments upon him in default of other comforts

The wind came up so furiously through the crevices in the floor, and the snow sifted down so plentifully from the roof, that the tired man could not rest.   Excepting on one occasion, however, when he thought he heard Casey get up, and turned to see that it was not his step but that of his helpmate, he pretended to slumber, out of regard for and not to hurt the feelings of the kindly pair who had taken them in.

In the morning, early, McAndrew and Maguire clambered down the adder and awakened the rest with demands for beer. They were very thirsty. McKenna arose, gave the old lady her clothes, and she was soon ready to wait upon them. The detective noticed that she took her half gallon measure from beneath the foot of her bed, threw something that it contained out at the door, and then filled it half full of bee. from the keg. But he said nothing of this to his companions.

"I belave I'll take a sip o' gin," said the Secretary, as the Bodymaster and Maguire, in turn, drank deeply of the malt liquor. "I always try and get gin for my morning dram!"

This liquor was in a small bottle and clear and genuine. The beer he could not relish, considering the use to which the tin vessel in which it stood had been put during the night.

It was not until they had reached Shenandoah that McKenna informed his comrades of the sickening circumstance. Their stomachs were in such a peculiarly sensitive condition at the time, that a few explanatory words caused them to revolt. As a consequence both men were very sick. "Seasickness was no name for it," they said.

It chanced well for McKenna that, on this very day, and before Maguire and McAndrew recovered their appetites and their strength, he was compelled to go to another part of the county and remain during several nights. When he returned Maguire was away at his home and McAndrew had forgiven him.

"Faith, an' ye know well enough, it would have been both mane an' uncivil for me to say anythin' of it before the kind old couple!" was all the excuse the operative could offer. Not one of the three men drank ale at Mike Casey's house after that.

There was little of interest occurring in the region from the dates last mentioned, until early in the spring of 1875, when the Mollies determined to destroy the bridges on the Catawissa Railway, then as now run by the Philadelphia and

Reading Company. The reason given by Pat Brennan, one of the prime movers in the business, for the proposed out rage, was that considerable coal passed to market over the Catawissa line, and it would be necessary to stop shipments as well as production in that portion of country. McAndrew of Shenandoah, and Pat Butler, of Loss Creek, were expected to furnish the force of Mollies, and Brennan was to secure an equal number of men from outside sources. The several high and costly structures were to be set on fire simultaneously, after all trains had passed over, so that life would not be endangered. Brennan, found picking coal at Glover's dirt bank, was not a Mollie, but bad enough to be one. McKenna went to see him, pretending great anxiety to have a hand in the matter, at the order of McAndrew. Brennan implicated two brothers, named Welch, with many others, and said one meeting had already been held on the subject, by his friends, in the bush, but nothing had been permanently decided upon. Another gathering was appointed for the ensuing Tuesday night, to be attended by Mollies and outsiders, and the detective was invited to be present. He consented. McHugh was opposed to the project. Gibbons was greatly in favor of it. In a conversation held with the latter, the detective said :

"It is a big job, ye understand, an' it will take a good many men to do the thing. They must be as true as steel, at that."

"I know it," answered Gibbons. "An' are not the Hibernians the men who can be depended upon? They can do it, if anybody can."

"I know we're all right—but we're not alone. We can't possibly arrange everything so as to act before next Wednesday night."

"That's the truth!" responded Gibbons.

This was urged in order to gain time in which to notify Mr. Franklin, so that, if McKenna might not succeed in dis couraging the Mollies and preventing the destructive effort a force could be sent to capture the would-be incendiaries before the match had done its duty. It was finally decided that a second meeting should be held the ensuing Tuesday night, at nine o'clock, at Number Three Hill, when the details should be attended to, and quickly following that should come the destruction of the obnoxious bridges. The following evening—Wednesday—all were expected to convene at Ringtown Mountain, near the Catholic cemetery, duly equipped for work, and, after brief consultation, at once proceed to do the task proposed. Axes and other tools were to be procured and brought to the second meeting, with plenty of powder and fuses for exploding some of the heavier abut-ments.

The detective afterward saw Pat Butler, and informed him of the proposed affair. Butler was inclined to be cautious. He fully approved the business, but feared the outsiders might harm the Mollies—in other words, inform against them —and wanted every one specially sworn to secrecy. He knew very well that there would be a large reward offered for the capture of those interested in destroying the bridges, and believed those not in the society would be the first to sell out. This was in McAndrew's presence. The Shenandoah Bodymaster thought it made little difference whether the men were sworn or not, as they gave away secrets held under oath about as freely as when not bound by an obligation. A pledge would not stop them from in-forming, if they were so disposed. John Thompson, of Num-ber Three Hill, and John Dean, said they agreed to the arrangement, would attend the meeting, and provide some powder. There was no way for the detective except to go in with the incendiaries. In no other manner could he learn the exact time when the deed was to be committed; in no other way was the thing to be prevented and the would be bridge-burners apprehended. There was danger that he might be captured with the rest, or killed; but the damage to the company, in case the game was not frustrated, would be very great, beside the loss of life to innocent passengers, who would, if the bridges were destroyed at the time proposed, some of them, be hurled, without a word of warning, into eternity. These were among the nigh probabilities. The detective could but run the hazard. Certainly, he must keep in with the conspirators, and see that his whole duty was performed.

CHAPTER XXVI.

A CALAMITY AVERTED.

MR. FRANKLIN was, the same evening, duly instructed where the detective intended to be the next night and informed of the probability that he would succeed in frustrating the designs of the bridge-burners, at even the last moment, as he had his own plans, should there come a failure in creating a disturbance which would result in a disbandment of the two forces engaged in the matter—the Mollies. as well as non-Mollies. The agent also suggested and described a medium through which the Superintendent might communicate with him, by telegraph, before the arrival of the decisive time, should he find it important to do so. Up to the hour of leaving Shenandoah, to attend the Tuesday night meeting in the bush, however, no telegram came, hence McKenna knew that he was entrusted with the entire management of his side of the transaction, the Agency being left to take care of the other.

Tuesday, April 6, 1875, came, bright and cloudless, as though dark desires and hellish passions were not swaying the human breast, and danger threatening the lives of these who reveled in the clear sunlight of the present, buoyant and hopeful for the future. Passing the day in talking with the principal Mollies interested in the bridge enterprise, the Secretary started, at about eight in the evening, accompanied by Pat Butler—who still seemed determined to wait and learn what the outsiders had to say about the thing before he committed himself and his division to the scheme—for the place on the verge of the mountain. Butler was more than half inclined, the Shenandoah Secretary was pleased to see, to let the outsiders have the plot their own way and allow the same parties to perform the work of destruction by themselves. McAndrew, who soon joined Butler and McKenna, was also averse to receiving any assistance from those not within the order. Still all were agreed to attend the preliminary meeting, hence they gathered, under the starlight, at Number Three Hill.

McKenna was not afraid of the outside citizens executing the job, unaided, after having fully disclosed their ideas to the Mollies, and was equally certain that the brotherhood would refuse to do it under similar circumstances, hence his obvious labor was to foment division, and make its performance impossible for either party. This he proceeded to do, and found it no easy task. Strong words had to be employed with the Mollies, most of whom were greatly in favor of the undertaking, to make them willing to abandon it. His principal reliance he found to be the jealousy of the society regarding the interference of all other combinations, and its disinclination to join in an overt act with people not members. Using this as his *piece de resistance*, in the commencement, he added to it, from time to time, such suggestive incidents as came to mind.

"I'll go to the divil, or just anywhere," he said, "with the right sort of people, but these strangers I'm not so quick to follow! I'm forninst colloguin' wid men not known to be friends.

"So am I!" said Pat Butler, a hardy little fellow, with black hair, a keen eye, and a look of resolution on his sharp face.

"And I," echoed McAndrew.

The scene presented at Number Three Hill was impressive, but almost shrouded in darkness. Seated on rocks, bits of logs, and heaps of earth, and leaning against the bodies of stunted trees, the men were grouped, recognizing each other by their shapes and the sound of their voices. The stars gave just light enough, at that hour and season of the year, to make human faces and figures dimly visible.

Brennan, who had been so forward in the inception of the job, hearing, early in the day, from a voluntary emissary of McKenna, that Shenandoah Division was greatly opposed to the joint movement, did not make his appearance at Number Three on that particular evening, nor did any of the non-Mollies, who had been promised, assemble at the spot. The following persons were there: John Thompson, John Dean, Pat Butler, John Gibbons, Frank McAndrew, Fenton Cooney, Mike Doyle, Ed Sweeney, Mike Casey, Chas. Hayes, Mike Murphy, Pat Whalen, and James McKenna.

Not a pipe was smoked in that silent conclave. Men spoke in whispers, and moved with stealthy tread, for fear that a spark of fire or loud word might disclose the whereabouts of the conspirators. McKenna stood among the rest, leaning against the trunk of a tree, expecting every moment to hear the sound of approaching footsteps announcing the arrival of the allies of the Mollies; but in this way an hour passed and nobody came; then, as silently as they had come together, the crowd dispersed, and the enterprise was a pronounced failure.

At McHale's saloon, in Shenandoah, an hour later, the principal Mollies reconvened, in a convivial way, when, no others being present, drinks were procured and all pledged themselves never to have anything to do with business of a

12*

serious character when any outsider was to be interested. Especially were they to refuse co-operation where they themselves were not the persons to plan an entire movement.

The same night Gibbons informed McKenna that he had been several days trying to induce Thompson, of Number Three Hill, to aid him in a plan by which the company— the Philadelphia and Reading Coal and Iron Company— would be greatly injured. The idea was to go, in the dark, and run a loaded truck, then standing at Grover's Breaker, down the railroad track, when a train would be coming from an opposite direction. It must then occur that the train, locomotive and cars, would come in collision with the coal car and all be smashed in pieces. Thompson had thus far refused, as he was sure that the engineer, fireman, and brakemen, and possibly others, would be killed. Beside he thought the engine might naturally be crowded with workmen, returning to their homes, and he was not favorable to killing innocent persons merely in order to spite one corporation. Gibbons argued that the train would not be thrown off, only the truck smashed, track torn up, and consequent delay in shipping coal insured.

Here was another thing that the detective must have an eye upon. It added to the now constant pressure upon his mind. The elements were around. Violence was in the air. McKenna should have a care for himself, and for the great purpose of all his thoughts and acts. He knew not what the morrow might bring forth.

At this time it was calculated by those who had every facility for knowing, that there were thirty thousand members of the Ancient Order of Hibernians—otherwise the Mollie Maguires—in the State of Pennsylvania, and, in the county of Schuylkill alone, where my agents were most actively operating, some two thousand five hundred. These figures may be exaggerated, or may not, but it is undoubtedly true that there were enough in the Commonwealth to carry the elections and to produce wide-spread terror in the coal regions. So invincible was their power, that they had but to say the word and a priceless life was thenceforth worth no more than the powder burnt in its destruction. The County Delegate, Kehoe, needed only to crook his little finger or call upon the officers of any adjoining county for help, in any nefarious undertaking, and it was forthcoming. From the assassination of a man to the burning of a breaker, or the whipping of a boss who refused to obey an order to leave the country, he had but to command to be obeyed. The same rule applied—only not to so wide an extent—with the Body-masters of the different divisions. Over their subordinates these officials exercised complete control. Sometimes, it was true, as in the matter of Gomer James, at Shenandoah, the members undertook to lead. But in McAndrew the vengeful McHugh and Hurley found their match. He, when repeatedly urged, even as late as the first of May, 1875, utterly refused to have anything done, ending all cavil by once more promising that, when the resumption came—if ever it did come—and the attention of the people would be diverted from their society, he would get the men from Northumberland County and have the Welshman silenced. Finding that they had not sufficient force at command to put him out, the bloodthirsty trio were compelled to wait. That is, for a time, they did wait, and McAndrew still remained at the head of affairs.

Considering the increasing turbulence prevailing in the coal country, and the rapid accumulation of crime since the dullness in the mining business had set in, I, at this time, deemed it advisable to visit Philadelphia, and hold a consultation with Mr. Franklin and McParlan, *alias* McKenna. This was, therefore, accomplished on the 28th of April, 1875. After talking the matter over with Mr. Franklin, and fully exchanging views as to the future, Mr. F. B. Gowen,

President of the Philadelphia and Reading Railway and of
the Coal and Iron Company of the same name, was sent
for.   He was ill at the time, but came promptly, and we held
a long and absorbing talk with him in my private parlor.
The work of the past two years was passed in review, supported by copies of the reports from the Philadelphia
Agency and much said about the task remaining to be performed, having in sight the early breaking up of the powerful Mollie organization.   From all we had heard, the society
was now more powerful than ever before.   Its numbers
were rapidly increasing, its work becoming more desperate.
Evidently something must be entered upon that would have
the effect of reducing the latter, and ending the bloody deeds
of the monsters who were deliberately planning to sacrifice
human life and millions of property.

Mr. Gowen was disposed to defer to my judgment in the
business, knowing that, for many months, I had made a study
of the society, its rules and *modus operandi* in accomplishing
its sanguinary purposes.   He believed that I could best suggest the plot for the coming campaign, which everything portended was to be a bitter one.

" Mr. Gowen," said I, upon receiving this information,
"I wish, in this connection, to ask you a legal question.
Should I bring to the State a number of my operatives,
and have them sworn in as Coal and Iron Police, under
General Pleasants, and if they, in consequence of reports
received through detective McParlan, were to go to a
certain locality and there make the arrest of persons in the
act of committing crimes, would they be compelled subsequently to reveal the source of their knowledge ?   That is
can such service be performed without at present uncover
ing McParlan to the Mollie Maguires ? "

I was anxious that McParlan—otherwise the good Mollie,
James McKenna—should remain *incognito* for as great a
length of time as possible, and when no longer useful in this

way, to be secretly removed to some safe place, as I was aware of the fact that, without his voluntary consent, his testimony in convicting the Mollies could not be used. I had pledged him my word for that, and was not the man to change, whatever consequences might impend.

Mr. Gowen replied :

" It will not be actually necessary to disclose our source of information ! "

" Very well," I added. " I am pleased that it is so ! This being settled, I will have a good and trusted *employé* sent here from Chicago, with orders to go thoroughly through the country and over the ground, secure an understanding of the localities in which it is supposed outrages may be committed, and select a proper rendezvous for such persons as he may need for his support. At this point, McParlan, *alias* McKenna, can send to or give them such information as he may secure, in time for the prevention of crime or the capture, in the very act, of its perpetrators. I want five or six of my best and most resolute *attachés*, with an equal number of the Coal and Iron Police, who have been duly tried and found fearless and capable, placed under control of the thief operative who may be sent, thus forming a company of twelve, to be at all times at command, to prevent murders and act upon such suggestions as Messrs. Franklin and McParlan may furnish. I think, in due season, we may succeed in breaking up this body of assassins and cut-throats, and, in the course of a few months, perform labor which will strike terror even to the black heart of the organization ! "

" Anything and everything that we can legally give, you shall have ! I suggest Capt. Heisler, who has been Chief of the Coal and Iron Police, as your lieutenant from that force. He is an intelligent and courageous man, familiar with the topography of the entire locality, and the most suitable officer I can select for the duty. When you are ready for work, let us know, and he and a picked six of the police shall be ordered to report to your local Superinten dent. We must also communicate with General Pleasants, who, as chief engineer, is General Superindendent of the Coal and Iron Police, and he will see that your agents are sworn in and made regular members of the corps. As for the details, and the management, I leave them, as heretofore, wholly in your hands, and will approve all suggestions made by you ! "

I thanked Mr. Gowen for the confidence still reposed in me, and said I would endeavor to be worthy of it.

" I will at once telegraph to Chicago," I concluded, " for the men needed, and proceed to their organization. When prepared, I will consult you again."

Mr. Gowen then left, and I summoned McParlan to meet me. I was somewhat surprised to observe the change that two years had wrought in the appearance of my operative. While there was no doubt that once more I grasped McParlan by the hand, yet I could scarcely bring myself to believe it. The voice was familiar, and the eye, but all beside seemed different. Much of this transformation was probably owing to out-door exposure, the hard life he had lived, and the yellow wig, which he had been constrained to use after the loss of his hair. I was glad to see that his general health was quite sound again, and the young man still strong and hopeful for the success of his undertaking. Dressed once more, for a few hours at least, in his former decent habiliments, and having taken a path and enjoyed some manipulations in the barber's chair, with a dressing down of the artificial head-covering, he seemed more like his former self, and we held a long and profitable interview, during which he related, much more graphically than I can describe, some of the incidents of his life among the Mollies which I have woven into the warp and woof of this narration.

A dispatch, purporting to come from McKenna's sister saying she was to be married, and wanting him to come to

the wedding, had been sent, as per arrangement, preparatory
to the meeting with me, demanding the detective's presence
at the Agency.

McParlan's sister was not married, but I wanted to see
him; this he distinctly understood, but his friends in Shenandoah did not. It rested with the detective to answer all
the questions that McAndrew, Lawler, and the rest of the
Mollies might ask him regarding the nuptials and how he
enjoyed himself. I knew he was capable of inventing stories,
when on detective duty, which would hang together and
satisfy all his acquaintances. That night, with a lighter
heart and vigorous determination to labor for the extinction
of the hateful clan, McKenna bid me adieu and returned to
his former headquarters.

He told McAndrew a long tale about the magnificence of
his sister's wedding, the name of her husband, the articles
comprising the bridal supper, the brands of champagne and
wines they consumed, with other particulars too minute for
use in these pages. He ended by saying that he had met
his old partner in the " queer " business, and made a raise
of enough money to last him for some time—a large balance
having been invested in a speculation in the city, from which
he was to hear regularly by letter. This last item of information, as he expected it would, reached the post-office
within the course of a few days, and at once relieved the
mind of the delivery clerk as to a man of McKenna's character keeping up such an extended correspondence. The
aforesaid clerk would have told the public nothing, at any
rate, but it was just as well to have his thoughts at rest on
the subject. And, as the detective might have occasion to
spend money more freely, he felt compelled to make an
early exhibit of the source from whence the cash came.

In the meantime the Annual County Convention had
been held, and Kehoe duly elected County Delegate, having, until the occurrence of that event, been holding the

office under appointment of the State branch of the order. Now Kehoe was King of the Mollies in Schuylkill, in fact as well as in name. The wily fellow had accomplished his purpose. We shall see what he did with his power.

CHAPTER XXVII.

NEW FORCES IN THE FIELD.

In casting about me for a chief assistant of Mr. Franklin and co-worker with McParlan, in the coal country, I was quick in deciding that the very man, of all others among my large number of operatives, was Robert J. Linden, then of Chicago, a gentleman who had long been connected with the Agency, and in whose courage, judgment, and discretion I could place implicit reliance, and this from the reason that all of these qualities were united in his mind and body, and had received abundant trial during the time he had remained in my service. Capt. Linden was eminently qualified to assume a leading part in such a hazardous undertaking as we were to enter upon in Pennsylvania. A man of attractive personal appearance, captivating address, great·energy and perseverance, and with more than ordinary powers of perception, I knew he would make an excellent open operator, when the time might arrive for that kind of business. About forty years of age, tall, powerful in frame and physical organization, with black, close-curling hair, whiskers and mustache of the same texture and color, blue eyes, which were expressive of confidence, and just the kind of orbs to win the confidence of others, Linden was a person who could ably command my coal police. A native of Pennsylvania; at an early day a ship carpenter by trade; possessed of a fair education and many qualities of head and heart to entitle him to esteem and regard, I wished for no better man. He had performed labor for the Philadelphia office previous to 1871, was then detailed to Chicago, and engaged in the responsible position of Lieutenant on my local Preventive Watch. So well did he perform his duty there, that when my son William, several years since, went to Europe on business of the Agency, I appointed Linden to temporarily fill his place in the detective corps. He was yet acting as an Assistant Superintendent, and permanently located, with his estimable family, in Chicago. The only cause of hesitation that I felt in returning him to Pennsylvania, was found in the separation from his wife and children that must necessarily ensue. Still no other officer that I could spare from the west would fill the position so well, and he was therefore directed to report in Philadelphia at once. His experience in the navy, during the late war, had given him confidence and coolness under trying circumstances, with capacity for the training and management of bodies of men, and I was certain that there would be no needless delay in making his appearance, ready and willing to perform his task. Nor was I disappointed. Linden soon reached Philadelphia, accompanied by a detail of six stalwart men—partly chosen from the Chicago Preventive Watch, and partly from the Detective Department—and there received his orders and instructions. Without resting a single day, he entered upon his labors, taking the cars for Pottsville, Friday, the sixth of May, 1875. Once in that city, where he arrived a little after noon, he took his men to the Merchant's Hotel, directing them to remain and await his return, and then hunted out General Pleasants, to whom he delivered his letter of introduction. The General received him cordially and at once sent for Mr. Heisler. A long consultation between the three men ensued, during which plans were exhaustively discussed and arrangements carefully made to cover every conceivable condition of affairs. Then followed the induction of the men I had sent into the Coal and Iron Police, which ceremony transpired at the court-house and consisted in taking the usual oath of office. After this the six officers parted company, according to orders, going in pairs, in different directions, with strict instructions to make their headquarters at a certain place, and then survey carefully their field of operations, gaining, by actual experience, a correct knowledge of the shape and character of the country, the towns, villages, patches, collier ies, creeks and rivers, mountains and ravines, so that, in the performance of their work, they might have no trouble in finding their route, without inquiry, from one place to another, even in the darkness of night. Two men were sent to Locust Run, two to Boston Colliery, and two to Tunnel Colliery. Mr. Linden received a commission, showing that he was given full control of these policemen. Among the arrangements was a cipher for communicating with General Pleasants, and badges for the men to wear. Mr. Linden— or Captain Linden, as he was soon to be called—made a visit to Ashland on the eighth, where he tarried for several days gaining such information as might prove of value during the summer. At Ashland, on the fourteenth, he was introduced to his assistants, chosen from the Coal and Iron Police, by Mr. Heisler, and found them of the right class, the majority having served with honor as soldiers during the war.

Soon afterward the Captain was made acquainted with Barney Dolan, of Big Mine Run, which is not far from Ashland.

In the meantime, McKenna had visited Ashland, and meeting Linden privately at a hotel, they adjourned to a place where they conversed over a social glass of beer. It did not consume many minutes to agree upon a means of communication and a point in the bush where, the proper signal being given by either party, they might subsequently meet and hold private discourse. It was so fixed that one could send a letter to the other without the possibility of any third person suspecting their correspondence. There was only one thing that seemed impossible to be provided for and guarded against. This was the necessity existing for Linden suddenly going from place to place, as the acts of the Mollies might demand. All they were enabled to do in this regard was to promise to write each other, as often as it would be prudent, and plainly set forth the spot removing to, at as early an hour as practicable. McKenna would hardly know in advance when he might need Linden, and Linden would probably be unable to say, should violence and outrage continue to increase, where he might be most in demand. Still, every precaution was taken to have their whereabouts known one to the other. After their meeting, McKenna returned to his friends and Linden to his head-quarters.

To go back a few days : On the third of May, and sub sequent to McKenna's first council with Linden, the former took the train for Pottsville, where he was under promise to meet County Delegate Kehoe. Court was in session, and their business, connected with the trial of Dan Dougherty, for killing the Chief Burgess of Mahanoy City, resulted, as before stated, in the defendant's acquittal. Among those that the detective encountered during this visit were Alex. Campbell, of Summit Hill, and John Gallagher, with many other Mollie Maguires, all of whom were deeply interested in the result of Dougherty's case. There was great rejoicing indulged in, and much drink consumed, when their friend secured release. He was quickly taken possession of by his brother Mollies, and in their company made a night of it. Schuylkill County Jail was voted a good place for most people, but for a Mollie past endurance.

The return of Dougherty to Mahanoy City, an event occurring about the ninth of May, was made remarkable by a prompt renewal of hostilities between the lately liberated man and Jesse Major, a brother of Dougherty's former victim. Major was at the time accompanied by Wm. M. Thomas, *alias* "Bully Bill," a notorious desperado, who was known to be opposed to the Mollies and always ready to pull a revolver and shoot, upon the slightest possible provocation. Dougherty was fired upon and narrowly escaped death. Instead of calming the strife between the Welsh and Irish miners, this encounter added fury to the fire, and it raged more fiercely. The detective heard of the circumstance on the following day, and made up his mind that, if the feud was kept up, it could be but a very short time before Mahanoy City would become a modern Gehenna.

In the meantime John Gibbons brought the startling information to the Mollies of Shenandoah, one morning, that preparations were going on, looking to the early resumption of work by the surrounding collieries, and, this time, the Coal and Iron Company seemed determined to protect their laborers with arms. He suggested that such a course must be properly met by the Hibernians, force with force. The rumor was, that the company had already stationed seven heavily armed policemen at Plank Ridge Colliery, fourteen at West Shenandoah Colliery, and eleven at Indian Ridge Colliery.

"And," said Gibbons, with an oath, "the next thing to be done is for the boys on our side to get their guns; for I hear that these new police are all armed wid repeating rifles. If Irish miners are to be forced into open war, we will at least have suitable arms!"

Gibbons was loudly applauded by the surrounding Mollies, and by none more vociferously than by Jim McKenna, whose enthusiasm over the prospect of a fight was unreasonable and knew no bounds.

The scene of warlike operations, judging by the number

of outrages committed, appeared just then to be transferred
to parts of Columbia and Northumberland Counties; hence,
in accordance with Mr. Franklin's orders, as well as to give
Linden a free course until he should be quite familiar with
his future field of campaign, McKenna resolved to pay a
visit to Canning, County Delegate, and resume the acquaintance of the Mollies thereabouts, with whom he had previously made himself popular.   As an excuse for the trip, one
day, after this idea was fully formed in his mind, he gave out
to Tom Donahue, brother of "Yellow Jack" Donahue, that
he had, when in the vicinity, not long before, formed a great
liking for the youngest daughter of the celebrated Pat Hester.
The latter was known to be at the head of the clan, as far as
deviltry was concerned, in that region.   Donahue he knew
to be an intimate friend of Hester, quite at home at his house,
and, McKenna had reason to believe, knew more of the late
troubles in that vicinity than some living in more close
neighborhood.   Therefore, assuming a sober air, the operative made known his wish to go to see Miss Hester, but he
was rather bashful, and did not exactly know how to accomplish a fair beginning of his proposed courtship.   He told his
friend Tom, that "everything depended upon a good commencement."   This was assented to by Donahue, who was
on a protracted spree, at Girardville, where this conversation
occurred, in Jack Kehoe's hotel.

The idea of the devil-may-care Jim McKenna having experienced a qualm of the tender passion caused Donahue to
smile, but the confession of embarrassment made him nearly
go into convulsions of merriment.   Such a thing as bashfulness connected with McKenna—proverbial, the country
over, for the brassiness of his entire composition—was altogether too much for Donahue.   He roared with laughter, but
soon found voice to exclaim:

"An' is it yourself that ye are, or some *cruddy gorsoon*,
right from the auld sod?   Be me sowl, I niver entertained a

thought that ye had a shadow of bashfulness in your whole body until this minit !"

"Sure," answered McKenna, blushing all over his face, like a verdant boy being interrogated by a handsome schoolmistress, "an' I can't be brass through and through ! There must be some tenderness in a fellow—an' mine is Pat Hester's younger daughter. I'm free to confess it's a new thing for me, but there must be a starting, and I want to see her ! I'm not much acquainted with Pat, her father, an' what I'm axin' of you is to go wid me to his house an' give me an introduction to the whole family. I'll trate ye well if ye'l lo it !"

"I've only been away from there, this day's but was wake," responded Donahue; "beside, I'm out of money, an' can't get enough for me whisky, let alone gallavantin' around like a country parson. It costs cash to ride on the cars, an' I have none of the commodity, good, bad, or indifferent !"

"That nade make no difference," returned McKenna, "fur I'll stand the expense ! You see I've had good luck in a 'quare' way, lately, an' can afford a bit of a lark ! Jist join in wid me, we'll go to Hester's, have a good time, an' be back here in a few days !"

"I promised Jack Kehoe I'd help him wid his garden fence ; but I'll see ! If he'll let me off, I'm yer man, an I'll introduce ye to Pat Hester and all the young Hesters wid pleasure !"

Kehoe was glad enough to get rid of Donahue, for a while—though he might have particular use for such as he in a little time—as Tom drank more whisky, by half, than would hire a man who could perform twice as much work. So the two men started.

While *en route*, after having swallowed a few drinks, Donahue proved very loquacious, and wanted to tell the detective all about the recent destruction of Empire Colliery

near Excelsior, but McKenna gently stopped him, saying :
" It is a courtin' we are goin', an' not to a match at telling long
yarns!" This, as the officer had expected, only aroused
the pugnacity of his companion, and prompted him, from
pure obstinacy, to keep up the conversation. Once more
recurring to the subject, he went on—the hearer apparently
absorbed in contemplation of the happiness in store, through
sparking Hester's daughter, but, in reality, noting in his
mind the most trivial incident Donahue alluded to—and was
telling, not only of burnings in which he had been engaged,
but in pointing out those yet to be consummated in the
locality. In this way the fellow was literally pumped dry.
Occasionally McKenna would interrupt the flow of criminal
talk with :

" But phat about Pat Hester's daughter ? "

" To h—l wid Pat Hester's daughter!" would be the
impatient reply of the drunken Mollie, and then he would
proceed, with much volubility and extravagance of gesture,
to unfold a new rascality, tell of late outrages, and who had
performed them, with a detail of fact and incident convincing the detective that, with Donahue at least, the old saying, *in vino veritas*, was as correct in modern times as in
the days of Imperial Rome, for the more whisky Donahue
drank the more recklessly he spoke the truth, and the more
McKenna opposed his thus talking, the more he would
insist upon dwelling on the very topics that the operative
desired to hear about. In this way, out came the fact of
the recent burning of a bridge at the junction, when the
watchman had run after and fired upon the incendiaries.
Donahue confessed to having burnt the telegraph office in
the neighborhood, himself, and said he was not yet through.
In several of the deeds he was not a participant, but he
knew something concerning all of them and who were the
real perpetrators.

When the cars reached Locust Gap, McKenna and his

by this time, maudlin companion, alighted, and went directly
to the residence of Dennis F. Canning, the County Delegate of Northumberland, but learned from Mrs. Canning
that her husband was absent, in Philadelphia, on business.
They could not remain there, so adjourned to Scott's tavern,
where Donahue soon made himself ridiculous by quarreling
with everybody, and the agent was pleased to lead him away
on the road to Locust Gap Junction, near which place
Hester resided. After a fatiguing walk, the drunken man
rallied a little and was sufficiently himself to point out certain bridges that they had tried hard to burn. Donahue
concluded, from their ill success, that kerosene oil was not
sufficient for setting fire to heavy timbers. It might do with
small trash, but utterly failed when applied to large beams
and girders. The watchman at this bridge was a brother of
Mrs. Hester, and Donahue said the structure would yet have
to go. Had not the powder been mismanaged it must have
met destruction some weeks before.

At this period another well-timed query about Miss Hester
set Donahue's tongue running regarding the attack on Hel-
fenstein's, or Ben Franklin Breaker, which he pointed out.

"It made a devilish fine blaze!" the Mollie said, in a tone
of exultation, "an' the cowardly watchmen made no show
of resistance!"

This breaker, after repeated notifications to its owners
that it was in danger, had been left to the care of one or two
useless and cowardly attendants, and was leveled to the
ground. Donahue said that Enterprise would have been left
standing, had not the bosses continued to put good miners'
out and blacklegs in, after notification to stop it. Then that
structure had to go the way of the others.

"Here we are at Pat Hester's at last," said Donahue, as
they gained the locality.

They entered the house and McKenna was placed on
friendly terms with Mrs. Hester and the boys—for Hester

and a large family, several lads, and two blooming daughters. Presently Donahue retired to the sitting-room to visit the girls, leaving the operative to be entertained by the old lady. This was a joke that McKenna appreciated, but the tables were quickly turned upon Donahue, who was surprised, a moment later, to see his former companion walk into the parlor with Mrs. Hester, who gave him a favorable introduction to her daughters. They were both handsome misses, as McKenna had previously been informed, and received him very graciously. The conversation soon assumed a kindly and interesting phase, despite Donahue's condition. Even that tough customer was somewhat sobered by his long walk on the railroad track.

Hester came home to dinner. In the meantime, McKenna had talked his best to the fair one of his choice, whose name was Maria, and she seemed to take his blarney with a good grace, but really giving him, in joke, as good as he sent.

Pat Hester was a rather large, heavy man, with dark eyes and hair, the latter worn long and turned under at the ends, with massive and stolid, but by no means evil-looking features. He had a slightly wicked expression in the eye, arching eyebrows, thin lips and a narrow chin-whisker, the beard in hue a little lighter than the hair. In all, he was not a man to fall in love with at first sight, yet wearing a decent outward appearance, seemingly smart, and not ill-natured unless provoked. When Hester reached home, after over seeing a gang of laborers working on a railroad bridge, he met and was presented to McKenna. Taking a natural fancy for him, Pat immediately suspected his object, and gave the young man encouragement, that, if the lady was entirely willing, the father had no sort of objection to the courtship. But after dinner, and the departure of Hester to his labor, the arrival of Pat McCool and Ned Skivington, the latter ex-County Delegate, interfered considerably with the enjoyment of the ladies' society, and the greater part of

13

the afternoon was passed by the Mollies in the bar-room. McCool was an old acquaintance of McKenna's, as he has many a time tasted his liquor in Shenandoah. Of course he spoke favorably ot the Secretary and made much of him. Skivington was also very friendly. Toward night the men walked cut upon the track and met Hester returning. While passing a bridge, just before, Donahue had whispered to McKenna:

"See that bridge! Now, for two hundred dollars from Pat Hester, I'd see it well down wid the ground, but I'll be hanged if I'd do it for nothing!"

This was as good as a hint to the hearer that Donahue had been speaking to Hester about destroying the bridge and disagreed with him as to the amount to be received for the undertaking.

McKenna accepted the information with many nods, winks, and grimaces, expressive of rapt attention and interest, without hazarding an opinion on the subject for or against burning the bridge. But he thought that here was another warning to be sent to Mr. Franklin.

That night there was an interesting group gathered in Pat Hester's parlor. The center lamp shone on the principal characters, bringing them out in bold relief. Donahue sat in a big arm-chair, asleep. Whisky had at last overpowered the redoubtable relative of "Yellow Jack," and he slept, his head hanging to one side, and occasionally starting up to show that he still lived, and to save his neck from entire dislocation. Pat Hester and his wife—the latter somewhat advanced in years, yet spruce as a sunflower and as lively as a cricket—were opponents in a game of euchre; the lady having McKenna as a partner, while Pat played with his oldest son. One of the Misses Hester was busy sewing, and the other—the younger, and McKenna's particular affinity—sat at his elbow, telling him how to marshal his cards in order to defeat her respected father and brother at the game.

She was bright and interesting, and no fault can be found with the detective if he permitted his eyes to wander occasionally from his hand to gaze into the blue depths of those of the lady at his side. Knowing Pat Hester, as he did, there was no danger that he would allow himself to go too far in his wooing. Indeed, there chanced to be a charming girl living over at Tamaqua, that he had met at the Polish wedding, and on whom much of his thoughts in that direction were lavished. He could not forget the touch of those light hands, and the velvet kisses he had received on the cheek so many weeks before. Yet he had never met Miss Higgins the second time. He believed he would see her some day, however, and determined to remain heart-whole until that moment. Miss Hester's case was a hopeless one. Still her assistance in euchre was very convenient, and he could not help admiring the grace and vivacity of the girl, notwithstanding her connections. When two games had been finished, and success was about equal on either side, the house was closed, and all, excepting McKenna and the young ladies, retired. It was not quite morning when this trio separated, mutually pleased with each other and the manner in which they had passed their time.

The next day McKenna left, receiving a warm and pressing invitation to repeat his visit, which he was not slow in promising.

On the way home, Donahue, who had nearly recovered from his spree, only to engage in another, gave the detective, in confidence, the circumstances attending the cutting of the wire cable at Gordon Plane—thus dropping down the cars and entailing much loss and delay for the company—upon the space below, but fortunately taking no lives. He also told him of the cruel beating of a boss, on the fourteenth of the month, at Mt. Laffee, both outrages perpetrated by the Mollies. But he was not so communicative in giving the authors of those deeds, if he knew them, which might be suspected, as he was in the locality at the time.

When McKenna returned to Shenandoah, he found more trouble awaiting him. McAndrew, the Bodymaster, having for a long time been out of work, was determined to go to Luzerne County, where somebody offered him employment in the mines, near Wilkesbarre, and, on the night of the seventeenth of May, gave notice, in open division, that he would have to resign, or leave the books, papers, and business in McKenna's hands while he should be absent. All expressed regret that he must go, and none more sincerely than the Secretary, in whose care the division would be, in such an event, as there was no Vice-President and no other person considered capable of occupying the managing position. After the close of the meeting, McKenna tried his best to make McAndrew believe it his duty to remain, whatever might happen, and even went as far as to promise to use his own best efforts, and the entire influence of the Mollies, in obtaining work for him if he would stay ; but McAndrew's mind was fully made up. Go he would, and on the eighteenth he started, the operative regretfully accompanying him to the train and wishing him " a safe journey, good luck, and a quick return." Here was a trial for the detective. Here was that under which he well might tremble. The Mollies all aroused—the wicked element in power—work hard to get—murder and assassination riding rampant over the country, and he, the officer sent to ferret out and report their operations and their misdeeds, acting as the head of one of the most sanguinary divisions in Schuykill County. What if the order might chance to agree upon the killing of Jesse Major, or Gomer James, or Wm. M. Thomas, or any one of the number who had been secretly threatened with death ? What if Jack Kehoe were to call upon him for men to assassinate somebody ? Evidently it would require his finest ability to prevent himself from being drawn into the execution of crime, which was foreign to his duty. What should he do ? In which direction should he turn ?

CHAPTER XXVIII.

THE DETECTIVE IN SORE TRIBULATION.

McKenna's fears were not without foundation, as was shown from the action taken by members of his division the very day succeeding the one on which McAndrew, the Bodymaster, shook the dust of Shenandoah from his shoes and sought work near Wilkesbarre. On the morning of the eighteenth of May, the troubled Secretary was met at the street corner by Doyle and Garvey, who said they were on the way to his boarding-house, as Gibbons desired to see him immediately, down in the bush. The three men set out for the place of meeting, and meantime the mind of the detective was sorely agitated. What were these men about to do with him ? Had they penetrated his disguise, now many months worn, and, as he thought, quite thick enough to defy the sharpest scrutiny ? Were they taking him out to meet the fate he well knew must follow quick upon discovery of his real mission in the mines ? But, despite dark reflections, keeping up a firm outward appearance and passing merry jokes, upon the usual subjects, without as much as a quaver in the tone of his voice, or a perceptible tremor in his nerves, he walked along ; whether to his own death, or a conference to end in the murder of another, he could only guess.

In the bush, not far from Muff Lawler's house, a little later, were congregated Gibbons, Doyle, Garvey, Fenton Cooney, and James McKenna. Gibbons was the spokes man, and gruffly informed the Secretary that, now McAndrew was gone, Gomer James must be made away with.

"I propose," said he, "that two men be obtained from Mahanoy Plane, and two from Mahanoy City, to go with me an' Doyle, here, an' we'll soon end the cursed Welshman!"

"How is it to be done?" asked McKenna, and he did earnestly wish McAndrew was safe home again.

"I'll jist tell ye!" roughly responded Gibbons, while he smoked his pipe composedly, knocking off the burnt tobacco with the tip of his little finger, showing as much coolness as if sitting in his own chimney corner, talking to a friend about the weather. There was a cold, malevolent glitter in his restless eye which told those who knew him that he was wholly in earnest. "I'll tell ye! All Doyle an' I wants is fur the four men to kape a good watch, part on one side, an' part on the other side of the road that Gomer James passes over, an' we two'll attend to the rest! Gomer is now watchman at the Little Drift, an' we can catch him aisy like, early in the mornin', when he's goin' home from work. The patch is not so very far from here, but far enough, an' before anybody'll be up an' around, we can be back home, an' the Mahanoy men well on their road for the Plane!"

"Av coorse," said McKenna, appreciating that, to show cowardice or hesitation, under the circumstances, would prove sure if not immediate death, "if the majority's raally in favor of the thing, we'll certainly have it done! I consent to whativer the division may ask!"

The men present were united in the demand, and so expressed themselves. All wanted Gomer James killed. The detective, much against his will, was forced to appear as bloodthirsty as his companions. He must not only agree to, but assume a part in, the dreadful act. Thoughts flashed through his quickened brain with lightning-like rapidity. Ideas were plenty—in fact, too plentiful—but which way?

should turn, and how escape this terrible business, at first he
did not clearly see. Finally a suggestion came, like a
reflected gleam of sunlight to the prisoner in his rayless cell,
and he said :

"You are just right, Gibbons ! That's exactly the way to
manage ; an' I'll go, this very day, to Mahanoy Plane, see
Callaghan, an get two of the men. I'll take Garvey wid
me, an' Cooney is appointed to go wid you, to Mahanoy
City, to mate the Bodymasther and get the others. Then
we'll return here, the morrow, an' have everything ready for
business the next day mornin' !"

"All right," answered Gibbons.

Cooney consented to his part in the programme, and the
little meeting broke up, its members scattering in various
paths, and entering Shenandoah from different directions, to
avoid any remarks of the people.

This horrid mission the operative was loth to perform. It
came of McAndrew stubbornly refusing to stop in Shenandoah without work, and leaving the burden of the division
to devolve upon him. He well knew there would be no
chance that day to communicate with Mr. Franklin, who
alone could notify Gomer James of this new danger, as
Garvey was sure to remain close by him, and what he was to
do he was quite unable to determine. The assassination
must be prevented, at the risk of his own life, if need be ;
but how he was to reach the much-desired result remained
among the problems that he could not explain. Trusting to
chance, and an Irishman's ready wit, he took the cars in
Garvey's company, and went to Mahanoy Plane, as both told
inquirers, "to look for employment."

At Mahanoy Plane, in the afternoon, the two Mollies presented themselves before Callaghan, and in Garvey's hearing,
the operative made demand of that Bodymaster's division for
two men who were "capable of doin' a clane job." Callaghan said he was quite willing, but the members of his body

were nearly all young and inexperienced, and he doubted if he could find two who would serve the purpose. Still, he promised to make the effort.

The detective and his friend then left, saying they would call at an early hour in the afternoon, prepared to return to Shenandoah with the persons appointed. Before leaving Callaghan, the Secretary treated twice, and he and Garvey sallied out to find what was to be seen at the Plane. They first visited Joe Murphy's house, where they had more liquor, and, after taking the rounds of all the saloons, both begun to feel they had swallowed something more powerful than water —McKenna, especially, finding himself so badly under the influence that he exhibited it in his walk and conversation, the former fast becoming vibratory, and the latter boisterous. When they reappeared at Callaghan's, it was nearly dark, and the Bodymaster informed them he had not found the needed men. He said he did not despair, however, and, after treating once or twice, went out to continue the search. In his absence McKenna was entirely overcome, fell sprawling over on a long bench, and soon relapsed into a drunken stupor, from which neither Garvey nor Callaghan, with use of every known appliance, could succeed in awakening him. It was fully nine o'clock at night, and Garvey had taken the train for Shenandoah, before the drunken Secretary was made sufficiently sensible to understand that he must get up. So sottish was his condition that Callaghan found himself forced to secure a bed for him for the night, and assist in putting him under its cover.

The detective had, at least, postponed his own participation in the James matter, and was almost certain Gibbons would delay any attempt to kill the Welshman until he returned. Still there was a remote chance of his pursuing an opposite course. But McKenna was perfectly helpless. No dispatch could be sent to Philadelphia from that small place without creating suspicion. The best he could do was to sit up in bed, write a few lines in pencil, setting forth the danger James was in, seal it, stamp it, having recourse to the improvised stamp depository in his boot-leg, and after midnight, when all in the house were supposed to be asleep, steal softly down-stairs, in his stockings, with *brogues* in hand, and go to the post-office. All of this he succeeded in doing, and in safely mailing his letter, and got back to his couch without discovery. There was the risk that Gibbons had obtained his men from Mahanoy City, and might be even then waiting for Gomer James, ready to take his life. He found enough in this thought to banish refreshing sleep. But McKenna remained in his room until people were stirring for another day, and then rising, walked about in the cool air until Callaghan made his appearance in the barroom.

"Did ye get the men?" inquired McKenna, after greeting the tavern keeper.

"Divil a man!" answered Callaghan.

"An' do ye mane to?"

"Sure, an' I do!"

"An' phatever was't that ye gave me for whisky, last night? I'm half in the belafe that, to get out of sendin' the men to do me biddin', ye tried to poison me!"—adding: "I niver felt so quare in my head in all me life!"

"Deil a bit of poison was there in it! The whisky was the very best! You must have mixed your drinks after comin' to the Plane!"

It was of no avail for the operative to be angry with Callaghan, as he would make nothing by it. Therefore, leaving word with the Bodymaster to send his men over when they were ready, McKenna proceeded to Shenandoah. There he found a great excitement prevailing over two fires that had occurred the previous night, one at Excelsior Colliery, already spoken of, the other being the burning of the railway signal tower at Mahanoy Plane. Not much was said about

13*

the Secretary's failure to secure the two men from Callaghan, as Garvey had returned the night before, very much under the influence of liquor, reporting McKenna as on the road, drunk, without the Mollies sent for, and as Gibbons had been no more successful, having failed entirely. Thus the Secretary was once more excused for being intoxicated when intrusted with urgent business.

Hurley, Doyle, Monaghan, and Gibbons had lain in wait for Gomer James, however, the second morning, and he had not made his appearance as expected.

The operative was more easy in his mind, as he knew that, through Capt. Linden, or some other person, James must surely have received warning to keep himself continually under protection, out of harm's way.

A few days later, Hurley related how he and the others had, on one occasion, gone out to fix Gomer James, and he, Hurley, was armed with a rifle. They lay out nearly all night, hoping to see and catch him, and had Monaghan done the right thing, they would have killed the Welshman, as he actually passed their ambush, the ex-constable failing to inform them who he was until too late. As it chanced, Doyle had his pistol leveled at him, but was prevented from shooting by Garvey, who said he might be hitting an innocent man.

At another time, the young Welshman arrived when Gibbons, Hurley, Cooney, Garvey, Doyle, Monaghan, Finnell, and Thompson, all armed, were waiting for him. Still he traversed the road in safety. Hurley would have dropped him at a venture, only he was just loading the rifle at the time. When ready, the lucky man was concealed from view.

"Well, what are you going to do now?" inquired the operative.

"We are sure to get him yet!" answered Hurley. "But first let us go and see some remains of the man, Cosgrove.

If they will come down with more money, then we can return here, and if the rest all back out, I'll do the job on my own private account! I suppose you'll lend a hand?"

This to McKenna.

"Oh, yes! That's all right!" responded the Secretary, approvingly.

So money *was* at the bottom of it.

The life of the young Welshman hung upon an attenuated thread. Still he remained a watchman, only having himself changed from a night to a day hand. Gibbons and Hurley everywhere sought his life, but McKenna managed to keep clear of it. At last Gibbons boldly said he would go to Jack Kehoe in person, and demand for Hurley and himself a commission to kill Gomer James. They wanted no help and could easily perform the task by themselves.

The ensuing Sunday morning, Mike Doyle was at Cooney's, where McKenna boarded. He said everything had been arranged for Gomer James, and three men were to arrive from Girardville the next day, when the Secretary must be ready to do his share. The time set for the act was Monday night, May 24, 1875. Again were the thoughts of the officer turned to saving the intrepid but foolhardy young man. It was not possible that the Mollies suspected him of having warned James, causing him to cease traveling his former path at night, but Doyle seemed to be placed with the Secretary and clung industriously to him through the entire day, and he had no chance to write or telegraph a line to Mr. Franklin. Doyle, contrary to his usual custom, refused to drink, and his apparent task was to keep McKenna duly sober for the expected meeting with Kehoe's promised assassins. That was undoubtedly his object in remaining nigh the detective. He must have been instructed by some one to do so, as it was not characteristic of Mike Doyle to refuse good liquor, or restrain himself from a debauch, when acting wholly from his own impulses.

The detective began heartily to curse the day that he ever allowed himself to sit in the Secretary's chair, and exercised his wits thinking up some way of shirking official responsibilities, which, considering the condition the country was in, he found to clash with his duty to the Agency and to the public. He wished McAndrew might return, and even thought of sending him word that Mrs. McAndrew was very ill—but learned, upon visiting her, she was never better in her life—and that would not succeed. It subsequently occurred to him that he intended going away to Wilkesbarre, after more counterfeit money. But this pretence fell through, as Hurley and Gibbons both said he could send a letter. Then he called a meeting of the division, brought before it and read aloud the printed constitution and by-laws of the order, which provided for the election, each year, of a Vice-President and an Assistant Secretary, neither of which chairs had ever been filled. The suggestion was that Thomas Hurley be elected Vice-President until the annual day for choosing officers came around, and Gibbons to have the position of Assistant Secretary. Both of these men absolutely refused to serve—both were illiterate, both had characters too well known in the community—and a majority of the members present at the meeting unanimously supported a resolution to the effect that Bodymaster, Secretary, and Treasurer were officers enough for that lodge. Here McKenna's work came to naught. He was unable to find anything satisfactory which would take the responsibility off his shoulders and permit him to go to Luzerne County, as he desired, and had to let it rest, fearing that any very marked pertinacity might call the attention of the brotherhood to his efforts to avoid a duty assumed when he took the position he held.

The occurrence of a great fire in the wood, which spread from patch to patch, and from mountain to mountain, carrying destruction and consternation along its track, in the extinguishment of which everybody about the vicinity was eagaged, prevented the present execution of the James assassination. The employment of every available man in fighting fire made it impossible the Mollies should then seek the young man's life. Still, it was only a short time that this work kept them from bloody thoughts and bloodier deeds.

James must have received a notice of what was going on, as once more he resigned his position and left the vicinity. The men who, upon this occasion, were selected to do for Gomer James were James Bradley, of Loss Creek, Tom Connory, *alias* " Derrick," of Connor's Patch, and Anthony Monaghan, *alias* " Rappa Jack," of Rappahannock. They were duly notified of James' disappearance. But Gibbons was not the man to give up a thing upon which his heart was set, as it was on the murder of the Welshman, and the detective knew that he must keep an earnest and close watch of both Hurley and Gibbons, or they would yet accomplish the deed. Hence McKenna greatly affected Gibbons' company, night and day.

In a little while Gibbons hatched a plan to get James back as watchman at the old breaker. It was to gather half a dozen men, and fire a volley in the air, at night, to frighten the men who had taken Gomer James' place, when some one could report it to the boss, who would very naturally say: " When James was night-watchman, such things did not happen ; if they did, somebody got hurt, for Gomer was no coward ! "

This plan, it was thought by some, would cause Gomer James to be reinstated.

Cooney was of the opinion that it must fail, as James had proceeded deliberately to get drunk, when he knew that such conduct would surely end 'n his discharge. It appeared to him that the Welshman wanted a chance to leave, and had in some way discovered that the Mollies were once more in search of him.

To quiet the matter more effectually, McKenna promised Gibbons that he would try and make a trade with some Division-master for men to follow James, wherever he might be, and kill him. But he never did anything of the sort, nor had he so intended when making the proposition.

McKenna was supported in his acts by Jack Kehoe, who, a little later, swore that he would not be dictated to, and that if McKenna, who was, in his sight, acting Bodymaster of Shenandoah Division, allowed Hurley and Gibbons to tell him what he should and should not do, he would consider it his duty, as County Delegate, to look after him, the Secretary, and have him cut off.

The detective at the same time learned that Kehoe had just returned from Mahanoy City, where he found the English and Welsh all assembled about the public square, and no Irishman, or woman, could pass without being insulted. Even the Celts who were not, and never had been Mollies, he said, begged him to do something to end this unendurable state of suffering. They did not 'care what was done if it only quieted the Modocs, who were acting worse than their namesakes of the lava-beds in the far west.

"I have sent Tom Donahue," said the County Delegate, "up to Locust Gap, to see Dennis Canning, County Delegate of Northumberland, but learned that he had gone to Pittsburg and was at work there; an' I now intend getting Chris Donnelly, of Mt. Laffee, County Treasurer; Wm. Gavin, of Big Mine Run, County Secretary; Mike O'Brien, Bodymaster at Mahanoy City—and I invite you, McKenna, to be present—to hold a convention, on the first of June, at Clark's, in Mahanoy, an' we will see what is to be done wid the whelps, now barkin' so lustily. Perhaps it might be the thing to jist bouldly an' publicly challenge the whole pack to come out an' fight us. Some think we had best attack em in the night an' shoot down every one we meet, sparin' only women and children! I hate shedding of human blood, but these are mighty not times, an something will have to be put to work to give us our rights !"

"Sure, an' I can't but applaud your acts, Kehoe !" responded McKenna. "Fur wan that ye have invited, ye may count on my bein' at Clark's promptly on the day.'

The County Delegate expressed his pleasure, and said, if all the gentlemen were like the Shenandoah Secretary the Modocs would soon be silenced. The men then parted Kehoe to attend to home measures, and deal out whisky for his customers, and the detective to report to Mr. Franklin and prepare for the great convention.

CHAPTER XXIX.

THE INQUISITION OF TEN.

OTHER events crowding upon their attention seemed for a time to guard the threatened Gomer James from the bullets of his sworn assassins. The Welshman still lived and pursued his usual avocations, wherever he might be, unharmed and unmolested.

At the annual borough election Jack Kehoe was unanimously chosen High Constable of Girardville. He was not only King of the Mollies of Schuylkill, but had the power of arrest and charge of the municipal prisoners. If the latter chanced to be of the order, they were handled tenderly and fared sumptuously. If of the Chain Gang, the Modoc, or Sheet Iron sort, he bundled them into jail without gloves, and fed them upon whatever might be cheap and unsavory. Surely, Jack Kehoe was a rising luminary in the heavens—on on the earth—and his luck fast improving.

A few days before the date appointed for the convention at Mahanoy City, McKenna went to see Michael O'Brien and had a talk with him about the troubles in his vicinity. O'Brien was anxious to have three or four men, who could be depended upon, come over to Mahanoy, and he would appoint persons from his own division to show the strangers their work, which was to "fetch" Wm. M. Thomas and Jesse Major. He was of the opinion that, if these parties, and two or three others, were well out of the way, there might ensue a reign of peace in the community; but just as long as they lived, trouble would surely come. O'Brien said he had given Kehoe the situation of affairs.

While in Mahanoy one McDonell reported to the Shenandoah Secretary that he had recently conversed with Thomas, who seemed reckless and stubborn, remarking to the effect that it made little difference to him, since the Dan Dougherty shooting, how he carried himself, the Mollies were sure to get him, wherever he might hide. Some one had lately informed Thomas that, the next time he was assaulted, it would be in open daylight, by a man on horseback. McDonell learned that Bill carried arms on his person, and boasted his readiness to receive the Mollies whenever and in whatever manner they chose to meet him. Of the truth of this the members of the society had all the proof needed. What they wanted was to find somebody, unknown to the citizens and to Bill, that Thomas might be murdered and no trace be left of the murderers.

The next day, while McKenna was present, Hurley came to Cooney's, in Shenandoah, and asked the master of the house to pass out to him, through a window, his rifle, which had, during several days, been left there for safe-keeping. Some visitors were in the building at the time, with Mrs. Cooney, and Hurley did not care to have them see him receive the gun. This looked like business to the detective, but he was unable to stop in Shenandoah to find out what might be in preparation, as the approaching meeting in Mahanoy City demanded immediate att. ....n.

McAndrew, who was yet working at Port Griffith, could not go to the convention, and McKenna was the man to fill his place. Before the day arrived, the operative saw Kehoe at Girardville. There he met Jack Donahue, John Reagan, the latter Bodymaster at St. Clair, and some other Mollies. Mrs. Kehoe's child was sick, and Dr. Carr visited it, bringing Reagan up with him in his carriage. Dr. Sherman, of Girardville, was also there in consultation. Kehoe, after a little time, called McKenna, Donahue, and Reagan into the kitchen, at the rear of his bar, and some private conversation ensued upon the lately appointed meeting at Mahanoy City. Kehoe was anxious that Reagan and McKenna should be there, ending his introduction of the subject with a request that the latter should go, that afternoon, and inform O'Brien, Bodymaster of Mahanoy City Division, to be ready to receive them. This he promised to do. Subsequently Kehoe asked :

"Do either of you know any good *old* men, who are sharp on the shoot? I want some capable of doing a very particular work, an' doing it swiftly and surely!"

"Well, ye are posted as to Shenandoah Division," returned McKenna, "an' know that we are nearly all young men, an' of no great experience. I don't think any could be depended upon in a case of importance!"

"As for me," here broke in Reagan, "I belave I have one man that'll jist fill the bill an' put in good work whenever ye make the call on me!"

Further conference on this topic, at the time, was broken off by the coming down the stairs of Drs. Sherman and Carr. With the latter, after a treat from the disciple of Esculapius, Reagan rode away homeward.

It was on this occasion that Kehoe developed a plan through which a constable by the name of Lamison should be killed. It seems that the officer alluded to, in arresting a Mollie named Rusk, at Kingston, not long before, had shot the Irishman, who violently resisted. Beside, the same official had fired upon and wounded a lad, named Leville, who was saucy while on his way home from a foot-race. For these offenses the High Constable and King of the Mollies wanted Lamison assassinated. He desired that a warrant should be sworn out for his victim's arrest, to be served by himself, and while on the road to Girardville, a masked mob of Mollies might pounce upon and easily overpower Kehoe, and in the mêlée, shoot down and kill his prisoner. Tom Donahue, who was participating in the conversation, sagely suggested that Lamison would possibly have a hearing at Kingston and secure bail, thus knocking Kehoe's fine scheme into atoms. He was in favor of having Lamison planted under the 'daisies, on the general principle, as he coarsely put it, that "dead dogs wag no tails," but wanted the job done scientifically and without a chance of failure.

Sunday, the first of June, 1875, came, one of the balmiest of spring days. The snow had long since dissolved, swelling the mountain streams, the verdure brightened up, and winter no longer lingered in the lap of spring. The life-giving sap rose from the warm earth, coursed along and filled the bloodless veins, and brought bud and blossom to the forest trees.

But all this harmony in nature found no counterpart in the minds of the residents of the country cursed by the Mollie Maguires. On the contrary, the storm of passion and hate in human hearts was unassuaged, and swept forward, seeming to gather strength and fury as it desolated hearth-stones and filled graves with gory victims.

The detective was early at Mahanoy City, and in joining his brethren at the Emerald House, Michael Clark proprietor. This man Clark, as before stated, was not a Mollie Maguire, but his two sons belonged to the order. The hotel was a two-story, basement and attic affair, the outside painted brown, with the eaves and two dormer-windows facing the main street of the city. The first floor front was lighted by large show windows, for which there were no shades or screens to veil the array of bottles and decanters behind the bar, or the men there congregating to enjoy their liquor. There was a door at the center, giving entrance to the saloon and bar, and another at the side by which the upper apartments were reached without troubling other inmates.

In the rear of the public room was, first, a long dining-hall common to such places, and then the kitchen. All were very plainly furnished. At the end of the lot was the bank of the river. Upstairs, in the front part of the house, was one spacious, well-lighted apartment, carpeted and decently stocked with furniture, in which meetings were held, and it was lighted, by day, with four windows. Back of this were bedrooms. On the garret floor were also a number of sleeping apartments. The business of the writer is with the assembly room, where the conspirators congregated. There, at half-past ten in the forenoon, seated around a large table, were John Kehoe, County Delegate of Schuylkill; Chris Donnelly, of Mt. Laffee, County Treasurer; Wm. Gavin, of Big Mine Run, County Secretary; John Donahue, *alias* "Yellow Jack," Bodymaster of Tuscarora; Dennis F. Canning, County Delegate of Northumberland, residing at Locust Gap; Wm. Gomerly, Bodymaster of St. Nicholas; James Roarty, Bodymaster at Coaldale; Mike O'Brien, Bodymaster at Mahanoy City, with his Secretary, Francis McHugh, and James McKenna, representing Shenandoah Division, and also acting as my detective. In the bar below there were other Mollies, and with them James Kerrigan, Bodymaster of Tamaqua Division. Kehoe sat in the place of authority, made the opening prayer, and organized the meeting. He then delivered a brief speech, saying that he supposed all were acquainted with the object of the convention, and without further explanation, appointed a committee of two to bring Dan Dougherty before the meeting. This was done, and Dan came in. He was a well-favored young Irishman, with dark hair and mustache, eyes of the same color, nose straight, face rather full, and cheeks red and healthful, despite the wounds he had received from Major, and the dread he appeared to be in of the relatives of the deceased Chief Burgess, and of Bully Bill. Dougherty was a miner by occupation, dressed well, and had the reputation of being ordinarily a sober man. Of about medium height and weight, his physical status did honor to his twenty-four years.

"Dan, show us your coat," said Kehoe.

Dougherty obeyed, and, removing the garment, exhibited bullet-holes perforating the cloth in two or three places.

"Who do ye think did it?" queried the County Delegate.

"I belave it was Jesse Major, but I couldn't swear to him on the book!"

"Didn't the police try to catch him?"

"No! An' there was an officer not four yards from the man at the time! I axed him why. 'Sure, and I'd be shot down in me tracks if I raised a hand,' said he, an' he went off about his business as if nothin' had happened!"

This caused a buzz, evidently of anger, to pass around the table.

"What men do ye think are at the head of all the late troubles in this city?" asked Kehoe, who had remained standing from the time that Dougherty entered the apartment.

"The which? Who is it? Faith, an, I can think of no one exceptin' Jesse and James Major, an' Bully Bill! If the toes of these three were turned up, ther'd be peaceable times in Mahanoy!"

"That'll do," said Kehoe. "You may retire."

Dougherty cast a searching glance around the board, seemed satisfied, put on his coat, and left the chamber.

For a moment after the closing of the door, silence reigned

in the inquisition-room, and the inquisitors said not a word.

Chris Donnelly was the first to speak:

" These things are getting altogether too bad ; Last night the train coming from Pottsville, by way of Tamaqua, was searched by Jesse and Wm. Major, and a number of others, all armed, and the company allowed it without a word ! I suppose it is because the Majors hire a big vein. I think we must put a stop to such goings on ! "

Kehoe resumed his seat, placed his elbows on the table, rested his hatchet-face on his two hands, and awaited developments.

"For one," resumed Donnelly, who had not left his chair while speaking, " I'll get two good men, an' go myself, and have the Majors' business at once attended to ! "

Here Jack Donahue—" Yellow Jack "—stood on his feet, and remarked :

" We, of this side the mountain, are thankful to ye of the part beyant the mountain ; but we can attend to the affair, at present. You, Donnelly, nade not move just yet ! Afther Sunday, if we need you, I'll send word by a man to Potts -ille, an' tell you what's to be done."

Kehoe, after some more talk, appointed Mike O'Brien and James McKenna a committee to see what should be done with Wm. M. Thomas.

The detective brazened it out, and expressed a willingness to attend to his duty, at the same time suggesting that counsel from older heads would be in order. O'Brien tacitly deferred management of this portion of the business to McKenna, which was satisfactory to the agent, as it ran through his mind that, if permitted to hold the helm all through, Bill Thomas would not be in any especial danger of losing his life.

" I'm in favor of shootin' Bully Bill, bowldly right on the strate, in open daylight ! " exclaimed Kehoe.

O'Brien hinted that such a course would be sure to g·t the boys in a scrape, and added :

"Bill can best be taken on the road home to Shoemaker's Patch. Then he can be dropped, an' the men make sure their escape!"

"Yes, that is the best plan," here put in Dennis Canning, the Northumberland delegate, who had previously said little. He was a gentlemanly-appearing person, showing nothing in his face to indicate a sanguinary disposition. Yet he took part in the cold-blooded proceedings of the convention, without a chill passing over him, and seemed as much concerned regarding the murder of Thomas as the others.

"Let it be so, then," resumed the King of all the Mollie, in Schuylkill, and he lifted his bearded chin from his thin hands, and looked sharply over at McKenna.

"To you, an' your division, Jim McKenna, I lave the picking out of four or five good men, safe to be intrusted with such a difficult matther! Jist notify the division to come together an' select 'em, an' have 'em come over an' report to Mike O'Brien, here, who will find them a boardin'-place, payin' for their kapin' out of the county fund. Let them not be later than Saturday afternoon. If they can't make their point on Bully Bill in three days, you relave them and sind over fresh fellows, an' kape it up until the work be done. O'Brien will appoint those to lead the Shenandoah boys up to Bill, an' ingineer the business through! Fail they must not! If they do, let them beware the power of the order! If Shenandoah can't succeed, Roarty must sind men, an all the rest in turn, until the Modocs cry enough!"

The Shenandoah Secretary made known his acceptance of the charge, and said he would see the division notified and convened.

Canning inquired if any men were wanted from his part of the State, but Donnelly replied ·

'No! the job is a small one, and we can attend to it
ourselves!"

At first, and before the convention was called to order,
the presence of the young man, Frank McHugh, had been
objected to, but O'Brien said he was his Secretary, and insisted he should remain. Subsequently McHugh, a tall,
very juvenile personage, with sandy hair and blue eyes—a
mere boy, in point of fact—was directed to act as Secretary,
and fabricate a record of proceedings which would show to
outsiders, should chance reveal the fact of a meeting being
held, transaction of business on some entirely different matter than the murder of Thomas and the Majors.

Then, all having been arranged, the Mollies adjourned
to dinner, of which they partook in Clark's dining-room
below.

Kehoe enjoyed his food, and remarked to McKenna, in a
low voice : " I think the reign of the Modocs is comin' to an
end, and Irishmen will soon have law in Mahanoy City, as
in other parts of the State ! "

The King of the Mollies was elate and jubilant, and the
operative was compelled to appear so, but he was far from
feeling content with the share Kehoe had put upon him.
It would not do to refuse, nor was it safe to exhibit reluc-
tance.

When my agent reached home, he found the Mollies experiencing most intense excitement, caused by a report of
Ned Monaghan, that the Coal and Iron Company had sent
for and secured policemen, from a distance, all heavily
armed, and stationed them at their different colleries. To
this was added the story of Gibbons, that the Governor had
ordered out the Militia, to support the Coal and Iron Police,
and see that resumption of work in the region was not interfered with on the part of the members of the Laborers'
Union, or others. Even then forty or fifty men, loaded
down with repeating rifles and ammunition, were alighting at

the depot. Heisler, they said, was in command of the police, in person. One who has net seen the locality and known its people will hardly be able to appreciate the uproar in the different patches, and in the taverns and strongholds of the Mollies under such a condition of affairs. Men were quite wild, and flew from place to place, with reddened faces and determined looks, telling the news to their brethren, and eagerly asking what was to be done.

Mike Doyle met McKenna, that night, at his boarding-house, and at once proposed to be one of the men to go to Mahanoy City.

Tom Hurley was anxious to take a part, and wanted to deposit his card, formerly obtained for traveling purposes, and receive the "goods," so that he might be eligible.

The detective, before he retired, the night of the first of June, sent Monaghan to summon Thomas Munley, of Gilberton, a member of his lodge, with orders for Munley to notify others in the vicinity to meet at the hall, in Shenandoah, the evening of the third, at seven o'clock. The Secretary personally gave notice to Gibbons and the others mentioned that their presence was needed on the occasion.

Leaving the proceedings connected with the strike of the Mollies and the members of the Laborers' Union to be related in another chapter, I must now continue the incidents bearing upon the attempt to murder Wm. M. Thomas, and carry the recital to completion.

Monaghan returned from Gilberton, Wednesday, saying he had notified Thomas Munley, who promised to inform the others of what was wanted.

The night of the third of June came, and, from the turmoil prevalent in the city, the Secretary deemed it imprudent to hold the division meeting at the usual hall, hence the members were notified to gather in the wood, on the side of Ringtown Mountain, north of the city. When McKenna reached the rendezvous he found present John Gibbons,

Thomas Munley, Darcey, Monaghan, Garvey, and Mike Doyle, all members of Shenandoah Division, and soon after the opening Tom Hurley came along and joined the clan. Garvey said :

" I suppose ye all know what's called us together, an' it only rests with ye to make a choice, an' as McKenna does not care to do it, let us talk among ourselves, an' agree who is to go and make away with Thomas."

After canvassing the subject, it was decided that Gibbons, Doyle, Hurley, and James McKenna should go to Mahanoy City on the business. At least the three mentioned were selected, and they desired the Secretary's company, which he could not refuse to give. The date fixed for departure was the evening of the fifth of the month. When this proceeding was ended the body adjourned, at nigh eleven o'clock, the conspirators going into town, one by one, as on former occasions, in order that the citizens might not see too many Mollies together.

The next morning the streets were filled with soldiers and Coal and Iron Police, among the latter being Capt. Heisler but that made no difference. The arrangement to shoot Thomas must be carried out. Gibbons came along about four in the afternoon, armed with two navy revolvers, secured from Thompson and McCormick, and, at about half past four, the same day, the Mollies set out on foot over the mountain for Mahanoy City. They could not have selected a more congenial and yet more unpleasant night for the journey. The rain was falling in torrents and there were heavy shocks of thunder and sharp bolts of lightning in the sky. But, after walking more than three hours, the men reached Clark's hotel, in Mahanoy, where they found O'Brien prepared to receive them.

While trudging over the wet earth and slippery rocks the operative had concocted a scheme, which he believed would surely save the life of the man, Thomas, and relieve his mind

14

of an oppressive weight. As soon as all were well seated in Clark's kitchen, beyond the bar, he called O'Brien away for a short stroll. They went around the corner, and McKenna said to the leader of the clan in Mahanoy City:

"Do you mind the soldiers in the strates, an' the Coal Polace?"

"Yes, I do!" answered the Bodymaster, "an' I don't half like the appearance of aither! Its all owin' to the mob, I suppose!"

"Now, O'Brien, I'm as willin' to sell my life for the good of the order as you are, or as any man can be, but it looks the height of folly for us to undertake this job on Thomas while the soldiers are around! If we kill him, as we may, an' make the laste noise over it, we'll be pounced upon at once by the Militia or old Heisler—or both, perhaps—an' then we'll be caught and hanged! Isn't the life of any wan of us worth that of a dozen like Bully Bill? To spake truth, I'm in favor of all of us goin' quietly home, an' trying for Thomas on another occasion. The odds are too many against us this time!"

O'Brien cogitated over the change suggested for a moment and then responded:

"You're right, McKenna, as you always are! Troth! as you say, my life is better nor those of a dozen like Bill Thomas, an' I quite agree wid you that the very best thing to be done is to do nothing—at laste for this night!"

The two men soon went back to the Emerald House, and to the kitchen. Frank McHugh, the Secretary of Mahanoy City Division, had just arrived, and O'Brien made the proposition to Hurley, Gibbons, and Doyle in precisely the words previously employed by the detective. He explained the difficulties before them in so forcible a manner that even Hurley, always the first to enter a fight and the last to give it up, agreed it was for the best to retrace their steps to Shenandoah and not be seen by any one in Mahanoy.

McKenna said he was firmly of the opinion that the work should be deferred; but did not like to assume the responsibility of ordering it without a previous conference with O'Brien. Now that O'Brien was good enough to be the first to put forward the idea he felt willing to make known that he held the same view of the subject. This was peculiarly flattering to O'Brien, and forever sealed his lips as to the real originator of the plan, and was a clincher of the proposed settlement. It was thus decided. After a few calls at Clark's bar for refreshments, the weary men set out in the darkness for the return to Shenandoah.

While going home the four Mollies were haited by the police at Foundry Colliery, but after a short parley were permitted to resume their tedious journey. To avoid similar annoyances the party struck into a narrow path over the mountain. On the way they overtook a stranger, carrying a small paper parcel. At first he was shy of them, probably thinking they might want to murder him, but McKenna assured the stranger they were harmless fellows, lost in the darkness, and if he had no objection, as they seemed going in the same direction, they would keep in company. The man said but little. He "knew every foot of the ground," however, and demonstrated the fact, when in the vicinity of Lanigan's Patch, by missing his bearings and finally bringing himself and companions into a marsh, where they stuck fast in the mire to the imminent danger of their boots and damage to their clothing and tempers. After wandering about in the swamp, running against trees and snags, and occasionally falling down in the mud and water, they escaped from the place and met no further accident. It was about midnight when McKenna turned in at Cooney's, in Shenandoah, and sought his bed-chamber and much-needed sleep.

CHAPTER XXX.

ANOTHER VICTIM OF THE MOLLIES.

For a few days after the return of the unsuccessful delegation engaged in the work of killing Wm. M. Thomas, in accordance with the order of the Mahanoy City Convention, quiet reigned and nothing further was done in that direction. It will be remembered that the date fixed for the assassination was Saturday, the fifth of June. From the fact that McKenna judged it foolhardy, on account of the presence of Militia, to make the trial, it had been temporarily abandoned. In truth, the assassination was just as practicable then as it ever would be, from the isolated position in which the proposed victim was working. It served the detective's purpose to have the matter rest, at least until his reports could reach the Agency in Philadelphia, when he hoped, should the efforts be renewed, there would come officers on the ground to capture the would-be murderers, or at least save Thomas' life. But McKenna had no means of knowing how extremely busy Capt. Linden and his Coal and Iron force were at that particular moment. The detective was only inside the Mollie ring, and his friends were kept as much as possible in the dark as to police movements. In reality, he had about all that he could attend to—and so did the members of the open force. None found much leisure for amusement.

The Mollie Maguires, having passed sentence of death upon Thomas, it was not to be forgotten. Die he must. Some delay might occur, but the end in view was never relinquished. Meanwhile, Hurley, Gibbons, and Doyle were taken over to Mahanoy City and boarded, at the expense of the murderous society, in the house of a Mrs. Cosgrove until such time as O'Brien, the Bodymaster, might have every thing prepared for them. At the end of three days' stay, according to Kehoe's order, O'Brien having signally failed in leading them up to their prey, the trio went back to Shenandoah. There they tarried for a time, doing absolutely nothing.

In the interim McKenna experienced a return of disease, for several days was confined to his room, and much longer to his house. He suffered intensely, and was under the doctor's care, part of the time being delirious. That journey over the mountains, exposure to wet and cold air, with the accompanying excitement and mental pressure, all had their share in inducing a relapse of the intermittent fever, with which he had formerly been attacked, and for a time it threatened to assume a typhoid and very dangerous phase.

About the first day that the detective was strong enough to sit up in his chair, take an occasional walk to the door, and enjoy the warm sunshine, his heart was gladdened with the news that McAndrew had come home, his job in Luzerne County having terminated. McKenna was never more pleased in his life than when he grasped the hand of his superior officer, and McAndrew seemed equally joyful to see the face of his friend and division Secretary. Their interview, which occurred at Cooney's, was long and confidential. McKenna informed the President of nearly everything that and happened during his absence, including the orders the members were under from the Mahanoy Convention to kill Thomas, and at once gave into his possession all the lodge books and papers. It appeared to him, when this was accomplished, that health had been restored as through the working of a miracle, and the blood coursed more calmly in his veins. At least a very heavy load was lifted from his overburdened mind, and he breathed more freely than for weeks before, counting from the day of McAndrew's departure for Wilkesbarre. He held no longer the place of acting Bodymaster and thanked his lucky stars that he did not.

Time passed until the 27th of June. McAndrew had resumed active leadership of the Mollies in Shenandoah, and the detective yet continued ill, but was apparently fast convalescing. He had been sitting at the door of his boarding-house, enjoying the beautiful sunset, and wishing that his strength were once fully restored, when he heard footsteps, and soon McAndrew made his appearance and took a seat near him. They had only just begun talking of the weather and other matters, when Tom Hurley came up and joined the party. Shortly afterward John Morris, a very young, but solid man, with plenty of yellow hair, blue eyes, and heavy features, formed one of the group. Then Mike Doyle arrived, as he said, "jist from Number Three Hill." Mike Carey was already inside Cooney's, and emerged from the house, adding one more to the company. Following quickly a few words on comparatively trivial subjects, McAndrew inquired:

"Are any of yez going to Mahanoy City?"

"I am !" exclaimed Hurley.

These words were echoed by Doyle and Morris.

"Well, that's jist as it should be; for I have orders from Kehoe, if any man hesitates to obey me commands, to have him cut off for life at the very next meeting!" Then he added, turning to Carey:

"You must go to Number Three, and tell John Gibbons, who is now at home, that I want to see him here directly!"

"All right!" answered Carey, and he withdrew.

The men left with the detective to await the arrival of Gibbons did not say much to each other. They were more reticent than usual. The operative did not feel at all like talking. His active thoughts were trying to work out a difficult problem, something like this: In what manner could he forward news to Thomas that the assassins were again on his track?

How should he telegraph Mr. Franklin, that he might advise Linden to protect Bully Bill at the hazard of his own life ?. The only hope left was, that Carey, who had been his constant nurse and attendant, might be needed to go to Mahanoy with the rest, in case Gibbons were to refuse. He looked upon the golden sun, as it went down behind the somber hills, and just the last glimpse he caught of the orb, it appeared to him that its color had changed to a blood red. Would it rise on murder and violence ? His heart misgave him that it might, unless something could be thought of to reverse the present order of things. The detective was sure that no suspicion yet attached to him. He was known to be sick and incapable of physicial exertion, and McAndrew was there, at the head of the division. His orders must be listened to and obeyed. In his soul McKenna wished Gibbons might be absent, or unable, from some cause, to carry out his part of the arrangement. But his spirits sunk and his form trembled, so that he had to complain of a returning chill, caused by the night air, when he saw Carey, side by side with Gibbons, making his way up the path in the direction of the house. In a few minutes Gibbons reported. After the usual greetings, he took off his hat, wiped the perspiration from his forehead, and inquired :

"Well, McAndrew, what's the matther now ? "

The Bodymaster cast his eyes around, to see that all within hearing were Mollies, was evidently satisfied, and answered :

" These men here—Morris, Doyle, and Hurley—are going, by order of the County Delegate and our division, to Mahanoy City, to shoot Bill Thomas, in the morning, as he goes to his work ! I want to know if you are to be along ? '

" I'm agreed," said Gibbons, " as I don't want to stop around this neighborhood, anyhow, for I think I may be arrested for a few words I hev had with one of the bosses of Hecksher's Colliery—the fool thinks I mane to shoot him !

I don't care if I take part in the matter! Jist put a man in my place in the breast an' I'm wid yez!"

"Carey can take a hand at that; so there's nothin' to prevent the four of ye lavin' at once!" said McAndrew. "An' Dan Sweeney shall work for Morris, that he may miss no time—an' Hurley is not at work—so he'll lose nothing. Are ye well prepared for the business? Have ye all got proper weapons?"

The responses were in the affirmative, though no pistols were exhibited, and it only remained for Gibbons, who was in his shirt sleeves, to get a coat.

"I say, McKenna! You can lend me the old gray coat? You'll have no use for it until to-morrow, when I'll give it back to ye!'

This was said by Gibbons.

"The coat hangs within! Jist rache it, an' wear it, an' welcome," said the operative. To refuse would have seemed particularly suspicious.

The prevailing twilight deepened into darkness, and still the Mollies had not started on their errand of bloodshed, but, at about nine o'clock, the stars then shining out brightly, gave them light enough by which to see the pathway, and, bidding the Bodymaster, Secretary, and Mike Carey good-by, they quietly departed.

When their retreating footsteps could no longer be heard, McAndrew ordered the operative to go to bed, "unless he wanted more chills," and took his own route homeward.

"Yes, I'll retire directly," answered McKenna, who looked around to find Carey lightly dozing on the doorstep. He had no thought of going to his room without at least making an effort, even in his weak condition, to save Thomas or have the assassins arrested in the act. His plans were indistinctly formed, but he was determined to make a desperate movement in some direction. Linden's whereabouts, since his own recent illness, the detective knew

nothing of. The only plan, therefore, possible of accomplishment, was to send off a cipher dispatch to Mr. Franklin. In default of that he must try and deposit a written
message in the post-office, addressed to his Philadelphia
correspondent. The latter must naturally be too late, still
it would show that he was trying to do his duty by the man
whose life stood in jeopardy. Waiting until he thought
Carey was soundly asleep, McKenna noiselessly arose from
his bench, walked rather unsteadily to the door, and tried to
pass into the house beyond the slumbering Mollie. As he
did so, Carey roused himself, hurriedly rubbed his eyes, and
said :

"That's right! Let's get to bed!"

"I'm not slapy, an' am goin' to write a letther to me
sister before I retire," said McKenna.

"Very well!" responded Carey, "an' as I'm to slape wid
ye the night, ye kin sit up and write, while I'll jist rest me
for the morrow's work for Morris!"

Here was a predicament. The man was right. Transient
visitors were monopolizing the spare beds in the house, and
Cooney had provided, before retiring, that Carey would share
the detective's couch. What should he do?

"Upon the whole," finally said the operative, "I don'
feel slapy—you see I've had rather more of the bed, the past
wake, than wur pleasant—an' so I'll sit in here, an' rest me
eyes, without any light, for a while. You had better go up
so as to be arley awake fur your breakfast!"

"Oh, as fur that matther, divil a bit do I care fur slape,
aither! The bedroom is close, this fine avenin', an' I'll
kape ye company until it's made a little cooler!"

And Carey placed his knees against one door-post and
his head and back to the other, thus completely blocking up
the passage-way, and soon begun to snore like the good
sleeper that he was.

Every moment he thus wasted passed like a long hour to

14*

the impatient operative. The obstinacy of his companion was enough to provoke the ire of a more tranquil mind than he was the possessor of, and he nervously paced the floor of the small apartment, while his thoughts fairly burnt in his brain. Why was he ill? Why so weak that he could not thrust the miserable Carey out of his way, or gag and bind him with cords until he could fly to the telegraph office and send off that telegram? The idea of stunning him, as he slept, with a blow on the head from a club, even suggested itself, but was soon given up as too cruel for the situation. There were no means of getting out of the room, excepting through a window, and when he sought an exit in that way, Carey awoke once more and stared about him.

"Are ye gettin' luny agin, McKenna, that ye want to wait there by the windy, wid the cool air blowin' on ye? You'll have more of them chills! Sthand back!"

This was a sensible order for the sick man to obey, and it would cause a suspicion of insanity to refuse, hence he re-sumed his walk.

Later he turned to Carey and said :

"I tell ye, agin, ye had best get to bed! If ye don't, there'll be one miner late at the shaft-house in the mornin'! Lave me to myself! I can't slape, the night, wid the idea of the work that's to be done restin' on me conscience, so I'll stay below, where it is comfortable for me! Why in thunder don't you go to bed?"

"Faix," replied Carey, "an if the truth must be towld, I'm ordered by the docther never to lave ye until the mornin'. He says ye are touched in the head wid the faver an' the medicin', an' more's the token, I think he's quite right, for wasn't ye within an ace of throwin' yerself out at the windy, only jist now? Oh, no! Mike Carey knows how to obey orders, an wont give ye a chance to make away wid yerself until ye have back yer own siven sinses."

"The divil take you, an' the docther too! I'm just as

sound and sane this blessed minute as you are—or he
either—an' all I want is pace and quiet, an' that ye same
determined I sha'n't have ! "

The detective, now completely angry, began to walk the
room with rapid strides and gaze about him in the darkness,
searching for some weapon with which to demolish his too
careful guardian and nurse.

Seeing this, Carey shut the door, locked it, put the key in
his pocket, and, walking up to McKenna, took him gently
by the arm, saying :

"Come now, be aisy ! Don't look so fierce, but come
wid me to your room an' go straight to bed ! "

Had Carey known exactly the condition of the detective's
mind, he might have hesitated. It was well he did not, and
he persisted in his cajoling and pacificatory measures, until
the ludicrousness of the situation striking McKenna's
thoughts, he burst into a fit of loud laughter, and consented
—as that was the only alternative—to go to his room. But
neither of the men slept. One turned and tossed feverishly
and uneasily in the bed, and made such a disturbance that
the other was no sooner in a blissful slumber than he was
as suddenly aroused. At last, in sheer desperation, Carey
arose, dressed himself, and the operative was in hopes he
would go elsewhere, but he did not. On the contrary,
planting the back of the only chair in the room against the
closed and bolted door, he leaned backward, resting his
head near the latch, and soon slept soundly.

It was not until nearly sunrise that McKenna, almost
crazy with excitement and suspense, was left to himself.
Then Carey had to get his breakfast and be off to the colliery. It was now too late for McKenna to act, had he been
bodily able, and he sunk down, helpless, on his pillow, perfectly exhausted ; and deep lethargy came to his physical
and mental relief.

After breakfast, the morning of the 28th—a meal that,

strange to say, the operative ate with a better appetite than usual—he went to his room to prepare a report. Carefully locking the door, and hanging his hat over the keyhole, which he had a shrewd suspicion the chambermaid was in the habit of interviewing occasionally, to find out, if possible, the business in which he was engaged while fastened within, he seated himself at the table and started to write.

That hat was a terrible eyesore to the aforesaid maid-of-all-work, and she wondered many a time, as she subsequently confessed, "How it was that McKenna made his room so dark, exceptin' he were holding converse with the devil!"

It was light enough in the room for the detective, however, and the felt hat sufficed to keep prying eyes from discovering his employment. On this particular occasion the agent was doomed to disappointment, as he had hardly begun his highly important correspondence when he beheld Mike Doyle coming toward the house. Hastily throwing the writing materials into his valise, and carefully securing that depository, he unlocked his door and patiently waited, knowing that Doyle would probably wish to see him alone. In this supposition he was right, as the man soon afterward climbed wearily up the stairs. Doyle occupied a seat. McKenna once more shut the door, and, as soon as his visitor was a little rested, asked:

"Well, Mike, I suppose ye have missed him again?"

"No! We fixed him jist as he came into the colliery stable!"

'An' is that thrue?" inquired the detective, trying to appear cool and indifferent.

"Yes! But I must not stop here palaverin' wid you, when the rest of the boys are on the mountain, jist starvin' wid hunger and thirst!"

"Well, I'll get some whisky an' go up wid ye!'

"You go wid me? Why, you're sick, lad; an' last night

I said to Gibbons that ye looked like a passible braze might blow ye away like a flash o' smoke!"

"But I'm betther this mornin'—have passed the crisis of me disase, the docther has it—an' a bit of exercise will do me no harrum in the worruld!"

"Well, if you can sthand it I ken," said Doyle, and, after securing a little extra clothing for himself, the detective started for Ringtown Mountain. Happily, the spot was no more than three hundred yards distant from Cooney's residence, and they were soon in the presence of Hurley, Gibbons, and Morris, who were found sitting upon logs, rocks, and the ground, all covered with dust and perspiration, completely exhausted by their morning's work and the succeeding rapid journey from the Patch to Shenandoah.

Tom Hurley was the first to talk of the murder. In answer to McKenna's query, he said, in substance:

"Oh, Bully Bill's safe enough for the coroner by this time! When we got to Mahanoy City, we went direct to Mike O'Brien's house, as told by Frank McAndrew, an' Mike took us to Mrs. Costello's, where he got us some whisky and somethin' to eat, and a bottle of the raal stuff to take wid us, an' about daylight, with his directions, we started for the Patch, where Thomas lived. We went and sat by the drift-mouth, an' watched Thomas' house until he came out and went up to the colliery stable, the big doors of which were sprung wide open. After he had been in a while, an' talked wid the stable boss, an' the boss had left, we jist walked slowly up to the place. I stepped into the side door of the statle, through the blacksmith's shop, an' Gibbons in the other, an' blazed away at him, as he stood, wid one hand on a horse's mane. The fellow was game to the last. He had no weapon, but he just threw his black hat in my face, an' then, after bein' hit three or four times, ran behind the horses. I fired again, an he was worse hit, an' rather staggered. After that, Gibbons and Doyle sent him three or four, an' he fell, so did was of the horses, an' then John Morris, he came up, put in his pistol an' fired the last shot. Bully Bill never said wan word afther that, but lay quiet like, partly under the horse that was down. I have an idea that Bill Thomas won't shoot any more of us in this world. He's surely done for!"

The conversation was continued by the other men. John Morris said that Doyle put in his shots like a man, but Gibbons turned as pale as a sheet of paper. In turn Hurley and Doyle asserted that John Morris had shaken so with fear, when aiming at Thomas, that he shot and severely injured a second dumb beast. Each one made his statement, but the several relations were of the same general ten— that Thomas had been killed, that morning, at the colliery stable in Shoemaker's Patch.

The detective, after hearing the story of all the men and listening with evident interest, putting in a word to the effect that the victim had been rightly served—while, in his heart, he felt that a dastardly murder had been committed—returned to Shenandoah, hunted out Frank McAndrew, gave him news of the condition of their companions and their need of some kind of refreshment. He concluded:

"You get them some food, an' I'll take up some more whisky!"

McAndrew consented, went to his house, procured a supply of cold boiled ham, bread and butter and cheese, while McKenna bought a second bottle of good liquor, and they went in company to the mountain. In McAndrew's presence, the detective heard another rehearsal of the particulars of the attack and its termination, not materially differing from the one already detailed.

Gibbons wanted McAndrew and McKenna to give him a card, and he would leave at once, stopping at Kehoe's to secure money for traveling expenses. Having in view the continuance of the assassin within his convenient reach, the Secretary said he had no printed blanks, but when he, Gibbons, had once located, he could send him a letter and he would by that time be able to forward the card duly attested by the County Delegate. To this arrangement the man assented, and, in a short time, after obtaining change of clothing—taking care to return McKenna's coat—Gibbons departed and the rest of the assassins separated, each person taking a different route, for their homes. Hurley, Doyle, and Morris were to return to the colliery that evening, and resume their usual avocations, which they did.

The same day, my agent sent to Philadelphia a succinct account of all he had seen and heard. It was wonderful how McKenna improved in health. The excitement of the morning and night had seemingly checked his chill, put a stop to the fever, his appetite increased, and strength and nerve soon resumed sway. In the afternoon Mr. Linden reached Shenandoah, and, receiving the signal from McKenna, followed him to their place of meeting and verbally received the information the detective had already dispatched to Mr. Franklin.

The next official visit made by Linden was to Shoemaker's Patch.

CHAPTER XXXI.

HOLDING THE BREAKER.

WHEN the troubles of the first of June arose, and the Militia were ordered out by Governor Hartranft, Gen. Pleasant called Mr. Linden to him and said :

"I see by a report of Mr. Pinkerton's agent in Shenandoan—and we also have it from other good authority—that the strikers, including the Mollie Maguires and the members of the Miners' and Laborers' Union, are openly threatening the destruction of some of the company's more expensive works in Schuylkill County, among the rest West Shenandoah Colliery, which is only defended by two private watchmen. Can your men occupy and hold that breaker?"

"We can, or die in the attempt!" was the characteristic response.

"I admire your courage, Mr. Linden," said Gen. Pleasant, "but I am somewhat in doubt as to the result. However, there is no other course to pursue. Your men, headed by yourself, armed with the Winchester rifles and navy sixes, must make the trial!"

"We will leave on the next train," Linden answered

And they did go to Shenandoah, as was reported to McKenna by Gibbons and Hurley, arriving there the day following the one on which the first attack upon Thomas was to have been made. The militia-men were daily expected, but it was questioned in the minds of some whether its members were all to be depended upon in an emergency. That there were relatives of Mollies in the ranks was well known. Capt. Linden and eighteen men took charge of West Shenandoah Colliery, with the determination to defend and keep it working, preventing the miners from being driven away, if among the possibilities to do so.

The second of June the Mollies and other strikers made great preparations for a dance at Number Three Hill. Word was sent by special messengers that all who could should assemble on the night of that day for a monster workingman's parade, which was appointed for the third. Early in the morning the crowd began pouring in. There were delegates from Connor's Patch, Loss Creek, Number Three, Raven Run, and Griscom's Patch, as well as from Shenandoah. In the evening fires blazed from all the hillsides surrounding the collieries. There was the greatest and wildest excitement. The labor picnic at Number Three had seven or eight hundred persons in attendance.

There was plenty of music, and drink, and dancing, but the principal work seemed to be organizing for the exercises of the next day, and the evident object of these was to frighten people, who were quietly at work, away from the mines. The presence of the roughest characters in the country, armed to the teeth—some having as many as three revolvers displayed ostentatiously in their belts—and the open talk of the crowd, was sufficient to tell Linden and his devoted band that the morrow boded no good for them. Still they stood manfully at their posts, guarding every point and keeping off the approach of and attacks from all stragglers. Capt. Heisler, with more men, came to the rescue, and the Militia were expected by every train. Telegraphic messages kept the wires busy and messengers hurriedly going and coming.

Among the miners, the Welsh, English, German, and Poles mingled, and heartily joined hands with the Irish. For once feuds were forgotten, and nationalities all made common cause. The destruction of the collieries, or entire submission to the behests of those on the strike, had been decided upon.

While the music sounded, and dancing was going on at Number Three, McKenna held a secret conference with Linden. He gave him all the information regarding the proposed action for the morrow that he had been able to gather, and assured his friend he would have fierce work to do if he did not abandon the breaker.

"We can die there, then!" said Linden. "I will never give it up! Rather than that, may every man in my command—officers and all—be murdered! Let the strikers come! Some of them will bite the dust! I can tell them, we will be found well prepared!".

"I'll do everything in my power, at all events," responded

McKenna, "to discourage violence! Did any of the Chicago men recognize me, to-day?"

"I think not! If they did, they had sense enough not to speak of it!"

"I trust they may do the same thing to-morrow! If they come to shooting, I'm sure I'll get out of the range of those Winchesters on the double quick!"

Linden advised him to remember to do so, as he could not tell what might occur.

"They—the police—look upon you as the worst and most desperate character in the Mollie crowd!"

"I know it!" said McKenna, "but they'll learn their mistake one of these days!"

It was noticeable that, when communicating with Linden, the detective dropped his well-worn brogue, and conversed in his ordinary tone, using few Celtic terms.

The conference was brief, and with a "good night" the detectives separated, McKenna returning to the camp-fires, and Linden seeking sleep upon his bed of hay.

When he reached Number Three, McKenna learned that a portion of his brother Mollies, fearing to face the consequences of the parade—as it was called—but, as it really was, a mob, comprising all the elements of a commune and a riot—had fled to Ringtown Mountain and there organized a local guard, or reserve force. Among these stay-at-home heroes—who received loud shouts, hisses of derision, and the appellation of "craven-hearted cowards"—was Mike, *alias* Muff Lawler. He would have nothing to do with the celebration, sneaked away and hid himself at Ringtown. The operative, having in mind the pusillanimous manner in which the same man had retreated from Dick Flynn, at Colorado Colliery, months before, leaving him to face the infuriated fellow alone, was not much surprised that Lawler had no appetite for the next day's work, but said nothing. In fact, if the truth were told, the detective did not really blame Mike for his later action, and, had not duty called him to take part in the proceedings, would have adopted a similar course. But he must stay and see the affair through. It was not his time to run away.

The night passed without the occurrence of any overt act. The morning of the third had but fairly opened when new delegations commenced coming in, and Marshals Walker and Johnson begun the work of forming the line. Impromptu flags were prepared, the drums beat, and the uncouth assemblage was soon ready to march.

Fenton Cooney was deputed to take charge of the rear and form the stragglers. One Fitzpatrick, a boss at Heckler's, assisted.

Nine o'clock came, and as the crowd was about to move the Sheriff of Schuylkill County rode up, accompanied by a Superintendent of the Coal and Iron Company. The former inquired as to the cause of the assemblage.

" Only a bit of a parade," was the plausible response, and the two men, apparently satisfied, rode away.

The intention of the men was to have an imposing procession, ending at Mahanoy City, and, meantime, to force the miners, at every colliery in their way, to quit work and join, or go to their homes. They were determined to stop operations, if they had to kill the workmen. But the Sheriff was not informed of this portion of the programme.

When the mob reached West Shenandoah Colliery it mustered, despite the disaffection of a few, some seven hundred strong, all firmly resolved that mining should not proceed in the Mahanoy valley. They marched away at a brisk pace, and thought themselves invincible. But at the road skirting the works mentioned was revealed a sight for which they were all unprepared. The blackened walls of the breaker stood out boldly in relief against the blue sky ; the sun shone upon twenty armed men, ranged in a compact line, surrounding and cutting off approach to the mouth of the slope and the engine-house, with arms, bright and gleaming, forming an inclosure of human bodies. Their repeating rifles were threatening. That obstacle did not seem so easy to surmount, and the mob stood at the foot of the hill, wavered, and presently the Grand Marshal ordered a pause. Part of his force had crossed the Reading Railway track, just before it passes under the Lehigh bridge, and there they waited, undecided what course to pursue.

It was a trying moment for the police, under Linden, Heisler being unavoidably absent in the city.

"Are you going to send the men from the slope, and stop the works?" asked Walker, in a loud voice.

"Go on about your business!" answered Linden, resting one hand on his piece. "The men in the mine are under the protection of the law! They will stay where they are, and you must not molest them!"

"Forward!" commanded Walker. But his tone lacked confidence.

"Halt!" shouted Linden.

But few obeyed Walker's call—and they stepped back hastily, as though they had blundered, when, at a signal from Linden, a score of Winchester rifles promptly came to the shoulders of as many hardy and resolute men, ready for the expected order to "fire."

McKenna was the most eccentric and savage appearing Mollie Maguire in the whole seven hundred. His old, soft hat, knocked in at the sides, yellow hair flying wildly in the breeze, a long, patched, gray coat, with two revolvers in his belt, beside a big hickory club which he carried in his hand; even the men from Chicago looked upon him as a prominent target to receive the contents of their already directed weapons. By the side of the detective was a sleek bull-terrier, which he had carefully raised and just brought out, trained ready for the pit, its tongue protruding, and showing the white teeth appearing fully as murderous and ugly as his master.

The Mollies knew—if the rest did not—that each one of those bright gun-barrels could send sixteen deadly messen‐gers into their ranks without reloading. They also knew that Linden—"Captain Jack," as he there received christen ing--was at the head of the force and would fight to the last drop of blood in his body. His rifle would be aimed with those of his followers.

Walker realized the gravity of the situation in a moment, and did not repeat his order. Soon there was a whisper of consultation. McKenna suggested that "twenty times six‐teen wor three hundred an' twenty, an' that was the number that must fall before them Winchesters were exhausted! An' wur it all worth even fifty lives?"

The Marshal and other leading men thought not, and, scowling fiercely back at Linden and his Spartan band, they quietly moved on, in the direction of the bridge, leaving the breaker undisturbed. The muzzles of the Winchesters and the faces of the men behind them showed that the police were not to be trifled with.

The mob had decided—and wisely too—it was not a propi‐tious moment to compel Linden and his men to retire—that another time might as well be selected for seizing the colliery and forcing a suspension of work. Jack Delaney, Peirce Walker, Ben Johnson, Fitzpatrick, and John Gibbons, who had all been industrious in raising and organizing the rabble, it was noticed, found themselves among the foremost to recognize the force there was in Linden's metallic argument.

The awkward squad surged along toward Mahanoy City, forcing those it encountered to join the ranks.

At Hazleton a prisoner was rescued, and the law defied.

Fox's Colliery, which had begun to work, was stopped by force, and the men driven home.

The owners of Bowman's Colliery, hearing that the crowd

was coming, sent off their miners and discontinued operations before the advance guard hove in sight.

The Sheriff made a stand, with a few men, at Jackson's
Hill, but he was derided, loudly cursed; and the communists marched onward in spite of the law and its minions.

The Foundry Colliery was stopped, and its men ran away
in a fright.

Soon word was brought that three hundred men, from the
vicinity of Hazleton, had already entered Mahanoy City,
caused a disturbance, and some of their number been arrested by the police and placed in the lock-up.

At last Mahanoy City was gained, and its streets found
swarming with demoralized citizens. The mob had accumu
lated strength until it numbered over two thousand men, and
everything was swept, like chaff in a west wind, before it.
All business was suspended.

The first cry of the communists was, "To the rescue of the
Hazleton boys!" and the Chief Burgess, Eckman by name,
was hunted up and politely invited to release the men he had
in custody. He carefully examined the faces of the persons
surrounding him and consented. The prisoners soon formed
part of the line of the parade. The principal streets were
marched through. Disorder and lawlessness prevailed, but
as there was no one to oppose the rioters, little, if any, personal violence ensued. The striking miners had everything
their own way. The collieries were all blocked, and the men
sent home unharmed.

One colliery sounded its shrill whistle, adding to the pre
vailing confusion and alarm, the engineer having deserted
the works, carrying the cord attached to the mechanism with
him. A crowd rushed to the spot. Gibbons climbed upon
the boiler, which it was feared might explode, opened the
valve, the steam escaped, and the danger was over.

McKenna, the drum corps, and those who could pay
and dinner at Clark's Emerald House. Those who had no

money procured food, wherever possible, from the citizens. While he was eating, the detective heard firing on the street. Followed close by Doyle, Thompson, and McCormick, he rushed out to see what was the trouble. It seems that the mob, when about to attack Little Drift Colliery, had been met by a deputy sheriff, backed by a few city policemen. The officer had read the riot act and ordered the disturbers of the public peace to disperse, but without other effect than to cause them to go on faster toward the colliery. One, Tim Jolley, being excited, fired a shot into the mob, hitting nobody. Then a rush was made on the Sheriff, and shooting became general from and in all directions. Jolley was quickly knocked down, and his pockets searched. Some one carried off his watch and chain, another his money, and yet others secured his hat and outer clothing. Friday O'Donnell, according to his own story, did some rapid shooting at about that time, but was not aware whether he hit any one. Jim McAllister received a cut in the head, while engaged in throwing rocks at the officers. He had no weapon. McGinnis had a pistol wound in the head, but it was not a fatal one.

Finally, the officers having retreated without severe injury, the disorderly procession moved for the return march to Shenandoah, and the parade and the riot ended at the same time. Strange to say, not a person was killed in the entire day's transactions.

The Militia arrived that night, and thenceforward there were to be no more serious riots in the county—at least not as long as the soldiers remained. But violence and assassination did not cease. On the contrary, bad blood had been stirred. It would not settle until innocent men were murdered. A few arrests were made of the leading rioters, but no particular punishment was ever meted out to them. The Mollies swore *alibis*, without regard to truth or conscience.

About the sixth of June Tom Hurley, who had a brother

a member of the Girardville company of Militia, tried to accomplish, all by himself, the butchery of Capt Heisler. James Hurley was on duty with Heisler at West Shenandoah Colliery, and, late at night, Tom Hurley came up and spoke to them. In Heisler's temporary absence the brothers arranged that James should contrive to leave Heisler alone a few moments, when Tom could easily pick him off from an ambush. Heisler returned to his post and Tom bid the two "good night," saying he must go home. Walking but a short distance, however, he plunged into the underbrush, took a detour, and crawled stealthily up again within pistol range of Heisler and James Hurley. Finally he heard the latter say :

"Captain, it's coming chilly ! I'll just go to the office and get my overcoat !"

"No !" answered the Captain. "That will never do ! We are put here on guard, and here must stay !"

Heisler acted as if he suspected Tom, at least Jim had to remain where he was. Heisler's life, for a time, was safe.

In about half an hour, during which Tom Hurley, with pistol leveled full upon the Captain, remained watching in his place of concealment, Jim Hurley exclaimed :

"Faith, I've come out here with no arms on me at all ! I've left me revolver ! I'll go and get it !"

"No !" again answered Heisler. "You can take the rifle ! The navy six is enough for me !"

Cursing the stupidity of the man who refused to be left alone, so that he might kill him, Tom Hurley, after stopping where he was until nearly overcome by sleep, cautiously arose from the ground, and, without making a sound to indicate his presence, stooped low and moved skulkingly away. He told McKenna of his adventure, the next day and Linden was soon in possession of the fact. When subsequently consulted about his conduct on the occasion Capt. Heisler said he had heard considerable about Tom

Hurley, and believed that the brothers might attempt some trap upon him. Still, when he refused to be left alone, he had not the least suspicion that in so doing he twice thwarted the would-be assassins.

Jim Hurley was no more placed on guard at Shenandoah Colliery.

The resumption was not again interfered with, and by the sixteenth of June became quite general in the coal regions. Even the Mollies went to work, having stood out as 'ong as they deemed it possible, and finding that, without their aid, the company were able to continue their mining operations.

Mr. Linden, at about this time, met some adventures, which must be described.

CHAPTER XXXII.

LINDEN FORMS AN ACQUAINTANCE.

CAPTAIN LINDEN made a flying visit to Shoemaker's Patch, when once informed of the attempt upon the life of Wm. M. Thomas, where he met the injured man, frescoed and ornamented with plentiful patches and plasters, and bolstered up in bed, loudly proclaiming he was quite well enough to resume his daily work, and that he should do so on the morrow, despite the advice of an army of surgeons and nurses. Considering that he had received four serious gunshot wounds, one disabling the fingers of his right hand, two in the neck, and one penetrating the chest, this might be thought rather rash talk and conduct. Linden so believed, and endeavored to soothe and curb him. It was of no use. The madcap bruiser said he would kill anybody who tried to

prevent his going out the next day. And, in defiance of all
the laws of physic, pharmacy, surgery, and precedent, he did
walk to the stables the second morning subsequent to the
shooting. One of the bullets, hitting him in the neck, had
plowed a passage, through muscular fibre and cuticle, missing by only half an inch the inner jugular vein and adjacent
carotid artery, and, should the coats of any of these large
blood-courses slough away, his death would be certain and
speedy. Without awaiting this crisis, and with the first
plasters still on the hurts, the careless and reckless man resumed his job in the stables. Fortunately the injuries continued healthy, rapidly healed, and in a few weeks Thomas
was just as strong as ever, and as anxious to kill a Mollie
Maguire as before receiving the shots of his assailants.

Linden sought to learn all the particulars of the assault,
concealing the knowledge he had already received, and
therefore interrogated Thomas closely, generally securing
prompt responses to his queries. In answer to the question :

" Do you know any of your assailants ? "

Thomas answered :

" No ! But shall know some of them if ever I see them
again ! A feller generally recollects the faces of them what
pulls a pistol and shoves it inter his face ! Leastways I do ! "

" That's true ! " assented Linden.

" There was but four of 'em ! I'm sure of that ! I saw
em before they got nigh the stable, as they were sitting near
the drift-mouth, but thought nothing of it. It was no new
thing to find men there, and even strangers. I had been
talkin' a bit with the stable boss, when I again saw the
fellows, this time coming toward the stable. Still, I had no
suspicion of their purpose. The next thing I recollect was
a youngster, sticking a bright seven shooter in my face ! I
went fur him, and seized the pistol with my hand. It was
discharged as I caught it. I let go, and shied my hat in his
face, and just afterward another of the party came up and fired

at me ! After that, two more came and followed suit, when I thought it time to get shelter, so I went behind a horse, and they fired and hit the horse, and he fell, and I went down with one leg sorter under him, an' they looked in, saw me as they thought, dying—but I'll let them know I'm good for the lives of some of them bucks yet !—an' left the place It was about half-past six in the morning—just nigh sun-up, an' I could see them as plain as I can see you ! Of course I'd know the first one that shot, and I believe I'd recognize the rest if brought before them. I mean to live to see the scoundrels punished ! If the law will not do it, Bill Thomas will ! The sneaking, cowardly curs went up the hill like a shot, and were out of sight in two minutes, before anybody could catch them ! One walked a little lame. I recollect that, for I stood up as soon as I could and looked after them Dr. Bissell, of Mahanoy City, got here soon afterward and dressed my hurts. He had the impudence tell me I must keep my bed for the next ten days at least ! I'll see him and all his plasters, pots, and vials in h—l before I'll do that ! "

Linden tried hard to convince the wounded man that it was as much as his life was worth to venture out until the result of his hurts could be definitely ascertained, but made no impression upon the stubborn fellow. Seeing that this would not succeed, the officer tried another tack, and found Bill ready and willing to second his efforts in hunting up and arresting the would-be assassins. Said the operative :

" Now, Thomas, if you will not obey me, or your friends and physician, I do hope you will bear in mind what I say in another direction ! "

" What is it ? " asked the frescoed man, sullenly.

" I want a promise that, if any one asks who shot you, the answer shall be, ' I don't know !' "

" Neither *do I*—so that'll be no lie ! "

" Well, if people inquire what the four men were like, say.

for the present, that there was so much smoke you could not distinguish their faces or figures!"

"I'll do it, Captain" responded Bill, with an oath and a groan. "I'll do it! But what is it for? That's what I want to know!"

"I'll tell you! If these Mollies hear that you, their intended victim cannot recall their appearance—in fact, would not know them if they were to come again before you —they will be emboldened to remain in the neighborhood. In the meantime, I can be on the lookout, and you may rest assured, if I once get my hands on them, they'll be put in a safe place, where you can come and identify them! I have your description of the parties, and do not think I will be long in running them down! Do I have you, word?"

"Yes, Captain! I'll promise to be straight out in the business, if you think it'll help in bringing the crowd to jail! I do hope to see the day when the scoundrels will suffer for the deed!"

"They will be arrested, you may be sure, when found!"

Once more impressing upon Thomas' mind the necessity for silence and caution, Linden left the house, and, the same day, returned to Shenandoah. While Thomas was a desperado, had the reputation of an amateur pugilist and a rough customer, all this did not palliate the crime of his enemies. I was very anxious to have them captured, and work was at once commenced upon that portion of the business.

Wm. M. Thomas was of Welsh descent, and his real name was Willmad Frank, but he was generally known as Wm. M. Thomas—or "Bully Bill." Why people persisted in calling him by the latter coarse title, he told Linden, he had no knowledge. He did not particularly delight in the *alias*, yet it was quite appropriate, in slang parlance, being founded upon his daring and reckless personal character. His father's name was Frank. That should have been his own, but he was everywhere denominated Thomas.

When the Mollies heard that Bill was not dead, after all the powder and ball that had been wasted upon him, they were enraged. It was not policy for them to emit their wrathful feelings on the public streets and in the presence of strangers, but in their own secret circle they were loud in denunciations of Hurley, Gibbons, Doyle, and Morris, as foolish bunglers, who did not have the nerve to face " Bully Bill ! " The four worthies received little sympathy from those who knew their part in the tragedy, and those who did not were as likely to speak their feelings to their very faces as in the presence of others. Gibbons had gone. Morris, Doyle, and Hurley were at work. The general public merely read the published accounts of the attempted murder in the newspapers, and gave little thought to solving the riddle as to who had wrought the deed, or wherefore it had been done. It was charged upon the Mollie Maguires, however, as it was known that Thomas had made himself peculiarly obnoxious to that class, and it was supposed his end would one day come through use of their pistols. At present Wm. M. Thomas survived and swore eternal vengeance.

It was not difficult for McKenna and Linden to form a plan by which the latter should become acquainted with the prominent Mollies in and about Shenandoah. A time was appointed when Linden should encounter his brother detective at Cleary's saloon, where the clan mostly congregated, after the departure of McHugh, and after the little misunderstanding McKenna and his companions had had with Micky Cuff about his teeth. They entered the place separately, one day, finding themselves in the presence of Muff Lawler, John Delaney, of Number Three, and some others, when Linden pretended to recognize McKenna as an old acquaintance, from Buffalo, whose face he had not seen for several years. They shook hands heartily and were greatly rejoiced at the seemingly accidental encounter.

"Glad to see you again!" said Linden.

"It plazes me, too, tho' I can't say much for ae sarvice ye are in," answered the detective, scowling upon Linden rather ferociously.

"Oh, that need not part old friends!" responded Linden. "You know I always perform my duty, and as long as I say nothing about your Buffalo matter, and do not go out of my way to harm you or your friends, I don't see the need for quarreling! Come, let's have something in remembrance of old times!"

"I'm agreed!" responded McKenna, and he was prompt in walking up to the bar, followed by the assembled Mollies, all of whom drank at the Captain's expense. Had he not shown himself an old friend of McKenna, there were few of the Mollies who would have cared to take a glass in his company. They soon found him a gentleman of his word, and as he had promised not to hurt McKenna, they felt he would be equally lenient to that person's comrades. Lawler was particularly struck with the frank and manly manner of Linden, and said he was "proud to form his acquaintance!"

Before Linden left the crowd it increased considerably in numbers and its members were greatly under the influence of the liquor they had consumed.

The ice once broken, the Mollies did not wonder, or indulge suspicion, when they saw Linden and McKenna occasionally in company. It was not often they were found together, and then there were always others present, to prevent any private talk; but it was easy enough, when he wanted to meet the officer alone, for McKenna to write it— as well as the time and place of conference—on a bit of paper, in his room, in cipher, and, when occasion gave opportunity, quietly place the communication in Linden's hand, or in a side pocket of his coat.

On one occasion, the detective, having something particular to transmit, made the open boast in Cleary's that, his revolver being empty, he would "do" Linden out of a fresh charge. Slipping out of the room, a few minutes later, he walked to the previously-appointed rendezvous, at the old bridge, by the side of West Shenandoah Colliery, held the necessary business talk, secured some cartridges, and, in half an hour, was back at the saloon, exhibiting his loaded pistol, and chuckling over the sly manner in which ammunition had been obtained from the enemy.

As a natural consequence of his defense of the Colliery, and similar employment in other sections of the country, Linden was soon well known as a policeman who had been placed at the head of a special force ; but his connection with my Agency was carefully guarded until such time as it might be necessarily or unavoidably revealed.

At another time, Linden saw McKenna in Cleary's place, and, after a drink, in the course of conversation asked the Shenandoah Secretary if he had any objection to talk over old times, and if he should speak out before the company—nearly all Mollie Maguires.

"Av coorse you can !" said McKenna in a loud voice.

"We are all friends of Jim McKenna," remarked Muff Lawler ' so see to it that you don't say anything amiss of him !'

"No danger of that," responded Linden. "He's too good a chum of mine, and I have known him too long, to do or say anything to harm him !"

In the course of the conversation Linden accidentally let out the supposed fact that, while McKenna was the best-hearted man alive, and the truest friend, he would traffic in counterfeit money, if he had a chance, and when beset, was a very devil in a scuffle, as one fellow in Buffalo had found out when it was too late. McKenna said very little, and allowed his friend to freely chaff him to his face simply so sponding that he knew the source whence the stories came and did not care for them.

After Linden had gone, Muff Lawler took McKenna aside and whispered in his ear:

" I don't believe, Jim, that Linden would arrest you for any crime whatever ! He seems a jolly chap, and is too generous an' true to take in an old companion ! "

" He is mightily changed, if he is not all ye can say that't good," responded the detective; " but let us be wary, even of him ! He's a sworn peace officer, an' I know he'll do his duty, no matther who sthands in the way ! It is my intintion never to throw myself in his road, if I happen to be wanted for anything in particular ! "

" Well," resumed Muff, " ye may be all correct, but it seems to me that I could depind upon him and never be decaved ! "

Linden had thus built the foundation for what was fated to be a considerably extended and intimate acquaintance with the Mollie Maguires.

The shooting of Wm. Thomas, and its failure in a fatal result, caused extra exertions to be put forth by the members of the Mollie order, in different localities, to make trouble for the Coal and Iron Company, the Superintendents of which were determined to continue work in their own way.

Pat Butler, Bodymaster at Loss Creek, came to McKenna, a few days subsequent to the incidents just detailed, and said his men were anxious to put an end to shipping of coal over the Lehigh Valley Road, and wanted his assistance. The operative demurred, said McAndrew had returned, was the man to apply to, and finally refused to entertain any such proposition. A little later, rails were torn up on the road mentioned, and trains must have been smashed in pieces and people killed had not the engineer, who was on the alert, discovered the trouble in season. Butler, it will be remembered, was in favor of the Catawissa bridge-burning heretofore alluded to, and which had been given up when outsiders became interested. He was still solicitous that the job should be done, by Mollies alone, but McKenna boldly opposed the work, and after a while forced him to abandon the project.

The next plan was broached by Thompson, of Number Three, who sought aid in throwing the passenger train off the track of the Shenandoah Branch. McKenna caused a delay, urging want of men, and then agreed, but finally backed out, saying it was too dangerous to human life. So this was effectually stopped, and the men gathered for the purpose of its execution were sent home.

Determined to do something devilish, Thompson, Doyle, Murphy, and John Dean, came together and turned loose the brake of a horse car, loaded with iron, let it fly down, over the steep grade of the main line of the road, when they knew the passenger train was coming up from an opposite direction. Had not the flying and deadly missile—for it sped over the track like an arrow from a bow—been observed at Loss Creek Store, and a word of warning telegraphed the cars to get on the side track, hundreds of lives would have been wantonly sacrificed.

A little later, Tom Hurley and Jack Hilbert entered Penitentiary Drift, then being worked by a Mr. Schwartz, took away all the tools, powder, and harness, and the property they could not carry destroyed and emptied into the creek.

Soon after these things occurred the detective was given fresh cause for uneasiness, in the expressed determination of Frank McAndrew to once more leave for another mining locality in search of work. Should the Bodymaster carry out his threat the management of the division would again be left to McKenna, a consummation not devoutly to be wished. The detective, therefore, endeavored to show to the perverse McAndrew that the work already begun would soon result in a general resumption of mining all over the

15*

Mahanoy Valley, in spite of the strikers, when work would be as plentiful there as anywhere. All he had to do was to counsel quiet, do his best to put the men in good humor, and he would not be forced to remove from Shenandoah.

"This is all mighty fine," answered McAndrew. "Still, it's nothin' but talk, an', be gorra! it taks cash to buy the childer clothin' fur their wearin' and bread for their atin'! If I don't get somethin' to do in a week or two, I tell you, seriously, that Shenandoah won't see my face for a long while! I'll turn me back upon it wid all the speed imaginable!"

Would McAndrew desert the place, and once more leave the Secretary in the toils? McKenna determined that he should not go, if he could find anything to prevent. But what could he do to keep him at home?

CHAPTER XXXIII.

PRESIDENT GOWEN AND THE LEGISLATIVE COMMISSION.

THE Legislature of Pennsylvania, listening to the repeated demands of the dissatisfied and the call of the Anti-Monopoly Convention, heretofore alluded to, in 1875 appointed a committee to investigate the affairs of the Philadelphia and Reading Company. That commission convened at Atlantic City, New Jersey, the 29th of July, in the same year, and heard such testimony as the complainants could bring before it, as well as the pleadings of the able attorneys representing the prosecutors of the inquiry. Mr. Gowen, the President of the Philadelphia and Reading Railway Company, personally appeared before the committee and made answer to the charges. I have deemed it necessary, in order that the careful reader may fully comprehend this entire operation and the extent to which it reached, to give a brief abstract of the principal points in Mr. Gowen's exhaustive, comprehensive, and unanswerable argument, which is hereunto appended :

After furnishing a condensed history of the Reading Railroad Company, which was chartered in 1833, and opened to the coal regions in 1842—enlarging gradually from a line of fifty-eight miles of single track, in 1835, to over one thousand miles, in 1870—468 of these being in the coal fields alone—Mr. Gowen alluded in fitting terms to the various trials the Company had had in the Legislature, while he was counsel, opposing franchises to other companies securing liberty to mine iron and coal. He succeeded, at one time, by an amendment, in preventing an act, in favor of an antagonistic corporation, having any operation in Schuylkill County. Then the Company bought up large quantities of coal land and had the Franklin Coal Company incorporated. This was followed by the strike of 1871, after which the Reading management determined to enter the field as coal and iron miners and obtain a grant from the Legislature for the formation of an auxiliary coal and iron corporation. This gave rise to the Laurel Run Improvement Company. They bought one hundred thousand acres of land, and it was conveyed to the Company. Forty millions of dollars were thus expended.

Mr. Gowen subsequently traced, in brilliant and striking contrast, the respective positions of New York and Philadelphia, showing the benefits to be conferred upon Pennsylvania by preventing the grasping New York associations from obtaining a monopoly of the southern as they had of the northern coal fields.

The Reading Company, now that Mr. Gowen's plans have succeeded, ships from the city of Philadelphia alone two millions five hundred thousand tons of coal a year, in vessels; has shipped as much as ninety thousand tons a week, and the commerce and prosperity of the port of Philadelphia, as a shipping point, are much more dependent upon the industry which it brings to it than upon all others put together. It can now say to the manufacturer: " Here is a Company that owns lines of railroad in the heart of a rich agricultural region, where labor is plenty and always will be abundant, we own the coal mines, and you can come here to locate your works, in the confidence that self-interest alone, and the worship of the almighty dollar—generally supposed to be implanted in the breast of a corporation, without regard to any benevolent or philanthropic ideas in the minds of the gentlemen connected with the Company—will induce us to let you have this fuel at less than you can buy it from an individual."

After giving some pertinent figures regarding the productiveness of the coal region—alluded to in an opening chapter of this work—the President went on to state that, at the end of the year, while the Schuylkill had only increased, in 1870, to four millions eight hundred and fifty-one thousand eight hundred and fifty-five tons, or twenty-nine per cent., in the same time the Wyoming region increased from two millions nine hundred and forty-one thousand eight hundred and seventeen tons, to seven millions eight hundred and twenty-five thousand one hundred and twenty-eight tons, or one hundred and sixty per cent. Here was an increase of one hundred and sixty-six per cent., against twenty-nine, due to the fact that the Wyoming region was controlled by large corporations which could expend money in developing the land, and who were not liable to be prostrated by a monetary panic.

In the four years, from 1870 to 1874, the tonnage of the Schuylkill region has increased thirty-three and twenty-three one-hundredths per cent., and that of the Wyoming only eighteen and one one-hundredth per cent.

The peculiar business transactions of factors in Philadelphia were then ably discussed, and received at Mr Gowen's hands the exact treatment they deserved, when he turned his attention to the retail dealers, and some of the iniquities of their system, after which he examined, *seriatim*, the four principal charges made against the Company, in the following order : 1st, of detention of cars ; 2d, of short weights ; 3d, of an unfair distribution of cars ; and 4th, of a combination, or conspiracy, to control production, which, if proven, renders it amenable to the law, and which shows it to have been guilty of an abuse of its corporate franchises.

As to detention of cars, Mr. Gowen explained the cause to be unavoidable, at times, but said the Company always endeavored to deal justly by its patrons. Detentions were principally from accidents to trains and to cars. They employed a Missing Coal Agent, and did everything in their power to be prompt.

The speaker made a complete demurrer to the charge of short weight, and fairly turned the tables upon those fighting his corporation, exhibiting the result of a test given the retail dealers in Philadelphia, greatly to the discredit of the latter. In many cases these very honorable retailers sold from thirteen to sixteen and eighteen hundred pounds of coal for a ton, annually realizing a handsome percentage from their villainy.

Unequal distribution of cars was equally well refuted. Then the opponents of the company said : "Philadelphia is not the place to make the investigation in. We must 'beard the lion in his den.' We must go right up to Pottsville. The newspapers of Philadelphia are worth nothing. They are all in the interest of the Company, and as for Mr. Gowen, he will not venture ten miles out of Philadelphia, if he does, he will be shot by the miners. We will take the committee where everybody is opposed to the Company." It was just where Mr. Gowen wanted to go. His adversa ries had two weeks, and then there was an adjournment of nearly ten days more, in which to prepare for the Pottsville campaign. Mr. Bronson moved his headquarters to Pottsville, and examined the matter carefully. Mr. Gowen was present. Threats did not intimidate him. What was the result? The allegations were abandoned. Even the discharged employés of the Reading Company, when put on the witness' stand, said nothing to reflect upon its management.

As to the charge of unlawful confederation, the speaker was equally felicitous. The object in entering into alliance with the New York Companies was simply this—to announce as the future policy of the Company that the price of coal should be lowest at the mines, and increase with every mile of distance over which it was carried ; that it should be just that much higher in the city of New York than it was in the city of Philadelphia as was due to the increased distance of the former from the region where the coal was produced. It was so adjusted that, instead of coal being a dollar a ton cheaper in New York, the difference between the price of coal in the port of Philadelphia and in the city of New York was exactly one dollar a ton in favor of Philadelphia ; and coal in Boston was exactly so much higher than coal in Philadelphia as was due to the cost of carrying it from Philadelphia to Boston—namely, about one dollar and sixty cents per ton.

After speaking of the loss from deterioration of coal, by exposure to the atmosphere, the risk of capital invested, and faulty veins, Mr. Gowen thus alluded to troubles in the coal region : " It will not do to say that these troubles result from the inadequacy of the price paid for labor, because, without exception, the rates paid are the highest in the world. The high rates have had the effect of attracting to the coal region a surplus of labor, more than sufficient to do the work required ; and it is the effort of this surplus to receive as employment which it cannot really get that has led to all these disturbances." He would not be understood as reflecting in any manner upon the laboring class of the community. He believed ninety-five out of every one hundred of the men employed about the mines in the coal region to be decent, orderly, law-abiding, respectable men ; but there is among them a class of agitators—a few men, trained in the school of the Manchester cotton spinner—brought here for the purpose of creating confusion and to stir up dissension between the employer and the employed. Mr. Gowen here grew earnestly eloquent, and his language is quoted in full :

'I yield to no man living in the respect and admiration that I pay to the workingman. Let him who will erect an altar to the genius of labor, and, abject as an eastern devotee, I worship at its shrine,

> "'Gathering from the pavement crevice, as a floweret from the soil,
> The nobility of labor, the long pedigree of toil.'

"I ask your attention, therefore, for a few moments to my advocacy of the rights of labor. I stand here as the champion of the rights of labor—as the advocate of those who desire to work and who have been prevented from doing so. I stand here to arraign before you a class of two or three men out of every one hundred, who, by their machinations and by their agitation, have held in absolute idleness and starvation thousands and thousands of men for months. Why, gentlemen, look at what we have undergone. When people object to a profit of twenty-five or thirty cents upon the ton of coal, I ask them to look at what those who mine coal have had to submit to during the last six months. I have had printed for your use a statement, from the daily reports coming to me during the strike, of the outrages in the coal region. Here I want to correct an impression that goes out to the public, that these outrages are intended to injure the property of the employer. They are not. We do not believe that they are. They are perpetrated for no other purpose than to intimidate the workingmen themselves and to prevent them from going to work. I shall not read the list; it is at your service ; and you can look over it and see the position we have occupied for months. But let me mention a few of the glaring instances of tyranny and oppression. At a colliery, called the Ben Franklin Colliery, the employés of which were perfectly satisfied with their wages, had accepted the reduction early in the season, and were working peacefully and contentedly, the torch of the incendiary was applied to the breaker at night. These men, having families to support, working there contentedly and peacefully were driven out of employment by a few dangerous men, simply for the purpose of preventing them from earning their daily bread. I had some interest in the subject of the amount of their wages, and I asked the owner of the colliery what his miners were actually earning at the time when they were prevented from working by the burning of the structure in which they were employed, and he told me that the lowest miner on his pay-list earned sixty dollars a month, and the highest one hundred and thirty dollars ; and yet, although these men were peaceful, law-abiding men, they were driven out of employment by an incendiary fire. At another colliery within five or six miles of this, a band of twenty or thirty men, in the evening—almost in broad daylight—went to the breaker, and by force drove the men away and burnt the structure down. It belonged to a poor man. It was a small operation. The savings of his lifetime were probably gone, and his own employés, who had nothing against him, and who were perfectly willing to work, were thrown out of employment, and probably remain out of employment to this day."

All schemes for causing the miner to provide for himself, when sickness and trouble came, having been found unavail ing, from the improvidence of the men themselves, the Company announced, in January, 1876, a rule that, whenever a man was killed in its service, a certain sum should be paid for his funeral expenses ; that his widow should receive a fixed payment each week, in money, for a definite period, or so long as she remained a widow ; and that every minor child of the deceased, unable to work, should have a designated amount, weekly, all of which was to be paid out of the treasury of the Company. Even this charitable and beneficent plan was ridiculed by the people whose business it was to destroy confidence and create trouble in the coal region.

When Mr. Gowen concluded, the committee made its report, showing that there was no ground of action, and that was the last heard of Legislative intermeddling with the Company.

The reader will observe that Mr. Gowen's address appeals directly to the workingman, and that his blows are mainly showered upon the Mollie Maguires and their evil and violent associates. Wishing to show the good the miner is capable of doing, he speaks plainly, and without affectation, so that the illiterate can understand as clearly as the learned. He also desires to point out, and is successful in depicting, the benefits actually accruing to Philadelphia and the State of Pennsylvania through action of the two great companies that he so ably represents.

It was the sixth of July that the committee was in Pottsville, where they supposed Mr. Gowen would not dare to show himself; but in this the gentlemen prosecuting the case were entirely in error. Mr. Gowen was there. Thinking, as excitement ran high, and outrages were being almost daily and nightly perpetrated in all portions of the coal country, that the threats of the Mollie Maguires to kill the President of the Company, might, if unprevented, be carried out, I took precautions to block the enemies of that

gentleman in this regard. Detectives were sent from Philadelphia, unknown to him, to watch over Mr. Gowen, and
McParlan, *alias* McKenna, was ordered to Pottsville to see
that the Mollies were not allowed a chance of preparation
to strike at the President without the knowledge was communicated to others. It was during this excitement that
McKenna met with a mishap, which I must briefly describe.

He was, one fine morning, walking about the city, and
came upon a suspicious looking man, who, the detective
thought, was throwing himself more frequently than absolutely necessary in the presence of Mr. Gowen, and determined to see who he was and what disposition he made of
himself. Informing Linden of this intention, he started.
The person under surveillance first entered Dormer's Sheridan House, remained there a short time and, coming out,
went to Hughes' drinking place, in Center Street. In this
way he consumed the time until ten o'clock at night, Mc-
Kenna keeping continually on his trail, but entirely useen
and unsuspected by the visitor. This constituted some
twelve hours of continuous shadowing, and the operative
nad discovered nothing, except that his man consumed a
large quantity of liquor and walked very fast, occasionally
talking a short time with leading Mollies. He was well
tired of the business, but determined to see where the party
made his headquarters before he left him. It was surpris-
ing how many people that comparative stranger knew in
Pottsville, and equally miraculous how fast he flew over the
uneven ground, climbing the hills like a native, and never
stumbling or falling, even after imbibing whisky enough to
kill an ox. McKenna, meanwhile, had been unable to secure
anything to appease either hunger or thirst and was nearly
prostrated.

Finally the man traveled, at a late hour, on a hurried
walk, up Mahantongo Street, and, after a long and toilsome
pilgrimage, which the operative thought would never end,

paused before a small house in an eastern suburb of the zity, looked cautiously about, to see that nobody observed him, and then, leaping the garden fence, entered the rear door of the premises. A light still burned in the kitchen, and the detective, assuring himself by actual observation that his party did not live in the dwelling, but was courting the cook in the back apartment, secreted himself in the shadow of a large tree, on the opposite side of the street, and awaited results. The stranger stopped more than an hour. McKenna, his patience and strength quite spent, still persevered in maintaining his watch.

Presently he heard unsteady footsteps approaching, and, fearing discovery, the operative sat down on the sidewalk, took off his boot, and pretended to be very busily engaged in extracting some apocryphal sand and gravel which had worked into it through an indefinite hole in the upper-leather. To the surprise of McKenna, he was accosted by a thick, lubberly, short-set city policeman, evidently a German. Seeing the *pseudo* Mollie, he rolled along toward his resting-place, and, in a decidedly thick and drunken tone, demanded :

" What for you lofe about here, eh ? "

McKenna examined his boot more attentively, and answered respectfully :

" Begorra ! Me boot hurts me foot ! Sure, an' I am gittin' some gravel stones out of it, when I mane to start for home ! "

" Py tam ! I shows you what for you lounge around in der dark ! Get away from dis ! Marsch along on der schtreets ! "

Without waiting for McKenna to obey him, which he was preparing to do, by drawing on his boot—meanwhile keeping a sharp eye upon the door of the house in which his friend was concealed—the brutal and besotted wretch struck the detective a savage blow on the head with his heavy club

Although it was an entirely unprovoked attack, and the stroke brought blood freely from his forehead and nostrils, the agent gave no answer, and made no effort to retaliate. A second stroke, intended for his head, was parried skillfully with his arm, and he walked away, down the street. The vagabond policeman staggered along a few paces and fell down upon the walk, in a state of drunken unconsciousness. Continuing until he reached the shadow of the Catholic church, McKenna stopped, bound up his head as well as he could, and, then seeing his man emerge from the kitchen, he once more started in pursuit. It seems that the fellow had been merely paying a visit to his sweetheart, as he took the road for the country, and, after following him several miles, the operative dropped the trail and returned to his boarding-house.

The next day McKenna was a horrible sight to look upon. With eyes clad in mourning, scalp bound up in plasters, clothing torn and soiled, and limbs bruised, he thought he had learned quite enough of Pottsville and its policemen. And Pottsville had had enough of him, in his character of a Mollie Maguire. It is fair to say that the particular watchman spoken of did not remain on the force many weeks longer, his place having been filled by worthier material.

------◆------

CHAPTER XXXIV.

MURDER OF B. F. YOST.

In the interim, while many of the collieries were beginning to work, making up for lost time, and others putting machinery in order, preparing to do so, the Mollies kept themselves as active as ever, and McAndrew found himself so busily employed, attending to the interests of his division, that he was entirely unable to put his threat, to leave the neighborhood, into execution, had he continued of that mind. He was so chagrined by the failure of his comrades to kill Thomas, that, for a fortnight, he made it his principal daily duty to saunter about the streets, abusing the unsuccessful men as "blundering idiots" and " arrant cowards," drinking much whisky, and everywhere asserting that, if the job were to be tried again he would trust nobody, but just attend to it in person. At about this time the Bodymaster obtained employment in one of the Reading Company's mines, was well contented, and said no more about going away. As McKenna had kept his word, and helped him all he could, and really been instrumental in finding McAndrew something profitable to do, the Bodymaster was a firmer friend of the operative than ever. He proclaimed aloud, wherever he went, that there was "no better man living than Jim McKenna." Few were bold enough to dispute this statement. But for poor, unfortunate Mike Doyle, the Bodymaster chose only hard and insulting words. He was especially severe upon him, as it secured belief that he might easily have finished Thomas had he not run off the ground too early in the game.

It was now arranged that Gomer James should be shot, on or about the fifth of July, when a night picnic was to be held in the neighborhood of Shenandoah. McAndrew ever. went to Girardville, to see Kehoe and have him furnish four men to do the act, but the King of the Mollies said there were none in that place capable of transacting such delicate business. McAndrew traveled to Big Mine Run, found Barney Dolan, with a similar result, and returned to Girardville, where he met Larry Crean, Bodymaster, and that officer bluntly refused his request. Father Bridgeman had, only the previous Sabbath, denounced Kehoe and himself from the altar, and the Mollies were in a state of perturbation from that reason. Otherwise the County Delegate and the President of Girardville Division might have been more efficient and prompt in seconding McAndrew's proposition. As it was, that person felt constrained to go home, his aims as far from fulfillment as when he first departed from Shenandoah. He told McKenna, the same night, that Jack Kehoe was too mean to be half-way honest, and that he had barely given John Gibbons a dollar and fifty cents toward defraying expenses to Luzerne County, which was in contrast with the action of Tom Donahue, who donated two dollars in money, hired a horse and buggy, and drove Gibbons over to Rupert Station, where he was to take the train for Wilkesbarre—Tom Donahue being a poor man, while Kehoe was known to have plenty of money.

The detective now knew where John Gibbons was.

Finally, Pat Dolan, a brother of Barney, sent word to the troubled Bodymaster of Shenandoah that he would find some men, and lead them himself, and see that the James affair was satisfactorily settled. The party was surely expected to arrive in Shenandoah, at or before the picnic of the fifth of July.

It was near the same date that Pat Butler, of Loss Creek, made his advent in Shenandoah, caused McKenna and some others to meet him in the bush, and then and there gave out that he would, in a day or two, bring five men over to take the life of a boss named Forsythe, who had, in some manner, made himself repugnant to a few of the clan.

It was definitely arranged, through a suggestion from the operative, that a second meeting, to perfect the plan of attack, should convene, the following night, in a small school-house on Number Three Hill. By this postponement McKenna gained time in which to notify Superintendent Franklin, who, in turn, took measures for warning Mr. Forsythe, and this Mollie scheme of assassination was wholly defeated. Mr. Forsythe had urgent business elsewhere for a few weeks. Butler held his meeting ; McKenna attended, witnessed the discomfiture of the gentleman from Loss Creek, when he learned that Forsythe had been suddenly called away, and was as loud and vehement as the rest in execrating the ill-luck that dragged a doomed man from their murderous hands. Not a person present suspected that Forsythe had been informed of the plot to take his life. This was far from their thoughts. The disappointed gathering in the dark, at the rustic school-house, dispersed at an early hour, and the Mollies retired, unaccountably cheated of their prey, to their homes.

The fifth of July arrived, but not the men promised from Big Mine Run. Certainly they did not show themselves to the committee of Shenandoah Division, McKenna, John Morris, and Mike Darcy, appointed to receive and lead them up to their victim. 'To state the whole truth, this committee was purposely dispersed by McKenna, who had no desire to see James killed, and if Dolan's party came to the picnic there were none present to show them the least attention. It is more than probable they never reached the vicinity. The operative sent Morris to the base-ball ground, on a plea that he should bring home Tom Hurley. Morris at first obeyed orders, but found Hurley so drunk that he could not be forced away, hence went in for a spree on his own account and remained absent until past midnight. Darcy was dispatched in another direction, with a different excuse, and McKenna then waited alone—waited in the city of Shenandoah, where he conferred with Linden, informing him of the plans afloat, and telling him to have his men near the picnic grounds, in case his own schemes to prevent bloodshed should miscarry. Returning to the festivities, after it was entirely too late to expect the Big Mine Run men, the detective continued the watch. Dancing was ended and the lights nearly all put out when he left—and Gomer James had once more made a narrow escape. Why the young man would persist in staying in the neighborhood, after the repeated notifications he had received to leave, or fail to take precautions against sudden surprises, was more than the detectives could easily explain.

But the murderous order was more successful in other localities. It never paused or permitted its purposes to entirely fail. The work was often slow, while the assassins stayed their hands from week to week, but in few known instances were attempts, once prepared for, easily abandoned until the task had met at least partial performance. Wm. Thomas was a living evidence of the fact. Time was yet to bring forth many dead and silent witnesses to testify to the same thing.

The city of Tamaqua, in Schuylkill County, is a handsome place of five thousand inhabitants, located fifteen miles north-northeast of Pottsville, on the Catawissa Railroad, and connected with the Philadelphia and Reading Railway by a branch from Port Clinton. Like all the larger mountain towns of Pennsylvania, Tamaqua has narrow streets, brick sidewalks, steep ascents and descents, good hotels, fine business and residence structures, and a mixed population, in a great measure dependent upon the mining business for support. There are seven or eight churches, which ring out their musical chimes on the Sabbath day, with the usual complement of banks, offices, and warehouses. Broad Street is a principal thoroughfare. The town, or borough, has its nicipal officers, magistrates, and a small city police.

On the night of Monday, the fifth of July, 1875, the ordinarily quiet city was considerably excited over the conclusion of the observance of the national anniversary, which had absorbed attention during the day. There were many people upon the streets, among others a few visitors from adjoining localities. The police, at the time, consisted of only two men, Benj. F. Yost and Barney McCarron, the former a German and the latter of Irish descent, and they were ex-

pected, in addition to regular patrol service, to light and ex-
tinguish the gas lamps in the principal streets. Yost had
experienced considerable trouble with the Mollies, at the
head of whom was one James Kerrigan; had arrested the
latter for drunkenness on several occasions, and, as would
be natural in his position, sometimes felt compelled to use
his club to enforce obedience on the part of those apprehended. McCarron came in for his share of ill-will, but,
from his German parentage, Yost was peculiarly disliked.
Several times had he been threatened with violence, but,
being a fearless man, an old soldier, and veteran of many
battles, the policeman laughed at danger and kept on in the
performance of his duty. McCarron was also openly men-
aced.

Time passed until about midnight of the fifth, or the first
small hours before the dawn of the sixth, when McCarron
and Yost, passing Carroll's saloon, noted that the place was
still open, went into a hotel, where they saw and drank with
Kerrigan—described as a small, round-faced, short and
stubbed little Irishman, and a miner, but then out of employment. Subsequently they moved to the westward, on
Broad Street, extinguishing the lamps in their way. Soon
their task was almost done, and, before two o'clock in the
morning, the policemen turned toward Yost's residence, near
the corner of Broad and Lehigh Streets, to partake of a
lunch, preparatory to finishing up the night's work. They
had not put out all the lamps in the locality, but it was
customary, on their part, to have some refreshments before
ending the last half of the patrol, during which the city would
be in utter darkness, unless the moon shone—which it did
not—and, on this occasion, opened Yost's front gate, passed
to a rear door, used a latch key, went into the house, and
found a simple repast ready spread for them, Mrs. Yost
having long since retired to her chamber on the second floor
of the building. Having satisfied their appetites and en-
16

joyed some moments of repose, they emerged from the same door and went upon the street, prepared to turn off more lights. Hearing the noise below Mrs. Yost was awakened, arose, the night being warm, and sat by an open front window, sending a loving word and look to her husband, as he and his companion advanced to the performance of their duty. It was a few minutes after two o'clock when she saw Yost go toward the lamp at the corner, place the ladder against its iron post, lightly ascend two steps, extending his arm to shut off the gas. But his hand never reached the base of the lamp. The woman beheld two rapidly succeeding and alarming flashes of light, instantly followed by two loud reports, and her husband fell, his face still turned toward her, lighted up by the rays sent slantingly down from the still blazing gas jet. That was all her eyes saw. That was enough for her ears to hear. She ran madly down the stairs, thinly clad as she was, and into the street, through the front door, beyond the gate, and met the wounded man, staggering and weak with loss of blood, clinging to the fence looking toward his once happy home. Alas! happy home no more!

"My God, Ben, what is it?" asked Mrs. Yost, her face turning ghastly white.

The wounded policeman threw his arms pleadingly forward to her, and said, faintly:

"Sis, give me a kiss! I'm shot and I have to die!"

She ran very fast, but before it was possible to reach him, he came down upon the pavement, blood spurted from his mouth, and he was, for a few minutes, unconscious.

Meantime where was Barney McCarron?

Having separated from Yost upon the street, he was going slowly eastward, in the direction of Mr. Lebo's dwelling, leaving the other officer to care for the lamp near his own house, and had expected him to come up in a moment. But that moment was destined never to arrive. Not hearing

Yost's familiar footsteps, McCarron looked backward over his shoulder, at the very second of time that Mrs. Yost was gazing tenderly in the same direction. He heard the two pistol shots, saw the quick-following flashes, and knew that Yost was hit, as he dropped heavily to the earth. Two dark figures had left the shadow cast by a collection of shade trees near the fence, walked to within a few yards of the police-men, discharged their weapons and started on a brisk run toward the cemetery. McCarron immediately set out in pursuit. Gaining somewhat upon the assassins, when near a clump of bushes, he let fly two shots after them, and the men paused long enough to return the fire, fortunately with-out effect, and in a second resumed their precipitate retreat. He could merely see, in the brief moment they stood in the lamp-lignt, that one was a large man and the other somewhat smaller. It was useless to go further alone. Hastening at once to his wounded comrade, he aided some neighbors to convey him into the house that they had so recently left in such joyous mood. There Yost was placed on a lounge and word sent for a surgeon.

Dr. Solliday lived not far distant, and was soon on the spot, but, after a brief examination of the injured man, said he could live but a very short time. The bullet had passed in at the right side, between the eighth and ninth ribs, and hemorrhage would be sure to carry him off. There was no human skill that would avail anything. The end must come

Mrs. Yost heard the sentence, and burst into passionate weeping, clasping the fast-paling face of her dying husband in her two hands, and kissing his livid lips as if her caresses might renew his short lease of life.

"Do you understand?" said the physician. "You are sure to leave us in a very short time—possibly in one moment! Tell me, before it s too late, all you know of your mur-derers!"

The dying man's fast-glazing eyes slowly opened and

stared vacantly in the face of his frie xd.   But he recognised the necessity for action.

"I know," he answered, in German, "I know! You want the whole truth!"

"Yes!"

"Well! I was just outening the light when two men made up to me and fired! They came down from the direction of the cemetery, and, when they had done their work on me, ran back in the same way. They were two Irishmen. I truly think they shot me by mistake, meaning to kill Mc-Carron, there! They had threatened him, and he was afraid he would get it. They were two strangers. Still, I should not say that, for I have seen them before. They were both down at Jim Carroll's—a party of them—last night, and Barney pointed them out to me, or I showed them to him— I can't tell which, now—as we went by Carroll's!"

This was all that the dying man could say just then. After resting a space, during which his faithful mate knelt at the side of the sofa and bathed his brow with her tears, he motioned McCarron, who stood nigh, to move up closer, and said to him :

"Barney, who were those men that I pointed out to you— or you pointed out to me—which was it ?—as we passed Jim Carroll's saloon, last night ?   Didn't you remark, ' They're fellows from the other side ? ' "

By "the other side," Tamaqua people described the country the other side of, or beyond, the Schuylkill.

McCarron bowed his head and assented.   He remembered the time and event, but did not know the men.

To all his friends, Mr. Shindel, Mr Lebo, Mr. Shepp— the latter his brother-in-law—Mr. Houser, and others, the policeman made precisely similar declarations, knowing that he must die. He did not want to accuse anybody unjustly To Dr. Solliday, who questioned him once more, he said :

"One was a large man. and the other was smaller!"

"Was not one Jimmy Kerrigan?'

"No! He was larger! Kerrigan was not there! If so, I did not see him! And I had been with Kerrigan just before, at the United States Hotel, where he drank with me! Oh, no! He didn't do it!"

"Was it Duffy?"

The doctor was aware that Yost nad had trouble with man by that name.

"I am sure none of our men did it! They were strangers, believe me!"

To his brother-in-law, Daniel Shepp, the prostrate and dying man said, as he closely held his hands, and the life-blood slowly ebbed from his side:

"Oh, Dan! To think that I served so long in the army, was in so many hard-fought battles, and escaped all the bullets, to die now innocently!"

This was about the last that the brave officer said, excepting the utterance of some gentle words to his distracted wife. At a little past-nine o'clock, the morning of the sixth of June, 1875, seven hours subsequent to receiving his wound, Benj. F. Yost breathed his last breath on earth, and one of the most cruel murders of all the great number perpetrated by the Mollie Maguires was consummated. It was even then implicitly believed to have been the work of the order, as, outside its blood-stained ring, Yost did not have an enemy. The fact, also commonly credited, that the assassins were strangers in the borough, or at least not residents of it, gave color to this supposition.

The carnival of blood had fairly commenced. This deed was speedily to be followed by others of an equally mysterious nature, and no man could tell whose turn must come next.

McCarron gave it up, after questioning Yost, that neither Kerrigan nor Duffy, both of whom were enemies of the dead policeman, from the same cause, having been arrested by him while they were drunk, and, resisting, having felt the weight of his baton, had fired the fatal shot; still it could not be erased from his memory or belief that they possibly knew something about it. Thinking of the men he had noted at Carroll's, and to whom Yost had, on the occasion, made allusion, the partner of the deceased determined, unknown to any person, to make an investigation of the locality, and find if the same persons were still there. The hour was nigh half-past four in the morning. Yost was fast losing consciousness. McCarron went to Carroll's, but, after walking about the house and into the back yard, he saw no lights, heard no sounds, or anything to indicate that people were astir in the dwelling or saloon. Evidently all were in bed. Nothing could be discovered of either citizens or strangers, and he therefore returned to Yost's residence and there remained until taking the eternal farewell of his friend and companion.

B. F. Yost was thirty-three years of age, and universally respected in Tamaqua, his widow constituting not the only one that shed bitter tears over his untimely taking off. Hundreds of men and women in the city, who knew his brave, frank, and honest heart, and remembered the warm, firm grasp of his strong hand, felt that they could mingle their tears with those of the one left wholly bereaved and desolate by the murderous bullet of the cowardly assassin. Some of these thought that crime had now gone its length, and it was time its course was ended. They had only seen the beginning, but believed the end was in view. Among this class were many men of wealth and influence, and those who grieved to see the fair fame of their home smirched with innocent blood. They then determined, if they could prevent, violence should no longer reign in Schuylkill County.

CHAPTER XXXV.

McKENNA TAKES UP THE TRAIL AT TAMAQUA.

THE wounding of Thomas, and subsequent murder of Yost, were enough to assure me that more work of the same character would speedily follow, unless earnest endeavors were put forth to prevent. Do the best I could, the Mollie Maguires would cause blood to flow. Their thirst had been excited by the sight of the crimson tide, and other victims must be struck down before the appetite was appeased. Maddened by the goadings of the few turbulent spirits in their midst, I knew they would never stop until they found the unavoidable avenger on their track and the outraged law strong enough to punish, blood for blood, life for life, " eye for eye, tooth for tooth, hand for hand, foot for foot." It was my duty to commence the work, upon the small foundation furnished, in building up a force which should withstand the efforts of the league and successfully battle with the midnight foe. My plans were quickly formed, as quickly transmitted to Philadelphia, and Mr. Franklin gave them, as far as was thought advisable, to the operatives engaged in the mining country. Linden, laboring somewhat openly—though not ostensibly for me—was secretly to co-operate with McParlan, *alias* McKenna, who was by no means to be acknowledged by any one as in the most distant manner connected with the Agency. On the contrary, everything was to be done to keep down a suspicion, should one arise, ever so faintly foreshadowing any such relation. McParlan must be depended upon to perform the principal service, in keeping track and securing the arrest of the men who had attacked Thomas, as well as those who were guilty of assassinating policeman Yost. The substantial chain of circumstances and the testimony, must be so direct, unequivocal and convincing as to leave no chance loophole for the escape of the murderers, no scope for an *alibi*, before a single guilty man could be captured and brought to the prisoner's box. Never had a defendant, a member of this thoroughly organized association for murder and all sorts of crime, received punishment through the verdict of a jury, and many good men despaired of ever accomplishing such a work; but I truly considered that, if given plenty of time and saved from the intermeddling of others, I could surmount the trouble, and after a while drive the Mollie Maguires from their strongholds. I would not be spurred on to take precipitate action. My plans must all be brought to their proper denouement.

Assuming such safeguards as he might think for the best, McParlan was directed to go to Tamaqua and learn, if possible, who had killed Yost, and there lay the groundwork of a superstructure upon which the prosecution of the assassins might be founded. He was to obtain such information as he could, using his official relation with the order, as far as it might go, and any other artifice, or detective scheme, which should appear useful in gaining the desired results.

The command for a change of his base of operations reached McKenna on the fifteenth of July, and he at once prepared to obey.

Linden also received instructions to second McKenna, but to refrain from making his appearance in Tamaqua until requested by the other detective to do so.

The Superintendent's letter to McKenna did not find him in the enjoyment of the best of spirits for a most dangerous and difficult undertaking, from reasons which I will proceed to explain. The previous day, Frank McAndrew having moved into a house at Indian Ridge Breaker—or Davis' Breaker, as it was familiarly called—engaged with a number of Mollies in a great carousal, which lasted until midnight, and, having inveigled McKenna into the affair, succeeded in keeping him up and employed, there and elsewhere, all night. This, with a return of a chronic sore throat, from which he was suffering, made him almost ill again.

Indian Ridge Breaker is situated on the road by Lanagan's Patch, leading to Mahanoy City, from Shenandoah, and not far from the shebeen shop of Mrs. Bridget Monaghan, twice a widow, but far from ancient at that, although "fat, fair, and forty" was applicable as an imperfect description of the lady. She occupied the stone basement of a tumble-down, three-story wooden building, the upper floors of which were devoted to the midnight gambols of predatory cats and daily incursions of migratory rats—the hallways filled with webs of spiders that, with the mice, made nests in the corners of the vacant rooms —and her subterranean abode was, like that of handsome Micky Cuff, the habitation of geese, ducks, chickens, goats, and pigs, among which Mrs. Bridget walked, "monarch of all she surveyed." This was a favorite and frequent place of resort for McAndrew and other Mollies, and the stories that gained circulation concerning the flitting of spirits, clad all in white, through the upper corridors of the structure, at the dead hour of night, and the gleams of an occasional flame—burning pale, sickly, blue and ghastly, as some benighted miner was fain to report to his superstitious household—all may have been due to the meetings of the society in the otherwise untenanted place, and the failure of the impromptu janitor to put up a curtain close enough to prevent a ray of the single candle, lighting their deliberations, from escaping. It was a famous place for the telling of ghost stories, and McKenna, who was an adept at the relation of mysterious events, as well as singing songs and dancing flings and jigs, frequently held the Mollies spell-bound for hours, while he chronicled the scenes he had seen and the ghosts and ghouls he had heard about in the old country. His legends were in great demand, and some-

16*

times he indulged in the narration of one in the presence of
the widow, who, meanwhile, would draw herself up close to
the story-teller—story-teller in more respects than one, it is
to be feared—and declare that the company positively should
not leave her "hotel" until daylight, if she had to supply
the drinks and other comfortables at her own expense. I
was not difficult to win over the Mollies to remain and
"keep off the *banshee*," if she only put out the overflowing
noggin with a generous hand. And this she did. To the
credit of the widow be it said, the love of drink and indulgence in gossip were among the worst of her failings. In
every other regard she was considered a respectable and
honorable member of her kind of society.

During the repetition of these hair-raising and blood-curd
.ing fabrications, given in the detective's best vein, the Mollies
habitually and involuntarily threw off reserve and spoke
boastfully of their own adventures, not forgetting deeds they
had recently participated in. Through this action McKenna
received many a hint that he could use and improve upon
when the time came. It was easy, under such circumstances, to obtain the confidence of the most hardened of the
brotherhood.

The night spoken of, McAndrew, Ed Ferguson, and Mc-
Kenna, with several more of the gang, were at Wiggan's
Patch, and, returning to Shenandoah, the proposition was
made to wake up the widow and take a drink in her shop.
Accordingly, Ferguson knocked loudly at the rickety door.

"Who's there?" asked a woman's voice from within.

"Sure, it's Ed Ferguson, and some friends! Let us in,
Mrs. Monaghan!"

"All right!" said the lady, and in a few moments the
fastenings of the entrance were undone and the party entered, warmly welcomed by the landlady, who, from the prevalent heat of the night and sudden advent of her visitors,
had not donned any perceptible amount of clothing, but

proceeded to help them to liquor with the grace of a mer-
maid in its native element, without even unfastening the
strings of her dingy night-cap.

There was a feebly-burning lamp on the counter, which
illuminated the room, for it was by no means a large place,
showing the simple array of bottles on the shelves, the bed,
and other scanty furniture. But there was more in the apartment than, at first glance, the operative was willing to
believe. Seeing that Ferguson was moving uneasily about,
Mrs. Monaghan said :

"Have a care, Ed Ferguson ! Mind where ye put down
your two big fate, and don't step on me chickens, plaze !"

Having taken their drinks and paid for them, the men
were in for a lark, and Ferguson, knowing some of the
peculiarities of the widow, proceeded to make a search for
curiosities—and he found them. At the same time the detective was nearly dead with the foul and fetid atmosphere
filling the unventilated basement.

"What have we here?" said Ferguson, who, while
groping around where Bridget said "he had no business"—
under the bed—had caught somebody by the naked feet.
"A human being, as I live ! And a woman at that !"

He first dragged out in this ungraceful way a female—
Mollie Williams by name—who, stopping accidentally with
the landlady over night, had been frightened by the noise
the visitors made before entering and secreted herself beneath
the low bedstead with a part of the widow's portable property.
An inventory of other things discovered in the apartment
would read as follows :

. Widow Bridget Monaghan—very angry and flushed as to face and
scantily clad.

1 maiden lady, of uncertain age, ditto as to raiment, and badly scared.

5 goats, scattered about the floor very promiscuously.

37 chickens—including one plucky game-cock.

1 collection of new-washed female raiment, hanging damp on the line

5 ducks and a drake.

1 goose and a gander.

1 demijohn—contents, whisky.

2 tin pots for drinking purposes—of tin.

1 stove and furniture—badly cracked in places.

1 section of a log, for a chair—not cushioned.

1 collection of miscellaneous articles, on the shelves, intended for sale.

His comrades drank several times, but McKenna could not stomach the liquor in that den, and, taking a tin dinner pail, which he found, he washed it out and milked one of the goats, swallowing the warm fluid with a relish.

As a natural consequence of the time, place, and opportunity, McKenna was importuned for songs, which he sung, sitting beside the widow, on her bed, with Mollie Williams nigh, perched on the wooden excuse for a chair, and the equally interested men, sitting on their haunches, and in various extraordinary attitudes, around the room. The few following hours until morning were consumed in the relation of sundry soul-harrowing tales of ghosts, haunted houses and church-yards, hobgoblins and spirits, to which all listened in silence, only excepting an occasional interruption by the widow when proffering more liquor, until the young man's throat and tongue fairly gave out from too much exercise, and he was constrained to beg for a season of rest. The sun was rising when the company, very well soaked in bad liquor, oozed out of Mrs. Monaghan's cellar and started on a serpentine trail for home. As a consequence of inhaling so much bad air, and from protracted confinement in foul gases, the operative was so ill that, when he received Mr. Franklin's instructions to leave for Tamaqua, he felt more like keeping his bed and sending for a physician.

The uninitiated reader may be inclined to think my description of Mrs. Monaghan's groggery an exaggeration. The thought is pardonable, but I assure those who have followed me thus far in this recital, that, instead of being overcolored, the whole truth, in all its details, has not been told. It could not well be revealed without giving offense.

Mrs. Monaghan subsequently married a man by the name of Breyer, is yet living, and can, if she will, substantiate every point I have given in reference to this night's adventure in her residence.

To make matters more complicated, a letter came with Mr. Franklin's, from Linden, warning McKenna to look out, as he was suspected by one of the principal bankers of Shenandoah, of being a professional burglar, hanging about the city for no good purpose. So firmly fixed was the man of money and bonds in his belief, that he made the journey to Pottsville, interviewed a city detective, and tried hard to induce the officer to go to Shenandoah, see McKenna, and keep close watch of his movements. The capitalist said he could not tell when his vault might be attacked, and was fearful its valuable contents would fall, easy-made plunder, into the lap of that dreadful Irishman. Linden informed the Pottsville policeman that, although McKenna was rogue enough for almost anything, charged with a brutal murder in Buffalo, where he formerly knew him, and, as he believed, even then closely leagued with counterfeiters, yet he did not believe he would, or could, burst a burglar-proof safe. Linden further promised the banker's friend that he would take the matter in hand, go over to Shenandoah, and see what McKenna really did intend. He " knew *he* could worm the secret out of him." Here the matter dropped.

It was, after all, quite fortunate that this information met the detective when it did, as through it a plan was suggested to his sick brain by which he might easily depart from Shenandoah without engendering suspicion 'n the minds of the Mollies as to the real object in view. Dressing himself in his rougher attire, and packing a supply of better clothing in his valise, ready for starting, McKenna called on Frank McAndrew, in the afternoon, found a number of his friends present, and, taking the Bodymaster aside, held a short whispered consultation with him.

"Faix, I hev very bad news this mornin'," said the operative, assuming a solemn air, greatly in contrast with his usually radiant countenance.

"Phat is it?"

"I've got a letther from me sisther, an', would ye belave it? them beggarly Buffalo detectives hev been to her house, in Philadelphia, watchin' an' spyin' about, an' finally axin fur me an' me whereabouts!"

"Indade? But I make sure your sister didn't tell them?"

"But she did, then!" And McKenna put on an appearance of much anger. "She just said to them the last they aeard of me I was at Shenandoah, but didn't belave I wor there now! That was enough, I'm sure, fur they're as sharp as the edge of a razor, an' I expect they'll quickly be here afther me. Me sisther sent a letther, warnin' me, if I had raison to fear them, jist to make meself scarce! An' now I must go! I shall only tell you where I'm really goin'. If ye want me particular like, I'll be in Mahanoy City, or Pottsville occasionally, an' ye may write me at these places—but holt! perhaps 'twould be betther not to send me anything until ye hear from me! As soon as I'm settled a bit I'll let ye know. In the meanwhile kape dark! If anybody inquires for the address, say that ye don't know where I am—but I tould ye I wor goin' to see some friends in Canada—that'll put them on a false trail!"

"I'll mind all ye say," answered McAndrew, and he ' pulled a long face, when he thought how he would manage the division without his Secretary's assistance.

Taking a few drinks of beer with the persons in the room —for McAndrew kept a liquor supply by this time—the detective left the house, moved deliberately to his boarding-place, told a similar story to Cooney and his family, put his satchel in the hands of an Irish lad that he could trust, to be taken to him at the depot, and then appeared as usual among the remainder of his companions. A more despondent detective never was seen. He was sick; his head ached, and his whole system needed rest. Despite all, however, he managed to keep up a fair external demeanor, joked with his Mollie friends, and even sung a laughter-provoking ditty. When the time for the departure of the train arrived, he excused himself, walked rapidly to the depot, found his satchel and his messenger, tipped the boy a quarter of a dollar, seized the baggage, mounted the car, just as it started out, and, in a few moments, was trundling over the hills in the direction of Tamaqua. He fell asleep—after half an hour's uneasiness, fearing he might be recognized by some one, but discovered he was unknown to all about him—and was in a sound slumber when he reached the place of his destination. "Tamaqua!" shouted in a loud voice, by the brakeman awoke him, and he alighted at the depot as the locomotive gave a preparatory shriek and glided, with its serpent-like string of cars, along and around the mountain.

Notwithstanding the fact that McKenna had tasted nothing stronger than water, coffee, and Cronk beer, throughout the day—in truth during several days—he was so much over-powered, apparently with liquor, when he reached the front door of the Columbia House, the same night, that he fell sprawling across the threshold, his satchel flying in one direction and his hat in another. His old acquaintance, Marks, the landlord, was compelled to fly to his assistance, gather up his scattered goods and chattels, lead him to a seat, and finally escort him safely to a room and bed, the besotted guest all the while muttering to himself almost unintelligible Irish jargon, about some "*dawshy-dawshy, allana machree,* all the way from auld Erin," that he had been to call upon, and the "bastely *calliagh,*" her mother, had forbidden him the house, bad cess to her night-cap!" In truth, he was maudlin over some one that he named his "*colleen bawn,* wid the *rucket* head! ·

Marks left him upstairs, without a lamp, stretched on the bed, to find the way under the covers as best he might.

No sooner had the landlord made an exit than the detective ceased his mutterings, arose, ran lightly and soberly to the entrance, turned the key in the lock, and hung his hat cautiously over the knob, as was his custom. Then, weary and worn, and as sick as a man well could be and still retain his senses, he undressed himself and retired.

The few of McKenna's Tamaqua acquaintances who recognized him as he staggered up the street had no desire to trouble the man in his evidently advanced state of intoxication, and either turned off into by-streets and avoided his presence, or failed to look in his direction. The word was passed about the city, during the evening, that " that wild Irishman, from Shenandoah, Jim McKenna, was in town again, on a rousing spree, and would probably make things uncommon lively the ensuing day."

Meanwhile the overtasked operative was sleeping calmly and peacefully, and sweetly dreaming that he sat once more in his home, by the western shore of Lake Michigan, hearkening to the soft sound of the waves as they broke ripplingly upon the sandy beach, whispering tales of other days, that in his waking hours were almost effaced from remembrance. The morning sun shone brightly when the agent awoke, donned his miserable attire, and prepared to continue the simulated debauch, which, he knew, would serve as a veil for his real object in visiting Tamaqua, and in the end, he hoped, bring him in communication with the murlerers of Yost.

CHAPTER XXXVI.

IN THE MURDERER'S NEST.

AFTER breakfast, the detective accompanied the landlord to the bar and swallowed a powerful decoction of spirits, lemon, and sugar, commonly termed whisky-punch, which had the effect, in a little while, of tangling up his wits, weakening his joints, and causing his eyes to see everything in couples, even to the solitary chimney-tops of the houses in the city. At least, so it appeared. But he retained the sense of hearing sufficiently unimpaired to receive the full benefit of Marks' reflection, directed to the hangers-on of the tavern, as he quit the house, and of which the agent was the subject—to the effect that it was "a great pity he, McKenna, had no head for resisting the stupefying influences of strong drink." This forms the substance of the remark, but not exactly the language, which was very coarse, and intensified by sundry adjectives and expletives not mentioned to ears polite.

One of the first places honored with the detective's presence after quitting the Columbia House, was Carroll's, where, as he had been informed by Superintendent Franklin, Yost and McCarron saw the strangers, "from the other side," suspected of having committed the murder, the morning of the sixth of that month. The saloon and residence of James Carroll—all included in one building—was on Broad Street, no great distance from the United States Hotel. After calling on Patrick Nolan, another liquor-seller with whom he was familiar, and from whom he obtained more liquor, thus adding to his appearance of drunkenness, the operative went direct to Carroll's. Union

House. Fortunately, the proprietor of the place and his wife were the only occupants of the bar-room. McKenna passed Carroll the sign for the quarter, while the proprietor stood in the doorway, and Carroll answered correctly, then warmly greeted him as a brother. The detective introduced himself:

"I am James McKenna, of Shenandoah! I think you know me by report, but not by sight! Have often heard of you, as Secretary of Tamaqua Division!"

At this juncture, Mrs. Carroll, who had been standing nigh, discreetly withdrew, and Carroll said: "Jim Mc Kenna? 'Heard of you?' I think I have! You are right welcome here!"

"I'm jist afther having a bit of a spree, as ye'll doubtless observe wid half an eye, an ain't nigh so steady as I wor yesterday, an' don't know as much by half, but I greet ye kindly! Supposin', now, you fit yourself inter the space behint the bar an' the shelves, an' pour me out some gin? I'm particularly partial to pure Holland!"

"Of course I will," replied Carroll, and he served some liquor, taking a stiff glass himself.

"I can't stay but a little time," said McKenna, seating himself before the counter and balancing his body insteadily "fur I must get to Summit Hill, beyant, this afternoon, fur to see Aleck Campbell!"

"Campbell is all right!"

"Yes! Campbell is one of the thruest men in the county, an' one that I have taken a particular likin' fur!"

"You know Aleck and I are brothers-in-law?"

"Sure, an' I hed no sich idea!"

"We are! An', if you stay in the neighborhood, you must spake of me to him! It'll be a good thing for you to do!"

"I'll remember that, depend upon't!"

"I suppose you've read of the Yost matter?" said Carroll

"Oh, I saw somethin' of it in the papers, but nev no knowledge of the particulars! I belave, however, that the Dutch policeman desarved all he got!"

"It was a clane trick, an' well done!"

"Some of the people in town are sayin' that McCarron—isn't that his name?—did the whole thing!" suggested McKenna.

This groundless charge the detective had constructed, from whole cloth, to draw Carroll out, but the saloon keeper did not choose to say much. He responded:

"There was mighty little difference in the two—McCarron an' Yost! I think Yost was a trifle the manest, but not much!"

This was considerable for Carroll to say, before a comparative stranger, even though known as a good Mollie, but contained no information; so, after another glass of gin, which the detective dexterously threw out at the door, after having changed the glasses and drank the water placed on the counter with the liquor, McKenna took his leave, perceptibly the worse for his morning drams, and boarded the cars for Storm Hill, leaving his satchel at the Columbia House.

Arrived at his destination, the officer continued his appearance of intoxication, and, after staggering about and entering one or two saloons, rolled himself into Alex. Campbell's house, finding the proprietor at home, surrounded by several other Mollies, all of whom seemed engaged in doing nothing in particular, excepting the rapid consumption of the contents of the bottles behind the counter. The reception accorded McKenna was generous, finding that he had a few dollars to expend, and Campbell and the rest being eager to assist in that operation. When they had taken some rounds, of which the detective was compelled to imbibe fully his share, Campbell put on his coat, and signaling to McKenna, the two started for a walk. They first made a call at Pat Me-

Kenna's—whose relative James McKenna, the operative, had already made himself out to be—where an unusually warm greeting awaited him. All of his second cousins were happy to resume a companionship previously begun. This saloon was kept by Pat McKenna, the father of the Old Mines Bodymaster. Pat, junior, was not at home. The whole country swarmed with Mollies, and Campbell, Fisher, and Pat McKenna, junior, were the leading spirits in the division, Fisher being at that date County Delegate of Carbon County.

As the agent considered the dangerous company he was in, and the extra-hazardous duty he was performing, at the very stronghold of the party that he was almost convinced had assassinated the Tamaqua policeman—although he had not gained any positive proof of their guilt—his mind was so unduly excited, brain so highly stimulated and alert that he might make no false step, speak no suspicious word, the liquor he swallowed produced no more effect upon his organism than so much water. Under similar circumstances a man will drink, from hour to hour, all day, and never be really intoxicated until the mental strain may be removal by the taking away of the cause of danger, when sleep, or stupor, will promptly supervene. Thus the detective joined with Campbell, the McKennas, and others, and was not too far gone to swallow several drams, after the walk in Campbell's company to the Summit. There Tom Fisher resided. He was also a tavern-keeper.

As McParlan—I shall call him by his true surname, while describing his associations with the Carbon County McKennas, to avoid confusion of titles in the reader's memory—and Alex. Campbell were tramping over the hills to Summit, the agent, during a pause in the conversation, inquired if news of the Bill Thomas affair had reached Storm Hill.

"Indade an' it has!" returned Campbell; "an' I hear it wur your men that did it!"

"I guess ye have it purty straight, then," said McParlan, not caring to spoil a story which was working tangibly in his interest, and which would draw his companion on to say more. "But ye must not let it out on me! I caution ye, there's many inquiries goin on as to who performed that job!"

"All right!" responded Campbell. "Although the thing ended in failure, it was well meant, and you were not to blame!"

"There's *lashins* of betther men for such a thing than one can get in Shenandoah!"

"I belave ye! Your fellows couldn't do so clane a job as that down in Tamaqua!"

Here was very delicate ground. The tracer must say exactly the right thing, if he desired to learn more. He was very drunk, as Campbell truly believed, yet managed to reply:

"Be the great piper! but that wor a trick to be proud of! Indade, the best thing of the kind I ever heard about!"

The tavern-keeper looked proudly but searchingly at Mc-Parlan for a second, seemed satisfied that he was trustworthy, and exclaimed:

"Well, it do gain our lads credit! I wouldn't have bothered my head about it, only it was on a trade, you know!"

As a natural consequence of the direction of his professional duty, McParlan ardently desired to learn who was to be killed in exchange for the shooting of Yost, and the names of the men Campbell was just confessing he had sent to Tamaqua, but he knew his business too well—inebriated as he appeared to be—to put a leading inquiry in that direction. Campbell then closed his mouth, possibly thinking he was already more communicative than would be pronounced exactly prudent, even with a man and a brother Mollie who confessed to having secured and furnished the parties for the shooting of Wm. M. Thomas, and said no more on the subject

They found Fisher very much intoxicated and unwilling to do anything but drink.

By this time it was night, and, although considerably "under the influence," Campbell left the detective at Fisher's and went out to attend the meeting of a building association, of which he was a member.

McParlan was forced by the proprietor of the place to remain with Fisher that night. He would listen to none of his alleged reasons for returning to Campbell's. It was late when the operative retired, and in a few moments sleep and weariness overpowered him.

Friday morning, after breakfast and a parting glass with County Delegate Fisher, who urged him soon to come there again—certainly before leaving the vicinity—the officer returned to Storm Hill and went directly to the saloon of the elder McKenna, where he encountered Pat McKenna, the Bodymaster, who introduced the visitor to his wife, with whom he had not long before been united. There were a number of Mollies about the place, and they experienced little trouble in inducing McParlan to give them some songs and dances. Among the former, "Pat Dolan," printed in an early chapter of this work, was a great favorite and several times *encored*. At the second singing every man in the bar-room joined in the chorus:

> "Wid my riggadum-du—an' to h—l wid the crew
> Wouldn't help to free our nation;
> When I look back, I count 'em slack,
> Wouldn't join our combination."

In the jigs and reels there were some who took part, and all beat time to the dancer's heel-and-toe refrain. Both performances gave great satisfaction, and at once seated McParlan firmly in the good graces of all the Irish people of Storm Hill.

Pat McKenna, during the day, made a statement to the

detective sustaining what Campbell had previously said, and more might have been gathered from the same source had not the place been so crowded with patrons. The Body-master was a little more cautious than Campbell had been, and the officer did not press him, however badly he wanted to have the names of the men who had been sent to put Yost out of the way. That night McParlan, *alias* Mc-Kenna, remained at the house of his *quasi* and convenient cousin, Pat McKenna, and enjoyed a good night's sleep, which, considering his arduous labors and long-continued excitement of mind, he greatly needed.

Saturday, the seventeenth of July, was a sunny and rather sultry summer's day. In the forenoon, McParlan entered the bar of McKenna, senior, and was there joined by Mike McKenna, a younger son of the tavern-keeper, and brother of Pat, the Bodymaster. When all had taken some drinks together, McParlan found a seat in the shade, not far away, saying he felt very sick, after such a prolonged debauch, and young Mike followed. Protected by the spreading branches of a tree, the pretended cousin indulged his propensity for romancing—in the interest of the public—to its full extent, rehearsing with additions and embellishments, the absorbing particulars of the many "clane jobs" in which he had par-ticipated—all purely figments of the brain from commence-ment to end, but given in such minuteness of detail, and appearance of candor and frankness, that the interested hearer took them in without doubt or distrust of their truth-fulness. Mike believed implicitly in Jim McKenna.

When the searcher after knowledge had exhausted his store of material and talked himself hoarse, Mike thought it his turn to say something, and while he had little to urge for himself, sung pæans to the prowess of his elder brother, Pat McKenna, the Bodymaster. He spun many fine tales of no particular value to his single auditor, but to all of which the operative affected to give earnest and undivided attention.

In a little while, without in the least appearing to do so McParlan brought the young fellow around to the main question, and he plainly stated that the men who had killed Yost were Hugh McGehan and James Boyle, both then living at Summit Hill.

" Ye see, sir, it wor a bargain wid the boys around Tamaqua, by Campbell, who jist wants some of them, wan of these fine days, to do for Jones, who is a sort of Sub-Superintendent at Old Mines. He is Charlie Parrish's tool, an' but fur this fellow   ve been at work long ago ! Hugh McGehan is   best man at a clane job in all the county, an 'it's a pity fur him to have to lave now, after lyin' idle so long !"

" I was sure in my own mind, before, who had done the trick ! But, be jabers, it wor a well-laid plan, an' mighty nice wor it carried out ! I suppose Jones will be taken off directly the excitement of the last affair blows over !"

McParlan was trying to learn facts by appearing to have them partly in possession.

" I thought ye knew somethin' of the matther," continued Mike, "but don't ye brathe divil a word to Pat, me big brother, that I hev been chatterin' here wid ye, fur he'd be worse nor a mad dog over it ! I don't know when Jones is to be shot—an' possibly the thing has been given over—but when Aleck Campbell makes up his mind to a thing it generally has to be done sooner or later, so I rather opine that it will come off yet !"

" I suppose it was Boyle who fired the shot that brought Yost down ?"

" You're wrong there, then, for it wor McGehan's pistol what performed the thing nately ! But there's brother Pat, an I must be goin' ! Don't you say anythin' !"

" Depend upon me !" said McParlan.

They entered the bar-room, the operative hoping he might meet Boyle, described to him as a low-sized, stoutish man, with dark hair and mustache. But Boyle was not among the new visitors. McParlan treated to the best, paid his reckoning, and, with Mike, went to Campbell's, where the afternoon was spent at cards. The games ended when Pat McKenna came in, just from his work at the mine. This person was a fine physical type of a man, six feet four inches in height, well built and proportioned, of fair complexion, and apparently twenty-five years of age. He was glad to see McParlan again and accompanied him to his father's house, and they had drinks at Pat's own expense, who then proceeded home to change his clothing. Mike, meanwhile, took occasion once more to caution the operative against saying anything about their talk of the forenoon. He was reassured when McParlan suggested that he was no *cruddy* idiot, and reiterated his promise to observe great care over his lips. " Trust me to know better than to blather over what is tould me in confidence ! " were his concluding words.

Subsequently, Pat McKenna, when given the opportunity, confirmed his brother's revelations, confessing that men from his division had shot Yost, but he would go no further. The names he kept to himself. The detective slept, that night, at the residence of young Pat McKenna, retiring at the early hour of three A.M.

The following Sunday, McParlan, accompanied by Pat McKenna, the Bodymaster, went to Coaldale, the residence of James Roarty, at the head of the division there, ostensibly to see what Jack Donahue had done about the Major business. A man named McNellis went with them. The weather being very warm, all were glad when they came to a shady spot. Roarty was easily found and took them to the house of another Mollie, called Bonner, where they enjoyed refreshments. When questioned, Roarty said he did not know what Chris Donnelly, of Mt. Laffee, and Yellow Jack Donahue, of Tuscarora, were doing on or about the

17

fifth, as he, Roarty, and Kerrigan and two others—n
not given—were in Tamaqua, on their way to Big V
when Carroll gave them a letter, telling the three to wait for
further orders. The meeting took place, he heard, and
Chris Donnelly and his armed men were on the ground, but
Donahue would not permit them to act, as he was fearful,
from the fact that the Majors had quit working at their
usual place ; they might be in receipt of notification of foul
play awaiting them. "They will get a pill yet," exclaimed
Roarty, "as Bully Bill did ! By the way, you acted your
part well in that same, but the rest made asses of themselves
by not stoppin' to see their man's toes turned up, before
leavin' the stable !"

Roarty also alluded to the Tamaqua "clane job," but
disclosed nothing more of consequence. That he had
personally been interested in the Yost murder, at its inception, whether he actually assisted in the killing or not, the
detective was fully sensible before the end of Mike Mc-
Kenna's recital. They returned to Pat McKenna's house
in season for dinner, finding the rooms swarming with
Mollies. McParlan counted over thirty active members
about the place, all indulging in a boisterous bacchanal.
During the afternoon he was introduced as " Jim McKenna,
Secretary of Shenandoah Division," by Alex. Campbell and
Pat McKenna, Jr., to Hugh McGehan. He shook the
blood-stained murderer's hand without flinching, and immediately invited all hands to present themselves at the bar at
his cost. McGehan I have partly described in giving the
dying declaration of Yost. It may be added that he was
of rather light complexion, had dark eyes, face clean-shaven
—at this time—short, or pug nose, was five feet nine inches
in stature, straight and well built, weighing from one hundred
and sixty to one hundred and seventy-five pounds, and apparently a smart, well-spoken fellow. He dressed, when
out of his shifting clothes, in very good taste. But McGehan

not remain long in the company saying he had other fish to fry."

Monday, without seeing Boyle, as he knew he was work· ing in the shaft, and not likely to leave very soon, McParlan boarded the train for Tamaqua, having nearly recovered from what he was pleased to denominate the "bad effects of the poteen he had taken the week before." , Arriving at Tamaqua, he entered Carroll's saloon, with the interior of which he was by that time quite intimate, and there found Roarty. The people of the house were glad to see him once more, and Roarty, hearing that McKenna—the detec- tive may once more be called by his assumed name—was about to start for Shenandoah, had come to Carroll's to take leave of him. Roarty was working a night shift near that place. The operative employed every known means, with- out asking the question direct, to make Roarty say who had done the Yost murder, and which men were to act for the Tamaqua Division in repaying the job; but the miner either did not know, or would not venture to say.

The same night McKenna once more appeared on his old stamping ground, at Shenandoah, but took care not to be seen by any excepting McAndrew and Cooney. McAndrew informed him quietly, that Linden had been there to warn the Secretary, as two strange men were not long before in- quiring for him at Pottsville. The Mollies had determined, if they visited Shenandoah—having no doubt but they were the Buffalo detectives—to give them a good beating and the advice to go elsewhere as quickly as possible. Thus far the Buffalo officers had not shown themselves in the place. Remaining in Shenandoah, *perdu*, for a few days, recovering strength, and writing on his reports, which had been unavoida- bly neglected, McKenna once more bid his friends farewell and returned to Tamaqua, saying he had business in Luzerne County with an old acquaintance. The last-mentioned hint was taken as foreshadowing a trip to meet some counterfeiters and replenish his purse with uncurrent funds. Mc Andrew pressed his hand warmly, saying he hoped he'd "kape out of harm's way!"

"I'll do that, if I can, jist depend upon it!" responded the detective. "If the men I have described to ye come here, look out for 'em, will ye?"

"They'll be attended to!" was the promise of McAndrew.

Had any unhappy stranger filling this description : "Tall, long-nosed, bald-headed, squint-eyed, knock-kneed, pigeon-toed, hump-backed, and cracked-voiced," appeared about this date, in Shenandoah, he certainly would have needed protection. As few persons on earth have the misfortune to possess all these unfortunate characteristics, it is presumable that no one was injured. In truth, McAndrew wrote a letter to the detective, when he found out where he was, saying, among other things, that the " Buffalo detectives had not yet arrived, though Capt. Linden reported having seen men looking like them in Ashland."

At Tamaqua, the operative whispered in the ears of his Mollie acquaintances that it seemed necessary, from certain reasons—two of the same being Buffalo detectives—that he should keep dark and well away from Shenandoah, for a short season. He was free to say he did not relish being carried back to Buffalo in irons, as he certainly would be if the officers found him. From the same cause he refused to appear very often in public, kept his room much during the day —to sleep and write, in reality—only coming out after night fall and joining the Mollies in Carroll's or at other haunts and meeting places.

At the Columbia House, where he made his temporary home, he met a man named Miller, an old acquaintance, who told him the city had fairly swarmed with detectives, representing all parts of the country, dating from the occurrence of the Yost murder. It was thought that suspicion pointed to Kerrigan and Duffy as actors in the case. The operative kept his own counsel, saying he "guessed all the detectives in Pennsylvania would not be able to fix the crime upon any one in particular ! '

Sunday, the twenty-sixth of July—twenty days subsequent to the murder—McKenna met Carroll in the evening, at his house, and after some drinks, the saloon-keeper took the agent aside and confided to him that, while the latter was absent at Storm Hill, detectives had been there to see him, Carroll—one claiming to be a mechanic in search of employment, and saying Gus McAffee, a Scotchman, working in a foundry, was an old friend. His name was Hendrick. Carroll laughed at the gawky acts of the pretended workman—but, as he believed, actual detective—and reported that he would appear in his, Carroll's saloon, every day, treat all hands, and never drink anything but beer, himself. The fact that he pretended to be "temperance," while he gave others strong liquor, excited the tavern-keeper's suspicions at once, and, as a natural result, Hendrick left, with the hint that his calling was known and he had been looking in the wrong place. The same word was taken to McAffee. Beside, the detective wore two or three different kinds of hats. Another followed. He made nothing out of Carroll, but was bluntly informed that he was a detective. A third fellow came and took Kerrigan to a saloon and got him very drunk, but made nothing in the way of solving the mystery.

"I can tell you," concluded Carroll, warming up and gaining confidence in McKenna, "the night the Yost job was to be done, I had loaned my pistol to a man in Tuscarora, an' the boys brought but one between them, an' I was forced to give them an old, single-barrel, breech-loading one that I had!"

"That wor not much in the way of weapons to undertake such a thing wid!" suggested McKenna.

"True for ye! But the job was done clanely, as you'll admit! By the same token, they fetched my wife on the stand at the coroner's inquest, an' before lavin home she cried, an' said she had seen me turn over the pistol to some men, an' belaved I, Kerrigan, Roarty, and Duffy knew all about the affair. Fur all that, my old woman made a fust-rate witness, an' let out nothing ! There wus somethin' said about a man that was aslape on my front steps, the night of the killin'. He wasn't one of 'em ! That wor Jo McGehan, who lives at Coaldale, an' he was drunk as a piper, at the same time. He's a white-haired, heavy fellow, is Jo, an' a brother-in-law of big John Gallagher ! "

" Isn't he, at the same time, a brother of my friend, Hugh McGehan ! " inquired the detective, carelessly.

" I don't know," was the response ; but Carroll immediately added : " When I saw the two policemen pass my house to gether—Yost and McCarron—I wanted the men not to do the job that night, but they swore they had been over before for the purpose, and they would not be balked—do it they did ! "

Mrs. Carroll had sworn, before the coroner, that she knew Tom Duffy had not been one of the murderers, for he slept at her house, was not absent, and could not have gone out without her knowledge, and that she had never heard Duffy or Kerrigan use threats against Yost.

The detective had knowledge, from the bullet which was extracted from Yost's side, where it had lodged, that the shooting was done with a revolver carrying a number thirty or thirty-two cartridge. It was his duty to find that particular pistol. To ai l in the search he was furnished with a new revolver, from Philadelphia, bearing a thirty-two cartridge. This he constantly carried, claiming that he had stolen it, in Tamaqua, and, on one or two special occasions, exhibiting the weapon with part of the loading abstracted, remarking that it was of little use to him, as he did not dare, from the circumstance of its illegal ownership, ask for or purchase any cartridges to fit it. How he employed the Smith and Wesson to good effect may be related hereafter.

CHAPTER XXXVII.

KERRIGAN'S SISTER-IN-LAW

THE following Tuesday, Carroll having accepted employ-ment at the new depot of the Philadelphia and Reading Company, McKenna would be unable to see him until after the day's work was done, and therefore turned his attention elsewhere. A man named McNellis, with whom he held some talk at Summit, as before noticed, met him at the Colum-bia House and in his company the operative set out to find Kerrigan, hoping to light upon the pistol with which Yost had been killed. McNellis said he also wanted to see Ker-rigan, but did not, at the time, divulge the particular business he had in view. As McNellis was a Mollie, and McKenna was another, they were soon on friendly terms and convers-ing on various subjects with considerable familiarity, thus passing the afternoon together, in Carroll's saloon ; and the man from Summit Hill grew somewhat excited, through the liquor he had imbibed, while his companion, intoxicated early in the day—as he had pretended—was in reality a little the worse for his potations, but by no means as fully over-come as he appeared. They interchanged opinions upon all topics, excepting the weather, which was decidedly hot, and ultimately decided that they were two of the arbiters of the fate of nations—in other words electors—and the decision of the forthcoming State campaign rested in their hands. The policy of the Reading Railway and Coal and Iron Company received due attention, and it was remarkable how nearly their ideas regarding those great corporations tallied. Mc-Nellis reprobated the management. McKenna abused Mr. Gowen and the entire association, from its lowest to its

highest official. After exhausting their capacity for conceal
ing spirituous liquors about their persons, and the supply of
subjects for argument, McKenna agreed to accompany the
Summit Hill man to Kerrigan's residence, known to be a
little outside of the borough limits, hoping to find the Bodymaster at home. On the route, by way of the cemetery,
they passed the house of Yost and the fatal street lamp, seeing which McNellis said something about a matter then being
negotiated, which would exceed that deed in interest to the
order, but, as he made no more definite allusion to the subject, the agent refrained from comment, merely remarking,
for about the hundredth time: "Be jabers, that wor a nate,
clane job!" And to this McNellis, for the hundredth time,
gave earnest assent.

Kerrigan's house formed a portion of a long row, or block,
of tall buildings, with stone basements and wooden upper
stories, standing on a high embankment, accessible over the
cut by a staircase. The little Tamaqua Mollie, with his big
wife and three unruly children, occupied the basement and
floor above, while the third story and garret were uninhab-
ited. If Jimmy Kerrigan was physically a small fellow,
measuring but two or three inches above five feet in his
stockings, he had a spouse of rather more than average size.
She was also something of a virago, and, as the neighbors
said, drove the Bodymaster with a tight rein—while he lorded
it over the Mollies—and had so held him in check for many
years.

It will be remembered that, in 1874, Tamaqua boasted no
division of the order. In 1875 it had one, to which some
of the best and worst of the Irish Catholic inhabitants belonged

Mrs. Kerrigan said, when visited by McKenna and Mc-
Nellis, that her husband would be back from his work, at
Col. Coke's Colliery, in a short time, and they could amuse
themselves at the front, while she entertained a neighbor

They took the hint that, in her enlightened view, they were a little too far gone in drink to be company for respectable ladies, and she wished them to remain at a distance, which they did, and occupied themselves with the children, chickens, and pigs, until they saw Kerrigan, in his shifting suit, coming along the ravine. Just as he arrived and they joined him at the house corner, McKenna's sight was refreshed by the appearance, coming from Kerrigan's residence, of a young woman, fashionably dressed, and carrying her parasol, whose face and figure seemed wonderfully familiar to him. Who could she be? Without pausing to look at him, as she came nigh, after once passing, the lady cast a shy and modest glance in his direction over her shoulder. Surely, he had seen that face somewhere. "Who is that lady?" asked McKenna, turning to Kerrigan, who was speaking with McNellis, and pointing toward Mrs. Kerrigan's caller.

"Who is she?" said the Bodymaster. "Why, sure an' that's me own sisther-in-law, Miss Mary Ann Higgins!"

It here burst upon the senses of the bewildered operative that it was the same lovely girl who made him feel, for a time, so supremely ridiculous at the Polish wedding, and the soft touch of whose lips lingered so pleasantly upon his cheek many weeks afterward.

"Then that is your sister-in-law? Bedad, but I must nev an introduction!"

"That ye surely shall hev!" returned Kerrigan. "She'll he here to-morrow avenin', wid her sisther, which is Mrs. Kerrigan, an' if you makes it convaynint to drop in, I'll let ye well acquainted in jist no time at all!"

"I'll be here!" answered McKenna, who could not keep his eyes off the handsome Miss Higgins, as long as she was within his line of vision.

Entering the house, Jimmy introduced McNellis and Mc Kenna to his better and greater half, and they received her apology for keeping them so long outside. It was:

17*

"Since the Yost affair, I have bin so much worritted by polace officers and their dirty spies, that, unless I know who the new-comers are, all hev to kape well outside until the man of the house is at home!"

"That's right!" said Kerrigan.

"Certainly!" echoed the two strangers—strangers to her, but not to her husband—and McKenna, especially, cursed all detectives and policemen with such downright earnestness that he completely won the heart of Mrs. Kerrigan.

"Sure, Misther Kerrigan," said McNellis, "an' I am sint to tell ye not to go beyant, to-night—if ye know what that manes, which I don't. At any rate, the word is you're not to come over the-night!"

"I perfectly understhand!" replied Kerrigan.

"Hugh McGehan an' Bill Mulhall have just got in from Luzerne County!"

"I'm glad to hear of that!" remarked the Bodymaster. "They are the boys for a swate thing!"

There was little more conversation until after supper, of which all partook with keen appetite, when Kerrigan put on his coat, and McNellis reiterated the remark about "not goin' over, because the boys were back."

"Be the way," exclaimed Jimmy. "Will ye do me a small favor?"

"Certainly I will!" answered McNellis.

"I want ye to take Roarty over his revolver! It has been here long enough!'

Kerrigan started to go upstairs, when McKenna brought out his pistol, at the same time saying:

"Just look at this little beauty! Wasn't that a raise to make for wan night's worruk?"

Kerrigan took the repeater, weighed it carefully in his hand, worked the lock, pronouncing it a splendid affair, then said:

"Wait here a bit, an' I'll show you the one what kilt Yost!"

The detective had evidently struck a vein that bid fair to prove productive, but he controlled his countenance to the expression of doubt in unmistakable terms, saying:

"I guess not by these lights!"

"But I will!" reiterated Jimmy. He left the room ascending the dark staircase, and soon returned with a black, rather old-fashioned five-shooter, which he transferred to McKenna, employing the words:

"That's the gun what brought down the peeler, Yost!"

All present had taken in much whisky, after eating, and McKenna judged most of Kerrigan's share was gathering in his head. So delivering himself, at least, he was again informed he held the weapon that had "fixed the Dutch policeman!"

The pistol carried a number thirty-two cartridge, and, although he was convinced of the truth of Kerrigan's allegation, it served his purpose to give out disbelief.

"I guess you're wanderin' a bit, there!" exclaimed the operative, "fur isn't it currently reported that Barney McCarron, Yost's own partner, shot him, because of a recent quarrel they'd had?"

"Oh! that's a swate enough story!" was the quick retort of the Bodymaster, "but you'll allow that I know somethin' of a job that I planned be myself, an' wor there on hand, when it wor all done!"

Here was a direct confession of one of the murderers, which was more than McKenna had expected. But at once dropping his assumption of disbelief, he acquiesced in the statement that Kerrigan really should be well informed, and begun to talk of the pistol, which was, in the operative's presence, turned over to McNellis for transportation to its owner, James Roarty, of Storm Hill.

Subsequently the trio went to Carroll's, and found the

saloon-keeper at home. But McKenna warned Kerrigan that, for his own sake, it was best they two should not be seen together on the street, and Jimmy walked alone, while McNellis and the operative traveled in company. While going toward town, McKenna again handled the old revolver, and found it to be of rather peculiar construction. In order to take out the cylinder a screw had to be unloosed in front of said cylinder. The weapon was fully loaded, and had one rusty screw, evidently not a part of it when leaving the manufactory. Somebody had given it repairs. But where, and who? These were questions to be solved in the future.

Before nine o'clock McNellis started for Storm Hill, carrying the tell-tale pistol with him. Subsequently Kerrigan and Carroll engaged in games at cards. At ten P.M. the "babe" — a name given the Tamaqua Bodymaster, but not on account of his known innocence—and McKenna visited a point on the hill, near the old cemetery, and sat down on a bank of earth together to have a talk. Kerrigan expressed a feeling of great bitterness toward Yost and McCarron, saying he had once been arrested by the policemen for taking the part of Duffy. Warming up a little, and deftly urged on by the detective, Kerrigan, in the end, made a revelation, substantially confirming young Mike McKenna's statements. He said he got his men in their positions, the night of the fifth, then went down town, where he drank with the policeman whose life was to be taken, and saw that Duffy was well in bed at Carroll's and all was right for the deed. He assured McKenna that not a man in his division, excepting Carroll, knew anything about it. He did not want them informed. Although the act was brought around by the order, it was enough for him—the President of the division—to be aware of it, and when the ordinary members came to be called on to do a job for Campbell in return, they would suspect, but could swear to nothing. Before the shooting, he went

to the spot and remained in the vicinity, in concealment, until he saw that his men had put in their work. In a few
minutes he retreated, with the rest, through the run and over
the hill, and kept with them until coming out near Breslin's,
at the White Bear Tavern. There he left the others, they
going to their houses at Storm Hill, where they must have
arrived at about five in the morning. The tale was continued
in about this way :

"I got home early, an' me ould woman wanted to know
where I'd been, an' I told her a lie, an' so got rid of it.
Faith, I wor to go this very night an' lay in wait, wid two
nen, an' shoot a boss, who richly deserves it, but, on account of the word McNellis brought, that McGehan hev
come back, it is put off till another day ! It wouldn't do to
have anything occur, ye see, the very time McGehan got
here ! Let him get to work at the breast first !"

This was further confirmation of Mike McKenna. Mc-
Gehan was certainly the taller man of the two who had murdered Yost. It was more than probable that Boyle was the
other.

"You'd better belave," concluded the Bodymaster, "I
took off me boots an' moved aisy enough, that mornin',
fur there's a German family livin' next door, an' I wor afraid
I'd be heard by them. But I made up to me house, begun
to scrape wid me nails at the door, an' Mrs. Kerrigan knew
what it meant, an' let me softly in. I jist tould her I'd been
drunk and stopped out all night, as I've done before, an'
didn't want the neighbors to know it ! Jist as sure as you're
over there, an' I'm over here, I've never brathed a single
word of it, only wonst to Jack Donahue ! He said it wor a
good job an' I was entitled to credit for me skill ! I tell ye
what 'tis, McKenna, ye want to be very careful how ye talk
wid strangers, at the hotel, for the place hev been fairly
swarmin wid detectives these few days past ! Some of 'em
may hev stolen the sign, ye see, an' still be detectives !'

"I know my business!" replied McKenna, "an' devil a word will they get out of me at all!"

At midnight the couple separated, my agent going to his hotel and Kerrigan staggering awkwardly homeward, as full of self-importance and spirits as he could be and retain power of locomotion.

The ensuing day McKenna met and conferred with Linden, who was thus fully informed of his progress. After this, he made up his mind that it had become his plain and open duty to cultivate the intimate companionship of Kerrigan, who was proving such a valuable informant. In order to gain further grace in the Bodymaster's eyes—also to please himself, it may well be believed—he resolved to give desperate siege to the heart of the handsome sister of Mrs. Kerrigan. To resolve was to act. Visiting the barber, he caused his wig to be properly dressed, face well cleansed, and beard and mustache nicely trimmed. Then attiring himself in his best clothing—none too fine at that, but much better than the garments he usually wore—he thought he was ready to start on the wooing expedition. It appears McKenna had soon learned to forget Pat Hester's daughter. But then, he argued, Miss Higgins was the earlier claimant for his attention. Had she not commenced the courtship at the Polish wedding? He was very sure of that. His sympathies could not have been earnestly enlisted with the other lady. In Miss Higgins he really believed he might easily be permanently interested. While this was the case, he felt forced to confess he was not so much paying attention to Miss Higgins, for Miss Higgins' own sake, as for the sake of her wicked little brother-in-law, whose cruel works would yet bring him within prison walls, if not beneath the gallows tree.

Kerrigan's little, round face expanded in a broad grin when he saw the particular pains McKenna was taking to make himself genteel, and he put on his best manner as he pro-sented the young man to his fair sister-in-law. Jimmy was somewhat puzzled when Miss Higgins blushed crimson, as she extended her hand, and remarked that she "believed she had seen the gentleman once before."

"Yes!" explained McKenna, the red blood also mantling his forehead and face. "I remember meeting you at a party, some months ago!" But he added, for her encouragement, in a low tone of voice: "Never fear, Miss! I'll say nothing further about it!"

"Thank you," said Miss Higgins, below her breath.

They were very commonplace words, as the detective afterward thought, but they sounded very musical to his ear, that evening, coming from the handsome young lady's lips.

In a short time, by using the free-and-airy style now so natural to him, McKenna succeeded in putting all present completely at their ease, and Miss Higgins, as well as her sister, Mrs. Kerrigan, begun to think they had known him since they were children. As for Jimmy Kerrigan, he was already confidential with his brother Mollie from Shenandoah. But the whisky toddy soon put the "babe" out of the way, as he was forced to admit that he had taken several glasses before reaching home, and the liquor he drank with the family disagreed with it, getting up a reaction in his system making a recumbent position indispensable. Mrs. Kerrigan marched her liege lord off to bed. It was a very pleasant evening that the operative enjoyed with Mrs. Kerrigan and her unmarried sister, after the exodus of the noisy fellow claiming the house as his home, and when he bade the ladies good night, at a late hour, they united in cordial requests that he should visit them often. Miss Higgins, especially, was pressing, in her modest way, to have the caller not forget their humble place of residence.

"Sure, an' I will not!" said McKenna, "an', all in due sayson, I hope I may be able to take revinge on the young lady that so surprised me at the Polish wedding!'

This last remark in a whisper, at the door.

"Hush !" warningly exclaimed the lady, her face the color of a blooming rose. But Mrs. Kerrigan saw nothing, heard nothing.

"I'm as silent as the churchyard I'm goin' to walk beside," said the operative, with a roguish smile, as he took his final leave.

"She's a very fine girl," soliloquized the officer, while walking to the Columbia House. "What a pity she is of such a family ! And to think that I must get her brother-in-law hanged ! Oh, I never can hope to have ' Miss Higgins transformed into 'Mrs. McParlan !' Brother-in-law to a murderer ! No ! Never !"

Despite this decision the dreams of the detective, that night, were not fated to be entirely deserted by the girl by whom he had been victimized at the Krozenski nuptials.

It was soon whispered over Tamaqua by talkative spinsters and gossips of more advanced experience, that the wild fellow, Jim McKenna, had fallen desperately in love with Mary Ann Higgins, Kerrigan's wife's sister, was quitting the drink, fast sobering down, and, if his wooing sped successfully, bade fair soon to marry the object of his passion, settle in Tamaqua, and make an honorable and respectable member of society. Certainly the subjects of these conversations were frequently together, and just as surely McKenna was more regularly seen dressed in his best, a lady on his arm, of a Sabbath day, attending church, than ever before, and it was evident that, as far as he was concerned, it would not be his fault if the New Year did not look upon him a full-fledged Benedict. As for Miss Higgins, she kept her own counsel. It is more than probable that her heart really remained untouched and she accepted the attentions of McKenna, as any virtuous girl in her station would have done, more because the man was popular and generally pleasing, than from the reason of having placed her affections upon him.

It was at or about this time that McKenna received the following letter:

SHENANDOAH, July 30, 1875.

JAMES McKENNA:

DEAR SIR:—Them persons who you heard was around was Inquiring about you in Pottsville hall (Pennsylvania Hall probably) Captain Jack (Mr. Linden) was telling me, a few nights ago.

I remain, as ever,

Yours, in Friendship,

FRANK McANDREW.

P.S. They were asking Captain Jack if he knew any person of the same, and they told your weight and height and he said he knew nothing of you.

F. McA.

This work on the part of the detectives secured the enduring friendship of the Shenandoah Mollies, and confirmed Muff Lawler in his belief that Linden could be implicitly trusted. "If he would not give McKenna away to the officers from Buffalo," said Lawler, "why should we, who are also his friends, fear to confide in him?" Muff was right, as far as tangible results were concerned, but as the reader will easily see, his arguments rested upon unstable grounds. Linden was seeking, with McKenna, to obtain the good-will of the Mollies. This letter shows that their mutual labors were successful.

It was now McKenna's purpose to cause Kerrigan to repeat his confessions before Capt. Linden, or some other person who could be safely used as a witness, and a number of attempts were made to agree upon places of conference where this could be gone through with, but the recklessness of Kerrigan, and his carelessness in keeping prearranged appointments, caused the efforts to come to naught. He met the detective, but not at the hour fixed, and sometimes at a different locality. Linden was thus greatly inconvenienced and left to lie on the ground, behind a protecting fence or wall, for many weary hours, without seeing Kerrigan or taking down his expected account of the Yost murder. But on these occasions Kerrigan freely opened his heart to Mc-Kenna, giving him the most explicit delineation of about every fact connected with the crime, excepting the names of the murderers. These would come all in good time.

CHAPTER XXXVIII.

SLOWLY GAINING GROUND.

At the close of the month McKenna met Yellow Jack Donahue, who gave out that he had nearly given up the Major job, for the present, and feared his vengeance might fail of accomplishment, from treachery, some person evidently having warned the Majors, as they no longer worked in their accustomed places and were shy of going abroad alone at night. He suspected John Slattery, who knew of the preparations made to kill Thomas and the Majors, as the one giving them notice. In any event, he would not wholly throw it up, only hold the matter back until a favorable opportunity occurred. Donahue was by no means complimentary of the men composing his division, saying there was not one in the number to be trusted with an important transaction. He expressed himself freely regarding the affair Alex. Campbell was trying to accomplish, wisely concluding that he was quite foolhardy about it, too short a time having elapsed since the Tamaqua murder. The breeze that stroke had started should be allowed to subside before entering upon any fresh undertaking.

During this interview, the operative received from Donahue the fact, confidentially communicated, that it was
himself, the redoubtable "Yellow Jack," who shot Morgan
Powell, the circumstances attending which assassination have
already been related in these pages. The deed was done at
Summit Hill, December the second, 1871, and in it Donahue
was assisted by two men, whose names he did not give. He
said their escape, after the shooting, was very easy, as they
did not go ten yards from the spot where Powell dropped,
until the excitement cooled down, when, in the darkness,
they quietly departed for the bush, soon reaching their homes
in safety. The detective made mental note of this disclo-
ure, his subsequently written report throwing the first true
flood of light upon a dark crime, which had, for four years,
baffled the best efforts of the officers of justice. He wrote
all about the conversation to the Agency, that night. It
was not politic to press Donahue for a description of his
accomplices, but from points he had already gathered, Mc-
Parlan suspected Campbell and the McKennas were at
least interested. Donahue made himself very friendly with
the agent, praised him highly for the part he had taken, as
he supposed, in the Thomas matter; invited him to his
house, and, as he took his departure, swore that "those
Majors should yet come to their graves, even though he
had to draw a bead on them, bowldly, in open daylight!"

In Carroll's saloon, the same night, my representative
chanced upon an old friend, Dan Kelly, known to be Manus
Kull, *alias* "Kelly the Bum," a hard case then as now, and
open for almost anything outrageous. About every crime
in the great catalogue had been charged upon him, but he
was not understood as possessing a noticeably bad character
previous to attaching himself to the Mollie organization. In
the same company at Carroll's were James, or Friday
O'Donnell, and Kerrigan. The latter took early occasion to
tell McKenna he should "keep quiet about the Tamaqua

matter, as these fellows were too soft to intrust with anything connected with so serious a subject." He promised to obey, and upon that topic consequently remained silent. The men were engaged in a wild debauch, and all more or less mellow, but they took good care to have every outrider away from the room before the Summit affair came up for discussion. It was the intention to put some boss off his pins, and Kerrigan volunteered to walk to Mt. Laffee and find some men to accompany a detail of his own, so that the job might be concluded about the middle of the week. Who the party was the agent did not then learn.

While escorting Kerrigan to his home, late that night, McKenna noticed he was being clumsily shadowed by Barney McCarron, who, although very drunk himself, acted as though he had a half-formed idea in his thick pate that Kerrigan and McKenna were hatching some mischief, and therefore sought to throw himself in their way, to learn the particular business they were engaged upon. But his amateur detective work was done so awkwardly that Kerrigan quickly saw through it. Then the two Mollies made up a game to put the police man to more trouble, and they led him a wild-goose chase. Late at night, McKenna, still blunderingly traced by Mc-Carron, came to a halt at the Columbia House. He found the doors all fastened and no porter up to admit him. Just then McCarron came along.

"What are you trying to do?" asked the hiccoughing and worn-out policeman.

"Bedad, but I'm sakin' for an admission to me boardin'. house!' responded McKenna.

"Yes," put in Kerrigan, "he's shut out enthirely, an how he'll get within, is the question! It wor different wid me, when I wor in the lock-up! I wanted a way out! He wants a way in!"

McCarron laughed, and suggested that McKenna might try a window.

" Perhaps some of them may be unfastened ! "

" No ! I prefer you'd do that job for me ! " answered the agent, staggering and leaning against the side of the house. " You know you are an officer, an' can safely go in ! If I wor to do so, perhaps you'd jist arrest an' take me to jail for an attempted burglary ! "

Notwithstanding McCarron's repeated assurances that he would do no such thing, McKenna refused to touch a single shutter, or sash, and finally prevailed npon the policeman to seek entrance to his hotel through a casement and then unlock the front door for him. Kerrigan and the detective enjoyed the fun, beholding the unsteady efforts the drunken watchman made, raising the window and then ungracefully climbing into the house. But they soon gained entrance and went upstairs, after ·lighting a candle at the office counter, McCarron still following, Kerrigan noiselessly bringing up the rear. Once in McKenna's apartment, the policeman was offered a chair and Kerrigan told that he could go. The Bodymaster obeyed. And then McCarron set about the task of extracting information from McKenna regarding the Yost murder. The detective was acting the part of a drunken man to perfection, while McCarron was really much intoxicated, but trying to appear very wise and sober. Taking the flaring candle in his hand, he got down on his knees and endeavored, with an owlish assumption of superior intelligence, quite ridiculous in him at any time, to explain to his only auditor precisely how and where certain acts had been done, the night of the murder, illustrating his meaning by pointing out with uncertain finger, on the irregular figures of the carpet, an imaginary map of the locality and the proceedings. It was as much as the operative could possibly do to refrain from laughing in McCarron's face, to see the style in which he performed this part of his unaccustomed work. Meanwhile McCarron was trying his best to gain intelligence from his companion. He succeeded indiffer ently, as McKenna was, to all appearances, as ignorant as the man in the moon of everything connected with the Mollies. When the policeman had nearly spoiled the bedroom carpet with the melted tallow constantly dropping from his migratory candle, and exhausted himself in making drawings of the Yost matter, giving the position he occupied, and the places in which the murderers stood, over and over again, McKenna put a stop to the proceedings by politely asking the fellow to leave, as he wanted to obtain a little sleep before morning.

Seeing that he could gain nothing by his extraordinary efforts at "roping," the drunken guardian of the peace, after a while, took the hint and went stumbling down the staircase, muttering to himself about the "ignorance of some people." He had been unable to impose upon McKenna, and flattered himself that it was because of that person' stupidity. There was stupidity in the business, but it was in McCarron, not with McKenna.

The Sunday following, after visiting church, in the forenoon, with Miss Higgins, and subsequently taking her a pleasant evening's walk, the agent met Kerrigan again at Carroll's, and the pair went to the scene of the Yost murder together, the Bodymaster designating the vicinities which McCarron, on a previous occasion, had tried so hard to explain to the operative. Kerrigan marked the very spot on which McGehan and Boyle had stood, under the shadow of the trees, where he was waiting, armed only with a stone, to put in work if found necessary, then to lead the men away after their job was done, and gave him other information of great importance. He said that he, Kerrigan, was wearing the same pantaloons he had on the night of the murder only they were industriously patched by his wife. He ruptured them badly, running in the bush, and, the next morning, was asked by Mrs. Kerrigan how the holes were made. She was satisfied when he told her he fell down the bank by the house and nearly killed himself.

A little later, Kerrigan took a seat, near the Odd Fellows' Cemetery, on some rocks, and proceeded to dwell upon his own fortunes and those of some of his friends. The "babe," according to his own story, was born in Schuylkill County; had received no education, no schooling, in fact, since he was an infant; had been successively a coal-picker, a miner, and, during the late war, a soldier, in the cavalry branch of the service, under gallant Phil Sheridan. As to McGehan, he said he hailed from Donegal, Ireland, but had been partly reared in America. Alex. Campbell, reported the same historian, was married, and had a family, his wife being also a native of Donegal.

It was well toward morning when the two Mollies separated.

A meeting of the agent and Alex. Campbell, transpiring at Carroll's saloon, the fourth day of August, was productive of interesting results. The Summit Hill tavern-keeper and former Bodymaster zealously recommended McGehan as one of the best men in the country, and was happy to see that Hugh and Mulhall had found work at Tuscarora. He said, boastingly, that as soon as he could go to Mauch Chunk, for the necessary license, he proposed to set McGehan up in a saloon of his own, McKenna, Kerrigan, and Carroll being warmly pressed to honor the opening with their presence, which all promised. Then, stepping aside a little, Campbell let out to the detective more than he had ever before said .

"It was McGehan, himself, who fired the shot that killed Yost! Boyle was along, it is true, but McGehan's shot finished the business and the other did not save to discharge his pistol at all!"

This remark, coupled with the facts he had already obtained from Mike McKenna, Kerrigan, and Carroll, firmly convinced the inquirer there could be no mistake about the matter. The murderers of Yost were found. But where was the testimony with which to convict them, in the face of the omnipresent *alibi!* He did not despair of even ferreting out that, before finishing the good work. It was Campbell who had sent McNellis to Tamaqua, notifying Kerrigan he should stay at home the night fixed for the killing of some unsuspecting boss, as McGehan and Mulhall had that day chanced to return to Storm Hill.

Subsequent to the departure of Campbell for his home, McKenna took the saloon-keeper away from the house a little and said :

"Jim Carroll, you thought I didn't know who it wor that knocked Yost off his two feet!"

"I knew d——d well that you did know!" was Carroll's laconic return.

"Well, I don't blame ye at all for kapin' a tight rein on yer tongue! I'd ha' done the same, meself, had I been in your pair o' boots!"

"That's all right!" continued Carroll. "It was a mighty good thing, an' McGehan is the fellow for a clane job! Mulhall was in for it, with him, but some objected because he was a man of family, so Boyle took his place. I wanted to have it put off, when I saw McCarron and Yost come past here, in company, an' told the men to seek a better chance, another day, but McGehan said he'd been over here three times to do it, and he would not brook further delay. So they went and did it!"

"An' did it nately and aisily, too?' suggested McKenna.

Mrs. Carroll had her suspicions aroused, during the visit that McKenna was a Mollie, and so informed her husband. She thought he could not be so intimate with Jack Donahue, talking by the hour with him in the back yard, and with Jimmy Kerrigan, and remain only an outsider. She also accused Carroll of forming one of the order, but he laughed, and said: "You know better! What's the use of charging such a thing on me?" Yet he was Secretary of the division at the very time. This answer did not change Mrs. Carroll's mind. But she was too discreet and true a wife to disclose her thoughts on the subject to every one.

The same night Kerrigan was more than usually communicative, and related to the agent all about a trick he and Carroll were to play, in stealing a lot of hams, and a new copper boiler, out of the Columbia House cellar. The operative made up his mind the landlord should not be robbed, but said nothing. The attempt was subsequently made and some things carried off, but they had to be returned.

While the Bodymaster was in a talking humor, McKenna carelessly inquired :

" Now what about that Summit job ? "

" Oh, that's put off until the latter part of the month ! And Kerrigan sighed, and seemed to greatly regret the delay.

" Is it Zehner, or Jones, this time ? "

" Jones, av coorse ! " was the response. " An' it has to be done by daylight too, as he is a workin' boss ! I am not sure, yet, where he will be caught ! "

The sending of this report to Mr. Franklin, the detective very well knew, would cause the party threatened to receive notification of the danger he was in. The important missive was written and mailed before he slept.

Thursday, the fifth, occurred the funeral of John Dowling, one of the oldest members of the Ancient Order of Hibernians, otherwise the Mollie Maguires, in the State, and, as many were to come to Tamaqua from Shenandoah, McKenna suffered a convenient return of rheumatism, so he said, and kept his room, in consequence, all the day. None of his old companions sought him out, excepting Frank McAndrew, and he visited the Columbia House, was shown to his friend's apartment, and had a long visit with him. The Shenandoah Bodymaster had heard that McKenna was suspected of complicity with the Yost murder, and soberly warned him to have a care for himself, which advice the agent re-

18

ceived with a hearty laugh, saying, as he was innocent, he
"didn't care a snap of his fingers what people thought!"
He expressed himself as heartily tired of hiding so slosely
from the Buffalo detectives, and, but for a second letter,
which he had just received from his sister, saying the men
were still hanging around her house, he would emerge from
his cover, return to Shenandoah at once, and resume his old
occupations and amusements. As it was, he hoped soon to
hear that the New York officials were starting off for Canada,
on a false scent, when he would certainly hasten homeward.

"Ye can't be too careful, me boy!" was the admonition
with which McAndrew separated from his Secretary.

It was at the saloon and beer garden of Conrad Iffland,
on Broad Street, Tamaqua, that Linden and McKenna now
met to talk over the operation and arrange all their movements. Mrs. Iffland was a good-natured German lady, gen-
erously patronized by her countrymen and other lovers of
lager-beer, and she gave no particular attention to the detectives—hearing from her husband that Linden was all correct—as long as they paid for their refreshments. When
McKenna appeared on the streets with a peculiarly ugly
hat, or made a particular gesture with his hand, Linden
knew they were to meet at Iffland's immediately. A similar sign with the hand of Linden taught the same lesson to
McKenna. On the seventeenth of August, 1875, the two
men held a very important conversation at Mrs. Iffland's,
and made preparations, subsequently carried out, to meet
Campbell, McGehan, Boyle, and others, if possible, at
Mauch Chunk, where Campbell was to go to make application for McGehan's license. Linden then assumed the *rôle*
of the toper to perfection, and was finally invited by Campbell to join the company, slightly opposed by McKenna,
who claimed Linden was only a stranger who had accosted
him near his hotel, inquiring the way to the Mansion House.
In this manner Linden learned the faces of the men and

something of their habits and conversation. Conrad Iffland had no knowledge of McKenna's business, nor had his spouse, but both believed him to be the wickedest Mollie Maguire in Schuylkill County. As long as he was in Linden's society they tolerated him. Alone, or with Kerrigan, they would have turned him promptly away from their door. Knowing this, the operative never attempted an entrance, excepting he found that Linden was in the neighborhood.

It was not until the eighth of August, that McKenna made his reappearance in Shenandoah, and then remained but a short time. He was warmly greeted by his old-time associates, Morris, Hurley, and McAndrew, who said they had heard that the agent and the rest were to be arraigned for the attack upon Wm. M. Thomas. At least they feared preparations were being made for their apprehension. He soon quieted their suspicions, saying there was no testimony, and, if the contrary were true, they could easily prove an *alibi*.

The monthly meeting of the division was held, McKenna acting as Secretary, as usual. While in the company of his friends, he thought it strange he heard nothing more of the Gomer James affair, but concluded the feud had subsided and the Welshman was to be allowed to live in peace in the community. How sadly he was deceived the sequel may show.

CHAPTER XXXIX.

BLOODY SATURDAY.

EARLY in August, 1875, symptoms of smouldering disorder in the coal regions began to increase in severity and numbers. Seeing and appreciating this, Superintendent arranged to meet and hold council with McKenna and Linden in the vicinity of Mauch Chunk. Glen Onoko, one of the most entrancing of the many beautiful spots found in the vicinity of the city named, was the chosen place. In sight of Dual Vista, another extraordinary and charming resort, accordingly, the three men came together, and, in the quiet shadows of the everlasting hills—the Alps of America —covered by the close-woven branches of the overhanging trees, they seated themselves, and, at their leisure, fully discussed the situation and the work being performed. It was while returning from this meeting—the particulars of which may not find record here, as they will be developed in the history of the progress of events—that McKenna and Linden encountered Campbell, McGehan, and others, as mentioned in another connection. While Capt. Linden remained at Mauch Chunk and Superintendent Franklin returned to Philadelphia, McParlan—otherwise McKenna—was constrained to accompany Alex. Campbell and his jolly companions to their homes. The invitation was so pressing, and the chance so good for obtaining knowledge of facts bearing upon the Yost case, and the threatened assassination of Jones, that the watchful operative could not well refuse acceptance. Evening saw the collection of Mollies, McKenna among them, gathered in the smoking-car bound for Summit. In a seat, not far removed from them, but, to their eyes, so effectually steeped in liquor as to be almost unrecognizable —and in fact entirely unnoticed by Campbell—reposed the form of Linden, every nerve really strung to the highest tension, awake, cool, determined, and ready, at any moment, to take his brother detective's part, should he find himself in trouble. Happily nothing occurred to call for his assistance, and he feigned to sleep the time away, without molestation, until the drunken crowd left the car. Linden continued his journey to Tamaqua, and there awaited McParlan's arrival. Reaching Summit, Campbell pressed that operative to so main at his house all night, and he did so, after first viewing the basement in which the late Bodymaster was to assist McGehan to start his gin mill. The building was situated just above the post-office, in an eligible locality, and preparations were being made to celebrate the formal opening, to occur on the twelfth of the month, with appropriate observances. Campbell asked no questions, but naturally concluded, from McParlan's previous avowals, that his guest was in Mauch Chunk that day to obtain a new stock of counterfeit money, and a crisp ten dollar bill he had seen him have changed, when treating the company in a saloon, he was quite sure would not successfully pass examination at any banking house. In this he seriously erred, however, as the currency was genuine and just from the Shenandoah post-office, where McKenna had presented and received the cash upon my postal order for fifty dollars, to be used in paying current expenses.

"I tell you, Jim," said Campbell, "if I knew just where to get such flimsies as you find, at about fifty cents on the dollar, I don't know but I'd put aside me prejudices an' religious scruples an' make a small investment!"

McParlan was never communicative as to the source from whence his bank-bills came, but pleasantly returned:

"When ye git rid of the rest of yer scruples and religious principles, come to me wid the ready cash, an' I'll do what I've never done for any wan afore, lade ye right up to me partner in business, an' indorse ye to him as a shover of the quare that'll do to dale wid!"

Saying he would remember this, the other changed the subject to the expulsion of Tom Fisher from the order, as an inactive and inefficient leader, because he, Alex. Campbell, thought himself much better qualified for, and really wanted the conspicuous place. The Shenandoah Secretary replied he had never heard anything urged against Fisher, only that he was not in favor of putting the enemies of the order under the sod, but that was a serious objection to any Ancient Order man, hence he was in favor of cutting Fisher off and electing Campbell, who was a chief after his own heart, and would not hesitate to shoot a rascally Welsh boss in person, if it was found for the good of the society. The Summit official swallowed the bait, hook and all, and remarked, self-complacently, that he believed, after the Tamaqua Convention, already called for the 25th of August, he would have John P. Jones taken care of, whether Kerrigan came up with his assistance or not. There were now two men in his neighborhood, Hugh McGehan and James Roarty, who could not be matched for excellence in shuffling off the mortal coil for those needing such a job performed, and if he once sent them out, that mining boss would never again have a chance to refuse a friend of his work in the breast. Jones, the detective found out, resided at Storm Hill, about Lansford, not far from Mike O'Donnel's tavern, in a field just at the foot of an old plane near the pipe-line ascending to Summit Hill, and Campbell thought it one of the easiest things imaginable to take the man off just after sunrise, some fine morning, when on the way to Number Four Breaker, without a soul being the wiser for the job. "We'll fix him, yet!" was the late Bodymaster's conclusion of the talk, when suddenly interrupted by the entrance of Mrs. Campbell. "Not a word more!" was the sign made by the late Bodymaster, with a finger on his lip, and as readily understood by McParlan, who quickly changed the subject, saying, as a blind, he thought the "Company would very soon get sick of standing out against the Union and offer to compromise on as favorable a basis as that of 1874." Mrs. Campbell suspected nothing, and thought so too. Alex. Campbell knew it must come to that. After singing "Widow Machree," for the lady the detective retired to his apartment.

The second day after the grand opening—the fourteenth of

August, rendered memorable as "bloody Saturday" in the
coal regions—a fact, however, that had not yet reached the
knowledge of the little community at Summit Hill, where
few newspapers were taken and the telegraph operatives
were seriously uncommunicative—McParlan met his pretended relative, Pat McKenna, the Bodymaster, but learned
nothing new. At four o'clock the same afternoon he repaired to McGehan's saloon with Campbell, and found
Hugh, perfectly at his case, smoking a pipe as complacently
as though no innocent human blood stained the hand that
supported his head. They had a pleasant chat, McParlan
told one or two stories, and also took a whiff from his cutty-
pipe, and the three enjoyed themselves in this way for an
hour. At the end of that time, no strangers being about,
McParlan produced the new, nickel-plated pistol, which he
said he had taken from his hypothetical Welshman in Tamaqua, and handed it over to McGehan for his scrutiny.   He
clicked the lock critically, looked at the cylinder, and passed
it back, saying it was "an illigant affair, altogether."

" So it is ! " replied the owner of the repeater, putting it
away, " but divil a bit of good will it do me, in this or any
other matter, if I can't find some cartridges !   I don't dare
buy a single wan in the borough of Tamaqua, for fear the
gun may be traced to me ownership, an' I don't care to go
up on so small a job, when I can have bigger ones for the
axin' ! "

McGehan hesitated a moment, looked cautiously around
the room, was assured that no one outside the Mollie ring
heard him, and then answered, in a low tone of voice :

"The cartridges for Roarty's revolver might fit your
shooter, but I am not so sure that he has one left; an' he
too is a little timid about purchasing, as it wor his pistol
that I had to shoot Yost with ! "

" Is that so ? " carelessly remarked the detective, betray-
ing no sign of undue excitement over McGehan's voluntary

and tacit admission that he had killed the Tamaqua policeman, and at once adding : "Well, never mind ! I can use the two I have in the cylinder, in case of accident, an' as I'm a tolerable marksman, I think no more'll be actually wanted."

McParlan had the three missing cartridges, at the moment, safely secreted in his pocket. But McGehan was in for a clean breast of the whole matter—would not stop—and went on with the narration :

"Ye see, we came to do the job in this way ! Kerrigan an' Campbell, they had a trade between them, an' I an' Boyle was to go along, so was Roarty, who started on ahead. Kerrigan agreed to get the pistols for us. When we—Boyle and I—got over to Campbell's we heard a messenger had been there before us, comin' from Roarty's house, wid a word sayin' as how Roarty's wife was taken sick, an' for him to go straight for the doctor ; Roarty did so, but sent forward his pistol to represent him, to Carroll's house, where we were told to meet. When we reached Carroll's, sure an' Roarty's black pistol wor the only serviceable weapon in the whole company, an' Jim Carroll, he gave us a little, old, breech-loading, single-barrel affair, which was of no account. I took the big shooter, an' gave the other to Boyle, after Kerrigan had been out to try an' borrow another, an' returned empty-handed. An' I told Boyle, if he wakened, upon gettin' up to Yost, an' stirred a foot in retrate, I'd shoot him down too ! Kerrigan then went up Broad Street an' put us in our places, near the fence, in the shadow of some trees, an' after that went down town, saw the policemen together, and took a sip o' whisky wid Yost—more'n I'd ha' done in such a case—when he jist come back to us, by a winding route, sayin' all wor right, an' the men would be up by midnight, or a little later. They had to put out two lamps near by. One would be taken by Yost, to outen, and the other by McCarron. It wor nearly two o'clock

when they came, both together, which wer very different
from our expectations. But they came! Kerrigan wanted
to be there, armed wid two rocks in his hands, to bate out
Yost's brains, in case the pistols failed, but I ordered him
away and made him stand fifty yards off, rightly thinkin' he
wor too noticeable, from his small size, an' if any one saw
him he would be known an' remembered. Then the thing
wor done! Roarty's pistol did it! It's all nonsense to say
McCarron did not give chase, fur he did, an' fired two shots
at us, which I returned, an' then we ran away, Kerrigan, the
rat, along wid us! But I made him lave when we came
out at Breslin's White Bear tavern, an' I would have been
much better plazed had he remained away an' left us to find
our route by ourselves!"

"It wor a mighty slick thing!" exclaimed the operative
"an' I'm sure Tamaqua Division should be willin' to send
you over men to do your job whenever ye may ask it!"

Campbell was of the same belief, saying that Kerrigan
and Carroll were all right and would come up with their
help in due season.

The ensuing Sunday, at church, in company with Campbell, McParlan met James Roarty, and the latter accom
panied him to McGehan's. Then, in McGehan's presence,
he made more inquiry for cartridges for his supposed-to-be
stolen revolver, and Roarty answered:

"I believe I have some belonging to the revolver Mc-
Gehan used at Tamaqua!"

He made known his willingness to supply a charge to Mc-
Parlan. Then Roarty left, expecting soon to return, and
McParlan and McGehan passed the evening, to a late hour
waiting in the damp, cool basement, but Roarty did not
get back, probably being prevented by the rain, which was
falling, and finally the operative separated from his companion, returning to Campbell's for a bed.

During the detective's talk with McGehan he found the
18*

the murderer of Yost boarded with a young widow lady
named Mrs. Boyle, living near Number Four Breaker, who
was very fond of her lodger, and intended to become his
wife. It was more than probable, from this circumstance,
that, should McGehan be arrested, Mrs. Boyle would try to
swear him clear, by saying he had been in her company the
night of the fifth of July. How clearly McParlan saw future
events will be shown hereafter.

Well satisfied with his trip to Lansford and vicinity,
McKenna returned to Tamaqua with Alex. Campbell the
ensuing Monday, there to find very important news. Picking up a copy of the Pottsville *Miners' Journal,* for Monday, the 16th of August, the agent read aloud to his comrades an article, entitled "Bloody Saturday," of which the
following is a summary:

"Saturday was a horrible day for the people of the
Mahanoy Valley. The devil had business on his hands.
Two dastardly assassinations and one case of manslaughter,
beside several cases of lesser crimes, were his harvest. At
Girardville, possibly the most heinous act of the short but
bloody list was committed. A good citizen, and a mild,
inoffensive man, was murdered, in the person of Thomas
Gwyther, Justice of the Peace.

"Saturday, the miners in the Mahanoy Valley received
the first pay of any consequence since the strike, and the
result was that Girardville, in the evening, was crowded
with men in various stages of intoxication. The rougher
element grew absolutely rampant and defiant of lawful
restraint. Gangs of ruffians went about the streets, flourishing their revolvers. Though there were special policemen, they were powerless and cowed. One of the bands
was headed by a man named Hoary, who was heard to
exclaim, as he exhibited his weapon: 'Give me some one
to shoot! I'll kill the first man that insults me! In their
travels this party went to Jacob Wendel's tavern, and

jostled a number of persons in the bar room. Hoary struck and maltreated Mr. Sheisler. Squire Gwyther was sitting in the room, at the time, and to him Hoary's victim applied for a warrant. Before matters could advance any farther there, Wendel put Hoary and party out, and then let the Squire and the complainant out by the back way. They went to the Squire's office and he had begun to write out a warrant for Hoary's arrest, when that individual and his gang entered the office, threatening to kill both the Justice and the plaintiff if the warrant should be issued. They were got out and the door locked. The warrant was properly prepared, and the Squire stepped out to look for Hoary. He was standing near his own door at the corner, when he found a man a few yards off with a leveled gun. His daughter also saw the same man, and cried out, ' For God's sake, don't shoot father !' Almost immediately the gun was fired, the contents taking effect in the breast of the Justice and in a short while causing death. The assassin fled and escaped. A man named Thos. Love was arrested on suspicion, but he proved an *alibi* and was released. Subsequently it was ascertained that the assassin was Wm. Love, who is missing. Naturally, so bold a defiance of law and so dastardly a murder created the most intense excitement in the borough and vicinity, where the victim was known and esteemed.

"At Shenandoah a cool and premeditated murder was committed. The motive of this particular assassination is to be sought in the events of the past. On Monday night, August the 11th, 1873, a Welshman, named Tom Jones, was assaulted, knocked down and beaten by one Edward Cosgrove, in Shenandoah. Jones' friends ran to his rescue, and among them was a young fellow, called Gomer James, a Welsh miner. In the trouble which followed, Cosgrove was shot and killed, James was accused of his murder, arrested and tried. The testimony at the trial was not sufficient to

convict him and he was acquitted. His escape incensed
Cosgrove's friends, who believed James guilty, and threats
were made to take his life. Saturday last, the Rescue Hook
and Ladder Company, of Shenandoah, held a picnic, which
being well attended, was run far into the night. Gomer
James, somewhere about 11 o'clock, was inside a bar at this
picnic, waiting upon its patrons, and a number of men came
up. They asked for beer, and while James was drawing it
he was shot and killed. In the semi-darkness and confusion
the assassin escaped.

"A dispatch from Shenandoah, received last evening, says :
Gomer James was shot last evening, about 12 o'clock, at the
picnic grounds in Hecksher and Glover's Grove, the ball
passing through his heart, embedding itself in his back near
the skin. Dr. Quail, Coroner, assisted by Drs. Reagan and
Byers, held a *post-mortem* examination. Deputy Coroner
Dengler impaneled the following jury: T. J. Foster, R.
Stacker, Lyam Bloom, George A. Herring, A. H. Roades,
and H. C. Boyer. The jury adjourned until Monday morning to finish hearing the testimony, there being a large number of witnesses. The evidence so far is likely to point sus
picion on some one.'

"The usual results of a large pay were visible in Mahanoy,
Saturday night. There were numbers of drunken men on
the streets, and a lawless spirit seemed to animate some of
them. There were several encounters, in which individuals
got roughly handled, and a fight which cost the life of an
innocent citizen. A disturbance arose at Phillips' Pottsville
House, on Centre Street, between Wm. M. Thomas and a
man named James Dugan. Both drew revolvers, and fired
a number of shots at each other. Which fired first we could
not ascertain. Thomas was in an intoxicated condition.
He received a bullet in his left cheek, where it now is. A
man whose name is given as Christian Zimmerman, or Christian Brenhower, who was standing across the street, waiting

for his wife to come out of a store where she was shopping, received a bullet through his left lung. It was taken out of his back. Though alive at five o'clock yesterday afternoon, this unfortunate man was surely dying, having made his will. Yesterday Dugan was arrested and held by Squire Comrey in $800, for an aggravated assault and battery on William Thomas. Thomas was arrested and committed by Squire Groody in default of $1,800 bail, for an aggravated assault and battery on Dugan. He was lodged in the county jail yesterday afternoon by officer Gorman. So it appears no one has been arrested for the killing of the innocent man.

"A man, whose name we did not learn, received a flesh wound in a leg during the shooting. Another, called 'Carney,' a shoemaker, while standing on his own door-step, was assaulted by a party of young men, struck on the head with a billy, and had an oyster knife stuck into his back. His injuries are not serious!"

McKenna was astounded to find that Gomer James, after so much had been done for him, should have engaged in any public position, especially as booth-tender at a picnic, thus placing himself temptingly before the Mollies, who, for over two years, as he must have known, had been thirsting for his blood. He reached the very result that might have been expected from such criminal recklessness.

When Alex. Campbell learned that Gomer James was killed, he almost shed tears of delight. McKenna was forced, against his will, to participate in the general rejoicing which followed. It proved hard for him to put on the hateful mask, but, galling as it was, he had to wear it. The same afternoon, he returned to Mahanoy City, finding the country in a blaze of excitement, and none the more safe place of refuge for a man, well known as a prominent member of the Ancient Order of Hibernians, otherwise the Mollie Maguires, as he was. Remaining but a short time he went, by train, to Shenandoah, saying, when he met Mc

Andrew, Morris, and Lawler at that place, that his friends, the Buffalo detectives, had either been frightened off by recent occurrences, or gone away to Canada, on a false scent, and it was no longer necessary he should hide from them. All the Mollies were glad to meet him. The non-Mollies, as they were aware of his prolonged absence from the vicinity could not look upon him as at all chargeable with the killing of Gomer James, and therefore did not, at this time, particularly seek his life. They—the goodly citizens—merely glanced at him, out of the corners of their eyes, and some thought he was good enough to be hanged, but made no overt demonstrations.

McKenna had not been four hours in Shenandoah when he learned, through Muff Lawler, that there was little doubt who had done for the young Welshman. Mike Carey, who was present, with Lawler, McAndrew, Morris, and other Mollies, said in an impressive whisper:

" Hurley reached forward, over the counter, and fired, the bullet striking Gomer James full in his heart, an' he fell ! Before any one could go to his assistance he wor dead ! I saw the thing done myself ! "

It seems that Shenandoah Division was in session at the time of the assassination—eleven o'clock at night of the fourteenth—when Carey rushed in, before the members, and announced, " Tom Hurley has shot Gomer James ! " He was quickly stopped by McAndrew, and subsequently sharply reprimanded because of his thoughtlessness, in making such a statement before all the members. But it was doubtless true that Tom Hurley had done the deed.

As a result of this unexpected success, all the Mollies in Shenandoah engaged in a grand bacchanal, and few remained sober. To get rid of them, McKenna left the place and went to Girardville. Kehoe said that the murder of Squire Gwyther was the result of a drunken spree, and Love, he was glad to say, had made his escape. The young man, Thomas

Love, who had been arrested by High Constable Kehoe, in person, he knew, as well as any one, was quite innocent, but the brother, who was guilty, had traveled off, untrammeled.

This dark day was not the end of the reign of the assassins 'a Pennsylvania.

----------◆----------

CHAPTER XL.

MORE BOSSES DOOMED.

Now the Mollies having Gomer James dead and buried and out of their way, it was believed by some bloodshed would cease. But the attentive reader will have arrived at the conclusion that the end was not yet. For my own part, I must confess to having experienced occasional periods of disappointment. Here had I been, using my best efforts, seconded by the most effective help the Company could furnish, and notwithstanding our united action, despite the fact that we daily knew much of the order, assassinations were not being entirely prevented. This midnight society, to guard against surprise or capture, had its committees within committees, or, in other words, its secret affairs were seldom given to the general members, but were kept in charge of the leading officers and prominent personages. Hence, very few of the Mollies in Shenandoah were officially aware of the fact that Gomer James was to be put out of the way. McAndrew, Hurley, Morris, Munley, Monaghan, McKenna, and a few more knew it, and kept it to themselves—excepting the detective who reported it—as those in Tamaqua and Summit Hill retained among a few leading spirits the facts connected with the murder of Yost and the preparations for cutting off John P. Jones. But Jones was notified by Mr. Franklin, a

guard of men put in his house, and the boss instructed to
seek some other route, by which to reach his work, than the
pipe-line.   For a while he maintained a measure of caution,
but not during many weeks ; it became an old story.   Danger, as he thought, had been overestimated.   Carelessness
and the resumption of his former habits quickly followed this
conclusion

The convention, appointed for the twenty-fifth of August,
occurred at Carroll's house, the members occupying three
chambers in the upper part of the building.   Among those
convened on this interesting occasion were Jack Kehoe,
County Delegate ; Wm. Gavin, County Secretary ; Christopher Donnelly, County Treasurer ; Jerry Kane, of Mt.
Laffee ; Francis Keenan, of Forestville ; Frank O'Neill, of St
Clair ; James Roarty, of Coaldale ; John Donahue—"Yellow Jack"—of Tuscarora, and Michael O'Brien, of Mahanoy City.   Tom Hurley and John Morris, of Shenandoah,
were in one of the rooms for a few minutes.   Many outsiders
seemed to be in the city and in the building, but the parties
mentioned transacted all the business of the meeting.   Pat
Butler was on hand, but not as a legal part of the convention's committee—only as a sort of witness.   During the
session of the lesser body, which was devoted principally to
hearing grievances, expelling and readmitting members,
Tom Hurley came forward and made known that to him,
and to no one else, was the society indebted for the killing
of Gomer James.   Modesty, it appears, was far from a
prominent point in Hurley's character.   At least, on this day,
he not only boasted much of his peculiar service, but put
before the order, with no circumlocution or evasion, a direct
and open claim to a money reward for putting out of the
way the murderer of Cosgrove.   He thought he was entitled
to a large sum for his success.   James McKenna, the detective, acting as Secretary of the committee before which
Hurley's demand was made, was obliged to receive it, but

Pat Butler, of Loss Creek, presented himself before the same committee with the verbal demand of one McClain, of his division, who asserted that he, and not Hurley, had been the marksman who brought down the young Welshman. When Kehoe heard of the difference, he ordered Pat Butler and James McKenna to act as arbiters and to settle the difference by holding an investigation and reporting a decision, in writing, at a subsequent date, directing to him at his home in Girardville. They accepted the duty and appointed the succeeding Sabbath for the appearance, in Shenandoah, of the two men and their witnesses, when the case should be heard and adjusted according to its real merits. Kehoe would make no movement toward rewarding the man, who, he was free to say, deserved a fair recompense, until this trial had been concluded. Friends of Hurley were satisfied, they urged, that a dozen persons could swear Tom did the shooting. Every confidence was expressed that the blood-money would go to him and to no other person.

Jerry Kane, Pat Dolan, Frank Keenan, Jack Donahue, Mike O'Brien, and James McKenna, constituted the committee first spoken of as having been selected by the convention.

The convention and its committee, after transacting their legitimate business, adjourned, the members returning to their respective homes, only Hurley, Morris, and McKenna remaining at Tamaqua over night.

The Shenandoah Mollies were very anxious to enlist the Secretary in assisting to get bail for Chas. Hayes, who was in jail in Pottsville. He consented, and through his influence Marks, the proprietor of the Columbia House, was induced to sign Hayes' bond. This resulted in the young man's release, and earned for McKenna the gratitude of his many friends.

McAndrew, while in attendance upon the convention, was approached by Kerrigan and asked to send men to do the

Jones killing. The Shenandoah President answered, assuring him he would, if he could be made to see that assistance was, in return, ready for him when required. Kerrigan promised to furnish the needed men on a trade, and then McAndrew said he should have the help of his branch in doing anything reasonable.

McKenna went back to Shenandoah the day following the convention, accompanied by Morris and 'Hurley, and while on the way his comrades were anxious to know if the operative had recently seen anything of Linden. He answered that he had not.

"If I thought, for wan moment, Linden wor doin' anything on us, or on you, McKenna, I'd make him a target for me revolver as sure as ever I came up wid him!"

This sentiment of Hurley's was echoed by John Morris, who said he'd shoot Linden on sight, in such a contingency.

"Oh, ye naden't spend yer precious breath over Linden!" replied McKenna. "I know him pretty well! He's all as right as a trivet, as square as any man can be, and will never go back on his true friends!"

This quieted the fears of the two men for the time, and no more threats were indulged in during the journey. McKenna informed Linden by letter, that night, of his danger, at least regarding the empty menaces of Morris and Hurley, hinting that it might be well that his friend have a care for himself during the excitement prevailing, or he would possibly find the acts of the Mollies in question not so harmless as their savage words and looks.

The meeting to prove or refute Hurley's assertion that he killed Gomer James, as against the application of McClain for the same rare distinction, took place near Number Three Breaker, Sunday, the twenty-ninth of August. McKenna, Pat Butler, Hurley, and several of his witnesses, gathered in the bush at the appointed time. There was little or no evidence introduced, but Hurley's statement was reiterated

He said he, with his own hand, had killed the young Welsh-man, and demanded recompense for the act in no measured terms. His own mother, it seems, had been an eye-witness of the murderous work of the son. She had heard him swear he would shoot James or be killed himself. Hurley, had no compunctions of conscience in refusing to obey her command to go home, but repeated his oath that he "would fetch Gomer James that day, if it cost him his life!" Too well had he kept his word. Now he wanted the wages of his iniquity, the thirty pieces of silver for which, more than from feelings of revenge, he had shed human blood.

Butler's man, McClain, so the Loss Creek Bodymaster intimated, was afraid to meet Hurley, refused to put in an appearance before the committee, and there was no course left but to quietly acquiesce in Hurley's charge. This was done, and McKenna requested to prepare a written version of the decision arrived at and forward the same to the County Delegate. There the duty of the committee of two ended. The men dispersed to their houses, and Hurley had made another confession, before witnesses, of his guilt.

The following Monday, Hurley presented himself at Mc-Kenna's boarding-place, received the letter to Jack Kehoe, and departed in quest of the reward for his deed. It is not known that he ever received it. But, at a later date, Kehoe was heard by the detective to say that Hurley should be given five hundred dollars, by right, from the society's treas-ury for the important job he had performed. Jack was always very free-hearted as long as the money donated did not come from his own pocket. It is fair to presume that the murderer will have to wait until the gallows claims its own before fully realizing his worldly recompense for that cold-blooded assassination. After finishing this matter the two men adjourned to Tobin's ball-alley, where they had several games. The operative thought it necessary that he should be seen in company with Hurley, and at the same time remember, if he could, who observed the companionship.

It was very late when McKenna retired that night—rather quite early in the morning—and he was so completely fagged out by the labors of the day, not to speak of the drinks Hurley had compelled him to imbibe, that he slept until after sunrise. When he did regain consciousness he found another man reposing in the bed by his side. Sitting up, and somewhat astonished that such a liberty should be taken with his apartment, the agent learned that his companion was none other than Mike Doyle, who had evidently arrived after all Mrs. Cooney's couches were occupied and been sent to repose with him. So soundly was the operative sleeping that he was unaware of the fact that he had an un-bidden bedfellow. When he arose, which was soon after making the discovery, he saw, on the wash-stand, a Smith and Wesson revolver, about the size of the new one he carried, where it had probably been left by Doyle. This portended business, as he very well knew that Doyle had no weapon of his own, and he at once proceeded to rouse his partner and ask him what was in the wind.

"Where did ye get the repeater?" asked McKenna, pointing to the pistol, when Doyle had sufficiently rubbed his eyes to understand where he really was.

"Oh, I got it from Ned Monaghan," he replied, yawning, as if not above half pleased that he had been called so early.

"An' I suppose Monaghan is so rich that he can afford to be afther givin' away five-shooters to every man what comes along! Faix, I belave I'll have to get meself one that way!"

"No! I have only borrowed the pistol! There's a big job on hand! Me an' Jim an' Charlie O'Donnell, Charlie McAllister an' Munley are to go to Raven Run an' jist finish off Tom Sanger, the mining boss, an' take him afther he comes out to his dinner!"

"Is that all?" inquired McKenna, treating the matter lightly, but feeling, in truth, very much concerned, as he knew the persons mentioned and was very sure there would be bloody work whenever Friday O'Donnell had a share.

"I think, for my part, that's plenty an' to spare," returned Doyle, as he proceeded to dress himself. "I don't at all relish the thing ; But of course orders must be obeyed, an' I'm the last man to go back on the Bodymasther !"

Here was news for the detective—early news, at that. But what could he do with it ? By the time he was well down stairs to breakfast, Doyle signified his readiness for that meal. In the bar who should present himself but that early-bird, Tom Hurley, already well posted about the proposed Raven Run matter.

"Jim, lend me your old, gray coat !" said Doyle. "I came off without anything but a light one, an' I nade somethin' somewhat heavier !"

"Ye can take it, in welcome !" replied McKenna. And Doyle put the garment on and wore it at the dining-table. It was the same unfortunate coat John Gibbons had donned when starting upon the last expedition to take off Wm. M. Thomas. The agent soon saw that the new situation of affairs much resembled the former in other particulars. Not only had one of the proposed murderers secured the loan of his gray coat, but he was himself so hampered, through the close attendance of Hurley and others, that there was no opportunity to send a message of any sort to Mr. Franklin, at Philadelphia, or to Linden. In fact, as concerned the whereabouts of the latter individual, he was at the moment entirely ignorant. He might be in Lansford, looking after Jones, as he had been intending, or in Tamaqua, or in Ashland. Where he was he could not tell. But as McKenna was in the company of the Mollies, and could not avoid them on any pretext, however specious, it made little difference. An attempt

to send off word by telegraph would be the signal for sus
picion, and with men like his companions a shadow of doubt
was good enough pretext for an assassination.   Hence, hard
as it really was, he endeavored to quell his excitement, appear to enjoy the prospect, and lend seeming countenance
to that against which every thought, impulse, and instinct of
his nature recoiled.

Hurley told Doyle that if he went with the O'Donnel
crowd, he would have to act the manly part, and perform his
whole duty, or they would kill him as if he were only a mad
dog.   With this consoling remark the young murderer proceeded to give Doyle particular instructions in the fine art
of assassination, showing him minutely how a man should be
killed and how not killed.   He accompanied his remarks
with illustrations, made in his peculiar style, in the yard attached to Lawler's premises.

McKenna and Hurley, still in company—it appeared to
the operative that he would do almost anything to free him
self from Tom's friendly and unconscious surveillance—
strolled about the streets of the city, as usual taking the
prominent saloons in their route, and finally encountering
James, *alias* Friday O'Donnell—a tall, slimly-built, fair-com-
plexioned man, whose smooth face, dark eyes, brown hair
and genial expression of countenance, were no indication
of the murderous passions slumbering in his being—with
James McAllister, the latter a brother-in-law of Jack Kehoe.
McAllister was quickly photographed on the memory of the
detective.   Some twenty-four years of age, of florid complexion, a little freckled, light hair and mustache, and usually wel. appareled, he was an average representative of his
race, and by no means unhandsome in form and figure.   The
latter said that Chas. O'Donnell would soon be through his
work and had promised to join them.   Friday O'Donnell
carried two revolvers, which the agent saw were about the
same size as his own, bearing a number thirty-two cartridge.

In company, after Charles O'Donnell came, all repaired to Muff Lawler's residence.

While on the way, McKenna made every excuse possible to separate himself from Hurley, who stuck to him more closely than Carey had, through the night following the departure of the men to shoot Wm. Thomas, and finally, seeing that all his efforts were useless, he discontinued them and came to the conclusion that, whatever was to be done, it would be impossible for him to successfully interfere. The Mollies must take their course. His life would pay the forfeit of any indiscreet word or act. The news of the intended foray could not be forwarded to Philadelphia, neither was it possible to admonish the intended victim. There was nothing left for him but to endure the suspense, carry with him the horrible thought that a man was possibly being murdered in his neighborhood, and he impotent to warn or protect. "Where is Linden?" . "What can be keeping him?" "What shall I do?" were some of the questions which puzzled his brain while he was making his way to Lawler's house. When all the men arrived, and, well prepared for the deed, again left the locality so as to be early at Raven Run, the operative secretly hoped Hurley would start too, but he did not. On the contrary, fastening himself more closely to his person, he marched arm-in-arm with him to Frank McAndrew's place, and insisted upon treating to the drinks for all who gathered there. And this was no small number, as McAndrew had called a meeting of the leading members of the division for that afternoon, and they were convening at five o'clock, so that their business might be ended before nightfall. The liquor once consumed, there was no time to spare until the appointed hour, and Hurley and McKenna entered the division room, an upper chamber in the building, in company. There were only men composing the inside ring of the lodge present. To these, after prayer and the usual opening ceremonies, McAndrew sai the time for action had come. The Hibernians in other places were following the good example set by his branch, and he must not be idle. He had come to the conclusion that a boss named Reese must be cut off, and reported he had an order from Kerrigan, Bodymaster of Tamaqua Division, for three men to do an important job at Summit Hill. Jones was to be put out of the way, and "there must be no growling about it!" Mike Carey was chosen to go and assist in the Lansford scheme, but unqualifiedly refused. McAndrew was much angered, and exclaimed that such conduct would be punished as it deserved, when he had more time, and in a moment selected John McGrail, Thomas Munley, and Mike Darcey to go to Tamaqua and report to Kerrigan. As Munley lived at Gilberton and was not present, Ed Sweeney was detailed to inform him of the affair on hand, and instruct him when to start and where to report.

"The latest must not be later than to-morrow night!" ordered the Bodymaster.

McKenna was requested to visit Tamaqua at once, make all right with Kerrigan, deliver the men for his job, and secure those to do for Reese. There was nothing to be gained by refusal. He had to go. The thought struck him: "Here is a chance for a warning! It is my only opportunity!" He promptly accepted the mission and at once took cars for Tamaqua. It was a terrible ordeal, but from it there seemed to open no avenue of escape.

Here is the situation: Campbell striving to have John P Jones killed, and calling upon Kerrigan for men to do the deed. McAndrew to furnish these men to Kerrigan, and Kerrigan, to make the matter even, to repay in a batch of assassins for the killing of Reese. Shenandoah Division having its business transacted in the Sanger case by persons from Girardville, part of the number being relatives of Jack Kehoe. McAndrew was not informed—though McKenna was, through his chancing to sleep with Doyle—of the duty the O'Donnell delegation were to perform. When the operative thought over the complications by which he was surrounded he hardly knew which thing to do first. But, as soon as he reached Tamaqua, he closeted himself long enough at the Columbia House to indite a brief letter to Mr. Franklin, setting forth the critical condition of affairs, and breathed somewhat more freely when the dangerous paper was out of his possession, safely deposited in the post-office. He had done all he could, but without much hope that his endeavors would save the lives threatened.

CHAPTER XLI.

MURDER OF SANGER AND UREN.

LEAVING my agent in Tamaqua, a victim of three-fold suspense, I must now attempt to describe a double murder, perpetrated by the Mollie Maguires at Raven Run, near Ashland, Wednesday, the first of September, 1875, a little more than two weeks later than the killing of Gomer James and Squire Gwyther. The plain facts are here collected, as given by the detectives, from sources which are deemed reliable.

As Hiram Beninger, a carpenter connected with the colliery, was passing from his house to the breaker, at about six o'clock in the morning of the day mentioned, he noticed two men, apparently strangers, sitting on some car sills not far from the carpenter shop. One wore a soft hat and the other a cap with a broad velvet band. Both had their coat collars turned up as if to protect them from the chilling wind, and

19

their positions on the timbers were those of mere listlessness, as though waiting for the arrival of the working boss. It was a common occurrence to see parties thus early on the ground to make application for employment, and Beninger paid no attention to these. But for circumstances immediately following, possibly he might never have thought of them again.

John Nicolls, this same clear cool morning in September and at about the same hour, was walking on the Mammoth Colliery road, or the path leading to that colliery, when he discovered three men, also seemingly new to the neighborhood, resting themselves on the trucks with which coal is elevated from the shaft or plane. One of the fresh arrivals spoke pleasantly to Nicolls, saying, "Good-morning!" in a low tone of voice, and, as a man naturally would, Nicolls politely returned the salutation. After passing these three persons, Nicolls noticed two others, sitting just where the carpenter had found them, and Nicolls walked within a yard of their locality. One of the last-named persons, he remembered, wore a light-colored soft hat and brown coat, and looked closely in his face as he was going by. The other had on the velvet cap noticed by Beninger. The first, a light-complexioned, heavily-built man, spoke to Nicolls, saying: "You are going early to your work!" Nicolls answered: "Yes; rather early!" and went on his way. He recalled nothing particularly suspicious in the circumstance, excepting, as he subsequently remarked, the man having the cap pulled its visor down over his eyes. Mr. Nicolls only saw five men, concluded in his mind that they were travelers, probably seeking work, and but for subsequent events would soon have forgotten them altogether.

Ten or fifteen minutes afterward Thomas Sanger, a boss in Heaton & Co.'s Colliery, started from his home for the scene of his daily labor, taking tender leave of his wife at their garden gate, accompanied by Wm. Uren, who boarded

In his family and was also employed at the same mining works. Both bore their dinner-cans in their hands.

Sanger was a man greatly respected by his neighbors, about thirty-three years of age, and, while he had always been firm in his purpose, and true to his employers, had failed to make any enemies, excepting among the Mollies. He had, in his time, been duly threatened, but more recently believed the anger of his organized enemies was buried, forgotten, or appeased. But it proved a great mistake. Their murderous desires only slept.

Sanger and his companion, who was a miner, had not gone far when they were fired upon and both mortally wounded by the same strange men noticed by the carpenter and Mr. Nicolls. Beninger heard the shots, and rushing out, saw Robert Heaton, one of the proprietors of the colliery, firing his pistol at and running after two of the murderers. He heard "Red" Nick Purcell call for a gun. Two of the five assassins just then stopped in their retreat and began discharging their revolvers at Heaton, but he was not hit, and, holding boldly his ground, continued using his weapon, apparently without effect. Then all of the strange men turned and ran quickly up the mountain. Heaton followed as fast as he could, and when he had gained a little on them, stopped, and resting his pistol on a stump, to get steadier aim, continued to shoot. Still none were wounded. At least they did not slacken their speed, but made rapidly for the heavier timber and soon disappeared. Mr. Nicoll's saw the same sight. It may be said, to his credit, that Heaton never withdrew from the unequal chase until his cartridges were exhausted and the men beyond range of his bullets. Had any of the several other witnesses of the deed been prepared, and followed the example of Heaton, the gang of assassins would have been killed or captured. As it was, they were not further pursued at the moment and got away before reason prevailed and preparations were made for going on their trail. Then it was too late. The game was out of even rifle range.

After Sanger received his wound he was taken to the house of a neighbor, named Wheevil, where every attention was given him. Wm. Uren, who was also bleeding freely, was removed to the same residence. The surgeons were sent for, and Mrs. Sanger soon came in. Sanger lived but a little while. When his wife entered the room he said, in a faltering voice : "Sarah, come and kiss me! I am dying!" involuntarily echoing Yost's exclamation under similar circumstances. Neither of the wounded men retained consciousness long enough to give any coherent description of the manner in which they had been met, but there were witnesses in plenty, workmen going to their labor and others, who had seen the entire transaction.

Sanger had been three years with Heaton & Co., and always performed his duty faithfully. He had received two gunshot wounds, one through the right forearm, and the other in the groin, the last severing the femoral artery. There was no gleam of hope for him. He bled to death in a few minutes. Dr. A. B. Sherman, assisted by Doctors Yocum and Yeomans, of Ashland, did everything in the power of man, but without avail. Death was inevitable from the locality and extent of the hurt.

Uren was shot in the right groin, in about the same place as Sanger, an important artery in his leg being injured. He remained in a sort of stupor until death ensued, the next day.

Heaton was eating his breakfast when he heard the firing, and at once his mind reverted to the men he had seen sitting by the carpenter shop. There was something peculiar in their posture, and in the fact of their hats being over their eyes, and coat collars turned up. Believing they were the cause of the trouble, he seized his revolver and ran out. The first thing he encountered was Thomas Sanger, wounded, lying on the ground by a stump, near the house, bleeding

freely, where the murderers had left him ; still Sanger said ,
Don't stop for me, Bob, but give it to them ! " Heaton
caught sight of the departing assassins, and, as before
related, opened fire upon them, but without effect. He had
a fair view of one of the persons, when he turned on his heel
and fired back at him. But Mrs. Williams, a neighbor of
Heaton, had a better opportunity to judge of the same man.
Her young son, when he heard the shooting, was very anxious
to go out and join in Heaton's attempt to capture or kill the
assassins. He desired to do just what the others should
have done, but did not do, and his mother, naturally fearful
harm might come to him, had, with the assistance of her
daughter, dragged the lad back into the room after he had
reached the entrance, which was open. She threw her arms
around him and effectually barred his progress. Then the
murderer of Sanger—having brought the boss down, as he ran
for the protecting building, and even stopping to turn him
over on his back and deliberately fire a second shot into his
quivering and bleeding body—with smoking pistol still in
hand, passed Mrs. Williams' door. While engaged in preventing her son's exit, her mind filled with horror from what
had already happened, and dread of that which she thought
might occur, she noted each feature of the murderer's face
and every peculiarity of his form, as, with head raised and
defiant air, he swung his weapon over his head, walked
rapidly by her door and up the road. She said she could
never forget that man. His likeness haunted her, waking
and sleeping, for many nights, and she furnished her neighbors with a description which was afterwards very valuable.

. . . .

The two men who had accompanied McKenna to Tamaqua, quite unfit for duty when they reached their destination, were put to bed at Carroll's—which place they had
approached by three several routes, by previous arrangement
not having spoken together on the car—very soon after their

arrival. Drink had quite overpowered them. This left the
agent at liberty to walk about and think over the predicament
he was in. His nerves were not particularly braced
up by the perusal of a savage article in the Shenandoah
Herald, recommending the formation by the citizens of a
vigilance committee, which should summarily rid the country of the Mollie Maguires. He thought that such an organisation was the one thing needful to render his position quite
unendurable. His Mollie friends merely laughed at it.
They said : " Let the committee be appointed ! If it is, we
will then spare neither women, old men, nor children ! It
will be war to the knife, and the knife to the throat ! "

This was anything but cheerful talk for the Shenandoah
Secretary, but he was forced to acquiesce in it, however much
his heart misgave him. He well knew that it would be a
modern miracle, if such a combination was entered into,
should he fail in becoming its first victim. No Mollie
Maguire was better known. No Mollie was suspected of
having committed more crimes, and, meanwhile, he was perfectly innocent. McKenna certainly did not favor a vigilance committee. On the contrary, he was zealously opposed to anything of the sort. While thinking over these
unpleasant things the operative inquired of Carroll where
Kerrigan was. He pretended he did not know. Under
these circumstances it occurred to the agent that it was his
duty to send the men, brought there to perform a murder,
directly back to their homes. In the afternoon he did so,
informing them that he had been unable to find Kerrigan
which was true, and probably the Jones job had been postponed, which he did not know to be the fact, but which he
hoped might be so. No sooner were his parties off for
Shenandoah than McKenna set about a plan for putting
Linden and his men in the bush about Jones' house, propos-
ing to be near himself and see that the boss was not hurt.
After failing to find Linden or Kerrigan, he went to Carroll's

the hour being about ten at night, and luckily the saloon-keeper was alone.

"Were the men you had here to go to Old Mines?" asked Carroll.

"Yes! But as I couldn't run across Kerrigan, they have been sent home! I can get them again by merely telegraphing McAndrew to 'send me over a game chicken!' That's the signal agreed upon. Where is that fellow, Kerrigan, anyhow? Sure, you ought to know!"

I'll tell you, McKenna," whispered Carroll. "He has been off since Wednesday, wid two men from Mt. Laffee, an' I'm after thinkin' that, before this time, all is over in that case! The fellows came here wid a letther from Jerry Kane, an' gave it to me, an' I jist kept them inside until Kerrigan got in, which was about nine at night, an' they all left. It wur Mike Doyle and Ed Kelly that went wid Kerrigan. They brought no arms along, so if they wur arrested nothing would be found on them! Campbell has plenty of pistols.

Here the saloon-keeper had to attend to the wants of a customer and McKenna, completely bewildered, walked out of the place and over to his hotel. What was he to do? The probability was that Kerrigan and his men had shot Jones that very morning. Where should he find Linden? How should he act? After calm reflection he determined that he could do nothing. If Jones had been killed, it was not possible to aid him. Everything had been done that his inventive mind suggested to notify and guard the man. McKenna therefore took the cars and returned, heart-sick and despondent, to Shenandoah.

Linden's duty had called him elsewhere, and hence he can not be held at all responsible for a job he thought amply provided for. Still in doubt about Jones' fate, it was at Muff Lawler's house that the operative learned the result of the expedition by Friday O'Donnell and his men to Raven Run.

They regained the outskirts of Shenandoah at about eight o'clock, the morning of the murder, and the crowd, consisting of Mike Doyle, Friday and Chas. O'Donnell, Thos. Munley, and Chas. McAllister, entered the house, one by one, and each was made quickly comfortable.

Chas. McAllister lived with the O'Donnells at Wiggan's Patch, and was married to their sister.

The entire company were covered with dust and perspiration and expressed themselves as very thirsty. They certainly drank a great quantity of water, for men whose usual beverage was something stronger, and seemed recently to have traveled far and fast. Friday O'Donnell made no secret of the scene all were freshly from, and boasted that they had made a clean sweep of it, and, while it was the intention only to take off Sanger, they had killed another man, supposed to be a miner. He did not know but they had hurt others.

Chas. McAllister exhibited to McKenna a navy revolver and said that Chas. O'Donnell carried one of the same size. Doyle wore the Smith & Wesson he had previously seen, and Friday O'Donnell had two pistols. In Lawler's back kitchen, that morning, they talked over the murder for an hour, saying they had all traded clothing before the shooting, and, after finishing, swapped back again. Each murderer took part in the conversation, and related, in his own way, the share he had taken in the assassination. Their reports were not particularly at variance with the facts as set forth in this chapter, and hence the reader's mind, already sickened with relation of violence and bloodshed, need not be further harrowed up by their repetition here.

But what were McKenna's feelings at this period? To say that he was exceedingly anxious, is a very weak expression in which to convey the mental experiences of that eventful day. With what patience he could command, he awaited information of Kerrigan's work at Lansford.

CHAPTER XLII

QUITE a fraternal feeling had existed between the two men murdered on the first of September at Raven Run, Wm. Uren having been a native of the parish of Germoe, Cornwall, England, but a short distance from Sanger's birthplace. He entered the Greatwork tin mines at the early age of ten years, with his father, and remained until about nineteen, when he bid his relatives adieu and sailed for this country, landing at New York in the fall of 1872. After working nearly a year at Dover, New Jersey, he removed to Schuylkill County and was employed by the Messrs. Heaton as a coal miner. While in England Uren was a regular attendant at church and Sabbath-school. In Pennsylvania he kept up the same course, early enlisting as a teacher in a Sunday-school, which place he held at the time of his death. Uren, with other bosses and miners, including Sanger, was coffin-noticed by the Mollies as early as 1874, and in consequence Sanger invited the young man to board at his house. They soon formed an intimate and enduring friendship The winter of 1875 and following summer, to the day of the assassination, passing peaceably and without any apparent attempt to carry out the promises of the organization, as far as he and Sanger were concerned, Uren began to believe all danger passed or blown over. They thought nothing would actually be done. Thus had it always been No ing this world, for the fiends incarnate causing all the trouble in the coal region were abundantly capable of waiting for any length of time, keeping their wrath warm and pouring it, at any unsuspected moment, upon the devoted heads of their victims. Therefore, Uren, when set upon, was no better prepared to defend himself against the power of his enemies than his friend, Sanger. There was nothing that either could possibly do but to stand up like men before the deadly pistols and be shot cruelly down.

A more sorrowful scene than that enacted around the couch of the dying Uren was never witnessed. His fellow countryman, Sanger, was already gone. It was not long before he followed. The funeral of the two men, like their murder, was a double one, and both were buried in the same grave. The parents of Wm. Uren are yet living in England, with four sisters and five brothers. They receive no more assistance from their dutiful son and brother. They know their main help this side of the Atlantic has been cut off by the bullet of the assassin.

McKenna was again in Shenandoah when he received a note from Linden informing him of certain remarks that person had heard made by a citizen of Tamaqua concerning the Secretary. They were not exactly the kind of words generally causing a man to feel more secure of or harbor firmer belief in his personal safety. Said Linden in his letter:

" A citizen by the name of Boyd remarked to me to-day that the only chance for an excitement in dull Tamaqua was when that man with the big head (alluding to the wig, I suppose) and blue coat came upon the street. Then people began to say to each other, ' What a shame that such a fellow (this means you, McParlan) is allowed to live ! He ought to be strung up !' You need to keep a sharp lookout, wherever you are, for about everybody here is thinking that you are a suspicious fellow generally and a particularly bad Mollie ! "

This was not very inspiriting information for the officer to receive, and, the next day, was supplemented by the following, showing that Linden had called at Shenandoah and not been able to find or communicate with his fellow-operative :

"I was in conversation, yesterday, with several influential men, and it was the universal expression that all would soon have to emigrate or make the Mollies leave. They talked vigilance committee very earnestly. One of the party asked another if 'that fellow, McKenna, was about the city yet ?' He replied 'yes !' Then said the first speaker : ' That is the smartest business man of the society ! He has the best head and does the most work ; in short, is the most dangerous scamp among them !' You will observe that my former recommendation is enforced by this. Look sharp ! Don't be imprudent ! Have an eye out for breakers, day and night ! "

A wayfaring man has, before this, perused letters of a more calming and conciliatory tenor. Indeed McKenna remembered having read passages, even in yellow-covered romances of the blood-and-thunder style of literature, which, torturingly bad as they were, gave him much more unalloyed pleasure than those two missives from Linden. Yet he was thankful to their author for them. His intentions were good, and his recommendations among the best that could be made.

Here there arose another apparent conflict between duty and inclination. The first said: "Stay here and procure testimony which shall punish the assassins." The second chimed in with a broad hint to pack up his clothing and other goods, purchase a ticket for Chicago, and hasten away toward the setting sun. McParlan thought he had but just commenced his work. It would be time for him to desert the post if forced to do so, or when Mr Franklin might deem his duty in the country quite complete. In any event, he concluded to stay some time longer, even though the wishes of the citizens of Tamaqua and Shenandoah might be executed. He knew that, if the excited people of the vicinity could only be aware of his true purposes, they would willingly carry him in their arms, or draw him in a carriage, shielding him from harm with their own bodies; and this inward consciousness of rectitude, which buoyed him through many a stormy day in the years he had been in my service, kept his head above water and steadied his nerves while he continued his professional work. He knew that, if he lived yet a little longer, the residents of Schuylkill, Carbon, Columbia and Luzerne Counties would praise and bless him. If he died, they would discover that his life was sacrificed that they, and generations to them yet unborn, might have and enjoy protection from the Mollie Maguires, under the law, and secure immunity from the black dragon which for a score of years had made their land a terror and a shame in the nation.

These and similar ideas were passing through the brain of McKenna, the afternoon of the third of September, 1875, when the perusal of the evening newspaper confirmed his worst fears. John P. Jones was added to the long list of victims of the mysterious society. He had been shot that morning. The operative soon learned the principal facts connected with this assassination and embodied them in a report to the Agency.

John P. Jones left his house, which was in Lansford and contained his wife and seven children, at about seven o'clock in the morning, bound for the breaker where he was employed, carrying his dinner-pail in his hand, and following the pipe-line toward the old railway embankment, which he had been, by Mr. Zehner, Mr. Beard, and others, repeatedly urged not to take, as they were aware that his life was by no means safe. He felt, like Sanger and Uren, entirely satisfied that the Mollies, who had so long been confronting him, were of a more forgiving nature than the public credited them with being, or that their desire for his blood had been satiated by the several recent sacrifices. Instead of heeding advice, and extracting warning from the deaths lately occurring, and using a locomotive to carry him up and down the line, as he could easily have done, or even refusing to work unless some such course was observed, he put his revolver in his pocket and went off cheerfully to what proved his last journey.

The assassins, James Kerrigan, Mike Doyle, and Edward Kelly, were waiting for him. He saw them not, but continued his walk as though nothing more than usual stood before him. Not a premonition of impending evil; not a thought of coming death; not a glance around, to see if the cowardly assassin was in ambush prepared to kill him.

But they were there, lying in wait, Kerrigan, as usual, standing at a little distance and wholly unarmed. Jones left his home by a rear door and moved down the pipe-line When the trio of murderers reached the top of the path, he was some yards from the same position. He heard their footsteps and turned aside, patiently pausing for the others to pass. Still not a suspicion could have crossed his mind that he stood at the gateway of death. The men had no intention of permitting him to obtain a hint of their design. They halted, when close to him, and then Doyle and Kelly drew their pistols and fired on Jones. Each discharged one shot. Their victim made a spasmodic blow at his assailants with the tin dinner-pail, when Doyle fired again. Turning off toward the bushes, Jones raised his hands and cried out: "I'm shot! I'm shot!" In a moment he fell forward upon his face. After this, Doyle fired two more bullets into his already riddled body. The Superintendent had not time to draw or think of a weapon, and in a few minutes the life of the man was ended. His heart beat no more. While Doyle was finishing the savage job, his companions were running away across the mountains The reports of the pistols brought many workmen on the railroad to the spot, and Jones' corpse was immedi ately taken to his home. Several persons had seen the assassins retreating over the hill, and one man was so near them as to be frightened, thinking his turn to be shot would come next. He made rapid progress in placing himself out of harm's way.

The citizens of Tamaqua were not long in ignorance of the incidents attending the killing of Jones, and the excite- ment, which before had risen to a high pitch, reached the verge of general madness. People procured arms and went upon the streets in numbers. Men, women, and boys were aroused, and everybody appeared intent upon arresting or killing somebody. The Mollie Maguires alone kept quiet. Finally it was discovered, by some one who had been quietly following the little miner since the killing of Yost, that James Kerrigan was away from his home. Silently and doggedly a few persons kept watch over his house. Early in the forenoon he returned, remained but a short time, and was shortly afterward seen to start out with a small bundle in his hand, and, sticking from one pocket, a flask of liquor. Cautiously the men kept on his trail and tracked him until he reached a spring where Doyle and Kelly were waiting. He had no more than time to give them the refreshments, when the three Mollies, evidently warned by a preconcerted signal from Carroll, who walked along, making himself con- spicuous upon the railway track, started to run. But the people confronted and soon captured them. They had no arms about their persons, and when examined at the jail only some cartridges were found in their pockets. A little later, however, some officers, while making a search, un- earthed three pistols and a heavy club, secreted under the trees in the leaves near the spring. The sheriff, the next day, escorted Kerrigan, Kelly, and Doyle to Mauch Chunk, where they were committed to prison, to await trial, the crime having been committed in Carbon County.

The supposed murderers were in a safe place. Was there testimony upon which they could be convicted? It was doubtful. They were unquestionably the guilty parties, and might be well identified as far as descriptions went, but the actual witnesses were standing at such a distance from the scene it was possible that a jury, especially without having corroborating evidence, might be deceived and fail to find sufficient fact to warrant conviction.

One good effect, at least, was produced by the arrest of the three Mollies. The remainder of the members of the order were, for the time, struck dumb. Their hands were powerless. They could perform no further acts of violence, for fear of prejudicing the interests of their brothers then in custody. Peace would be assured, at least until the trials could take place. But that the defendants would be sworn clear by the oaths of the fraternity few were found to doubt.

As in one of the earlier murders of the year, the killing of Jones was, by many innocent and well-meaning but uninformed people, charged upon my detective, James McParlan, *alias* McKenna. I do not allude to this censoriously. They did not know what they were doing, and were judging from outward appearances alone. Seeing him, for a series of years, the associate of murderers, thieves, and Mollies, and apparently the toughest man among them, it was no more than reasonable they should suppose him really one of their number and a leader in many of their criminal works. Mr. Reese, of Shenandoah, whose life the operative had just been the means of preserving, sent word, on the tenth of September, a week subsequent to Jones' taking off, that he desired to see Mr. Linden. When they met, Reese told my officer that an Irishman named McKenna was supposed to have originated, planned, and assisted in executing the crime, concluding with the death of John P. Jones, of Lansford. He added that, so well were the good people of Tamaqua satisfied of the truth of this assumption, though they were without a particle of positive evidence, he, Mr. Reese, had no doubt, if McKenna appeared in the town, they would turn out in hundreds and hang him to the nearest tree. This state of feeling exhibits the closeness with which the operative was doing his work, and is another evidence of his skill. The reader who has followed me thus far can tell how entirely void of all criminal act or intent the record of that officer had been. The public now knows that he was laboring, even at the risk of losing his own life, to clear the country of those who had for years been perpetrating crimes of blood in the anthracite region. It understands that he went there for a purpose, and I hope to be able to show, before the close of this volume, that he was eminently successful in his undertaking.

This feeling, on the part of the deadly enemies of the Mollie Maguires, that McKenna was the deepest and most guilty man in that wicked organization, is an evidence of the discretion and tact the detective had continually exercised. Without seeming to be fully in sympathy with and inside the order, without an apparent acquiescence in its doings, his task would have been abortive. It was this confidence on the part of good people that he was a very bad man, and the belief on the side of the Mollies that he was as hard and as bloody a character as even Tom Hurley, Yellow Jack Donahue, or Jemmy Kerrigan, that gave witness of his standing and efficiency as a secret detective. The mere suspicion, by the fraternity, that he might possibly be other than the party he affected to be would surely have been seized upon as the signal for his death.

Despite his apprehensions, which were more excited by the promised formation in the coal region of a vigilance committee than by the information just recorded, or the idea that his identity would be revealed to his companions, the agent stuck courageously to his verbal contract with me ; did not desert his post, but stopping for a time in Shenan-

doah, busied himself, as before, in keeping inside the inner
sanctuary of the infernal society with which he was connected. He thought occasionally of going to Tamaqua and
resuming his attentions to Kerrigan's wife's sister, and eventually did so, but for the few days following the assassination
at Lansford he was almost continually in the company of
Thomas Hurley and the rest of the Shenandoah branch.
Hurley was fairly famishing for more blood. He had not
done, and could not do, enough. The scent of gore had
fallen on his senses and he longed for another draught.
One day he said to McKenna:

" I tell you, Jim, so long as there is a pot over the fire,
the fire must be kept to it!"—meaning that, as the era of
murders had begun, it must be continued. The inventive
genius of Hurley was constantly on the stretch, manufacturing cases in which the pistol might be used with effect. This
was one reason, undoubtedly, that McAndrew took it into
his head to have Reese put out of the path. McKenna was
the cause of the signal failure of that scheme.

In one of the operative's reports for this date, he wrote,
evidently feeling exactly and keenly the sentiment that his
pen expressed:

"I am sick and tired of this thing! I seem to make no
progress, and the terrible and long-continued state of excitement in the town and the country around here will one day
end in something more fearful than has yet occurred. I hear
of preparations for bloodshed in all directions. The sun
looks crimson to me, and the air is tainted with the smell
of blood. We must do something to stop the sanguinary
whirlwind that bids fair to destroy everything!"

Long before this I had arrived at a similar conclusion. A
crisis in the operation had arrived which demanded immediate, masterly work. Therefore, Mr. Franklin met Linden
in Pottsville, the ninth of September, and McKenna was
directed to communicate with them at the same place. He

had little difficulty in cutting loose from his associates, saying that he was forced to visit an adjoining town to meet his
principal in the bogus money business, and, after promising
that he would only be absent a few days, took cars by a
roundabout route and reached Pottsville the same night,
making sure that no doubts of the object of his mission had
been aroused in the minds of the Mollies, and that none of
the order were following him.

Affairs had reached the pass that Linden was, in some
places, known as my representative in the coal fields. It was
brought about by one of my open policemen unfortunately
shooting a man who acted suspiciously and also being himself wounded. O'Brien was arrested, tried, and in due time
acquitted. Linden acted as his friend and counselor, and
thus revealed his connection with the Agency. It was time,
however, the season being ripe for the act. Linden and
McKenna must not be known to communicate with each
other. Any attempt to do so which would be seen by the
Mollies must serve as an excuse for the agent's execution.
It was as much as his life was worth to be found with either
Linden or Franklin. Still a meeting was necessary, and he
did not falter. Putting up at a smaller house, McParlan
went, after darkness set in, to the Exchange Hotel, where
he knew Linden had his apartment, found that officer at
home, and there remained, locked in the sleeping-chamber,
until Mr. Franklin came. The three men held a very long
and interesting conversation, during which our plans for the
future were discussed. The operative detailed all that he
knew of the Gomer James, Sanger and Uren, and Jones
murders, aside from his written reports, of all of which Mr.
Franklin made extended notes. He also answered such
inquiries respecting names and localities as were put.
McKenna was kept in the room through the night, or until
nearly morning, when he left and repaired to his own boarding-place, not appearing on the streets again until the Super

tendent had left for Philadelphia and Linden was far away going toward the scene of his future operations in Carbon County.

In a day or two McKenna was summoned to Philadelphia, thence traveled to New York, and had a meeting with General Superintendant Geo. H. Bangs. The result of the jour. ney the ensuing pages will explain.

CHAPTER XLIII.

VIOLENCE FOR VIOLENCE.

It should have been mentioned that, on the sixteenth of August, James Riles, of Shenandoah, was attacked by a crowd of Mollies, headed by Charles McAllister, Ned Monaghan, and Tobin, while sitting on the steps of his own dwelling. Mr. Glover was near him at the time. Riles was not mortally wounded, though his life, for several weeks, hung as upon a thread, and his health is still much broken because of the injuries he received. A man named Delaney was another eye-witness of the outrage, but could do nothing to stop its progress. It was about nine o'clock at night when three men came suddenly up to Riles and put their pistols to his back. Immediately the victim felt a stinging sensation running through him and knew he was hit. Regaining his feet he ran up Delaney's steps, closely tracked by the Mollies. It seemed to him there was a great mob pursuing, and he flew through his neighbor's house as fast as he could, jumped out of the window, not knowing what he was doing, striking heavily against the hard street below, and received injuries which, added to the effects of the bullet, made him faint and almost unconscious. When Riles was lying in the

road the crowd cried : "Shoot him ! shoot him !" But he
managed to crawl into the residence of Wm. Kendrick, who
protected him, finally saving his life.   Thence he had
to be taken by the members of the Coal and Iron Police.
Before their arrival, however, the Mollies surrounded Ken
drick's house and excitedly demanded possession of Riles,
saying : "Give him to us !   Give him to us !"   One timid
citizen who was present tried to persuade Kendrick to com
ply, urging that the crowd would have him, in the end, and
if troubled in their fierce pursuit of blood might do violence
to the family of his brave preserver.   Kendrick flatly re-
.fused to pursue any such course and resolutely stood by the
wounded and supposed-to-be dying man.   For several days
Mr. Riles was supposed to be near death's door, but subse
quently recovered sufficiently to escape to Philadelphia.
There he was forced to remain in the hospital until restored
to partial health.   At the risk of his life, he then returned to
Shenandoah, sold his homestead and other property, and emigrated to Illinois.   He had seen enough of the Mollies.
Among his late assailants he recognized Ned Monaghan and
others, but was unable to swear to the men who actually
fired upon him.   Riles kept a saloon, and had incurred the
displeasure of the gang in some way unknown to himself.

The murder of Geo. K. Smith, already briefly alluded to,
which occurred at Audenried, Carbon County, the night of
Thursday, November 5, 1863, was totally unprovoked.   Mr.
G. W. Ulrich, now employed by Messrs. Wanamaker and
Brown, of Philadelphia, but then a clerk for Mr. Smith, gives
the following condensed statement of the incidents connected
with the atrocious crime :

"The night of the murder I had just returned from Mauch
Chunk.   I got home about half-past six P.M.   I boarded at
Smith's house.   When I went down to supper, I told Smith
I thought something serious was going to happen.   He
asked me why.   I replied because of what George Allen had

said about having heard that the night of that day was to be
the greatest ever known in Audenried, and because, during
the afternoon, several men were noticed prowling around
there, going about in different directions, and, on the even
ing before, there were others in the store for powder. Mr.
Smith laughed and said: 'Mr. Ulrich, they wont hurt you
or me I I stayed at Smith's house that night, at the request
of Mrs. Smith, because her husband was unwell. About five
minutes before eight o'clock, hearing a rap at the door, I,
upon opening it, found standing there a man whom I thought
to be a Welshman named Evan Jones. Asking him to stay
outside until I put the dog away, I shut the door, took the
animal by the collar and put him in the parlor, where Mrs.
Smith was. Then I went back, opened the door, and when
I did so a tall man, with a soldier's overcoat on, stepped in,
and the one I took to be Evan Jones followed. As soon as
I saw his face I found it was not Evan Jones. The taller
person asked if Mr. Smith was in. I at first said 'no,' but
afterward told him he was in, 'and very sick at that.' He
professed to have a letter for Smith, that a man had given
him in Mauch Chunk the same afternoon. I told him if he
would give it to me I could hand it to Mr. Smith. He
would not do that, as he said he was instructed to deliver it
personally. I then left the room and told Mrs. Smith. She
went up and saw the sick man, and he replied if the person
could not deliver the letter to her, he must wait until the next
day. Mrs. Smith and I returned to the room where the two
men were sitting. She told them what Smith had said. The
man answered: 'If I can't deliver it to him I must deliver
it to you!' He quickly put his hand to his back, and the
first thing I saw was the butt-end of a Colt's revolver. Be
fore he got it out altogether it went off, and his clothes
ght fire, the ball penetrating the floor on which we were
standing When the revolver was discharged Mrs. Smith
cried out 'Oh, my God I' and ran precipitately into the

library. Then the tall man caught me around the neck and the smaller man commenced beating me on my head and on the back of my shoulders with a billy. The tall man got his revolver out and put it to the side of my head. I threw up my left hand and the pistol went off, and the powder flew into my eyes and blinded me so that I could not see for some time. By this some fifteen or twenty persons had walked into the room where we were. The majority were disguised in soldiers' overcoats and in miners' clothes. They crowded over against the wall, and the tall man tried to shoot me again in the head. Once more I threw up my arm and the pistol ball passed over me. Another man stooped down behind me, on his knees, and put his pistol to my person and shot me in the leg while I was held by the other. I then broke away from the crowd, with the intention of going upstairs. They followed me too closely, however, and I could not get clear. As I reached the foot of the stairs, Mr. Smith came down and walked into the room where the men were. I went to the hall door and they knocked me down and fired two shots over me with the intention of hitting my body. After this, I turned around to find if I could see anything, and saw Mr. Smith standing by the crowd. A man came up behind him, put a pistol to his head, and fired. He fell dead upon the carpet. After finishing this, they fired three or four shots, and I thought they were shooting Mr. Smith's dead body, but they fired them at Mrs. Smith's sister, who was in the room adjoining. This is all I know, excepting that the others escaped."

No present arrests were made. Nobody could tell who the murderers were, excepting that they belonged to the Mollie Maguires, or had been set on and were accompanied by those suspected of forming that clan. When, some time after, suspected parties were captured, a mob released them from Mauch Chunk prison.

The work performed by McKenna while in New York

and Philadelphia was very important and constituted a portion of the first really aggressive acts of the Agency against
the formidable foe. It consisted in the preparation of classi-
fied and carefully arranged lists of all the Mollies, or members of the Ancient Order of Hibernians, in Luzerne, Northumberland, Columbia, Carbon, and Schuylkill Counties,
their residence, occupation, standing in the society, and
crimes they had been connected with. When completed,
the schedule was given very extensive circulation throughout the United States, by publication in the principal newspapers. It was but the prelude of the thunderbolt which
was soon to cast consternation into the hearts of the leaders
of the society. Our plans were formed for unrelenting and
unending warfare upon them. They had for years carried
everything unresistingly before them, but now a force, the
secret emissaries of which for nearly three years had been
ferreting out and marking their weak places, meanwhile
sharpening and charging their own weapons for use, was to
put its potent machinery suddenly in motion. Fresh detectives were sent to the support of those already on the
ground, unknown to the others, and every available adjunct
that ingenuity could devise and money and influence supply
was set at work to accomplish the defeat of the thus far un
opposed and victorious Mollie Maguires.

Meanwhile the order was as active as a hive of bees, no
longer forcibly aggressive, but moving purely in self-defense.
Their long day of murder had set in crimson, and the day
of their abnegation and shame was at the dawn. Money was
raised for the legal expenses of the prisoners. Evidence was
hunted up to falsify the truth and swear them clear. But on
the track of the brewers of this testimony was the stealthy
tread of a man they knew but suspected not, and to whose
care they intrusted their most secret transactions. Such a
game must only end, after a time, in the defeat of the society,
however strong and large in numbers. Hurley Morris

Monaghan, Mulhall, Sweeney, Clark, Gavin, Butler, Campbell, and Fisher, and many more, were absorbingly engaged, day and night, securing funds with which to engage attorneys for the cases of Kelly, Doyle, and Kerrigan. The members of Shenandoah Division were assessed two dollars each, by McAndrew, which was promptly paid, and the result went to swell the protection fund.

On the twenty-third of September, McAndrew gave a grand ball—which was attended by McKenna—at his own house, for the especial benefit of the prisoners. It was on this occasion that Morris proposed killing Mr. Foster, the editor of the Shenandoah *Herald*, but was strongly opposed by both McAndrew and McKenna, and the matter fell through. Mr. Fielders, the city editor of the same sheet, was present at this entertainment and listened to one or two songs which the detective sang, but he left the room when he heard that the wild Irishman was threatening to kill him. The hint was sent to Fielders purely in a spirit of mischief, by some of the Mollies, who thought to frighten the reporter. They did not succeed, but gave a permanently sharp point to his pencil, which, for several years, he has used in puncturing the hearts of the Mollie leaders. It is hardly necessary to say that McKenna never made a threat against any one, in sober earnest. The ball was successful, and brought considerable money to the treasury.

About the same date Linden was approached by Mike Lawler with a request to find him a place on the Coal and Iron Police, which was easy enough to promise but more difficult of fulfillment. Muff invited his friend into Cleary's saloon, where they soon found themselves in the enjoyment of the usual refreshments. McKenna, seeing the two in company, determined upon a little police business. He searched out Tom Hurley, John Morris, and Ned Monaghan, and with them visited the same drinking-place. While there he adroitly mentioned each man by name, and Linden, know-

ing that something important was up, made himself familiarly acquainted with the features and other peculiar points
of all the Mollies spoken of. But Linden and McParlan
were not apparently as friendly as usual. In fact, the former
took occasion to roundly abuse the latter for the part he
had taken at the time of the riot, and later, in fomenting
discord in the coal region. The Secretary replied sharply
that he thought he knew his business pretty well, and would
thank Linden to give particular attention to his own affairs
and leave those of other people alone.

Lawler was astonished, and, by words and winks, warned
McKenna not to treat the officer so roughly, hinting that
Linden was the best friend he had in the State, and more
than once had aided him when he was in imminent danger
from angry citizens of Tamaqua and Shenandoah. Mc-
Kenna put on an air of indifference, coarsely expressing
himself that it " made no difference to him. He could take
care of Number One ! "

Time passed, from the last of September, through November, until the tenth of December, 1875, and still my work
was never relinquished or relaxed.

Between two and three o'clock, the morning of the day
mentioned, occurred an outrage of which it was supposed
citizens of the neighborhood were perpetrators, the Mollies
taking, for the very first time, the place of victims. It was
at Wiggan's Patch, a colliery village, not far from Mahanoy
City, that a band of masked men forced an entrance to the
house of the O'Donnell's, where lived Friday O'Donnell, his
mother, and brother—all related by marriage to Jack
Kehoe—and in the mêlée that ensued shot and killed Mrs.
McAllister, a daughter of Mrs. O'Donnell, a sister-in-law of
Mrs. John Kehoe, and then took Charles O'Donnell into
the street, and riddled him with bullets, leaving him dead
where he fell.

This was fighting fire with fire, and the Mollie Maguires
20

experienced a new feeling of dread. The people, stung to
madness by the rapidly succeeding murders of the summer
and fall, were, it appeared, taking the law in their own
hands and giving payment for assassination in similar coin.
It looked natural that this should be so. There was a
breach of the law, it is true, but it was in the interests of
humanity and the law, and, coupled with the arrests of the
murderers of John P. Jones, had a wonderfully tranquillizing
effect upon the society, which, during the preceding months,
had disported itself riotously in human blood and caused a
dozen families to mourn in despair the taking off of some
of their members. Now all was outwardly quiet. Inwardly
human passion surged and boiled, and the hearts of the
Mollies were filled with hate and bitterness. Jack Kehoe,
the King of the Mollies in Schuylkill, was open and loud in
his denunciation of the cowardly murderers of his wife's
kinsman. He was averse to receiving the sauce he served
to his neighbors, and vowed dire vengeance upon the vigilance committee. Pretending to believe that the killing of
Mrs. McAllister had been wholly intentional, when some of
the O'Donnell family believed it purely accidental, he
deeply cursed all murderers of women. Forgetting, for the
moment, the several attempts the Mollies had made in the
same direction, he endeavored to create sympathy for Kelly
and Doyle—wasting no breath on Kerrigan—in which he
made a mistake—seeking to make their expected acquittal
the easier by arousing the prejudices of the people against
the men supposed to have formed a part of the committee
of safety How he prospered in this, the succeeding
pages will exhibit.

The Mollies were now confronted with an adversary as
mysterious and as dangerous as themselves, and were forced
into at least an appearance of submission. That they truly
intended to give over their misdeeds is doubtful. On the
contrary, should they succeed in evading punishment, it was

more than probable their deeds of the past would be eclipsed in inhumanity by those they hoped were to follow. They could not be allowed to escape the just reward of their many misdeeds. While seemingly giving expression only to great indignation, the society was secretly discussing the propriety of forming military companies and buying improved firearms. Some went so far in their divisions as to pass orders requiring each man to pay into the treasury a sum of money sufficient for the purchase of a rifle or carbine. In the face of the fear produced by the late arrest, and the midnight work of the vigilants, progress in the business of arming was tediously slow. It was the subject of comment at a county convention, held at Tamaqua in January, 1876. Men were to be sent to New York to obtain the guns, with three hundred rounds of cartridges, and each Mollie was expected to hold himself in readiness to march to the front at a moment's notice. But the movement failed. The guns were not even bargained for. All the bluster ended only in bluster.

Hugh McGehan, at this time, gave out that he had been fired upon, at night, while going from his saloon to the spring for a pail of water, and made a very narrow escape from death, the bullet striking him in the fleshy part of the shoulder There were several in the attacking party, one of whom Mc Gehan said he knew, but was wise enough not to name. Beside the real injury inflicted on McGehan, several bullets passed through and cut holes in his coat, showing that however hurried the aim of the attacking party had been, it was tolerably well taken, despite the surrounding darkness.

The publication of the list of Mollies raised a feeling in the society that they held a traitor in their midst. Each man fell to suspecting his neighbor. No one, excepting a member, they correctly argued, could ever have given the newspapers such full and accurate information. The question uppermost in all minds was, "Who is the apostate?" That he was well posted, controlled sources of intelligence

not available by or open to ordinary communicants of the
body, was evident to all. After a season of serious discussion, during which every point was covered, it was settled
that the journals had been supplied with the names by some
person residing in Schuylkill County. Soon suspicion began
to be directed to Muff Lawler, who was known to be so particularly kind to Linden, in whose society, for his own purposes, he had very frequently placed himself. Jack McClain,
of the same division, was charged with having assisted Muff
in collating the facts. McKenna, the actual culprit, without
saying a word to give direction to the idea, was freely acquitted. Had he not quarreled with Linden months before?
Had he not separated himself from Lawler? Was he not
the same wicked Mollie Maguire that he always had been
since his initiation? These queries were promptly answered
in the affirmative. The agent was even the recipient of
praise that he no longer found pleasure in the society of Lawler or Linden. There were some who charged the damaging
publication on Barney Dolan, but he gave the lie to it. As
Barney, with his brother, "Bear" Dolan, was in prison, at
Pottsville, where they had been sent for thirty days, convicted of breaking a Mrs. Sweeney's windows, he thought such an
accusation uncommonly hard upon him, and was very vehement in his denials

McKenna was now succeeded in the Secretaryship of
Shenandoah Division by Ned Monaghan, and new members
were being gradually received, until the Shenandoah branch
was one of the most important and flourishing in that part
of Pennsylvania. But fear pervaded the division hall.

Nor was it much better at Summit Hill, where McKenna
found it convenient to go on the sixteenth of January, 1876.
While visiting Alex. Campbell at his residence, the landlord
took Carroll and himself beyond ear-shot of their companions, and, with a very solemn face, assured them that traitors
were fast multiplying in the camp. His pet, Hugh McGehan

was just in receipt of another intimation that he would be called for. In fact, he had been "noticed." The missive bearing the startling intelligence had upon it the Mauch Chunk postmark, and informed Hugh that, as he had not given policeman Yost, of Tamaqua, much of a chance for his life, he and Boyle, accomplices in that cruel assassination, with Campbell, Roarty, Carroll, and Mullhall, who were all known, would have about an equal chance for theirs. Their fate was sealed. This document frightened the Sum-mit Hill Mollies. Campbell hardly knew what to do about it. Were some of the boys in jail too open-mouthed, or was the dastardly work of the first spying miscreant yet going on? The men who had so long murdered with a stab in the dark, under cover of a mask, hated this baleful mystery. The weapon aimed full upon them, it made their faces pale with fear. They finally decided that the warning paper must have been sent by some one who knew nothing whatever of their crimes, but had suspected something and sought to disturb them with silly menaces.

Soon afterward a crowd of men walked up to McGehan's house in the night and fired seven or eight bullets through its siding, but none touched the murderer of Yost. Muff Lawler, of Shenandoah, was similarly treated.

That there was a spy among the Mollies all were now agreed, but thus far no thought had gone abroad that Mc Kenna was the man. If Linden had something to do with the matter no one would be disappointed.

At Mauch Chunk, on his return, McParlan met one Teague McGinty, who drew him aside and informed him that he had very important news to communicate.

"What is it?"

"Shortly after last court I met Major Klutz, an' he took me out, and inquired if John McGinly wor a Mollie? I told him the right down truth, that he wor not! Then Klutz said that a man named Pinkerton sent one of his detectives to Mauch Chunk, and he had reported McGinly as a member of the order !"

"Who the divil is this man, Pinkerton ?" innocently asked McParlan, "an' where do he howld out !"

"He is a great one at catching rogues, an' lives in Philadelphia ! He has over a hundred men employed ! I wonder you have never heard of him !"

"It's all owin' to me ignorance, I suppose ! An' that's because I don't rade all of the papers. Beside, I have a very poor recollection of names ony how! I may hev heard sometime about Pinkerton. If so, I must hev forgotten it !"

If the informer was not Muff Lawler, then who was it ? Time would probably solve the riddle. McParlan was fearful that not much time would elapse, as matters were shaping themselves, before he would stand revealed as the person. Still he did not falter, and continued his labors as before.

CHAPTER XLIV.

TRIALS AND CONFESSIONS.

Some weeks before the occurrence of part of the events narrated in the last chapter, McKenna had suffered from a severe illness, and for several weeks was under the constant care of an eminent physician, at Wilkesbarre, who succeeded in restoring him to comparatively good health, beside giving him back a fair sprinkling of hair for the adornment of his previously shining and denuded scalp. The capillary substance, which had formerly been of a yellow, or light hue, when reproduced was of a dark, glossy brown, adding con siderably to his personal appearance. In fact, a number of his friends remarked that he was far more proud of the second than the first growth, because it made him more attractive to the ladies. However this may have been, when he again visited Tamaqua and gave further attention to Miss Higgins, it is true that he found more favor in her eyes than he had while sporting the red, straggling, and bushy wig. But he had little time in which to press his suit with Kerrigan's sister-in law, as Mrs. Kerrigan and her relatives were all industrious'y engaged in preparing testimony to prove the "Babe" innocent of crime. Inadvertently the sisters let fall hints, now and then, as to the course they were pursuing and the parties on whom they relied for making oath to Jimmy's whereabouts the day of the murder. Very naturally, these confidences were incorporated in the detective's reports, and, very naturally again, the prosecution was made aware of this and other portions of the line of defense to be adopted by the prisoners when brought to trial at Mauch Chunk.

Passing over a few weeks, during the expiration of which the Agency was employed in massing testimony in all the cases and placing it in good shape before the District Attorney, I now come to the first indictment of a Mollie Maguire, in this country, with a possible chance for ultimate conviction. This was on the eighteenth of January, 1876, at Mauch Chunk, Carbon County. The parties arraigned were Michael J. Doyle, of Mt. Laffee, Schuylkill County, and Edward Kelly, charged with the murder of John P. Jones. The circumstances of the crime have already been sufficiently detailed. At an earlier date the three murderers, Kelly, Doyle, and Kerrigan, had been jointly put on trial, entering the usual plea of "not guilty," and demanding a severance. The Commonwealth was represented by E. R. Siewers, Esq., the able District Attorney, Hon. F. W. Hughes, of Pottsville, Gen. Chas. Albright of Mauch

Chunk, and Hon. Allen Craig. For the defendant, Doyle, the Commonwealth choosing to try him first, appeared Hon. Lin. Bartholomew, Hon. J. B. Reilly, and John W Ryon, of Pottsville, Daniel Kalbfus, Esq., and Edward Mulhearn, Esq., of Mauch Chunk. On the twenty-first of January a jury had been obtained, consisting of Wm. Bloss, Jonas Beck, Joel Strohl, Dan'l Boyer, jr., Dan'l Remaly, Abraham Henry, Levi West, Levi Straub, Henry Long, Peter Cushman, Thos. A. Williams and Drake H. Long. The trial at Mauch Chunk was well attended by all the celebrities of the Carbon County bar, much surprise being exhibited that at last there seemed a possibility that a Mollie might be convicted of a crime. Great efforts were made by the leaders of the clan to show that not one of the three men charged with the deed could possibly have been present at the killing of Jones, as they really were elsewhere, but their trouble and expense came to naught, from the effective work the detectives had performed and were performing. The witnesses, so confidently expected to appear, were for once abashed and afraid to take the stand. They knew they could not swear to a lie and go unpunished. The old and well-tried *alibi* fell prostrate, no more to be resuscitated, it is to be hoped, in the criminal courts of the Commonwealth. Before the end of the cause, James Kerrigan, of Tamaqua, made known, in a proper way, to the prosecuting officer that he wanted to give State's testimony. After a careful consideration, he was accepted, placed before the court and made a confession about as follows :

"I live in Tamaqua and have been there six or seven years; am a man of family and work in the mines. I have known Alex. Campbell three or four years; met him first at Tamaqua, last September; he lived at Storm Hill and kept a tavern, selling whisky and porter. I did not know John Jones, but was acquainted with Michael Doyle and Edward Kelly. On the first of September last I had been workin.

at Alaska Colliery, in Tamaqua, for Mr. Richards, and was returning home from work in the evening, when I went into the hotel, kept by James Carroll, to get a drink. Mr. Lutz, of Tamaqua, was there, also Doyle and Kelly. I was going out, when Carroll followed me to the porch, asking me if I would take those men, Doyle and Kelly, over to Alex. Campbell's, at Storm Hill. I told him I would have to go to work at 11 o'clock, but after he coaxed me I promised. He then made me acquainted with them and I went home to wash myself and get supper, returning at twenty minutes past seven P.M. (I left work at about half-past five P.M., that day.) The colliery was nearly a mile from Carroll's place. When I got back from the house Carroll treated twice and walked with us as far as Freidenburgh's, giving me instructions not to tell any one that might ask where we were going. At the New York depot we met Mr. and Mrs. Griffiths and I bade them good evening. We then walked on to Storm Hill and found Alex. Campbell there, and his little brother-in-law, a boy of fourteen, with him. Campbell called me outside, bidding me wait until he had put on his coat, when he would accompany us to McGehan's, at Storm Hill, first treating us at his own bar. He told his little brother-in-law to say, if any one inquired for him in his absence, that he had gone to a wake. As we went into McGehan's, two or three men were coming out; one I know is name: Aubry and I think his given name is William. Alex. Campbell called for drinks and paid for them. Then he began to whisper, up by the bar. The next thing I observed was three revolvers. McGehan got them, and took the chambers out of two and began to oil them out of a can. After fixing them he gave one to Doyle and one to Kelly. Campbell handed one to me, but I refused and would not take it. He wanted me to go with the others and shoot John Jones, but I said I did not know him and would not go. They then agreed I should stay there that night and they

20*

would go with me to get work in the morning, as they wanted
to see and recognize the boss.

"McGehan and Campbell were saying that John Jones
had black-listed some men that had been working there, and
McGehan was one of the three, another being named Mar-
shall. Parish gave these men a letter to give John Jones
and Zehner, to be reinstated, but they ordered the men away
from the office, saying there was no work for them. Campbell said if Jones was shot Zehner would then run away. Mc-
Gehan said : 'By G——, if he does not cool off, after this,
we'll give him a ball !' McGehan said he was black-listed
at Judd's, also, and there were two men there that he wanted
put out of the way, B. Marble and John Turner.

"We started from McGehan's at seven A.M., and came down
to the Catholic church and on the road to Micky O'Donnel's
tavern, passing Micky at the depot, and went up the railroad
to Number Six, where Doyle went into a blacksmith's shop
and Kelly and I went up to a house above, where we asked
a woman if she sold anything. Doyle afterward came up
and we got a bowl of milk.

"We then went up to a Mrs. Davis, and finding she sold
porter, called for three bottles ; she asked Doyle where we
came from, and he told her Shenandoah. Then she gave us
tea and a good meal. We went out to the slope to look
for work, but leaving Doyle and Kelly, I went to Mc-
Gehan's ; still they could not see the boss, so came back and
met me. They failed again to find Jones, and about six P.M.
we all went to Alex. Campbell's, McGehan carrying the
pistols. As a wagon was passing I wanted to go home on
it, as I told them my wife would think me lost, but Campbell would not let me. Campbell treated us, on arriving at
his bar, and after supper I again wished to start for home,
but Campbell objected, wishing me to go up with the others
and shoot Jones at the house, as he would be coming from
the post-office about that time. While Doyle and Kelly went

Campbell made me get down on my knees and promise never to tell or speak of the matter, drunk or sober. He then bade me go up and see where they were. I met them this side of Micky O'Donnel's, and Doyle was sitting on a stone. Kelly said he had been into a house and asked if Jones was at home, and the person said he was not.

"On returning to Campbell's, this house was described to Alex., and he said it was Geo. Hooley's house, not Jones'. We stopped at Campbell's all that night, and they were fooling with the cartridges. Kelly said he would take Campbell's small revolver along in the morning, and shoot Jones as he was going to his work, and not let him off with one ball, but give him three or four. Michael Doyle had the old pistol and the black-jack, and Kelly had the other two. Campbell advised them they need not be a bit afraid, for no one would ever follow them, as Jones was not liked by the Welshmen or any one else. 'You can have this,' said Campbell, handing me a five dollar bill, 'and buy them some whisky and give them enough to pay their way home on the cars.' I gave the bill to my woman when I got to Tamaqua, and she got a pint of whisky of Mrs. Clark, who could not change the bill I took the liquor out to them at the spring where we were arrested.

"Campbell told Doyle and Kelly to be sure not to be seen at Carroll's in the day-time, but to go in the night and leave the pistols there, and then go home on the cars in the morning. He also told them this the night Carroll came up the railroad. Then Doyle said: 'By G——, they are after us! There is Carroll!' and he started to run. I joined the society in Campbell's cellar, thinking it the A. O. H. A man named Donahue put me through. I did not know it was the Mollie Maguires until Barney O'Hare was burned out at Tuscarora. Slattery got and paid Alex. Campbell to send the men. I was at Campbell's when they started.

"I made this statement before Doyle's conviction. I

received no reward from Campbell for showing the men the road, and the five dollar bill which we could not change I have since sent my wife from the prison by Wallace.

"The order of Mollie Maguires is an organization to murder, and the men do not speak of their plans at the public meetings but the Bodymasters employ men to do the work for them."

After this, Mrs. Kerrigan turned against her husband and said he might hang. She would not raise her hand to save him.

During the trial, McKenna, who was in attendance, ostensibly as a spectator, but really to find out all he could, came across a man named Durkin, who told him he was ready, in the event that the Mollies were convicted, to blow up the court-house edifice, killing judges, jury, attorneys, officials, and innocent spectators, having procured a can of nitroglycerine, which he had safely deposited in a shop near at hand. The agent informed the desperado that he was very foolish to concoct such a plot, and would be still more silly should he endeavor to put it into operation, as he could make sure of being captured and strung up by the vigilance committee, to the nearest tree. As the attempt was never made, it is probable that the reckless fellow was sufficiently frightened and wisely decided to abandon the idea.

Kerrigan's confession having corroborated, in every important particular, the stories of the other State's witnesses, on the first of the ensuing February the jury returned a verdict of "guilty of murder in the first degree," and, on the twenty-second, the Court sentenced Michael Doyle to death. This was noteworthy as the earliest conviction and disposal of a real Mollie in Pennsylvania, and the news spread rapidly, far and wide, carrying consternation and dismay into the ranks of the organization and shocking the nerves of the leaders everywhere in the State. During the progress of the trial the Mollies had been bold and defiant, and many of their principal men were on the spot, expecting, as they expected to live, to witness the defendant's release. How deeply they were disappointed McKenna was among the first to receive intelligence. He said that the unforeseen result had come upon the order like an earthquake in a quiet village. Everybody was dumbfounded.

Edward Kelly was placed at the bar before Judge Dreher, the twenty-ninth of the succeeding March, and although ably defended, met with a similar fate, a verdict of murder in the first degree having been returned by the jury on the twelfth of April following. Death-warrants were issued by the Governor in both cases, fixing the execution of Doyle for the third of May, and that of Kelly for the fourth of the same month. Writs of error in the Supreme Court, however, superseded the death-warrants, and all of the murderers of John P. Jones, and those implicated before and after the fact, at this date, are still unexecuted. In February, 1877, Edward Kelly made a voluntary confession, clearly showing that he had not been wrongfully charged or convicted, and substantiating the words of Kerrigan to the letter. He did not expect or ask for mercy, but, before dying, desired to purge himself of his crime, and was given the opportunity.

These cases failed in the Supreme Court, and in May, 1877, Gov. Hartranft signed the death-warrants, the executions to take place on the 21st of June following.

Returning to Shenandoah, after the adjournment of Carbon County Court, McKenna rejoined his friends, the Mollies, and silently acquiesced in the "sweet" prayers of all the organization for the "dear" judge and jury that had convicted one of their number. They were terribly mortified and annoyed through the failure of their plans, and were at a standstill.

Jerry Kane took the cue early, and fled from the country.

Hurley preceded him, and the remainder, now fugitives from justice, stopped awhile to see the full result of the matter.

Barney Dolan, the great, at this time was outspoken against Kehoe, exclaiming in his mild way, that all the pending troubles came from the County Delegate's own inefficiency and unpardonable blundering. He added complacently that, had he been the incumbent of the office of County Delegate, it could never have occurred. He would have taken ten or twelve good men, marched to Mauch Chunk, captured the jail, and released the prisoners. Barney was allowed to have and enjoy his boast, but there were those present who thought even he might not have saved the defendants from conviction.

Kerrigan turning State's evidence was the most stunning blow the Mollies had thus far received, but they knew not, at the time, how much heavier strokes were yet in preparation to fall upon their villainous heads. Some of the tribe, Jack Kehoe included, would not believe the report that a Body-master, especially one who knew so much of the cruel crimes of the society as Kerrigan, had assumed the work of informer. He even went as far as to say that some of the State's officers—Capt. Linden very probably—had originated the story for the purpose of inviting a person to do just what they accused Jimmy Kerrigan of doing. He was more inclined to the thought that Ned Monaghan, who had been seen, he alleged, at a suspiciously late hour, coming out of the editorial rooms of the Shenandoah *Herald*, was engaged in the character of spy, and accused him of having inaugurated the movement by publishing the names of the chief Mollies. "At least," concluded King Jack, "somebody in Shenandoah is at the head of the game for injuring the organization, and I am determined to learn who it may be!"

At this juncture McKenna suggested that, to make his own work more effective, he might be arrested on a trumped-up charge of having been in some way connected with the You

tragedy, after which, when incarcerated with other prisoners,
be could safely form plans for learning all their secrets, and
possibly obtain important confessions, in the presence and
hearing of other witnesses, which would lead to new arrests
and at least make sure the conviction of all that had been
captured. Linden urged the same thing upon Mr. Franklin,
and we were about to arrange the scheme in accordance
with the line indicated, when a series of startling events
transpired, which concluded the chances for such work
proving successful. The Mollies thought they had discovered
who was the traitor in their ring.

CHAPTER XLV.

SUSPICION AROUSED.

In February, McAndrew found himself the victim of a
panic regarding the society. He believed that Kerrigan was
only the Alpha and that Omega was not far away, and therefore requested the detective to go with him and help destroy
every book and paper in any manner connected with Shenandoah Division, A. O. H., otherwise the Mollie Maguires.
They quickly performed that task, and the test-paper, fabricated record of proceedings, constitution and by-laws, treasurer's receipts and vouchers, with the charter and blank
traveling cards, were converted into black and harmless
charcoal. The men who had so long carried the affairs of
the county with a high hand were now in a state of demoral-
ization. They appreciated that something dreadful lay in
their pathway. What goblin shape it might assume they
could not say, and it was the more horrible from its very

indistinctness. It might be a gallows tree. It might be a prison. It might be something more to be feared than either, and at last take the form of a vigilance committee. Whatever it might prove to be, they were determined to have no written evidences of their acts confronting them. In Kerrigan's case, the books and papers of Tamaqua branch were at his house when the constables searched it, but so well concealed were they that, after upsetting almost everything, and turning all the beds and mattresses inside out, they were still undiscovered.

The next news Shenandoah Division received was contained in a letter from Linden, written to McKenna, giving the latter a fraternal greeting and saying that, as he, James McKenna, was suspected, he had best make his way to foreign parts. "I may at any moment, have a warrant placed in my hands for your arrest," concluded this precious epistle, "and I really do not wish to be forced to lay hands upon you. If you have flown and I cannot find you, as a natural consequence I will be unable to put irons on my old chum from Buffalo!"

"I'll not budge wan single inch, to save them all from perdition!" exclaimed the operative, after reading the document to McAndrew and the crowd usually congregated at Cleary's. "I am innocent! I'll only be arrested, anyhow! An' if others stand by, why shouldn't I! Linden knows I will remain!"

The Mollies applauded him for this exhibition of mock courage. They would have acted in an entirely different manner had they known that it was precisely the response he had been expected to make to the well-concocted epistle, and that even then the proper papers were ready for McParlan's apprehension and confinement at Mauch Chunk.

Thomas Munley was arrested for the Sanger and Uren murder at about this date, with McAllister, and both were taken to Pottsville, where a hearing on an application for a writ of *habeas corpus* was had, and many of the members of the order were accordingly in the city. The detective found it necessary to confine himself very closely to his room, under medical treatment he was receiving, seldom venturing beyond a block from the boarding-house on Norwegian Street, and was feeling very despondent over the prospect of becoming totally blind unless there soon came a change for the better, when he received a call from Frank McAndrew, then a transient visitor at Pottsville in the interests of the prisoners. After a little friendly conversation, the Shenan-doah Bodymaster invited his Secretary to walk with him to the court-house. It would not do to deny the reasonable request, and the two emerged from the dwelling, arm-in-arm.

McAndrew was thoughtful for a moment, then exclaimed.

"Something queer occurred on the cars as I was coming down, this morning!"

"Phat wor that?" inquired McParlan.

"I know it's not true, but I must tell you for the danger there is in it! Some of the boys, Kehoe among the number, were making bets, as we rode along, that you'd appear on the witness stand, to-day, for the Commonwealth—in other words, that you were a secret spy, a detective! There! It's out! But, remember, I don't believe a word about it!"

"Me a spy? Me a detective?" exclaimed McKenna, with a show of virtuous indignation. "I will thank ye to name the man that dare insult me by saying so!'

"There is no occasion for anger!"

"I think, be me sowl, there *is* occasion for much of it! I won't have such a slander circulated about me! Sure, if ye are the friend ye say ye are, you'll out wid it an' give me the man's name!"

McAndrew hesitated a second, and then responded.

"Jack Kehoe was the person!"

"Jack Kehoe? Does he dare do that?

"I heard him whispering it to several. But, to the credit
of the men of the division, I must say they'll not entertain the
suspicion, which has risen in some way since the arrest of
Munley and the squealing of Jimmy Kerrigan!"

"Will ye go wid me, an' see Kehoe? I'll knock those
words down his throat, or he shall tell me where he got 'em,
or take them back!"

After consenting, the two men visited Danny Hughes
place—which at the time was a sort of headquarters for
the crew, since Dormer had sold out the Sheridan House and
adopted the peaceful calling of a pedler of wares and vegetables, in a wagon, over the hilly country—but Kehoe was not
there.

"An' hev ye heard the nonsensical charge they're circula-
tin' about me?" asked McKenna of the tavern-keeper.

"Yes! and I must confess that it staggered me! I am far
from belavin' anything of the sort! Kehoe didn't come down
here himself, but sent Mrs. Kehoe to me, wid a message,
like. She came into me saloon, she did, an' wanted me, for
Jack's sake, to say to every wan interested, to beware of you,
Jim McKenna, fur you wor a detective! At laste, that such
wor the report; an' that Jack had recaved it from responsible persons! That's all I know of the matter! Tho' Jack
Kehoe was to take his oath on the holy cross, I'd tell him he
lied! I'm not such a fool as to be scared at a shadow!"

"Thanks for your confidence in me," answered the agent
pleased that Hughes, who was an honest, free-spoken man,
snould refuse to credit the statement of even King Kehoe.
"I'll see this man, soon, an' he'll have to tell me who's the
father of this lie, or I'll surely make somebody suffer!"

"I would, if I were in your place," said Hughes. "No
person should slander me in that way an' live!"

The case before court resulted in the holding of Munley
for trial. This created more indignation, and the murderers began to look about them and inquire if this was the

State of Pennsylvania that they were in, or some territory where Mollies were unknown? With their surprise was mingled inveterate hate for those who were supposed to be following them for the purpose of their capture and punishment.

The time had now come, with McKenna, which he had so long dreaded. Suspicion, which he knew, from experience with many others, had generally proven fatal, was at last directed upon him. There was nothing for him to do but brazenly face the accusation down. He believed that not a living person knew anything of the actual facts. People might think him a detective, but he had the utmost confidence that they would be unable to bring an item of proof to support their belief. Nobody excepting Mr. Gowen, Mr. Linden, Mr. Franklin, Mr. Bangs, and myself had knowledge that he was James McParlan, the detective. He was confident no other man could learn anything of his business. Bishop Wood, of Philadelphia, was aware of the circumstance that an operative was in the coal region, as before explained, but he had no definite idea of the individual. Even had he been cognizant of his personality he still would have preserved the secret intact. "Then," the detective argued, "it must be merely a chance suspicion, which Jack Kehoe has himself originated, or some other highly imaginative person may have given to him." Come what would, he resolved to go at once to Shenandoah, thence to Girardville, and openly denounce the tale as a falsehood of the deepest dye. Kehoe kept out of the way while he was in Pottsville and the agent could not see him. In the evening of the same day, still accompanied by McAndrew, the agent took cars for Shenandoah. After sleeping there, he went alone to Girardville and marched direct to the house of the County Delegate.

"What is this I hear you are afther sayin' agin me?" inquired the visitor, facing Kehoe, who was in his own bar waiting upon customers when he entered, but the strangers having gone, the two men being quite alone at the time. "Tell me what you have been spreadin' over the country about me ! "

" I have told that you are not what you seem, but a detective ; an' I heard it some time ago ! " Then Kehoe laughed a cynical laugh, and added : " But I don't believe a word of the yarn ! "

He was evidently ill at ease and wanted to conciliate the heated individual before him, whose flushed face and uneasy movements indicated more than a usual degree of excitement, and he had no desire that the interview should end in a personal disturbance.

" I want to know, Misther Kehoe, who is goin' to prove this assertion ! Nobody can prove it, fur it is a downright lie ! You may appoint a trial fur me before the society ! I'll be there, an' let me stand forninst the thafe of the worruld who dare report me as an informer ! Let the order judge me ! An' if I find who is lyin' about me, it'll go hard wid him ! I'll shoot the scoundrel, if I hang fur it ! "

And McKenna made considerable bluster, thumped the counter with the butts of two revolvers, which he held in his hands and almost convinced Kehoe himself that he was not acting a part in his denials of the grave charge. At last the County Delegate informed McKenna that a conductor on the Reading Railroad, while he was riding from Ashland, at least when between Ashland and Girardville, had asked him, Kehoe, into the baggage car and inquired if he had seen McKenna lately, and added that he, the conductor, had heard that he was a detective. The reply that Kehoe made was not given.

" We'll have some proof of this ! " exclaimed the agent, having become more cool as the circumstance was detailed.

Subsequently Kehoe, who acted as though he discredited the rumor, agreed to give McKenna a hearing before a convention of Bodymas'ers, and, saying that, as he was himself rather nervous, the detective should make the necessary notices, signing the County Delegate's name to them. To this McKenna agreed, and, obtaining stamped envelopes and stationery, went upstairs to the family apartment, where he found Mrs. Kehoe with her childen, and, sitting at the table between the two front windows, he commenced writing. But he found his own fingers not in the exact plight to do duty in producing readable penmanship. Persevering, how. ever, he managed to get ready a few of the needed letters. Mrs. Kehoe received him pleasantly, as she always had. In a little while Kehoe, himself, left the bar and visited the sitting-room. He did not remain many minutes, but returned to his business below. Presently the detective heard his footsteps again ascending the staircase. When Kehoe entered the apartment the second time his face was of a more sickly color than usual and his hand trembled perceptibly as he passed a glass of liquor to the operative.

"This will steady your nerves," said Kehoe.

The tumbler and contents were accepted by McKenna. Saying he would taste of it soon, he thanked the agitated saloon-keeper and resumed work on his stack of letters. Mrs. Kehoe looked up inquiringly, as she continued her sewing, and the little girl, who had been playing with a ball and her pet kitten, gazed wonderingly upon Kehoe as he turned on his heel and journeyed down stairs again. McKenna did not particularly like the expression of Jack Kehoe's naturally smiling countenance. He pondered the circumstance for a moment and then, saying that the fumes of liquor, under certain conditions, made him ill, shoved the goblet from him with a preoccupied air and went on with his writing. He was in such haste to complete his work and place the letters, all enveloped, sealed, and directed in Kehoe's hands, that he quite forgot to imbibe the spirits, something Mrs. Kehoe had never observed in him before. He touched not a single drop to his lips.

It struck the mind of the operative, while he wrote, that Kehoe really believed in his guilt and had determined to silently and quietly put him out of the way with poison, hence he had decided to forego the potion so kindly brought to him. He might have been over-fearful of treachery, at that time, and without just cause, but quickly following events convinced him that he was not, and never could be, too cautious while dealing with Jack Kehoe. Had Mrs. Kehoe given him the beverage with her own hand, he would nave swallowed it without a suspicion, as he knew that she was with him in not crediting what they said to his disparagement, and her true womanly nature would not permit her to connive at his murder, even had he been her worst enemy.

The date mentioned for the proposed convention was about the first or second of March, the place, Ferguson's Hall, in Shenandoah.

When the work of getting ready the notices was properly finished, the result was shown to Kehoe. He approved and sealed the envelopes. They were given into his charge for deposit in the mail, and he went out, ostensibly to drop them in the box at the post-office.

McKenna remained at the Emerald House all night, sleeping with his revolver close by his side in the bed, fixed for use, and, not having been disturbed, early the ensuing morning took car and returned to Pottsville.

The report detailing these circumstances was of the utmost interest to me. I considered well the position in which the young man was placed, and consented, for his own sake, as well as for the good of the Company and the general public, that he should be arrested and thrown into prison. But, before the order could be carried out, the necessity giving rise to it had passed away.

Beside Kehoe, a number of other members of the organisation informed McKenna that they had heard he was a detective, Pat Butler, of Loss Creek, saying some of his men were early let into the secret and were very earnest in making a demand to have the matter promptly and properly considered.

"I hev the decided advantage of them in that," returned the operative, "fur haven't I already demanded and secured the calling of a county convention, to take action on me case? I have took early action on the matter by meself! Sure, an' if there's such a thing as justice in the State, I'll hev the matin' an' a fair trial on them villainous charges!"

Butler hoped he might come through all right, but was free to say things appeared very stormy, kindly advising the Shenandoah Mollie to keep an eye out for those who would seek to end the trouble easily by killing the one suspected, thus saving the formality of an investigation. Butler showed that he knew the Mollies thoroughly.

Saturday, the 26th of February, Kehoe made his appearance in Pottsville, in company with his brother-in-law, Manus O'Donnell, and the detective met the County Delegate again at Danny Hughes' house. Jack was full of business, having visited the city, as he said, to retain John W. Ryon, Esq., for the defense of McAllister, held with Munley for the murder of Sanger. There was not much transpired in the way of conversation between the King of the Mollies and the suspected man, Kehoe evidently being indignant with his former favorite that he had given him further trouble and work by refusing his recent sweet drop of poteen at Girard vil e.

In the afternoon the two came together once more.

"What is the news, now?" asked McKenna.

"The gettin' of a lawyer for McAllister is goin' to cost me two hundred dollars, sure," was the reply, "an' there is worse news nor that! I learn there are twenty-five hundred men banded together in this country for the purpose of prosecuting the Ancient Order, an' there is positive proof that we have detectives in our midst. These detectives even gets money to go aroun' an' spend among us, an' find out all our secrets, an' will soon turn around an' send us, some of us, to the penitentiary or hang us up by the neck! That's news, isn't it ? "

"True to ye, that is, an' bad news—sorry news enough! There has been somethin' of the same sort in me own mind for these many wakes. Somethin' crooked is surely goin' on, in wan place or another, an' that's the raison I'm doubly cautious where I goes, or what I says! But who tells ye these onpleasant things the day ? "

" I got them from John W. Ryon, this time, answered the County Delegate. " That's the very man! He's just afther tellin' me at his own private office ! "

There was no call for the denial of this. It did not apply directly to himself, and McKenna was content with the remark that it was possible Ryon told the truth. He knew, at all events, something was wrong in the coal region, or there could not be so many arrests. Whence came the difficulty it was not his province to explain. One thing he might do, and he did it, which was to again deny any claim to the despicable title of informer. Kehoe left the saloon in a few minutes, venturing nothing in answer to the last words uttered by his late associate, but with a sneer of disbelief on his face, as though to say he was convinced of the fact that there was a screw loose in the Mollie machinery, somewhere, and he entertained the belief that, if McKenna did not know where it was, nobody in the country could.

Time rolled around and the day preceding the one on which Kehoe had promised the convention to try McKenna arrived. During the forenoon the County Delegate once more appeared in Pottsville, and the accuser and accused again met in Danny Hughes' saloon, seemingly on fair terms with each other, exchanging civilities in a rather distant but not unfriendly manner, and enjoying a cigar in company.

" Are ye goin' up to Shenandoah this evenin' ? ' inquired Kehoe, carelessly.

" Yes ! I'm almost ready now," answered McKenna, ' an' I don't intind missing me appearance at the con- vention for me trial, to-morrow ! "

" That's right ! "

Kehoe, after this, said he would see McKenna later in the day and they could take the train together. It was his hour for an interview with Ryon. He mentioned, incidentally, that his wife was in the city, seeing some friends.

The detective made his report to the Agency, as usual, for the day, spoke of encountering the County Delegate, and informed Mr. Franklin that he was, at a certain hour the same evening, to start for Shenandoah. After mailing this, he re- turned to Hughes' place and particularly inquired for Kehoe. No person remembered seeing him after the conversation with McKenna, held some hours earlier.

Before nightfall the officer found himself in company with a man named Mullen, residing in the vicinity of Tuscarora. He had heard the tale concerning the detective business, and was fearful that, should there be any truth in it—of which he could not judge—there might be danger in having a conven- tion at Shenandoah. For his part, he had done nothing wrong, and was therefore not afraid, but he was lately listen- ing to the talk of some others, who readily concluded that McKenna merely wanted to get the officers and Bodymasters crowded together, at Ferguson's Hall, in Shenandoah, when he could have the whole band arrested by the Coal and Iron Police.

McKenna scouted the idea. All he wanted was a hearing He did not care where it occurred. Using his best endeav- ors, he tried to convince Mullen that such a foolish scheme would be illegal, as well as impossible, even though he had

21

the desire to execute it, which he had not. Mullen, at
last, seemed to be convinced of the honesty of the accused
Mollie's purpose in asking for a trial, and said he would see
how many of the officials he could cause to arrive at the
same understanding.

Before starting for Shenandoah, the accused sought out and
held a snort interview with Linden, telling him, for his sake,
not to have one of his policemen in Shenandoah on the morrow and to keep out of the city himself. A contrary course, he
thought, would raise suspicions that Mullen's friends were correct in their belief. Much against his inclination, Linden
promised compliance. He knew McKenna was running a
great risk, and it would have suited him better to be quite
near, for his protection.

"I believe I can fight them right through and make them
believe that I am no detective!" said McKenna.

"Very well! Do as you please," returned the Captain,
but I fear they will not be convinced! If you come away
with your life, you'll do better than I expect!"

"I am pretty well prepared against surprises," were the
last words of McKenna, "and if they don't overpower me,
or kill me with a shot from behind, I'll get along all
correct!"

The separation which ensued was not without feeling, as,
despite his defiant air and confident words, McParlan was
not perfectly sure that he would ever meet his partner
again. That night he started for Shenandoah on the late
train, but saw nothing of the County Delegate.

McParlan was in the smoking-car, just before reaching
Mahanoy City, when Manus O'Donnell came to him with
word that Mrs. Kehoe was in the ladies' car and desired to
see and speak with him. He waited until the train stopped,
then emerged from his coach and went to the rear, entering
the one the wife of Kehoe occupied. After the usual salu-
tations he inquired where Jack was, that he had not met him

and journeyed in his company, according to previous agree-ment. She believed he had gone up to Frackville on the afternoon train, while she had been to Tamaqua to see her mother. Returning to his own seat the young man began to deliberate. There was certainly something suspicious in the actions of his old associate—something he could not account for—and he made a mental resolution to be very careful of himself. Not that he knew anything particularly dangerous immediately threatening, but he was suspected, and the Mollies usually put suspected persons where they could do no harm. If they would give him a fair trial, as they were in duty bound, he thought he would move along safely. But Kehoe's failure to meet him and going to another place looked to him, under the circumstances, and in his excited mental condition, as though double dealing was going on. It would do no harm to be circumspect, hence, when the train slackened its speed and arrived at a certain crossing, where he had long been in the habit of alighting, it being a shorter route to his boarding-house, the detective kept his place, thought he saw—but was not sure of seeing—several men standing by the track, and rode on until the passenger depot was reached. Kehoe had told him to be sure to be up *that night.* Was it possible some harm was then intended? Without misadventure, he alighted, looked about the depot building, and saw no one. He had taken pains to send up word to McAndrew and his friends that he would be there by the evening express. For a long time, whenever he was expected, there would be from three to half a dozen of the members of his division ready in waiting to meet and give him welcome. On this particular occasion not a man sent him greeting, not a friend made his appearance at the platform. But he thought, as he walked up the street, this might have been accidental, or his letters from Pottsville had possibly miscarried or been delayed It was evident he was an unexpected or an unwelcome visitor. Which was it? Many knew he was to be up there that night. But not a person was at hand to ask him the news or go with him to take a drink. Something warned him all this was caused by a change of feeling on the part of his acquaintances.

As he moved through the town he did not seem as secure as he would have felt in his own room at the Agency in Philadelphia; but he carried on his person two loaded revolvers, his nerves were steady and his mind on the alert for an attack. He met some citizens, but no old acquaintances who were members of the organization.

When he reached James McHugh's saloon, he thought, as he was a member, he would speak with the proprietor They had always been tolerably good friends. McHugh was in front of his door and answered McKenna, asking him to enter the bar-room, which he did.

"Will you have something?" said McHugh.

"I don't mind taking a bottle of porter!" answered the agent. This was an unexpected response, as McKenna was noted for seldom touching any of the weaker fluids, but McHugh produced the bottle and fumbled about the cork excitedly, his face turning as white as a sheet meanwhile.

"An' phat is the matther wid ye, Jim McHugh?" inquired the visitor. "Hev ye got the shakin' ager, been sick, or wor ye drunk last night, or what?"

"Oh, it's only because I'm chilled through, standin' outside!" was the answer.

"Did ye hear what the divils hev ben tellin' of me?"

"Yes, McKenna, I have; but, between you an' I, there's no truth in the stories! I hope you'll come out all right an' I'll be around to-morrow, to see what's done at the convention!'

It struck the detective that McHugh had not exactly expected to meet him in his house that night. Could it be that a plan already made for killing him had fallen through?

But banishing all such ideas he left the saloon and kept on toward McAndrew's house. Passing the Lehigh depot he met another friend, Mike McDermott by name, who was also a member of his division and with whom he had always been well disposed and rather friendly. That night, after merely recognizing the former Secretary, McDermott hardly spoke, and passed along very quickly.

Just across the street from him McKenna now saw Edward Sweeney, another Mollie, with whom he had been quite intimate since his arrival in town.

"Is that you, Sweeney?" said McKenna.

"Yes! It is me!" was the answer. Sweeney was standing just near a lamp-post, but he crossed the street and joined the agent, who inquired:

"Have you seen McAndrew the night?"

"Yes, I have seen him!"

"How long since?"

"Not above an hour!"

"Do you think he's already gone to bed?"

"I guess not!"

Sweeney did not seem greatly inclined to talk, but continued to stop by McKenna's side, only once or twice dropping a step or two in the rear. Sweeney was a bad man He did not know fear. McKenna had once seen him walk up to a party who was drunk and threatening to kill everybody, and boldly take the man's gun away from him. If a job had to be done Sweeney was just the person who might be selected to do it.

"I say, Sweeney," exclaimed the operative, "I've had so much trouble wid me eyes, lately, that they are none of the best and I don't see very well! Will ye be kind enough to go on ahead and I can follow you widout danger of runnin' in the gutther or falling through these holes in the pavement!"

"Certainly!" said Sweeney, and he walked before the

operative, who made sure to keep him at the front, from that time until they arrived at McAndrew's place. So certain was McParlan that Sweeney meant him harm that he had fully determined, if the man turned suddenly, to shoot him down in his tracks. But his companion did not look around. When McAndrew's house was reached a man named Grady was posted outside and Doyle standing in the yard. They evidently expected him to arrive, and having waited his coming had put a sentinel at the gate and another by the door. Truly, this was showing him altogether too much consideration. It made him uncomfortable. He did not like it. There was something in it favoring the dark and mysterious.

CHAPTER XLVI.

MCANDREW SAVES A LIFE.

FROM what occurred later McParlan believed his friend Sweeney had been waiting for his coming, when he found that person on the street, near the lamp-post. But he said nothing, and gave no marked attention to the manner in which McAndrew's premises were watched, but entered as if everything had been about as usual. McAndrew received him graciously, and yet with a degree of constraint, probably, as McKenna thought, perfectly consistent with the changed relations now existing between them. After greetings, Sweeney came into the room, looked carefully around, said a few words, in a joking way, and went outside again. He remarked as he left the doorway that he was going home, but could not have done so, for, in a little while, he re-entered the bar, having a bit of snow in his hand. Watch

ing closely the movements of the man, while, to all outward
intents and purposes, earnestly engaged in smoking his pipe
and reading a newspaper, McKenna saw Sweeney toss the
piece of snow toward McAndrew, who was sitting by the
stove. McAndrew looked up, stretched out his legs, yawned
a little, gazed for one moment on the face of the detective,
then said: "My feet are sore! I guess I'll take off my
brogues!"

The Bodymaster suited action to his words and proceeded
to doff his wet and heavy miners' boots, and replace them
with a pair of easy slippers. At this, still silently and carefully observed by the seemingly absorbed McKenna, Sweeney
curled his lip disdainfully, and once more left the apartment.
From the movements he had seen the agent was almost sure
that something had been arranged—felt suspicious of everybody and everything—and the snow tossed by Sweeney, and
the taking off of McAndrew's boots, were, to his excited
imagination, signals having some reference to his own case.
But he had no desire to let those about him think he was in
fear of his life. It seemed far better to put on a bold, defiant front and face the music, which he did. At last, his pipe
being out, he asked:

"Well, McAndrew, what about the matin' for the morrow?
Be everythin' all ready?"

"Yes! I've engaged the hall and it is all right! I hope
there'll be a large attendance!"

"So do I! An' I don't care how soon the lies on me are
disposed of! It's mighty upsettin' to me nerves to have
such charges restin' again me reputation as an Ancient Order
man!"

McAndrew was, like Sweeney, not in a talkative mood,
and, after vainly attempting to draw him into a conversation,
the accused man bid his glum companion good night, left the
house and started on his journey toward Cooney's residence,
where he then made his temporary home. Once well in the

street, he cast his eyes anxiously around in the darkness, expecting to find Sweeney, or some other Mollie, lingering in the vicinity. But he did not. Everything was quiet somber, and in doubt. Something seemed to say to him, " Do not go home by the usual route, but take some other ! " and he accepted the suggestion as sensible, struck boldly into the swamp, at the risk of losing his footing, getting wet and muddy, finally crossed over, and came out in front of his boarding-house. His heart felt appreciably more buoyant when he saw a light shining from the window at Cooney's, and he knew the family were expecting him. He entered, was cordially received, but soon retired to his room. He afterward confessed to not sleeping much that night. After an unrefreshing season in bed, he arose early, swallowed his breakfast, and went over to see McAndrew. Thence he took a walk up-town, meeting Ned Monaghan and a fellow named Carlin, the latter being Bodymaster at St. Nicholas. Florence Mahony, of Turkey Run, was also seen, but the hall was otherwise deserted. Nobody seemed to come to the convention, and it struck the accused Mollie that Kehoe was surely playing him false, and had never forwarded the notifications prepared at his house. A little after ten o'clock, a couple of drunken men arrived from Mt. Laffee—or at least one was a little intoxicated and the other feigned to be so These fellows, Dennis Dowling and Mickey Doyle—not Michael J. Doyle, the Sanger and Uren murderer, but another person and no relative—said they had just stepped off the cars, when everybody in town knew no trains of any sort came in at that hour. They were Mollies, and Dowling was a big, red-complexioned man. After a time, all present made up their minds there would be no convention, and those in the hall adjourned to McAndrew's saloon, where Dowling asked McKenna what the meeting was about.

" Don't you know ? Didn't you understand what you were called together fur ? "

"No!"

"Well, somebody, I don't know who, have said that I am a detective—which is a lie—and I demanded a trial before the assembled Bodymasters of the county. Kehoe granted it, sent the orders, and here the hour is past and no convention comes. Even Kehoe himself kapes away!"

"I won't believe the story about you, McKenna," exclaimed Dowling. Thereupon, to express his peculiar satisfaction, McKenna, as was expected, invited the crowd to drink with him. None refused the chance. Then McAndrew took McKenna into a rear room and left him there. Doyle, who was drinking very hard, was soon very drunk and some one had to take him away and put him to bed.

The failure of the convention was a great disappointment to the agent. He readily charged the non-arrival of the delegates to Kehoe's door. It was more than probable he never intened to grant an investigation, but had held out the inducement in order to quiet McKenna, keep him in the locality, and manage, through some of his cut-throats, to have him murdered. The suspected Mollie made up his mind that he would pay the County Delegate a visit and institute strict inquiry as to the cause of the late adjournment. McAndrew insisted upon accompanying him, and, in order that he might have witnesses, he went out with his Bodymaster, hired horses and a sleigh, and paid for another cutter and horse for Monaghan. Dowling accompanied the ex-constable, McAndrew and McKenna leading the way over the snow-covered road to Girardville.

"How is this thing, any way, Frank?" asked McKenna of McAndrew, as the latter laid the lash upon the horses and they sped away swiftly over the hills. "I can't understand it at all! I am charged with guilt, am given an investigation before a county committee, the matin' fails, an' now Ned Monaghan and Dennis Dowling are goin' wid us to see Kehoe! What have they to do wid the subject,

21*

when there's no convention? It's all a muddle to me enthirely!"

McAndrew was driving over a particularly rough piece of
road at the moment and did not answer until smooth traveling was reached, then, when well out of the hearing of the
others, he said:

"Look here, McKenna, let me say a word to ye in confidence, while I have the opportunity! You had better look
out, for that man, who is riding in the sleigh behind you, cal-
culates to take your life! Dennis Dowling is the one!
Have you got your pistols ready?"

"Faith an' I always hev them, but little use will they be
to me if I get in a crowd an' Dowling lets on that I am to be
killed! Fur I know that he'll find plenty to help him! Innocent or guilty, it makes no difference!"

"Well, I have me revolver here, an' I mean to stand by
you! I'll lose my life for ye! I don't know whether you're
a detective or not, but I have nothing against you! I
always knew you to do the right thing by me an' those you
were with, an' until proven a traitor, which I can't believe ye
are, I'll keep with you! Why don't they try a man fairly,
an' not seek to take his life on mere suspicion?"

"I thank ye, Frank McAndrew!" was all the detective
could say as the slim hold he had upon the things of this
world was suddenly realized. "I'll sell me life dearly, as the
miscreants shall find if they make a movement to attack me.
I'll kape a sharp eye out for Mr. Dowling! That will I!"

From that moment, while riding, McParlan sat a little side-
ways, in the cutter, with one eye upon the couple behind them.

When they came to Anthony Munley's tavern, the four men
alighted and entering enjoyed something to refresh the inner
man. But McKenna avoided talking with Dowling, who,
more than once, endeavored to draw him into a wordy dispute. With his eye constantly upon the burly fellow and his
hand in his overcoat pocket, where slept snugly one of his

brace of trusty repeaters, he mixed with the crowd and
chatted unconcernedly about the general topics of the day
He was closely attended by McAndrew, and this was particularly noted by Dowling, who had no desire to interfere with
the Bodymaster's charge while thus under his immediate care.

After leaving Munley's, McAndrew positively informed
McKenna that he had saved him from death, and that
Kehoe, instead of keeping tne detective company on the cars,
as he had promised, came to Shenandoah by himself the
previous afternoon. He gathered together all the Mollies in
the place, spent a great amount of money among them, and,
in the presence of others, begged him, McAndrew, for God's
sake, to have that man, McKenna, killed, or he would "hang
half the people in Schuylkill County!"

"Did he say that?"

"I consented," continued McAndrew, not noticing the
inquiry, "and Kehoe went home satisfied. I didn't know
but you might be guilty, and, at first, I intended to act in
good faith toward my agreement with Jack, but my heart
afterward misgave me, and I couldn t do the thing! I
wouldn't do it! But others did prepare for your arrival at
the crossing, and as they were afraid to shoot you, because
it would make too much noise, twelve or fourteen of the
fellows gathered at the bank, knowin' you'd be up by the
late train—fur Kehoe had told us you were comin'—but you
did not get off then—your life was spared; and I was very
thankful it was so; and, from that moment, decided I would
have nothing to do with the affair. Some of the boys had
hatchets and clubs and axes, picks and iron bars, and others
such sledges as they use in the mines. If you had stepped
off the train, at that place, you would surely have been
killed, cast into a wagon, which was in waiting for the purpose, and then tossed down a deserted shaft, where, had
your body ever been discovered, it would have been supposed, by all exceptin' your oath-bound murderers, that you

had fallen in, in the darkness, and met an accidental death. Kehoe planned the whole thing, inspired the men with spirits, an' then informed 'em you had no relatives or friends in the world, an' you would never be inquired for! But, Jim, to save my sweet sowl, I couldn't hev any hand in it, an I staid at me house, an' when you jist popped in upon me there, last night, and I learned you had escaped the evil gang, an Sweeney hadn't been able to kill you while ye were walkin' wid him to my place, I blessed God that I hadn't stained me hands wid yer innocent blood! An' as Sweeney tossed the bit o' snow to me—I believe you saw it— I gave him answer, by the takin' off me boots, that, so long as you were wid me, you should be protected, and come to no harm; an' more'n that, I'd have no share in the affair from that moment forward. Sweeney went away mad! I couldn't help it! I was afraid they would wait for ye over night, or go to Cooney's an' kill ye, so, after ye were out, I watched ye, an' saw ye go across the swamp; and then I knew ye were safe! Jim, I mane to stand by ye to the last drop of my blood! If Dowling undertakes the job, this day, or Jack Kehoe himself interferes, they'll have to get to ye over my dead body!"

McParlan warmly pressed the hand of his friend, could not speak his gratitude, but determined that, thereafter, if he could do Frank McAndrew a good turn he would. But there was little time for talk, and none for forming schemes.

" You'll find I'm tellin' ye the truth, and that ye are in queer company this very minute!"

" I don't give a cent!" exclaimed the detective. "I'm in fur it, an' I am able, backed by you, to defend meself! They have accused me wrongfully, an' I mane to have justice! I'm goin' to Jack Kehoe's to face him down in it!"

McAndrew smiled.

" An' why do ye laugh? It may be fun for some, but I'm in no jesting humor!"

"I meant no harm, and was only thinkin' what Jack Kehoe will say or believe when he sees ye marchin' into his house, all alive an' well, when he at this time supposes ye are lyin at the bottom of the auld shaft, food for the rats!"

"I can't help what he may say or think! I'm goin' there, sure, an' if he wants me killed perhaps he'll have the bould ness to try the job with his own two hands!"

In a few minutes the four persons alighted from their respective conveyances in front of Kehoe's house, in Girardville, and McKenna suddenly made his appearance before the County Delegate, with McAndrew at his side. Monaghan and Dowling were not far away. Never was a man more surprised than Kehoe. He had twice essayed to clear that troublesome McKenna from his path, and the last time invoked, and thought he had secured the assistance of so many good men at the business that he believed he could not fail. Still, here was the man, McKenna, in the flesh, unharmed, and sternly confronting him. Evidently his plans had not worked well. McKenna still lived, and was in company with one of the very men who had promised him to aid in the assassin's bloody work. The County Delegate's crafty, narrow face was as white as a sheet of paper, and his whole body shivered with an ague fit. It needed the sound of McKenna's voice to recall him to himself.

"Well, Mister Kehoe, what about that county matin'? It seems the Bodymasters did not get together—at laste only a few of them—an' me trial seems to be a total failure!"

Jack placed some tumblers on the counter, in a crooked row, took down a bottle, spilled much of its contents untidily over the counter, succeeded in controlling his anger, resentment, and disappointment, and answered:

"Well, you see, I came to the conclusion that there was no use in tryin' you ——"

"That's what *I* thought at the start!" interrupted McKenna.

"There was little use in gettin' together a crowd : t Shen andoah ! "

"So you have taken a good deal of trouble to see that us crowd was gathered ? "

"There's no use talkin,' " answered Kehoe. "1 he trial can't take place ! "

"What am I to do, then ? Rest under this suspicion as long as you may choose to keep me down ? I'll not do it ! "

"If you don't desire to wait, you can go to Father O'Connor about it ! Maybe he'll tell you something ! "

"I'm only wantin' to find out who makes up these lyin' charges ! That I want to know ! The story of the conductor on the train is a downright lie ! It's too thin ! You never heard such a thing, but have got it up in order to have me put out of your way ! "

"Go to Father O'Connor ! It's all I have to say ! "

And Kehoe turned aside and spoke to others. But he kept his unsteady eye on McKenna.

"Well, I'll go to Father O'Connor ! He'll do me justice widout doubt ! An', Misther Kehoe, look here a little ! ' and the detective pulled his two heavy pistols from behind his back and again thumped the counter with their butts, loudly enforcing attention to his speech :

"I don't care for you, or fur any wan here, or in the county ! I'm an innocent, ill-used man, an' ye are tryin' to have me shot ; but listen to this ! I'm all ready, an' will sell me chances at the highest ! I'll go see Father O'Connor, an' then possibly I'll have a settlement wid you, Jack Kehoe ! "

Seeing that McKenna was becoming excited, and not knowing but Dowling might pluck up courage to shoot while in the room, McAndrew seized his friend by the arm, advised him to put up his pistols, and walked with him out of the place. He was right in this, as Phil Nash, Dave

Kelly and Tom Donahue, beside Dowling and Monaghan, had gathered there, any one of whom, had Kehoe said the word, would have finished the trouble with a pistol shot from the rear. McAndrew talked the matter over with the others, after McKenna was once in the sleigh, and it was determined to drive to Father O'Connor's house at once.

When the four men, McKenna, McAndrew, Monaghan, and Dowling, reached Callaghan's place, at Mahanoy Plane, who should be there ahead of them but Phil Nash and Tom Donahue. It was suspicious, the detective thought, but said nothing. They had heard that McKenna was going to see Father O'Connor, but might possibly have had other business at the Plane. Donahue and Nash took McAndrew some distance away, and held quite a talk with him. The agent was on the alert, and saw, from their gesticulations that the two men were endeavoring to induce his friend to do something, but he obstinately refused. Dowling and Monaghan finally joined the group and the remonstrances with McAndrew were resumed.

While the rest were talking, McKenna went to Father O'Connor's house with Callaghan, but was told the priest was absent in Philadelphia, and not expected back until the next day. By the time he got back the sleigh was ready. Dowling was very drunk and McAndrew in haste to leave. They entered the cutter and started, followed by Monaghan alone, as Dowling was too much overcome to take along.

"What was the matter at Callaghan's ?" inquired McKenna.

"The same thing," was McAndrew's reply. "They wanted to kill you right here ! Dowling tried hard to have me lend him my revolver ! But I wouldn't allow it ! Had they succeeded in disarming me, you could not have lived one minute. I would be unable to defend you, and not another in the crowd would interfere. Dowling was armed, but he didn't want to hurt me, and I told them sterr y they couldn't have their way wid you while ! lived."

"I was on the watch for Dowling," said the operative, "and had he made a motion toward me, I'd have shot him! My life is as dear to me as that of another man to him, an I'll not be murdered widout hurting some of them!"

But Dowling was too much intoxicated to do anything, and Monaghan, becoming disgusted, drove off and left him. Having failed to extract any satisfaction from Kehoe, or see Father O'Connor, McAndrew and McKenna, still accompanied by Monaghan, drove directly to Shenandoah. By the time they reached McAndrew's saloon, after putting up their teams and settling the livery bill, it was night. McAndrew took the operative to his home, where he remained undisturbed until his bedtime, when he started up to return to Cooney's, thinking he would again take the route through the swamp.

"Good night, Frank!" said McKenna. "It's time for me to be joggin'!"

"Where to?"

"To me boarding-house, av coorse!"

"Not to-night!" replied McAndrew, earnestly.

'An' why not?"

"Never mind why not; but you are to sleep wid me! My wife is away from home. There's plenty of room, an we are to be bedfellows!"

And the detective did sleep at McAndrew's, and, as the reader may well suppose, was very glad of the opportunity. Nothing occurred, however, to disturb the two men.

The ensuing morning, by the first train, McParlan returned to Pottsville, made out and mailed his report, and found a chance to communicate privately with Capt. Linden. He had appointed to meet McAndrew at Mahanoy Plane the afternoon of that day. Once more Linden urged him not to go without being shadowed by him, as he was sure they were laying plans for killing him. The operative said he would make one more attempt to prove his character good before the priest. Then, if unsuccessful, he could either abandon that course or allow his friend to keep him under surveillance.

CHAPTER XLVII.

THE LAST OF McKENNA.

WHEN the detective, in accordance with his promise, appeared that afternoon at Mahanoy Plane, he encountered Dennis Dowling and Tom Donahue still hanging about Callaghan's saloon. Both were a little more sober than on the previous day, but not a whit the less inclined to pick a quarrel with the man whose life they sought. It should be explained here that this man, Donahue, was neither "Yellow Jack" Donahue, nor was it the Tom Donahue, of Girardville, who had accompanied McKenna on his visit to Pat Hester's daughter, but a man in no way related to either of those mentioned. McAndrew arrived there also, true to appointment, saying he was in to see the affair through. It was fortunate for McKenna that he had such valuable assistance. Had he gone to the place alone it is more than probable he would have disappeared and no one ever been the wiser. When they were by themselves, McAndrew remarked :

"It was well that you stopped at my house, last night. If you had returned home, as you intended, I should never have seen you again alive. I met Cooney to-day, and he says men were waiting for you, and watching all through the night! They knocked at the door, asked if they could stay there, were refused, but kept coming and going until broad daylight, when they got away! They left an old carpet

sack, and other things, on the ground near the fence, a
make it appear they were tramps, but Mrs. Cooney thinks
although they were well disguised, that she recognized one
of the fellows as a resident of Shenandoah.

"Faith, an' I am beholden to ye once more, McAndrew!
When can I ever repay your kindness? I will try to do all
that I can, whenever I hev the chance!'

"Oh, that's all right!" returned the young man.

Again the visit to Father O'Connor was unsuccessful, as
that person had not yet arrived from Philadelphia. Returning to Callaghan's, McKenna reported his want of success.
McAndrew, Dowling, and the rest were talking together,
but no one offered him any violence. Bidding all "good
night," he went to Pottsville once more. He did not feel
that there was any actual necessity for going to Shenandoah
again that day. In fact, it occurred to him that, thereafter,
it might be as well to have somebody, upon whose aid he
could count, along with him whenever he made the journey.

I had telegraphed word to Mr. Franklin to have the detective clear his record, even at further risk, by persevering
until he saw Father O'Connor, but, as matter of precaution,
Mr. Linden should never leave him while there seemed the
least danger that he would run into serious trouble.

The operative, meantime, became convinced, through circumstances brought to his knowledge, that the Mollies had
penetrated his disguise—seen his cards. Somebody had
given them information about him. Who it was, he could
not tell. But that they were satisfied of his double part, he
was well aware. Nevertheless he said:

"I'll go to Mahanoy Plane just once more! Then, if all
is not made straight, you'll see me leave this country!"

"It's according to orders, I see, and, as I am to be with
you, I shall feel better about it!" said Linden.

Linden prepared for the journey, and, the next day, which
was Saturday, the fifth of March, after writing to Mr. Frank-

in, saying he was to go to Mahanoy Plane, to see Father
O'Connor, and adding : "If I am killed, Jack Kehoe is my
murderer," McParlan took the noon train for the place designated. Linden was aware of the localities the operative
would visit and at no time permitted him to stray far from
his presence. This time Father O'Connor was found at his
residence.

Callaghan was invited to go with him to interview the
clergyman, but refused, saying he had already been there
too many times. Beside, he and Father O'Connor had
passed some sharp words regarding a sermon which the
priest had delivered about the Mollie Maguires, or Ancient
Order of Hibernians. So the accused Mollie was forced to
go alone—excepting that Linden kept him in view. He
entered the house and was told the reverend gentleman
would see him in a moment. While sitting in a room,
waiting, McKenna heard footsteps in the hallway and then
came the voice of a man speaking. He recognized the
tone as belonging to one of the Mollies of the Mahanoy
Plane Division. Listening intently, he thought a chair was
drawn along the wall until near the door. Evidently some
one was preparing to hear every word that passed between
himself and the priest. This was enough to put him on his
guard and prompt the use of no language which would compromise him in the eyes of the Mollie Maguires. Soon
Father O'Connor arrived, and McKenna civilly addressed
him :

"I am James McKenna, Father O'Connor! I suppose
you have heard many ill things about me before this, but I
am not quite sure that I am as bad as reported. I know I
am not what you have represented me to be, a detective,
spy, informer! In tellin' me friends this, you hev hurt me
above remedy. I'm no detective! The order I belongs to
is a good wan—but its members are, some of them, charged
wid crimes—an' they'll kill me if they think I'm in league

and their enemies, which I surely am not! They are now quietly engaged in seekin' means of accomplishing me injury. You can stop it by saying that it is not true; that ye don't belave the tale told on me! I beg you to consider! I stands up for the Ancient Order of Hibernians, everywhere! They are the right sort! I hev belonged to 'em for seventeen years, and never saw anything wrong in them. Bishop Wood, an' all the rest, are astray in condemning them, an' if they'll only give us time we'll prove that we are not murderers and incendiaries an' all that's wicked!"

"I have heard about you, young man," calmly answered the priest, "and the language used need not be repeated. I assure you, however, that I have never used your *name* in connection with that of a detective! I confess I heard that you were a detective, and although I did not know you, I thought you might be, on occasion, cognizant of crimes long before their perpetration; crimes that I thought you should have prevented; and in doing as you did you acted as a stool-pigeon—a common phrase among men—and took part in bad acts in lieu of giving word to the authorities and having the perpetrators arrested and punished. I acknowledge I wrote a letter to John Kehoe, and gave it to a party to deliver. It was not sent, but brought back to me. I have told these unfortunate men that their time would surely come, that death would yet be their fate, and now they see that I gave them good counsel. They would not listen to my voice, would not leave their organization, and they must abide by the consequences. I can do no more for them. You can go to Father Ryan, of Mahanoy City, and Father O'Reilly, of Shenandoah, as they know more about it than I do. I learned of the detective matter only recently, and have been to Philadelphia to see how your relations are with another party. I need not name the man, for I found out nothing. You were seen around the vicinity

—or in Tamaqua—about the time Kelly and Loyle were arrested. You kept Kerrigan's company, just before Jones was shot!"

"But, indade, I had business in Tamaqua, Father O'Connor! I wor sparkin' Kerrigan's sister-in-law!"

This provoked a smile on the priest's face.

"Well, if that was all, there was nothing wrong in it; you had a right to pay attention to the young lady if you liked!"

"Of course I know that! An' to get the good-will of the sister-in-law, sure, didn't I hev to spark Kerrigan jist a little?"

Here some other persons wanted to see the clergyman, and McKenna took his leave, promising to visit the other priests and have the tangle straightened out, notifying Father O'Connor of it, so that he might, if he would, make due notice to the members of his congregation. The pastor stated that, when he was satisfied, he would be very happy to make a public correction.

But McKenna had no idea of going to see Fathers Ryan and O'Reilly. He had had quite enough of that kind of work.

McKenna was careful to speak loud while complimenting the Mollie Maguires, so that the eavesdropper might hear this part of the conversation if nothing else. As he went out at one door, he knew that Martin Dooley made his exit at another, and, had he given out anything derogatory to the order, he would never have escaped with his life.

After visiting Callaghan's, and telling the crowd assembled there that he had seen Father O'Connor, and it was all right, he agreed to have an interview with Father O'Reilly, at Shenandoah, the next day, and then took his final leave. While on his way out of the village the agent encountered Dooley, who quickly commenced to laugh. He was glad it was not Tom Donahue and Dowling he had met.

"Phat are you afther laughin' about?" asked McKenna.

"Oh, I heard ivery word of it ! "

"Every word of what ? "

" That passed while you was closeted wia Father O Cen nor ! "

" For shame !   Wor you list'ning ? "

" Sure, an' I was ! "

" Well, didn't I tell him some things about the society that not every *gorsoon* would have known ? "

" That you did !   Didn't you give the order a lift, tho' ? "

" That wor me rale intention ! "

"An' you have been a member for seventeen years, eh ? You told the whole truth about the A. O. H.—or the Mollies —but I don't believe you did about the age of your member- ship ! "

Dooley seemed highly pleased, and reported to all the men at Callaghan's that he never heard a man talk better sense to anybody than Jim McKenna put before Father O'Connor, during their short interview.   The crowd changed their feelings toward the agent, and were, at the moment, more inclined to doubt Kehoe than McKenna.   Dowling was quite drunk, as usual, but managed to put in :

" It's a mystery to me, anyhow !   I can't tell what to make of that fellow in the blue clothes !   He's a counterfeiter, a thief, a gentleman, a singer of songs and dancer of jigs, an', be gorra, now they say he's a detective !   It's a long way beyond me thoughts !   I gives it up !   I gives it up ! "

And Dowling called all hands to the bar, which was satis- factory to the landlord, at least.

Notwithstanding the detective had carried himself manfully before his foes, bearded Kehoe in his den, faced the priestly accuser, and defied the select band of assassins, now, while he knew that Linden was somewhere within sight of him—in truth he was in Mr. Davis' office, close at hand, all the while he had been with the priest, and even then was tracing Mc- Kenna's footsteps at a safe distance—as he made fast time toward Frackville, and the sun began to sink in the west, a feeling of dread came over him, a chilliness ran in his veins, which was nigh unto fear, and he walked faster than he had in a long time. Fortunately he overtook a Dutchman, driving to Frackville, and McKenna, not wishing to be caught in the dark on the mountains, asked the driver if he would give him a ride. The Dutchman consented, stopped his team, and the detective mounted the seat by his side, saying:

"I'm in a very great hurry! I hev a dispatch that me sisther is just dying, at Pottsville beyant, an' I fear I may not get to the train in sayson!"

"I'll drive a little faster!" said the obliging fellow, and he applied his black-snake whip to the animals' flanks and they went flying up the steep road, while Linden was some distance behind, but making good time, to catch up with the Dutchman's horses. McKenna looked back, and after a while, seeing his friend, told the Jehu that he thought there was no need of such hot haste, as they would probably get to the depot in time. But poor Linden had to walk all the way, and was glad enough when he saw the end of the journey. Both operatives took the same train for Pottsville, but were careful not to be seen communicating, and the next morning McKenna went by train to Philadelphia, no more to return as James McKenna. This was therefore, theoretically, if not in fact, the end of that personage so long known to the coal region and to the reader. No more would he appear as the wild Irishman of Shenandoah. When he again visited the locality—if he went there at all—it would be in his true character of James McParlan, the detective.

Let us now return to the trials of the Mollies already arrested. While he did not testify in the Kelly and Doyle cases, in March, 1876, at Mauch Chunk, McParlan was much in the locality and furnished very valuable information, greatly assisting the prosecution in their legal warfare upon the Mollie Maguires.

In April, 1876, I went to Philadelphia, and held another long, interesting and profitable consultation with Mr. F. B. Gowen and Superintendent Franklin. They had for some time been urging upon me the necessity for placing McParlan on the witness stand. With his assistance, I could easily see that many convictions might be made which, without his aid, never could occur. Still there was in my mind the verbal agreement I had entered into, nearly three years before, in my office in Chicago, that he the operative, should not be called upon to go before a court and give testimony. I would not go behind that statement, and was determined never to make the attempt. It was true that McParlan's usefulness as a detective in the coal region was gone, through the discovery which had been made rendering his departure from that part of Pennsylvania imperatively necessary.

Calling the detective to me, in my private office, we held an earnest and prolonged interview. Without saying anything to bias his mind, I plainly stated the situation, and asked him to consider whether it was better for him to go upon the stand or not. He could do as he chose, and I would remain firmly with him to the last. For some moments McParlan sat, with his head bowed down, seemingly in deep thought, saying nothing. He then raised his eyes, and replied:

"You remarked, just now, that Mr. Gowen would like to see me!"

"Yes, he so stated."

"Well, I can decide what is best to be done, after talking with him."

I then visited Mr. Gowen's house, where he was confined from sickness. He appointed a time when McParlan and I should meet him. We did meet him, at my office, in Philadelphia, and we held further talk over the matter. Mr. Gowen informed McParlan that all he desired was simply to bring the guilty men to justice. In his own quiet, business like manner, he placed the full circumstances of the case before him, offering, however, no hope of future or present reward, but describing plainly the duty he thought he owed to the public. When Mr. Gowen was through, McParlan thought over the subject for at least five minutes, none of us speaking, and Mr. Gowen and I almost breathlessly awaiting the result. At last McParlan said:

"I will come out in my true character as a detective, speak the truth in all the cases, wherever needed, and, so help me God, every assistance that I can give shall be rendered! Nothing shall be held back. With God's aid, I may be the means of doing much good!"

Mr. Gowen then left, and arrangements were made to carry out the decision.

I had consented, with this proviso, that, as soon as he should visit the coal region, and from that time until the precautions were all ended, he would place himself constantly, day and night, under the especial care of two of my bravest and most courageous men, who should be properly armed, and instructed to give him protection wherever he went. He did not deem this precaution at all necessary. I did, and McParlan agreed to it. Messrs. Gilchrist and Deacons, able and determined officers, have since that date acted as his guardsmen. That this was needful, several facts afterward transpiring abundantly prove. While two men would have been of little use in a combined attack, or if an assassin might come upon them suddenly in the night, I knew the Mollies would soon be so demoralized that the first would not occur, and no man would be willing to take the risk of killing another whom he knew was constantly under the eye of armed and watchful guardians. The fact that he had to move about the streets of Pottsville, Mauch Chunk, or Bloomsburg, protected by armed men, was galling to the detective's pride, but he finally began to see the demand for such care of himself, and never tried to evade those

22

guarding him. It is more than probable that his life would long since have been sacrificed, had I adopted a more reckless course, which I never contemplated doing.

Making arrests now begun in earnest, Mr. Linden having been duly authorized to attend to this department of the business under the direction and advice of Mr. Franklin, the district attorneys, and assisted by McParlan. Capture followed swiftly upon capture, commencing on the fourth of February, 1876, when Alexander Campbell, Bodymaster at Lansford, Carbon County, was apprehended, charged with the murder of John P. Jones, Sept. 3d, of the same year.

On the fifth of the same month, Hugh McGehan, of Carbon County, was arrested for the Yost murder, committed at Tamaqua, July 6, 1875. James Boyle was taken on the sixth and the capture of James Roarty, Bodymaster at Coledale, Schuylkill County, occurred on the seventh. On the eighth, James Carroll, of Tamaqua, then acting as Bodymaster at Tamaqua, was lodged in prison. There, on the ninth, he was joined by his coadjutor in the murder of B. F. Yost, Thomas Duffy, of Reevesdale. The last named was captured while at work, at Buckville.

The six murderers mentioned above were taken, one after the other, and so sudden was the descent upon them that they did not have a moment's warning, and the greatest excitement resulted throughout the coal region. Not only were the Mollies themselves greatly agitated, but the people of the vicinity arose in a mass and threats of lynching the prisoners were freely indulged in. Owing to the admirable arrangements of Capt. Linden, ably seconded by the officers and men of the Coal and Iron Police and local officials, everything passed off quietly, in a little while, and all of the defendants were safely lodged in Pottsville jail. Writs of *habeas corpus* were promptly taken out, made returnable on the thirteenth of February. On that day, Linden took James Kerrigan away from the Carbon County jail, at

Manch Chunk, in a special car, and landed him safely in Pottsville, ready for the hearing on the writ. The crowd at the court-house was so overpowering that President Judge Pershing declined to enter upon the case, and the numbers of citizens present had to be forcibly diminished before the cause could go on. Trouble was anticipated at this time from the Mollie Maguires, who were on the spot in crowds, and, while Capt. Linden was taking Kerrigan to the carriage in waiting, a member of the order, named Thomas Waldron, cried out, alluding to Kerrigan, "Drown the scoundrel! Drown him! A nod to one of the officers in attendance was sufficient, and Mr. Waldron was promptly arrested, taken before a magistrate, and put under bail. This quick settlement of his case quieted the order, and no further trouble occurred.

On the tenth of February followed the arrest of Thomas Munley, of Gilberton, on the affidavit of Capt. Linden, for the murder of Thomas Sanger, and Wm. Uren, at Raven Run, as related in these pages.

On the fourth of May, 1876, the trial of James Carroll, Thomas Duffy, James Roarty, Hugh McGehan, and James Boyle, for the murder of B. F. Yost, was commenced in Pottsville, before a full bench of Hon. C. L. Pershing, D. B. Green, and T. H. Walker. The jury was composed of the following gentlemen: Joel H. Betz, Thomas Bomboy, O. Miller, William Becker, Lewis Maul, Levi Stein, Paul Artz, Amos Forsman, Daniel Yeager, Benjamin Weller, Jules Kurten, and Jacob B. Hoffman. After hearing much of the testimony, and getting well along in the cause, Levi Stein, one of the jurors, and an estimable man, was taken very sick, and the court adjourned until the twenty-third of the same month. Mr. Stein never recovered sufficiently to reappear in the jury box, and after his death the remainder of the panel were discharged. The cause therefore went over. It was in this unfortunate trial that McParlan came upon the stand, stood revealed to the world as the former James McKenna, and made his astonishing revelations, which, for interest and novelty, have startled the civilized world. James Kerrigan, also made his *début* as a witness for the Commonwealth, and, but for the sad incident occurring, as related, the trial would have proven a triumph over the Mollies. Hon. F. B. Gowen, President of the Philadelphia and Reading Railroad Company and of the Philadelphia and Reading Coal and Iron Company, in this case first came forward as counsel, ungloved himself for the struggle, and by his boldness did much to reassure the depressed and suffering people of the coal region. It was a sad providence and calamity that terminated the trial so unhappily. The counsel engaged for the Commonwealth were George R. Kaercher, Esq., District Attorney, Hon. F. B. Gowen, Hon. F. W. Hughes, Gen. Charles Albright, and Guy E. Farquhar, Esq.; for the defense were Hon. Lin Bartholomew, John W. Ryon, Esq., and Daniel Kalbfus, Esq. It was an array of talent which attracted deserved attention from the people and the press, many citizens daily crowding the court room, and all the leading newspapers having representatives present. Everything, however, had to be repeated, because of the decease of Mr. Stein.

CHAPTER XLVIII.

A NOBLE EFFORT.

KERRIGAN, Doyle, and Kelly were already convicted of the murder of John P. Jones, and on the fourth of February, 1876, Alex. Campbell, the originator of the plan and the man for whom the assassination had been committed, was lodged in prison at Mauch Chunk. His trial commenced the twentieth of June ensuing. By the twenty-first the following jury had been obtained: Adam Meeker, Elias Berger R. J. Koch, Charles Horn, William Williams, Harrison Heim. bach, and Charles Zelner. A verdict of "murder in the first degree" was returned July 1st. An attempt was subsequently made to secure a new trial, an argument was heard on the twenty-fourth of July, and a second trial granted, which occurred on the twenty-first of January, 1877. He was a second time found guilty of murder in the first degree and sentenced by the court to be executed. He was also found guilty in the Morgan Powell murder.

In June, 1876, at Pottsville, occurred the trial of Thomas Munley and Charles McAllister, arrested Feb. 10th, in the same year, for the Sanger and Uren murder. This capture was made on the affidavit of R. J. Linden. The prisoner was taken at his house in Gilberton. McAllister demanding a separate trial, Geo. R. Kaercher, Esq., the District Attorney, elected to try Munley first, and the case commenced June 28th, before Judge D. B. Green, a jury having been found on the preceding day, composed of the following named persons: John T. Clouse, I. W. White, John Springer, Benj. H. Guldin, Thomas Fennell, Sr., Emanuel Gehris, Solomon Fidler, Daniel Zerbe, Frederick Alvord, Charles Brenneman, Jefferson Dull, and Daniel Donne. A verdict of "guilty of murder in the first degree" was returned on the twelfth of July. It was in this case that Hon. F. B. Gowen, assisting in the prosecution, made his memorable address against the Mollie Maguires, which I give almost entire. After alluding to the importance of the cause, the gravity of the case, a man being on trial for his life, and disclaiming any reflections as against the talented legal gentlemen engaged in the defense, Messrs. Lin. Bartholomew, John W. Ryon, M. M. L'Velle, and S. A. Garrett, he entered upon a minute history of the crime, not differing materially from that furnished in these pages, calling attention to the utterances of Mr. Sanger, while dying, and then said:

"What is the first defense? An *alibi*. That which comes most readily at the beck and call of every criminal who knows himself to be guilty; for, when every other defense fails, the ever-ready *alibi* is always on hand to be proved by a crowd of relatives and retainers, who come forward to say that a man charged with the commission of a particular offense, at a particular time, and in a particular place, was, on that very day, engaged in some lawful and legitimate calling many miles away. When established to the satisfaction of a jury, an *alibi* is the very best defense that can be offered, but, as it is always the defense that is resorted to by the guilty, and as it is the defense that is most easily manufactured, it becomes the duty of a jury most carefully to scrutinize and examine its truth; and in this case I am glad to say that I think you will have no trouble in disposing of it. By whom is this *alibi* proven? In the first place by Edward Munley, the father of the prisoner, and by Michael Munley, the prisoner's brother."

After showing how signally the *alibi* had failed, he said:

"I dismiss these two witnesses from the case. There is no palliation for such testimony, for there can be no palliation for perjury; and it has become too serious an offense in this county to be passed over, hereafter, in silence. But if there ever was a palliation for perjury, if there should be at the last great day, before the final Judge, any excuse for the enormity of this crime, it will be urged on behalf of a father who has striven to save his son from the gallows, and on behalf of one brother, who seeks to shield another from infamy and from shame."

. . . .

Addressing himself to the Mollie Maguires, he continued.

"I may say, however, before leaving this branch of the case, that now that the light of day is thrown upon the secret

workings of this association, human life is as safe in Schuylkill County as it is in any other part of this Commonwealth;
that as this association is broken down and trampled into the
dust, its leaders either in jail or fugitives from the just vengeance of the law, the administration of justice in this court
will be as certain as human life is safe throughout the whole
length and breadth of the county. The time has gone by
when the murderer, the incendiary, and the assassin can go
home reeking from the commission of crimes, confident in
the fact that he can appear before a jury and have an *alibi*
proved for him to allow him to escape punishment. There
will be no more false *alibis* in this county; the time for
them has gone forever. No more false *alibis*. No more
confident reliance upon the perjury of relatives and friends
to prove an *alibi* for him who was seen in the commission of
the act. No more dust thrown in the eyes of juries to blind
them from looking directly at the facts of a case; and I do
say that if there ever was anything to be proud of, to be glad
of, after the fact that we are enfranchised and disenthralled
from this despotism and this tyranny that has been hanging
over us, it is that the administration of justice will no longer
be polluted and disgraced by perjury and false swearing, for
the purpose of rescuing a criminal from the just vengeance
of the law.

"I now come to the testimony of McParlan. Many of
you know that some years ago I was the District Attorney of
this county. I am, therefore, not very much out of my old
paths, and not very much away from my old moorings, when
I am standing on behalf of the Commonwealth, in the Court
of Pottsville, demanding the conviction of a guilty man. It
was when I was District Attorney of this county, a young
man, charged with the prosecution of the pleas of the Commonwealth, that for the first time I made up my mind from
what I had seen, in innumerable instances, that there then
existed in this county a secret organization, banded together

for the commission of crime, and for the purpose of securing the escape or acquittal of any of its members charged with the commission of an offense.

"That conviction forced itself indelibly upon my mind. A man, who for two years acts as District Attorney in this county, prosecuting criminals who are brought before the court, must be either very obtuse or wilfully blind, if he could close his eyes to the existence of a fact as perceptible as this was then to me. I left this county with that settled conviction, and circumstances that occurred time and again, long after I withdrew from the prosecution of criminals, still more deeply fastened this conviction in my mind. Murder, violence, and arson, committed without detection, and apparently without motive, attested the correctness of that belief, and when the time arrived that I became so much interested in the prosperity of this county, and in the development of its mineral wealth, that I saw that it was a struggle between the good citizen and the bad citizen as to which should obtain the supremacy, I made up my mind that if human ingenuity, if long suffering and patient care, and toil that stopped at no obstacle, and would confront every danger, could succeed in exposing this secret organization to light of day, and bringing to well-earned justice the perpetrators of these awful crimes, I would undertake the task.

"I knew that it could only be done by secret detectives, and I had had enough experience, both as a lawyer, and as the head of a very large corporation, to know that the public municipal detectives employed by the police authorities of the cities, who operate only for rewards, are the last persons to whom you could trust a mission and an enterprise such as this. It was as important for us to know who was innocent as it was to know who was guilty.

"The detective who operates for rewards, who is only paid upon his conviction of the offender, has a motive to incite him to action which I would be the last man in the world to arouse. I knew, for I had had experience before. of the National Detective Agency of Allan Pinkerton, of Chicago, which was established by an intelligent and broad-minded Scotchman, established upon the only basis on which a successful detective agency can be established, and I applied to Mr. Pinkerton. His plan was simply this : ' I will secure an agent, or an officer,' said he, ' to ferret out the existence of this society. Whoever I get is to be paid so much a week, no matter if he finds out nothing. He is bound to me, never, under any circumstances, to take a reward for his services, from anybody, and, if he spends five years and obtains nothing in the way of information, he must have every month or every week exactly the same compensation as if every week he had traced a new murder and every month had discovered a new conspiracy. He is never to gain pecuniarily by the success of his undertaking ; but as a man who goes into this organization, as a detective, takes his life in his own hands, I will send no man on this mission of yours, Mr. Gowen, unless it be agreed, beforehand, and I can tell him so, that he never is to be known in connection with the enterprise.' Upon these terms this man, James McParlan, was selected. A young Irishman and a Catholic, but six or seven years in this country, eminently qualified by his peculiar Irish accomplishments to ingratiate himself with those to whom he was sent, he came here in the fall of 1873, and within six months he had so far won the confidence of the class of people who constituted this order that he was admitted as a member. Remember, now, here — and I advert to it lest I might forget it — that he came here pledged that he should not be used as a witness. Therefore, the only object of his coming was to put us upon the track, so that we could discover the crime when it was being perpetrated, and this is the best answer that can possibly be made to the charge that he wilfully withheld his knowledge when he might have saved human life. His only object here was to get knowl-

22*

edge. He never was to be used as a witness. His only desire was to find out when a murder was to be committed, to be with the perpetrators if he could, and to give notice to Captain Linden, who had an armed police force ready, so that they might be waiting at the very spot, and not only save the life of the intended victim, but arrest every man engaged in the perpetration of the offense, in order that there could be abundant evidence of their guilt. That was his whole object. Almost every night he made his report; and how well he has performed his duty, the security of human life and property in this county, to-day, as compared with what it was six months ago, is the best commentary I can make upon the subject.

"But Mr. L'Velle tells you that from the advent of Mr. McParlan into this county have all these crimes been committed. Remember the words: 'From the advent of McParlan into this county have all these crimes been committed.' I fear that Mr. L'Velle has not been long among you, or, if he has, his memory is sadly deficient, when he says that all these crimes have been committed since the advent of Mr. McParlan in Schuylkill County.

"MR. L'VELLE.—I antedated you in coming to Schuylkill County.

"MR. GOWEN.—Then your memory is very defective. Does the gentleman forget Dunne, who was murdered within two miles of this town? Does he forget Alexander Rae, who was stricken down near Mt. Carmel? Does he remember the assassination of William Littlehales? If he does not I am very sure that his colleague, Mr. Bartholomew, will not forget it, for I remember that I stood here, just where I stand now, some years ago, defending a couple of men for murder, who, with other good citizens, when the house of a boss had been attacked at Tuscarora by a mob intent upon murder, had behaved, not like some of those at Raven Run, but had sprung to arms, and had taken their old muskets, their rusty rifles, their pistols and their swords, some of them with no time to load their muskets save with the marbles with which their children had been playing, and had sprung to arms to defend the house that was attacked, and had shot down one of the assailants in his tracks, and were arrested and brought here charged with the crime of murder; my friend, Mr. Bartholomew, who was my colleague, joined with me in contending that our clients had done that which they ought to have done to protect themselves, and, as I was standing here, arguing that case, there came over from Coal Castle the news that William Littlehales had been murdered.

"Does the gentlemen forget all this? Does he forget George K. Smith and David Muir? Does he forget the assassins who made the attack upon Claude White? Does he forget Morgan Powell, and Langdon, who were killed, and Ferguson, who was beaten almost to death? Does he forget Patrick Barry, who, living with his wife and children in the house by the tunnel, when a band of assassins attacked him at night, placed his wife and little ones in the middle of the house and piled all the mattresses and blankets and pillows around them, and, when he had sheltered them as best he could, fought an angry horde of two or three hundred men, keeping them at bay until daylight, when they fled, leaving the long tracks of their blood behind them to show how well he had avenged himself upon his assailants?

"These coal fields for twenty years, I may say, have been the theatre of the commission of crimes such as our very nature revolts at. This very organization that we are now, for the first time, exposing to the light of day, has hung like a pall over the people of this county. Before it fear and terror fled cowering to homes which afforded no sanctuary against the vengeance of their pursuers. Behind it stalked darkness and despair, brooding like grim shadows over the desolated hearth and the ruined home, and throughout the length and breadth of this fair land there was heard the voice of wailing and of lamentation, of 'Rachel weeping for her children and refusing to be comforted, because they were not.' Nor is it alone those whose names I have mentioned —not alone the prominent, the upright, and the good citizens whose remains have been interred with pious care in the tombs of his fathers; but it is the hundreds of unknown victims, whose bones now lie mouldering over the face of this county. In hidden places and by silent paths, in the dark ravines of the mountains, and in secret ledges of the rocks, who shall say how many bodies of the victims of this order now await the final trump of God? And from these lonely sepulchres, there will go up to the God who gave them the spirits of these murdered victims, to take their places among the innumerable throng of witnesses at the last day, and to confront with their presence the members of this ghastly tribunal, when their solemn accusation is read from the plain command of the Decalogue, 'Thou shalt not kill.'

"But we are told that in the commission of these crimes, although Mr. Bartholomew admits that they existed long years before McParlan came into the county, this man abandoned his duty as a detective, and became an accomplice in the crime. And upon whose testimony does this charge rest? My friend invokes from you a careful attention to the facts of this case, and properly endeavors to exclude from it an examination of any other circumstances or any other facts than those which have been proved in the case.

"But upon whose testimony is McParlan an accomplice? Upon whose testimony is the charge made that McParlan engaged deliberately in the commission of offenses and secreted the offenders? Upon Ned Monaghan's and Patrick Coyle's, alone. Upon Ned Monaghan, for whom the doors of your jail open wide to-day, never probably to reopen until he comes out in company with Jack Kehoe, and the other murderers, to stand his trial for his life. Upon Monaghan, the Molly Maguire, the man who was on the Ringtown

Mountain helping to select the committee to kill William Thomas. Edward Monaghan, who, to-day, is as guilty of murder in the first degree as any other man now confined within the walls of your prison.

"And who is Patrick Coyle? A man who saw McParlan drawing a pistol and never heard him say or saw him do anything else, and because he did not see him do and did not hear him say anything, he swears he believes that McParlan was inciting to murder.

"What need I say further? An accomplice! McParlan an accomplice! Mr. Bartholomew tells you that he permitted Thomas Hurley to escape, and that he permitted Michael Doyle to escape. Neither Thomas Hurley nor Michael Doyle have escaped; but the excoriating denunciation which Mr. Bartholomew hurled against Thomas Hurley will effectually prevent him from defending Hurley, when he comes before this court for trial for murder. It will not be long before he comes here. It is simply a question between the Mollie Maguires on the one side and Pinkerton's Detective Agency on the other, and I know too well that Pinkerton's Detective Agency will win. There is not a place on the habitable globe where these men can find refuge and in which they will not be tracked down. Let them go to the Rocky Mountains, or to the shores of the Pacific; let them traverse the bleak deserts of Siberia, penetrate into the jungles of India, or wander over the wild steppes of Central Asia, and they will be dogged and tracked and brought to justice, just as surely as Thomas Munley is brought to justice to-day. The cat that holds the mouse in her grasp sometimes lets it go for a little while to play; but she knows well that at her will she can again have it secure within her claws; and Pinkerton's Agency may sometimes permit a man to believe that he is free who does not know that he may be traveling five thousand miles n the company of those whose vigilance never slumbers and whose eyes are never closed in sleep.

"They may not know that the time will come, but I say that so surely as I am standing before you to-day, the time will come, be it short or be it long, be it months or be it years, when every single murderer then living on the face of the earth, who has committed a crime in this county, since April, 1874, will answer for that crime before the presence of this court. 'The race is not always to the swift, nor the battle to the strong.' Those who, see what we are doing now have seen but little; for it is only the opening of the book of this vast conspiracy, and behind the meaner men who shot the pistol there stand others far more guilty than they who, with them, at some time will be brought to justice—

"'For Time at last sets all things even,
  And if we do but wait the hour,
  There never yet was human power
  That could evade, if unforgiven,
  The patient search and vigil long
  Of him who treasures up a wrong.'

"And now some words about this secret organization of Mollie Maguires. My friend, Mr. Bartholomew, is not correct in his statement of their history. If, after this case is over, and when you are permitted to read, you will get a little book called Trench's *Realities of Irish Life,* written by a relative of that celebrated Dean Trench, whose name is well known wherever English literature is read, you will find the history of this organization. It was known as the Ribbonmen of Ireland. It sprang up at a time when there was an organized resistance in Ireland to the payments of rents. The malcontents became known as Ribbonmen, and they generally made their attacks upon the agents of the non-resident landowners, or upon the constables or bailiffs who attempted to collect the rents. Their object was to intimidate and hold in terror all those to whom they owed money or who were employed in its collection. As a branch of this society, and growing out of it, sprang the men known as Mollie Maguires, and the name of their society simply arose from this circumstance, that, in the perpetration of their offenses, they dressed as women, and generally ducked or beat their victims, or inflicted some such punishment as in-fariated women would be likely to administer. Hence originated the name of the Mollie Maguires, which has been handed down to us at the present day ; and the organization of the Mollie Maguires, therefore, is identical with that of the Ribbonmen in Ireland, who have terrorized over the Irish people to so great an extent.

"How this association came into this county we do not know. We had suspected for many years, and we know now, that it is criminal in its character. That is proved beyond peradventure. It will not do to-day to say that it was only in particular localities in this county that it was a criminal organization, because the highest officer in the society in this county, the County Delegate, Jack Kehoe, the man who attended the State Convention, and was the representative of the whole order in this county, is at present, as you hear from the testimony, in prison awaiting his trial for murder. Whether this society, known as the Ancient Order of Hiber-nians, is beyond the limits of this county a good society or not I cannot tell ; but I have believed at some times that it was, and I am willing to be satisfied of that fact now, if there is any evidence of it. But there has been an attack made upon this organization, and up to this time we have not had furnished to us any evidence that in any place its objects were laudable or commendable. Criminal in its character, criminal in its purpose, it had frequently a political object. You will find the leaders of this society the prominent men in the townships. Through the instrumentality of their order, and by its power, they were able to secure offices for them-selves. You see here and now know that one of the

Commissioners of this county is a member of this order. You know that a previous Commissioner of this county was a member of this order, convicted of a high offense, and pardoned by the Governor. You know that another County Commissioner, before that, was a member of this order, convicted of an offense, and pardoned by the Governor. High constables, chiefs of police, candidates for associate judges, men who were trusted by their fellow-men, were all the time guilty of murder.

"But in addition to the criminal and the political motives, these people claim national characteristics. They claim that they were, *par excellence*, the representatives of the Irish of this country. They claim more than that, that they represent the Irish Catholics of this country. I shall say but little about the Irish, except that I am myself the son of an Irishman, proud of my ancestry, and proud of my race, and never ashamed of it, except when I see that Ireland has given birth to wretches such as these! These men call themselves Irishmen! These men parade on St. Patrick's Day and claim to be good Catholics! Where are the honest Irishmen of this county? Why do not they rise up and strike down these wretches that usurp the name of Irishmen? If a German commits an offense, and engages in murder, do all the other Germans take his part and establish a false *alibi* to defeat the ends of justice? If an American becomes a criminal, do the Americans protect him? Do they not say, 'Away with you! You have disgraced the country that bore you?' If an Englishman becomes an offender, do the English nation take him to their arms and make him a hero? Why, then, do not the honest Irishmen of this county come together in public meeting, and separate themselves widely from and denounce this organization? Upon what principle do these men, outcasts from society, the dregs of the earth, murderers and assassins, claim to be Irishmen and arrogate to themselves the national characteristics of the Irish people? It is a disgrace to Ireland that the honest Irish of this county, probably five or ten thousand in number, should permit a few hundred wretches like these to say that they are the true representatives of the Irishmen of Schuylkill County.

"Does an Irishman wonder why it is sometimes difficult to get a job in this county? Does he wonder why the boss at a colliery hesitates to employ him, when these people have been allowed to arrogate to themselves the Irish character and have been permitted to represent themselves to the people of this county as the proper representatives of Ireland? The time has come when there must be a line of demarcation drawn. The time has come when every honest Irishman in this county must separate himself from any suspicion of sympathy with this association. He must denounce its members as outcasts from the land that gave them birth. He must denounce them as covered with infamy and blackened with crime. He must say that they are not true Irishmen and that they are not representatives of Ireland.

"But far beyond this attempt to invoke your sympathy on account of their nationality is the attempt to invoke that sympathy on the ground that they belong to a persecuted religion. Was there ever such sublime, such tremendous impudence in the world, as that a member of this secret society, a society which has been denounced by its own Church, and each member of which has been excommunicated by the Archbishop of Philadelphia, and by the Pope himself, outcasts from society, and from the communion of their own religion, the door of the Church shut in their faces and the gates of heaven closed against them by the excommunication of their priests — these men, infidels and atheists, caring for no church, and worshiping no God, set themselves up in this community as the representatives of the Catholic faith.

> "'Just Allah! what must be thy look?
> When such a wretch before thee stands,
> Unblushing, with thy sacred book,
> Turning its leaves with blood-stained hands,
> And wresting from its page sublime
> His creed of lust and hate and crime.

"A few words more upon this subject of Irish Catholics. I was born and am a Protestant, but I was partially educated among the Catholics, and I have always had a kindly feeling for them, and when these assassins, through their counsel, speak of being Catholics, I desire to say to you here, in the first place, that they have been denounced by their Church and excommunicated by their prelates, and that I have the direct personal authority of Archbishop Wood himself to say that he denounces them all, and that he was fully cognisant of and approved of the means I took to bring them to justice. And, for myself, I can say that for many months before any other man in this world, except those connected with the Detective Agency, knew what was being done, Archbishop Wood, of Philadelphia, was the only confident I had and fully knew of the mission of the detective in this whole matter. So much, then, for the assumption of Mr. L'Velle that these men claim sympathy on account of their being Catholics. I can hardly reply calmly to such an argument. I believe that there must be different sects in this country, as there are in all countries, and I am one of those who believe that a good Catholic is better than a bad Protestant.

"MR. L'VELLE.—I repel that remark.

"MR. GOWEN.—Mr. L'Velle repels the remark! I cannot help it, and I reiterate the fact that although I am a Protestant, I have been taught to believe that a good Catholic is better than a bad Protestant.

"I have been taught to believe that the eyes of Justice are closed not only against individuals and corporations, but against nationalities and sects. I have been taught to believe that he is the good citizen who is truthful and honest, who is kind-hearted and affectionate, who lives in charity with all men, who gives freely of his means to the poor, and, whether he kneels before an altar or worships God in his own chamber, he is entitled to the favorable consideration of his fellow men. And I do know, oh! so well, that when our lives draw toward their close, and the opening portals of the tomb reveal to our eyes some glimpses of the boundless waters of that vast eternity upon which we will all embark, that then, at that dread moment, it will be to the recollection of the possessions of these simple virtues, this pure morality, this unostentatious charity that I have named, that we will all cling, in the sublime confidence that it will avail us most, when the time shall come that each one of us, Catholic and Protestant, Lutheran and Calvinist, Gentile and Jew, shall be stripped of the thin garb of the sectarian, and stand in equal favor before the great white throne of God.

"And now one word more upon this subject, and I dismiss it. Whenever you hear a complaint made against a man because he is an Irishman, or because he is a Catholic; whenever you hear any one, no matter who he may be, say that the outrages of this county are due to the Irishmen, or due to the Catholics do not, I beg of you, forget, in your secret hearts, that the highest prelates of that Church have cursed and excommunicated this order. Do not forget that whatever little credit may be due to him who has conceived the plan of exposing this association is due to one who is the son of an Irishman; and do not forget that a greater honor and a greater meed of praise than is due to any other is due to Detective McParlan, who is an Irishman by birth, and a Catholic by religion; and if those who profess to be Irish Catholics in this county have brought their nationality and their religion into disrepute, I beg of you to remember that both have been gloriously and successfully vindicated by an Irishman and a Catholic, in the person of James McParlan.

. . . .

' And now let us look to society in this county, as it was three months ago, when men retired to their homes at eight or nine o'clock in the evening and no one ventured beyond the precincts of his own door; when every man engaged in any enterprise of magnitude or connected with industrial pursuits left his home in the morning with his hand upon his pistol, unknowing whether he would again return alive ; when the very foundations of society were being overturned; when the administration of justice, which should always be regarded with reverence, had almost sunk into contempt ; when men doubted whether it was in the power of organized society to protect their lives and to secure their property ; and then reflect upon the change which a few weeks has brought forth. To-day I give you notice that there is no part of this county that is not as safe as the aisle in which I stand here now.

"Is there a man in this audience, looking at me now, and hearing me denounce this association, who longs to point his pistol at me ? I tell him that he has as good a chance here as he will ever have again. I tell him that it is just as safe to-day to murder in the temple of Justice as it is in the secret ravines of the mountains, or within the silent shadows of the woods. I tell him that human life is safe. I tell him that the members of his society, whom we desire to convict all, save one or two, are either safely lodged within the walls of your prison or are fugitives from justice, but almost within the grasp of the detectives, who are upon their heels. I tell him that if there is another murder in this county, committed by this organization, every one of the five hundred members of the order in this county, or out of it, who connives at it, will be guilty of murder in the first degree, and can be hanged by the neck until he is dead, not by vigilance committees, but according to the solemn forms of justice, after being defended by able and experienced counsel; and I tell him that, if there is another murder in this county by this society, there will be an inquisition for blood with which nothing that has been known in the annals of criminal jurisprudence can compare. And to whom are we indebted for this security, of which I now boast? To whom do we owe all this? Under the Divine Providence of God, to whom be all the honor and all the glory, we owe this safety to James McParlan, and if there ever was a man to whom the people of this county should erect a monument, it is James McParlan, the detective. . . . . . .

"McParlan is a detective, engaged in the performance of a professional duty, who enters upon his quest with the avowed purpose of trying to make all those with whom he was brought in contact believe that he is one of them. He is not an accomplice. He went there for the purpose of aiding the officers of the law in discovering and punishing guilt, and even were he an accomplice, even if every particle of testimony we have had during the last two weeks from the lips of James McParlan had fallen on that stand from the lips of Friday O'Donnell, or from the lips of Michael Doyle, it would have been not only corroborated, but strengthened and attested by the evidence of identification alone.

"But suppose there was no evidence of identification, I desire now to show you what corroborative testimony beyond that of identification we have of the facts proved by McParlan himself. I have taken the trouble, during the time Mr. L'Velle was speaking yesterday, to go over, with one of my colleagues, nearly the whole of the testimony in this case, so that I might be able to point out to you the various places in which and the manner by which McParlan is corroborated by other witnesses. I will now call your attention to this testimony, in detail, in the order in which it was given

and, having done so and fixed it upon your mind, I
endeavor to make some few arguments based upon this
roborative testimony, if any such were needed to enabl
jury of intelligent men to determine whether they will
credence to the testimony of McParlan.

"McParlan says that Munley told him that McAllister
O'Donnell, called for him, Munley, on the evening of
thirty-first of August. Remember, McParlan says that Mu
told him at Michael Lawler's that McAllister and O'Don
called for him the previous evening. How could McPa
have known this if Munley did not tell it to him? W
that in your minds for one instant. How could McPa
have found this fact out, if Munley had not told him?
but our friends may say that McParlan swears that Mu
said so, but the statement is not true, and here comes in
corroborative testimony. Frederick Hunniken, a witness
duced by the Commonwealth, says that on the evening of
thirty-first of August a stranger came to Wiggan's Patch
talked with the O'Donnells, and that James O'Donnell
the stranger went toward Gilberton together. Then Ja
Patton says that on the evening of the thirty-first of Aug
Darcy and Munley joined a party near Gilberton, and L
Richardson says that on the evening of the thirty-first, D
and Munley joined a party from Wiggan's Patch; and Sa
Ann Gessford and George Gessford both testified that
saw Munley with Darcy and some other men between e
and nine o'clock on the evening of the thirty-first, at the C
Roads, by the old Flour Barrel, near Gilberton. There
now one, two, three, four, five witnesses, in different part
the county, who have testified to a state of facts of wl
McParlan could have had no knowledge whatever, un
informed by Munley. Where can you find better corrob
tive evidence than this? How did McParlan know, if
made up this story to tell, that the O'Donnells came
Munley in the evening, and that they went off togeth

unley in a

Did McParlan know Luke Richardson or Mr. or Mrs. Gessford? Had he ever communicated with either of them? And yet James McParlan comes forward and gives us a statement which was told to him by Munley, and we produce five witnesses to prove that when Munley made that statement he told the truth.

"Again, McParlan says that Munley had on dark pantaloons of a grayish color. How could McParlan describe Munley's pantaloons, if he had not seen him on that morning? If he attempted to make up a story, is it likely that he would have discovered exactly the proper kind of pantaloons? James Williams and Roberts say that on that day Munley was dressed in gray pantaloons; Robert Heaton describes them as darkish; Melinda Bickelman says that they were pepper and salt, and Munley's family, themselves, have to admit that they were of a grayish color—one of them said of a brownish color, and still another said that they were gray, but had a kind of a dark stripe in them. Here is corroborative testimony again.

"Further on in his testimony McParlan says that Munley told him that after O'Donnell began the attack, he ran up and shot Sanger near the fence at the house, and that Charles O'Donnell, Doyle, and McAllister fired shots to intimidate the crowd. That is exactly as Patrick Burns describes it, and as Melinda Bickelman describes it. The two men that followed Sanger down the road and killed him were Friday O'Donnell and this prisoner, Thomas Munley. McAllister ran around to intercept Sanger, and the other two men fired shots to intimidate the crowd. How, under heaven, did McParlan know this, unless Munley told him. Where can there be stronger corroborative testimony than this?

"Again, McParlan swears that after some conversation at Lawler's, when these five men came in on the morning of the first of September, the two O'Donnells and McAllister left for home. How did McParlan know that, unless he saw it?

Our friends may say, where is the evidence of that? We answer by saying that Edward Fox, a witness produced by the Commonwealth, says that James O'Donnell, with two men, came to his engine-house, on a path between Wiggan's Patch and Shenandoah, dusty and thirsty as if from traveling, at eleven o'clock on the morning of the first of September. It seems to me as if there was some almost supernatural or divine agency pointing out to the officers of justice and the agents of the Commonwealth the evidence that would corroborate the testimony of this man McParlan. How could McParlan make up a story of this kind, unless he had seen the men? He swears these three men left together, and these three men are found together, and separated from the other two.

"Again, McParlan goes further, for he tells you what became of the other two. He says that after Doyle had gone to his boarding-house and changed his clothes, Doyle, Hurley, Munley, and himself went to Tobin's ball-alley, in Shenandoah; and Philip Weissner and William J. Fulton, two witnesses produced by the Commonwealth, testified that they met Munley in Shenandoah, with some other men, at ten o'clock on the morning of the first of September, at the corner of Coal Street and Chestnut Street.

"McParlan also says that Munley left Shenandoah for home about one o'clock in the afternoon on the first of September, and Mrs. Smith, Mrs. Richardson, Mrs. Lambert, and Mrs. Hayes, all saw Munley coming home to his house at Gilberton between two and three o'clock, just about the time at which he would have arrived if he left Shenandoah at one o'clock.

"McParlan also swears that Munley returned to Shenandoah in the evening, and attended a meeting of the Mollie Maguires, when men were selected to murder John P. Jones. Philip Weissner swears that he met Munley on the evening of the first of September, about five o'clock, on his way to

Shenandoah, and Mrs. Smith saw him leave his ton.e, after changing his clothes, on the evening of the first of September, in company with Darcy, who was one of the Mollie Maguires, and who was one of the men at the meeting in the bush on the evening   the first of September.   Where can you have stronger corroborative testimony than this?   Ask yourselves the question: how could James McParlan have known this? It is true, and it is proved by fifteen or twenty witnesses who have placed these men just at the spot and just at the time. How did McParlan know this, unless Munley told him?   Ask yourselves that question, and then ask yourselves whether, if this man McParlan was Friday O'Donnell himself, and had testified to this state of facts, would you as jurors require any other corroborative evidence than that which has been laid before you?

"The only other portion of the defense to which it is necessary for me now to revert is the testimony of the men around Raven Run, who saw some of this occurrence, but could not recognize Thomas Munley.   In the first place, we believe, though we have no right to make charges, but we do believe that there were a number of men on this stand, who, from the manner in which they gave their testimony, revealed the fact that they knew a great deal more than they intended to tell; and when an Irishman from the same county as this prisoner so testifies on cross-examination that you must believe, notwithstanding his denial of the fact, that he was a member of tne same organization, and always prefaces his testimony as to the prisoner's being one of the murderers by saying, 'Not to the best of my opinion,' you will see the easy way by which he bargained with his conscience for getting over the obligation of the oath which he had taken to tell the truth.

"What does all this testimony amount to?   Here were four days taken up with the examination of forty or fifty witnesses, and at the utmost all that each or any of them

23

could say was that Friday O'Donnell was not Thomas Munley. Why, we knew that before. Friday O'Donnell was the leader of this gang. Friday O'Donnell was the man who had the principal hand in it; he was the man who took the prominent part in the murder; he was the man whom nearly all the witnesses saw and described by his clothing and by his stature; and every one of them swore, with great vehemence, that Friday O'Donnell was not Thomas Munley. God knows, gentlemen, we knew this before; we knew that Friday O'Donnell was not Thomas Munley, but when they were questioned, they either had to admit that they could not tell whether the prisoner was one of the other four men, or that they had not seen the other four men sufficiently to enable them to identify them thereafter.

"I have said to you before that it seems to me as if there had been a divine interposition for the investigation and punishment of crime in this county. Remember that Mc-Parlan came here pledged that he should not be used as a witness. We placed no reliance upon him as a witness. We could not arrest a man because he told us anything about him, because he was protected by the pledge we had given him that he was not to be exposed, and was never to be known in the investigation; and I tell you that, no matter what the consequence would have been, when I became an instrument to lead him into the danger to which he was subjected when he took his life into his own hand and entered into the secret councils of this order, I would have been the last man in the world to have asked him to relieve me from the pledge which had been made to him. You have heard that his mission became known to this order, how or by what manner I am not at liberty to tell you to day, for it is not in evidence. We have the fact, though, that his mission became known to this society, and we have the fact that those from whose vengeance he was to be protected, by ignorance of his true character acquired information that enabled them to know that he was playing a false part in their organization, and that he was in reality a detec tive; and he was compelled to leave the county. And then I saw before me my path as clear as day. Then I saw that some miraculous interposition of providence had been vouch safed to permit us to use the testimony and the knowledge of this man McParlan. Then I breathed freer, and trod with elate step; then I knew that I had within my hands the power to crush these villains; then, and on the day when he took his place upon the witness stand, I took my seat at this table as counsel for the Commonwealth, and the warrants were executed which consigned to the prison every one of these criminals, with the exception of one or two and of those who had run away when Jimmy Kerrigan turned State's evidence. When, in all the history of criminal jurisprudence, did ever such a change of society come over a county as that which came over this county on the morning that Mc Parlan first became a witness, and on the morning when Jack Kehoe, the County Delegate, with twelve or fifteen other men, handcuffed to a chain, were marched from the high places they had occupied to take their solitary cells as felons within the walls of your prison?

"When I came to this court-house, on that memorable day, the court-room was crowded with the sympathizing friends of these criminals, but where are they to-day? They may be here, but they give no sign, and we know nothing of them, and we care not if they are here. The whole county sprang up like a giant unbound, and never, except in dramatic literature, has there been revealed such an awaken ing and such a change.

" There is an old drama called the ' Inconstant,' in which the hero of the play is beguiled into a den of infamy, and when he is confronted by miscreants he for the first time realizes the danger in which he is placed. He feels that his money is to be taken and that his life will be sacrificed

He has with him, however, a faithful page, and turning toward the outlaws he addresses them as if he was unaware of their true character. He shakes them by the hand, presents one with his watch, and another with his purse; he is hail fellow well met' with them, and he invites them to join him in a carouse, and offers to send his page for wine. The outlaws hear it and consent, and he says to his page: 'Bring me the wine—the blood-red wine marked 100.' The page departs, well knowing that the message refers not to wine but to a company of soldiers numbering one hundred and wearing a red uniform. After breathless suspense the page returns, and in answer to the frantic demand, 'The wine, boy, the wine!' answers: 'Coming, sir,' and the tramp of armed men is heard. Then the entrapped man grows bold. He pulls one outlaw by the nose, and cuffs another on the ear, and the soldiers enter and march them off to jail. So it was with us when McParlan came upon the stand. He was the blood-red wine marked 100. Then we knew we were free men. Then we cared no longer for the Mollie Maguires. Then we could go to Patsy Collins, the Commissioner of this county, and say to him: 'Build well the walls of the new addition of the prison; dig the foundations deep and make them strong; put in good masonry and iron bars, for, as the Lord liveth, the time will come when, side by side with William Love, the murderer of Squire Gwyther, you will enter the walls that you are now building for others.' Then we could say to Jack Kehoe, the high constable of a great borough in this county: 'We have no fear of you.' Then we could say to Ned Monaghan, chief of police, and murderer, and assassin: 'Behind you the scaffold is prepared for your reception.' Then we could say to Pat Conry, Commissioner of this county: The time has ceased when a Governor of this State dares to pardon a Mollie Maguire—you have had your last pardon.' Then we could say to John Slattery, who was almost

elected judge of .his court : We know that of you that it
were better you had not been born than that it should be
known.' Then all of us looked up. Then at last we were
free, and I came to this county and walked through it as
safely as in the most crowded thoroughfares of Philadelphia.

"There is one other dramatic illustration which I remem
ber and to which I cannot help adverting, as it so clearly
paints the scene which has been enacted so lately in this
county. It occurs in Bulwer's drama of Richelieu. You
remember that Richelieu, the Prime Minister of Louis XIII.
was threatened by a secret conspiracy, led by a great noble
man, dramatized as De Baradas, and headed in the army by
the very brother of the King himself. You will remember
that the statesman, realizing that his power over the King
was gone, and that the conspirators had acquired absolute
control over the mind of the monarch, set a page upon the
track to discover the evidence of the conspiracy, so that he
could lay it before the monarch in the presence of the conspirators themselves. You will also remember, if you have
read the drama, the thrilling description of the manner in
which the page, at the point of the poniard, wrested the
parchment evidence of this conspiracy from one of the chief
conspirators, at a time when the monarch was holding court,
and when the prime minister, almost dead with rage and cha-
grin, fear and disappointment, had almost ceased to hope
for success. It was at this moment that the page, wearied,
bleeding, and breathless, rushes in behind Richelieu and
hands him the parchment, which is laid before the monarch,
who, for the first time, learns that he has been betrayed, and
that the army of Spain is on the march to Paris. He says.
'Good heavens, the Spaniards ! Where will they be next
week ?' And Richelieu, rising up, exclaimed : 'There, at
my feet ! and issuing his orders for the arrest of the con-
tors, turns to the chief, and exclaims : 'Ho, there,'

Count De Baradas, thou hast lost the stake,' and that stake was his head.

"So when we discovered the criminal nature of this organisation, and when the evidence of this conspiracy was brought forward to us by McParlan, we issued our warrants for the arrest of the conspirators, and we turned to these men, with the Commissioner of the county at their head, and we said to them: ' Ha ! you have lost the stake.' They played a deep game, and they played for a great stake. They played to secure the property of this county, by endangering the lives of their fellow-citizens. They had agents as chiefs of police, and as constables and commissioners, and they had one of their number almost on the bench itself. God alone knows what would have happened to us if they had gotten him there, and then elected a jury commissioner besides. With Mollie Maguires as judges, and Mollie Maguires as constables, and Mollie Maguires as commissioners, and Mollie Maguires as witnesses, what would have been the history of this good old county? Think of this for a moment! Can you think where then we would have drifted, and to what it would have led us? Can you imagine the condition of the people of this county, with murderers upon the bench, and in the jury box, and in control of all the principal offices of the county. I lived in the apprehension of all this for two years and a half alone, and God knows that when the time comes that all I know may be told to the world, it will reveal a history such as will make every American citizen hang his head with shame. I have seen a society of murderers and assassins having its members in the highest places of this county. I have seen them elected to fill the positions of constables and police officers. I have seen a trusted member of that band of murderers a Commissioner of the county. I have seen this organization wield a political power in the State which has controlled the elections of a great Commonwealth. I have received the information of meetings between some of the highest officers of the State, and the chief of the murderers, at which large sums of money were paid to secure the votes of this infernal association to turn the tide of a State election. God knows, if ever in the world there was a revelation as deep and as damning as that now laid open to the people of this Commonwealth for the first time.

"I have one other allusion to make to a remark made by my friend Mr. L'Velle in his argument yesterday. At some time or other I thought it would be dragged into the case. Mr. L'Velle, acting for the prisoner, and defending him as his counsel, has said to you that it is the old story of capital against labor. I think I have shown to you how impudent is the claim that these men set up to be the representatives of the Irish race. I am sure I have shown to you the unblushing audacity of their claim that they are the representatives of the Catholic religion; but I now stand here on behalf of the laboring people of this county, the people who have suffered more throughout the length and breadth of this land by the actions of these men than any other— I stand here to protest, with all the power that God has given me, against the monstrous assumption that these villains are the representatives of the laboring people of Schuylkill County. You know very well in what estimation in the public prints the laboring people of this county have been held in consequence of the acts of this society. Two or three hundred assassins have given a name to the whole people of this county, and now, when they are put upon trial for murder, they say it is the old story of capital against labor. On behalf of every honest laboring man in this county on behalf of every man subjected to the primeval curse of the Almighty, that by the sweat of his face he shall earn his daily bread, I protest with indignation against the assumption that these men are the representatives of labor. It is too early in the history of what I have done in this county to say aught of myself in connection with labor, but those

who know me well will bear witness that on every occasion
in which I had to take any public part in the conflicts
between capital and labor, I have taken pains to assert my
belief that the laboring people of this county were as
upright, as honest, as law-abiding, and as moral as those of
any other community in the State. I took the pains to
show that there was a secret association banded together for
the purpose of committing outrages which had given a
notorious character not only to the laboring people of the
county, but to the whole county itself. Look abroad upon
this great county, diversified by a thousand industries and
beautified by nature to an extent such as few counties in the
Commonwealth enjoy. Why is not this a hive of industry,
and the chosen seat of the investment of capital? Why
do not people from all parts of the country come to these
mountains to enjoy the salubrity of the climate, and to revel
in the beauties which nature has spread before us? Why is
it that a curse and a blight has rested for so long upon this
county? Why is it that mothers and wives in far-distant
cities have shuddered when their sons and husbands have
told them that business led them to the mining regions of
Pennsylvania?

"Because, fostered and protected here in the mountains
of this county, was a band of assassins and murderers that
brought reproach upon the whole county itself. For the
first time now they are exposed, and we know where were
their secret places, and who were their chosen leaders, and
knowing this, we can stand up before the whole country and
say, 'Now all are safe in this county; come here with your
money; come here with your enterprises; come here with
your families, and make this country your residence; help
us to build up this people and you will be safe,' and by your
aid, gentlemen, we will show to the world that not by vigi
lance committees, and not by secret associations, but by
open, public justice the name of the law has been vind

eated, and the foul stain that had rested upon us has been wiped out forever.

"A few words more, and I am done. I feel that I have occupied more of your time than I ought to have taken, but 'out of the fullness of the heart the mouth speaketh,' and if I have said aught which some of you might think had better have been left unsaid, you must remember the strong provocation that I have had. You must remember what I have been doing for nearly three years. You must remember what a seal I had to put upon my lips. You must remember that it was only when Mr. McParlan consented to become a witness that I could speak of that, the weight of which was enough to crush me to the dust.

"I feel, indeed, that if I failed in my duty, if I should shrink from the task which was before me, that if I failed to speak, the very stones would cry out. Standing before you now with the bright beams of victory streaming upon our banners, how well I can recall the feelings with which I entered upon the contest which is now so near the end Do not think it egotism if I say, with the hero of romance that

" ' When first I took this venturous quest,
        I swore upon the rood,
    ·Neither to turn to right nor left,
        For evil or for good.
    My forward path too well I ween,
    Lies yonder fearful ranks between ;
    For man unarmed 'twere bootless here
    With tigers and with fiends to cope.
    Yet if I turn, what wait me there,
    Save famine, dire and fell despair ?
    Other conclusion let me try,
    Since, choose howe'er I list, I die.
    Forward lies faith and knightly fame,
    Behind are perjury and shame ;
    In life or death, I keep my word.'

"And when all had been discovered, and McParlan consented to become a witness, I said that I would come up into this county, where I first had learned to practice law that I would take my place among the ranks of the counsel for the Commonwealth, and that I would stand side by side with him in the prosecution of these offenses until the last one was wiped from off the calendar of your criminal courts. And let it take weeks, or let it take months, or let it take years, I have buckled on my harness and entered for the fight, and, God willing, I shall bear it out as bravely and as well as I can, until justice is vindicated, and the county of Schuylkill is free.

"My friend, Mr. L'Velle, makes a plea to you for mercy. He pleads to you for the mother and the wife of this prisoner, and he asks you to let mercy enter into your hearts, and to restore this prisoner to his home. Are there no others who plead for mercy? Have I no clients asking mercy at your hands? Why is this young woman made a widow in the early morning of her life? What crime had her husband committed that he was shot down like a dog? Oh, she pleads to you for mercy, more eloquently, even if more silently, than any one on behalf of the family of this prisoner. I plead to you on behalf of the whole people of this county I plead for mercy on behalf of the whole people of this State. On behalf of the orphans, the fatherless, and the widows, whose protectors have been stricken down before you, I plead to you for mercy. I invoke the spirits of the dead, and ask them silently to pass before you in this court-house. I invoke the spirits of Dunn, of Littlehales, of Muir, of Smith, of Rae, and the many victims of this foul conspiracy, to aid me in pleading for mercy. I ask you to listen to the cries of the wounded, to the shrieks of the dying, and the mournful funereal wailings over the bodies of the dead. If I close my eyes I hear voices against which you cannot close your ears, and which are pleading for mercy, oh! so strongly, that my poor words are but as the empty air.

> "'I hear the dying sufferer cry,
> With his crushed face turned to the sky;
>   I see him crawl in agony
> To the foul pool, and bow his head into its bloody slime, and die!'

"Oh! think once more upon your own county, almost one vast sepulchre, where rest the half-buried bodies of the victims of this infernal order—victims whose skeleton hands, bleached by the sun and by the wind, are stretching up from out the thin covering of earth that wraps their bodies in all the eloquence of silent prayer, beseeching you to have mercy upon your fellow-men.

"Oh! gentlemen, I beg to you for mercy, but to this prisoner let it be such mercy as the father, whose slaughtered infant lies beside him, gives to the wolf that has mangled the corpse; such mercy as the seed of the woman bestows upon the serpent whose head is crushed beneath its heel; and when you yield such mercy to assassins such as these, you yield a mercy and grant a protection to society at large, which looks to you now as its only refuge.

"And now the duty which I owe to this case is almost performed, and I commit it to your hands. For three years I have been engaged in an investigation, the result of which has now become known to the community. Two or three days after the commission of this offense I believed, from the information which came to me, that Thomas Munley was one of the assassins of Sanger. I had no evidence that I could use, for it was not until McParlan consented to become a witness that I could furnish the information that led to the arrest of this prisoner. I believe I have done my duty; for God's sake, let me beg of you not to shrink from doing yours. Solemn judges of the law and of the facts—august ministers in the temple of justice—robed for sacrifice, I bring before you this prisoner and lay him upon your altar, bound and fastened by such cords of testimony as all the ingenuity of counsel cannot unloosen, and, trembling at the momentous issues involved in your answer, I ask you, will you let him go? If you perform your duty without favor and without affection, if, in the pursuit of what appears to me to be your plain and bounden duty, you will say, almost without leaving the box, that this man is guilty of murder in the first degree, you will do that which I believe to be just, and you will do that which will protect society and save the lives of hundreds and thousands of your fellow-men. But if you should falter—if, from any false sympathy, you should unbind this prisoner and let him go, I tremble for the consequences to society. Who then would be safe? For you to do this would be to hold up this prisoner's hands, and the hands of all his fellows and associates, to place the dagger and the pistol in their grasp, and with the torch of the incendiary, to send them again throughout this land to play their part of murder, of arson, and of crime.

"I have done all that I could to expose the criminal character of this organization. Laying aside all other duties, giving up everything else that I had to do, I have tried to devote myself to this cause, for I believe it to be the highest duty that I could be called upon to perform. I am glad, at the conclusion of this case, to return my thanks to the able gentlemen who have been associated with me, and especially to the District Attorney, under whose administration these crimes have come to light. He was an old student of mine when I was in this county, and I was glad to know that it was he who filled the office when this conspiracy was first brought to light. He has done his duty faithfully and nobly, in the face of danger, without fear, or favor, or affection. I know that we have a Court that will not shrink from whatever duty may be imposed upon it, and I believe, from what I have seen of you, that you will walk unshrinkingly in the plain paths of duty that are opened before you. Do this, gentlemen, and I am sure that, linked together with that of Mc-Parlan and of others who have aided in this *glorious crusade* your names will be enshrined for long coming years in the grateful recollections of an enfranchised and redeemed people."

This remarkable address had its effect upon the jury and upon the public feeling in the State, and such a demand was there for it that a very large edition in pamphlet form was quickly exhausted. It was read with avidity and greatly commended wherever circulated. With Mr. Kaercher and Mr. Gowen in this case were associated Hon. F. W. Hughes Gen. Chas. Albright, and Guy E. Farquhar, Esq.

Before the conclusion of the Munley case a jury was im paneled, on the sixth and seventh of July, to try over again the case against Hugh McGehan, James Carroll, James Roarty. James Boyle, and Thomas Duffy, in the matter of the Yost murder, the other defendants in the same cause demanding separate trials. After a full and careful hearing the jury rendered a verdict of "guilty of murder in the first degree," against the prisoners. The speeches of Gen. Albright and Hon. F. W. Hughes—both very able and eloquent—were also published and very widely read, the interest in the trial as well as their own intrinsic value having created a demand for them. The counsel for the defense and prosecution was the same as in the Munley case. All the defendants named above were sentenced to be hanged on the sixteenth of August. Their cases were carried to the Supreme Court, arguments held, and a *nol. pros.* finally entered, confirming the sentence of the court below.

John Kehoe, Michael O'Brien, Chris Donnelly, John Donahue, *alias* "Yellow Jack," James Roarty, Dennis F. Canning, Frank McHugh, John Gibbons, and John Morr's were arrested on the sixth of May, 1876, charged with conspiracy, at the famous Mahanoy City Convention of the first of June, 1875, to kill Wm. M. Thomas and Jesse Major. They were tried at Pottsville before President Judge Pershing and Associates Green and Walker, commencing August 9 and ending August 14, 1876. The trial for conspiracy attracted the gentlemen of the bar from all parts of the State, and during its continuance the court-room was daily crowded to the point of suffocation with ladies and gentlemen, some of them having traveled hundreds of miles to have a view of the Mollies, the jury, the court and officials, and the witnesses for the prosecution. McParlan's testimony was intensely interesting, and such a public call for its particulars was there among the legal fraternity and the general reading public, that the entire evidence of the trial was printed in a pamphlet of nearly three hundred pages, and a very large edition quickly exhausted. The newspapers had special correspondents on the ground, and the illustrated journals of New York sent their artists to Pottsville to make drawings of the court and surroundings. The leading facts contained in this extraordinary suit have been given in the course of the preceding narrative. With the exception of the young man, Frank McHugh, who gave evidence for the Commonwealth, the defendants were all found guilty according to the counts in the several indictments, and sentenced to seven years' confinement each in the penitentiary. McHugh has not been sentenced, having been recommended to the mercy of the court by the jury.

CHAPTER XLIX.

CLOSING THE RECORD.

AFTER this came the arrest of the murderers—or those interested in the murder—of Gomer James. Thomas Hurley, having for the time made his escape—though it is reasonable to suppose that he will, with other fugitives from justice, some day be caught and punished—Chris Donnelly, John Donahue, Michael O'Brien, Pat Dolan, Sr., Pat Butler, and Frank O'Neill were arraigned at Pottsville on the 17th of August, 1876. James Roarty, charged with aiding and abetting in the killing of Gomer James, was, with the others found guilty. Chris Donnelly was given two years in the penitentiary, while Patrick Butler, partly in consideration of his having given State's evidence, met similar leniency. John Donahue, having already received sentence of death, was not sentenced. Mike O'Brien was sent to prison for two years. Patrick Dolan, Sr., was sentenced to eighteen months' imprisonment. Frank O'Neill also received two years.

September 23, of the same year, John Slattery, John Stanton, Michael Doolan, Chas. Mullhearn, Ned Monaghan, John Kehoe, Chris Donnelly, Dennis F. Canning, Michael O'Brien, Frank O'Neill and Pat Dolan, Sr., were arraigned for conspiracy to murder Wm. and Jesse Major, stood their trial, and all but John Stanton were found guilty, and sentenced to imprisonment as follows: O'Neill, five years; O'Brien, five years; Canning, seven years; Donnelly, five years; Kehoe, seven years, and Ned Monaghan, seven years.

At the same term of court, Thomas Donahue was sentenced to two years' imprisonment for aiding in the escape of John Gibbons, one of the men assaulting Wm. M. Thomas.

September 22, 1876, Muff Lawler was brought to court, as accessory after the fact to the murder of Sanger and Uren, found guilty, but not sentenced, having enrolled himself among those willing to aid the State in convicting men more guilty. James Duffy was sent one year for perjury. Mrs. Bridget Hyland, Bernard M. Boyle, and Kate Boyle, having been rather too fast in swearing their friends clear, were found guilty of perjury and given two and three years each at the State prison.

The murder of F. W. S. Langdon, by the Mollie Maguires, at Audenried, in Schuylkill County, committed July 14, 1862, implicated John Kehoe, County Delegate, John Campbell, and Neill Dougherty. Campbell and Dougherty were arrested, and with Kehoe brought to trial at Pottsville, January 2, 1877, found guilty of murder in the second degree and sentenced, Campbell for nine, and Dougherty five years to the State penitentiary. Kehoe was brought in guilty of murder in the first degree, and sentenced to be executed the 16th of April in the same year, but his cause was taken to the Supreme Court, where it will doubtless be decided in accordance with the testimony and its merits.

In November, 1876, Chas. McAllister was convicted of an assault, with intent to kill, upon James Riles, at Shenandoah. Sentence thus far has been deferred.

All of the above were Schuylkill County cases.

In Carbon County arrests were made almost simultaneously. John Donahue, Thomas P. Fisher, Patrick Mc-Kenna, Alex. Campbell, Patrick O'Donnell, and John Malloy, were taken, charged with the murder of Morgan Powell, at Summit Hill, December 2, 1871. The defendants were tried, at different terms of the Carbon County Court, at Mauch Chunk, James McParlan frequently appearing—as in most of the suits in Schuylkill County—on the witness stand and testifying to the confessions and admissions of the Mollies. They were found guilty as follows : Donahue of murder in the first degree ; Fisher of murder in the first degree, and sentenced to death ; Pat McKenna of murder in the first degree, and sentenced to nine years' imprisonment ; Patrick O'Donnell, as accessory, and sentenced to five years' imprisonment.

In Columbia County, February 24, 1877, Pat Hester, Pat Tully, and Peter McHugh, were arraigned for the murder of Alex. Rae. The circumstances of the crime have been related in these pages. The court was held at Bloomsburg, the county-seat, and attracted a very large attendance. McParlan was present, and his testimony was fully corroborated by Dan Kelly, *alias* Manus Kull, and Mike, *alias* Muff Lawler, was also a witness. An interview between McParlan and the last-named personage is thus described by an eye-witness :

"At about a quarter to ten this morning, February 12, 1877, the stage from Rupert Station rattled up the street, into town, and disgorged its occupants in front of the Exchange Hotel. With Messrs. Hughes and Ryon, from Pottsville, the redoubtable Muff Lawler made his appearance. The meeting between Lawler and his old friend McParlan —Muff once knew him as McKenna, and initiated him into Shenandoah Division of the Mollies, a few years ago—was particularly interesting. Stretching out his hand, McParlan inquired of Lawler, as he indulged in a warm shake : ' Have you the "goods" for the last quarter ? '

" ' I have not ! ' was the blushing reply.

" ' Well, now, that's a pity,' said McParlan, ' as I wanted to get the quarreling toast ! ' "

Several witnesses of the scene were convulsed with laughter.

I had at the time the " goods " for the quarter ending the first of February, 1877, in my office, and at once sent them by telegraph to McParlan, so that he might not have to inquire about them of Muff Lawler. They were as follows :

" DAY WORDS : *Question*—How does Erin stand ?
　　　　　　　Answer—The Russians will be victorious !
" NIGHT WORDS : *Question*—The nights are getting short !
　　　　　　　Answer—We'll soon have the Spring !
" QUARRELING WORDS : *Question*—Don't be outrageous !
　　　　　　　Answer—I never was such ! "

The sign of recognition was made as follows :

" *Question*—With the thumb and forefinger of the right hand, take hold of the lapel of the vest between the top buttons, or button-holes.

" *Answer*—Draw the back of the left hand across the chin."

The leaders of this society can make up their minds that henceforth, as in the past, I will not remain in ignorance of their most secret transactions. It is simply out of their power to prevent this. As long as it is a society, and as long as its signs, mummeries, and passwords are used for purposes of murder and assassination, so long will its imported " goods " remain my " goods " in the interests of humanity and justice.

It was the ninth of February, 1877, that the trial at Bloomsburg approached a crisis. Sitting in the prisoner's dock, Pat Hester smiled when he saw Dan Kelly, *alias* Manus Kull, *alias* "Kelly the Bum," in the witness-box. But his humor changed to dire dismay as he discovered that there were still other witnesses, who fully corroborated what Kelly made oath to. Dan Kelly's story of the Rae assassination was about as follows :

He met Pat Hester, Peter McHugh and Ned Skivington at Big Mine Run, in Barney Dolan's place, on the sixteenth of October, 1868, the day preceding that of the murder. Hester was on his way, he said, down the mountain with Skivington, but had missed the train and returned to Dolan's, where all had something to drink. Afterward they walked to Ashland, and entered Donahue's saloon. There Hester informed the witness that he had lost something by not going down the mountain that day, adding, "But there is a good thing to be had to-morrow, for Rae will go to Bell's Tunnel, and there is money in it for us !" It was then agreed that Hester, McHugh, Tully, Skivington, Brian Campbell, Jim Bradley, Billy Muldowney and Dan Kelly should go and rob Rae. Roger Lafferty, *alias* Johnstone, went across the street and procured some powder and bullets, returned and loaded the pistols, each one of the persons named having a weapon. After this they had more liquor and stayed there all night All but Lafferty went out in the morning to meet and rob Rae. But when they got as far as Germantown, Muldowney left, saying that he was too lame to keep on. After they got above the toll-gate, Hester and Skivington left, and Hester handed witness, Kelly, his pistol, saying : "Kelly, your pistol is no good ! Take mine ! for I know it's sure !" And he remarked that he would go to Shamokin, to purchase hair to mix with lime to make mortar for plastering. Skivington was off also, wanting to go to work in the mine to throw aside suspicion from the rest. All the others went as far as the water-barrel, and remained there. They then begun talking about Rae and his son, and finally concluded that, if the lad should chance to be riding with his father that

morning, as he often did, they would send the boy home
with the horse, if they had to shoot Rae. The object was
plunder, not murder, unless the latter was necessary to secure
the money. Bradley, who was not known in Centralia, went
and procured a quart of whisky and some crackers. When
he got back all hands drank and ate. Five of the number
present did not know Rae if they saw him, so Daltor, who
was acquainted with him, walked out on the road to signal
the others should their victim arrive. Soon a man came
along in a wagon, but as Dalton did not shake his hat the
person was allowed to pass. Still another man moved up
while the assassins waited in ambush, driving a horse attached to a light wagon, and he was permitted to go his way
unharmed, as Dalton again failed to give the notice. He
presently stepped out into the road to see who was coming
and returned to his former position. Quickly afterward a
buggy hove in view and the assassins saw that Dalton was
standing in plain sight, shaking his hat, and they knew that
the driver was Alex. Rae. When the vehicle reached the
watering-trough, all jumped out upon their victim. Rae
alighted from the buggy when the men ordered him to, and
quickly handed his watch and pocket-book to Kelly, the witness, but said nothing. He was confronted by a squad of
heavily armed ruffians. What was there for him to say?
Kelly asked McHugh what should be done with the man?
McHugh replied: "I won't be hunted around the world by
any living man," when the shooting began. Rae ran toward the woods, and Tully went up to him, put his pistol
to his head, and shot him near the ear. Seeing that the
man was sure to die, all ran up the mountain, where
they divided the money, about sixty dollars, and the
witness remembered that Dalton received a ten dollar bill
with a corner torn off. Tully and McHugh and Kelly
got in at Graham's some time that day, and in the afternoon
witness drove to Locust Gap with a beer-seller. He got home
at half-past three. They killed Rae at about nine o'clock.

He struck the ground upon his face, and they left him where he fell, after putting the horse and buggy out of sight in the wood. Kelly acknowledged that he fired two shots, but could not say how many the others fired. Dalton did not shoot at all. All of the rest discharged their weapons at the man. He was sure he saw Tully fire. One shot hit Rae in the cheek. He left Hester's pistol at Graham's and had given his own to Bradley. Hester's weapon was a sort of navy pistol and held five cartridges. It was loaded at Donahue's house. Dalton had a small pistol and McHugh's was not as large as Kelly's. McHugh had a seven-shooter Hester met him the same night in Graham's, at about nine o'clock, when the rest were there. The next he saw of Hester was three days later, when he rode in his wagon with him from the Gap to Ashland. Hester received none of the money taken from Rae. It was Hester's idea that Ray would have eighteen or nineteen thousand dollars with him, but when he heard how small a sum had been realized he said it was not worth dividing, so took none of it. About the seventeenth of November, after Donahue and Duffy had been arrested, Jack Smith told Hester of the capture, and he remarked it was about time for him to go, and he did go, without telling his confederates where he went. They all separated, remained away a month or two, and returned. When they got back Hester was in jail. He said he had been to Illinois, but it would look better to go back, as he might be taken there. A woman got Rae's pocket-book. The watch—a gold one—witness gave to Mike Graham, to keep for him. He took it from him afterward and left it with Con Garrah for ten dollars. Garrah restored it, when Kelly gave it to McGuire for ten dollars and turned the money over to Garrah. The watch was subsequently broken up with rocks and thrown into a creek, for fear it might lead to trouble

The attorneys for the defense were unable, after many efforts to shake Kelly's testimony in the least. Despite his bad character for truth and veracity, it was the conviction of everybody that he, for once in his checkered career, was bent upon telling the straightforward truth. It had its weight with the jury.

Judge Elwell presided at the session of court, and Hon. F. W. Hughes assisted the District Attorney in the prosecution, John W. Ryon, Esq., of Pottsville, and others, appearing for the defendants.

On the 24th, the jury returned a verdict in the three cases of "guilty of murder in the first degree." This was not unexpected by the general public, but formed a complete surprise to Pat Hester and his Mollie friends. So confident had Hester been of release, that, the day before the reception of the decree, he sent word to Locust Gap, ordering a grand supper prepared at his house in commemoration of his discharge and triumphant acquittal. While he did not actually fire the shot that killed Rae, he was virtually as guilty as those who did, having originated the job, and justice will, without doubt, be meted out to him.

Hester, Tully, and McHugh found that they had but one course to adopt, and got a new trial; but all has failed, the Supreme Court has affirmed the judgment against the prisoners, and sentence of death is their doom.

While these trials were going on, the Mollies were not idle. They moved every string possible to pull in money and influence to defend their brethren in the coal region. Contributions were levied by the National head of the order, in New York, upon the subordinate divisions of the country for a large amount of money—some place it as high as $30,000—part of which was to be expended in clearing the criminals, and the rest, I have reason to believe, in paying assassins to go to Pottsville and take the lives of McParlan and all of my employés in that section of country. But the refusal of one of the Philadelphia lodges to respond to this levy brought the matter to the notice of the public press and stopped at least a portion of the funds from going forward to the National officers. New Orleans and some other dis

tant branches had sent their share without knowing exactly
the purpose for which it was to be employed, but it is presumable that not more than one-half of the assessment was
ever realized, and that must have been expended in paying
for legal services.

During the session of court, at which occurred the trial
of Kehoe and others for conspiracy to murder Wm. M.
Thomas, I learned that an attempt would be made to assassinate Mr. Gowen, McParlan, and the entire court. It
seems at first there was an informal meeting of the Mollies,
in Pottsville, and it was arranged that twenty-four men should
be chosen to go to the court-house, twelve to sit on the back
row of seats, and twelve on the front tier, near the prisoners.
All were to be armed with loaded revolvers. Those on the
front row of seats were, at a given signal, to rise and simultaneously fire upon the judges, the attorneys for the Commonwealth—Mr. Gowen especially—and the officers, including
McParlan and Capt. Linden, and the members of the Coal
and Iron Police. Those on the back seat were to kill off
those left by the first platoon, when all were to rush in, seize
the prisoners and with them fight their way out and make
their escape to the hills. An influential member of the
order, and a county official, hearing of this arrangement,
after the twenty-four men had actually been appointed, made
his appearance at their rendezvous and informed the ringleaders in the movement that such an act was evidence of
sheer madness. "If you do this, boys," said he, "there will
not be an Irishman left in Schuylkill County, and what is
more, if you persist in the plot, I shall consider it my bounden
duty to go at once and have every mother's son of you
arrested! It can't be done, and it shall not be done!"

This, for the time, broke up the conspiracy. Subsequently
a young Mollie Maguire made his boast, in the presence of
several friends, that he would go to the court-house, any time
when he could hear that Mr. Gowen was alone, and shoot
him down. He was soon told that the President of the Read-

ing Railway, and the personal head of the prosecution of the members of the bloodthirsty organization, was writing, all by himself, in a jury room. The assassin walked into the apartment, his hand upon his revolver, and was about to produce it and fire, when an officer of the Coal and Iron Police having business with the gentleman threatened, unexpectedly appeared on the scene. As the would-be murderer had no reasonable excuse for remaining, he took his hand away from his pistol, and, thwarted in his design, sneaked out of the place. These and other equally foolish acts of the Mollies were duly reported to Mr. Gowen, and he was advised that he must take some precautions or his life would pay the forfeit of criminal rashness. Up to that date he had not as much as worn a pistol, or any other weapon, upon his person, and it is questionable if he ever did subsequently. He is a brave, frank man, but depended too much, I think, upon the justness of his cause, for with the Mollie Maguires the common instincts of human nature are outraged and disregarded. Still he was not attacked. While there were hundreds present thirsting for his blood, he turned upon the Mollies the heaviest deluge of invective that they have ever received.

But one New York newspaper, I believe, has ever openly taken the part of the Mollie Maguires. That was the *Irish World*. The animus of its article was contained in an attack upon Mr. Gowen and James McParlan, calling one "the head of a coal monopoly," and the other his "hired informer." As the editor possibly had to do something to earn his proportion of the $30,000 received for the defense of the Mollies, and as his modicum of the labor was so insignificant and trivial, I have not the heart to devote space to an answer. He is sufficiently replied to, perhaps, by the verdicts of the courts of justice, which point to something more serious than the editorial writer in question had in mind at the time of the preparation of his weak and idle philippic.

A well informed writer in the *American Law Review*, the

January, 1877, seems to have taken a more sensible impression of the matter, and found interest enough in the trials of the Mollies to devote twenty-eight pages of valuable space to the calm and dispassionate discussion of the subject from a legal standpoint.

.   .   .   .

The work of several years is now nearly finished. About seventy persons have been arrested in the coal region. Of those twelve have been, by a jury of their countrymen, found guilty of murder in the first degree; four of murder in the second degree; and four of being accessory to murder: sixteen of conspiracy to murder; six of perjury; one of assault with intent to kill; eight of aiding and abetting a murder; one of assault and battery; one for aiding in the escape of a murderer, and several others of lesser crimes. The sum-total of the time of these sentences to imprisonment foots up one hundred and twenty-four years and eight months. Eleven have received sentence of death.

On May 21st, 1877, Governor Hartranft issued warrants for the execution of eight of the murderers, viz. :—Alexander Campbell, convicted of complicity in the killing of John P. Jones; James Carroll, Hugh McGehan, James Boyle, and James Roarty, convicted of the murder of Benj. F. Yost; Patrick Hester, Peter McHugh, and Patrick Tully, convicted of the murder of Alexander W. Rea. Campbell was hanged at Mauch Chunck on the 21st of June, in company with Michael Doyle and Edward Kelly, concerned in the murder with him. Carroll, McGehan, Boyle, and Roarty expiated their crime on the same day, on the gallows from which Thomas Munley was suspended for the murder of William Sanger and James Urens; and Hester, McHugh and Tully will be executed at Bloomsburg on the 9th day of August next, which will be the first executions that have ever taken place in Columbia County.

THE END.

CPSIA information can be obtained
at www.ICGtesting.com
Printed in the USA
BVOW06*0249281117
501425BV00010B/82/P

9 781340 906078